Fourth Edition

ORGANIZATIONAL BEHAVIOR IN EDUCATION

Robert G. Owens
Hofstra University

ALLYN AND BACON
Boston London Toronto Sydney Tokyo Singapore

Library of Congress Cataloging-in-Publication Data

OWENS, ROBERT G.
 Organizational behavior in education / Robert G. Owens. — 4th ed.
  p.   cm.
 Includes bibliographical references (p.) and indexes.
 ISBN 0-13-642547-X
 1. School management and organization—United States.
 2. Organizational behavior. I. Title.
 LB2806.O9 1991
 371.2—dc20   90-38278
                                                     CIP

The first and second edition published as
Organizational Behavior in Schools.

Copyright © 1991 by Allyn and Bacon
A Division of Simon & Schuster, Inc.
160 Gould Street
Needham Heights, MA 02194

Copyright © 1987, 1981, 1970 by Prentice-Hall, Inc.

Printed in the United States of America

10 9 8 7 6 5 4 3   95 94 93 92

ISBN 0-13-642547-X
ISBN 0-13-638867-1

To my wife, Barbara,
without whose love, help, and encouragement
this book would never have been

CONTENTS

PREFACE   ix

Part I—Theoretical Foundations of Organizational Behavior

Chapter One
MAINSTREAMS OF ORGANIZATIONAL THOUGHT   1

Public Administration as a Beginning, *2*
Impact of the Industrial Revolution, *3*
The Rise of Classical Organizational Theory, 1910–1935, *7*
The Human Relations Movement, 1935–1950, *10*
The Organizational Behavior Movement, 1950–1975, *13*
Educational Administration Stirs, *16*
Emerging Developments in Organizational Thought, 1975–Present, *18*
Collapse of Traditional Organizational Theory, *20*
Rise in Qualitative Research Methods, *21*
Nontheoretical Influences on Organizational Thought, *30*
The School Reform Movement, *33*
Human Resources Development, *35*
Summary, *36*
Suggested Reading, *38*
Notes, *38*

Chapter Two
ORGANIZATIONAL THEORY   42

Organizational Theory, *42*
Two Major Theoretic Orientations to Organization, *43*
Bureaucratic Theory, *44*
Human Resources Management Theory, *47*
Theory *X* and Theory *Y*, *48*
Summary, *53*
Suggested Reading, *54*
Notes, *54*

Chapter Three
SYSTEMS THEORY AND ORGANIZATIONAL BEHAVIOR   56

General Systems Theory, *57*
Social Systems Theory, *58*
Role Theory, *62*
The Concept of Role Related to Social Systems Theory, *68*
Sociotechnical Systems Theory, *75*
Contingency Theory, *77*
Summary, *84*
Suggested Reading, *85*
Notes, *86*

Part II—Concepts of Organizational Behavior in Education

Chapter Four
WOMEN'S ISSUES IN ORGANIZATIONAL BEHAVIOR   88

Androcentrism, *89*
The Feminocentric Critique, *90*
Two Studies of Women's Issues, *94*
Some Findings of Feminocentric Research, *97*
Summary, *99*
Suggested Reading, *99*
Notes, *99*

Chapter Five
MOTIVATION   102

Introduction, *102*
Some Theoretical Approaches to Motivation, *106*
Maslow's Hierarchy-of-Needs Theory, *107*
Herzberg's Two-Factor Theory of Motivation, *114*
Integrating Herzberg's and Maslow's Theories, *118*

Expectancy Models of Motivation, *119*
Styles of Organizational Behavior, *122*
Job Enrichment, *126*
Summary, *128*
Suggested Reading, *128*
Notes, *129*

Chapter Six
LEADERSHIP   132

Definition, *132*
The Leader and the Group, *134*
Two-Dimensional Leadership Theory, *136*
Contingency Theories of Leadership, *142*
Fiedler's Contingency Theory of Leadership, *143*
Vroom's and Yetton's Normative Contingency Theory, *149*
Reddin's 3-D Theory of Leadership, *151*
Hershey's and Blanchard's Situational Theory of Leadership, *155*
Leadership in Schools: New Perspectives, *158*
Summary, *161*
Suggested Reading, *163*
Notes, *163*

Chapter Seven
ORGANIZATIONAL CULTURE AND ORGANIZATIONAL CLIMATE   166

Defining and Describing Organizational Climate and Culture, *167*
Recent Research on Organizational Culture, *168*
Organizational Culture and Organizational Climate Compared
    and Contrasted, *171*
Describing and Assessing Organizational Culture in Schools, *180*
Relationship Between Organizational Culture and Organizational
    Effectiveness, *181*
Describing and Assessing Organizational Climate in Schools, *186*
Organizational Climate Description Questionnaire (OCDQ), *186*
Organizational Climate Index (OCI), *188*
Profile of a School (POS), *193*
Summary, *204*
Suggested Reading, *205*
Notes, *206*

Chapter Eight
ORGANIZATIONAL CHANGE   210

The Tradition of Change in American Education, *211*
Empirical-Rational Strategies of Change, *214*
Power-Coercive Strategies of Change, *218*

A Third Strategy: Organizational Self-Renewal, *219*
Research on the Effectiveness of OD, *234*
Summary, *237*
Suggested Reading, *239*
Notes, *240*

Chapter Nine
CONFLICT IN ORGANIZATIONS   243

The Nature of Conflict in Organizations, *244*
The Dynamics of Organizational Conflict, *248*
Approaches to Organizational Conflict, *252*
A Contingency Approach to Diagnosis of Conflict, *256*
Summary, *258*
Suggested Reading, *260*
Notes, *261*

Chapter Ten
DECISION MAKING   262

Individual Versus Organizational Decison Making, *262*
Rationality in Decision Making, *264*
Limits on Rationality in Decision Making, *267*
Issues in Participative Decision Making, *277*
Team Administration, *281*
A Paradigm for Decision Making, *283*
Summary, *285*
Suggested Reading, *285*
Notes, *286*

Chapter Eleven
THE HOLOGRAPHIC IMPERATIVE AND QUALITATIVE RESEARCH   288

The Holographic Imperative, *288*
Describing and Assessing Organizational Culture in Schools, *289*
"Sounds in a Silent World," *303*
Summary, *304*
Suggested Reading, *304*
Notes, *305*

INDEXES

Author Index, *307*
Subject Index, *315*

PREFACE

These are the best of times and the worst of times in American education. As the pressure for reform and improvement of schooling continues to mount yet no royal road to success appears to convey us smoothly and surely to the goal of educational excellence, many become discouraged. At the same time, our understanding of schools and the behavior of people in them is better today, more sophisticated, than it has ever been. This is not to suggest that our knowledge is complete and perfect; it is still in the process of becoming, and that process will continue into the future. Nevertheless, opportunities for educational leadership—indeed, the need for educational leadership—have never been more abundant than they are today. If ever there was a time for leaders to find opportunity in adversity, the time in American education is now.

This book is for people who want to be leaders in education. We live in an era in which the legal power of administrators to control and direct others is being progressively circumscribed both by law and by increasing unwillingness of people to accept arbitrary authority. This has heightened our awareness that the power of educational leaders emanates not so much from their legal clout as from their ability to elicit the enthusiastic voluntary involvement of others—including students, teachers, community residents, and those in the official hierarchy—in the never-ending processes of creating and perfecting the educational institution. Thus, educational organizations require leaders who are not only educational experts but who are skilled organizational diagnosticians as well. Such leaders have expert knowledge of how organizations function and, therefore, how to analyze and solve problems of increasing the work effectiveness of people in them.

Two major and closely interrelated developments continue to unfold in the center stage of educational administration today. One is the growing use of non-quantitative, nonstatistical research methods, such as observational field methods, which has led to fundamentally fresh perspectives in understanding organizational

ix

behavior. The other is increased understanding of the importance of organizational culture in the exercise of educational leadership.

Qualitative research methods. As American organizations of all kinds ran into trouble in the 1970s—businesses losing out in international competition, schools losing the confidence of their constituencies—the time-honored remedies of management did not work very well. That caused students of organization to question a lot of old assumptions about the supposed bureaucratic logic and order that had long shaped and structured the way that organizational research was conducted. Increasingly, investigators actually began to go into organizations to see for themselves what was happening instead of sending around questionnaires.

The importance of organizational culture. That led to the discovery that, as some people had suspected all along, the culture of the organizations in which we work exerts great influence on our thinking and our behavior. Often greater, indeed, than the power of official policies, programs, rules, and regulations. While shrewd observers of the human scene, such as authors and playwrights—and a few sociologists and anthropologists—have demonstrated this to us again and again over the years, it has only recently emerged as a major, central theme in the study of organizations. This is powerful knowledge for leaders to have. But, at the same time, it dashes any hope that some may have harbored that there are some quick and simple ways to solve organizational problems in education.

These intertwined themes—the new perspectives on organization, especially organizational culture—arising from qualitative research form a central core of the theme of the book.

This edition of *Organizational Behavior in Education* reflects recent developments in the constantly growing body of knowledge about organizations and behavior of people at work in them that educational leaders may find helpful. Chapter 1 has been updated in view of the demise of formalistic theorizing that had tended to make much of scholarly research and academic thinking of the "theory movement" so barren and largely irrelevant. The emphasis is on understanding organizational behavior as it actually exists in educational organizations, not as either an applied science or a set of abstract principles with all the precision that such metaphors imply. The focus introduced in Chapter 1 is on the human dimensions of organization, and that is a theme around which all of the rest of the text is organized. Thus, the ideas introduced there are revisited in later chapters as they are explored in greater depth, and their relationships in the mosaic that makes up organizational behavior are examined. This spiral plan of development of the book's theme and information should help readers to synthesize, integrate, and internalize the material as they move through the text.

Chapter 4, "Women's Issues in Organizational Behavior," is entirely new. These are powerful issues but still woefully underrepresented in the literature of organizational behavior. Exploration of them may well represent the cutting edge of some of the most potentially fruitful (should I say germinal?) contemporary research in the scholarship of organizational behavior.

Organizational culture and climate remains the central arena in understanding organizational behavior in education. It continues to grow in promise of not only understanding organizational behavior in education but also of using that understanding to inform administrative practice. In Chapter 7 the material on organizational culture and climate has been reorganized, integrated, and enlarged to reflect this development.

As I have pointed out, one of the significant advances in research on organizational behavior in education has been in the increase in the use of qualitative, or ethnographic, research methods. This is not a new theme in this edition, but it is woven more firmly and consistently into the spiral development of the book. In addition, the more technical material on qualitative research methods has been organized into a separate Chapter 11.

The process of writing and rewriting a book such as this inevitably involves many people and, I suppose, all authors find it difficult to express their acknowledgment and appreciation adequately. I have had many intellectual mentors to whom I am indebted. Important among them are my colleagues at Hofstra University who were not only individually supportive but collectively, as well, by creating in the Department of Administration and Policy Studies a lively and caring intellectual culture that is rare in American universities. My students at Hofstra, important actors in that culture, have been of immense help in providing feedback and asking tough questions.

Many colleagues in North America and the Commonwealth countries who have used earlier editions as a textbook in their classes have been very helpful in sharing their experiences with me. Eddy J. VanMeter, Eugene Ratsoy, and Patricia A. Schmuck were especially generous and supportive in their critiques. It is no exaggeration to say that Egon G. Guba has not only been a mentor who has taught me much about epistemology and qualitative research methods, but has been an academic model and, frankly, inspiration as well. I am particularly indebted to Charol Shakeshaft and Colleen S. Bell for their patient guidance in my efforts to understand women's issues in organizational behavior. Carl R. Steinhoff provided incisive critiques that were very helpful in developing an understanding of organizational culture and organizational climate.

Many readers have no idea of the importance of their comments to authors. Much of what appears in this edition of *Organizational Behavior in Education* has been influenced by reactions from colleagues and students who have used it in their classes. I am deeply indebted to those who have taken the time to write, to call on the telephone, or to talk with me at conventions and meetings about their experiences with this book. Feedback such as that helps me to continue to develop the book so that it will be as useful as possible to readers.

Finally, I would like to thank the Prentice-Hall reviewers: Patricia A. Schmuck, Lewis & Clark College, Portland, Oregon, and William A. Woods, North Dakota State University, Fargo, North Dakota.

ROBERT G. OWENS
Hofstra University

ORGANIZATIONAL BEHAVIOR IN EDUCATION

1

MAINSTREAMS
OF ORGANIZATIONAL
THOUGHT

"The professional draws upon the knowledge of science and his colleagues, and upon knowledge gained through personal experience. The degree to which he relies upon the first two of these rather than the third one is one of the ways in which the professional may be distinguished from the layman."

—Douglas McGregor[1]

In a typical university, administration is not generally regarded as an academic discipline. For example, business administration is usually taught in a school or college devoted to business, with its own specialized faculty. Public administration also is usually organized as a distinct unit in a university, such as a college, school, or a department. Hospital administration is under the aegis of the medical school. We do not often find a school in a university devoted to the professional practice of administration, as such.

Educational administration is, generally, taught within the framework of the school of education—sometimes comprising a department of the school but often less formally structured and known simply as a "program." In colleges of education and schools of education, the teaching of administration is commonly even further fragmented and diffused: the school guidance and counseling faculty may offer courses in the administration of guidance programs, as may special education and the physical education faculty, and so with each of many "special fields" in the school of education. In fact, in a school or college of education, many faculty members may be found teaching administration in a wide variety of unrelated courses. The content of these courses and the ways in which they are taught are usually developed independently with little or no reference to each other. More than likely, there is virtually no contact between the faculty members who are teaching administration courses in the school of education and the faculty members in other parts of the institution who are also preparing students for administrative responsibilities.

This arrangement is the typical and traditional way in which administration is studied and taught. It is based on some time-honored and generally held viewpoints, three of which are:

1. The administrator of an organization must have a high level of technical knowledge of the area to be administered. For example, to be successful as an elementary school

1

principal it is assumed that one must possess considerable knowledge of the teaching of young children. And a director of athletics must have a high level of competence in teaching physical education. Moreover, we might suppose, the top administrator of a great scientific and technical university must, himself or herself, be a competent scientist or technical person.

2. Whatever the art or science of administration includes, it is best taught and learned in practical application to specific situations. This viewpoint suggests that, to a large extent, the tasks that administrators face are quite different in various specialized fields. This view would hold that the tasks and functions of, say, a hospital administrator are uniquely and distinctively different from those of the principal of a large high school.

3. Administration, as a body of knowledge and practice, is neither an academic discipline nor a profession. This viewpoint considers the knowledge content of administration, and its professional manifestations in terms of organized practice, too inadequate to warrant it a place among the recognized academic disciplines and the professions.

These views are slowly changing—reflecting fundamental developments that have already affected major changes in the practice of administration in and out of education and forecasting still further changes.

PUBLIC ADMINISTRATION AS A BEGINNING

In one sense, administration is one of the most ancient of all human endeavors. There is little question, for example, that the Egyptians organized and administered vast complex enterprises that required sophisticated planning, complex organization, skilled leadership, and detailed coordination at least two thousand years before the birth of Christ. To put it in perspective, it has been estimated that the task of constructing the Pyramids—which took one hundred thousand men twenty years to complete—was equivalent to administering an organization three times the size of the Shell Oil Company.

Similarly, the Chinese are known to have had highly systematic, large-scale administrative systems at about the same time as the Pyramids were built, which used many of the management concepts still in use today. Moses, implementing the plan given to him by his father-in-law by which the people of Israel would be ruled, is cited in modern management textbooks as establishing the pyramidal design of organization still so much in vogue today. The administrative system of the Catholic church, a far-flung organization at one time numbering nearly a half-million cardinals, archbishops, bishops, and parish priests, is still studied for its remarkably centralized administrative system and is compared with the vastly more complex administrative system of modern-day General Motors. And, of course, great military leaders from Alexander the Great to Caesar, to Napoleon, to Douglas MacArthur have long been studied for what they can teach us about planning, organizing, leading, and motivating.

Nearer to us in time, and better known to most of us, are the ideas and concepts that underlay the establishment of the reputable civil services of Europe and Great Britain in the nineteenth century. Two key notions provided the essential rationale for the civil services:

1. The idea that administration is an activity that can be studied and taught separately from the content of what is being administered. For example, a mail carrier need not

administer a postal service, nor must tax attorneys administer the collection of taxes. This gave rise to the notion that administration could, in itself, have a productive work role in the organization.

2. The belief that decisions about the policies and purposes of government belong to the realm of political action but that these decisions are best implemented by civil servants whose jobs are not dependent on the whims of politics and who are free to develop good administrative procedures. This includes much more than the mere creation of a civil service as an alternative to corruption and the "spoils system." This belief is based on the concept that a disinterested administrative organization can become more effective than one that is involved in the policy-making process. In the twentieth century, the Secretariat of the United Nations and the Foreign Service of the United States State Department are good illustrations of this concept in action.

In the United States in the nineteenth century, the term "administration" was also used in the context of government, and the ideas it represented gave rise to the growth of public administration, although "civil service" in America tended to connote a system designed to insure honesty and fairness rather than the expertness associated with the European and British systems. Woodrow Wilson crystallized early thinking about the professionalization of administration with the publication of his now-famous essay, "The Study of Administration," in 1887. He felt that the improvement of administrative techniques depended on scholarly study and learning in the specialized field of administration itself.

"The object of administrative study," he wrote in an often-quoted statement, "is to rescue executive methods from the confusion and costliness of empirical study and set them upon foundations laid deep in stable principle."[2] A thirty-one-year-old assistant professor when he published this article, Wilson was far ahead of his time in arguing earnestly for the inclusion of the study of administration as a subject fit for serious treatment by universities. Forty years were to pass before the first textbook on the principles in public administration for which he called was published (1927). The search for principles was essential to the development of an administrative science, as differentiated from administrative folklore or custom.

IMPACT OF THE INDUSTRIAL REVOLUTION

At about the close of the nineteenth century—the time of Woodrow Wilson's scholarly contributions—Western European and American businessmen were stepping up their efforts to increase profits from industry. It was generally believed in that burgeoning era of industry that greater profitability required lowering the unit cost of producing goods. One way to do this, of course, was to step up mass production through the use of such innovations as the assembly line. The leadership of pioneering industrial giants, such as Henry Ford, is widely recognized in connection with such technological breakthroughs. In this era of industrial expansion, the key people were the engineers and technically oriented scientists—as they are in our own day of technological revolution. These were the people who could build the machines and then combine them into assembly line units. This was the era of the engineering consultant and the drive for efficiency.

Frederick W. Taylor is a name well known to many students of administration. He had been an engineer at the Midvale and the Bethlehem steel companies at the close of the 1800s and, in the early 1900s, became one of the top engineering consultants in American industry. We know that Taylor had read Wilson's essay and had been influenced by it. From about 1900 to 1915, as he worked to solve practical production problems in factories all over America, Taylor developed what later became known as his four "principles of scientific management." They were:

1. Eliminate the guesswork of rule-of-thumb approaches to deciding how each worker is to do a job by adopting scientific measurements to break the job down into a series of small, related tasks;
2. Use more scientific, systematic methods for selecting workers and training them for specific jobs;
3. Establish the concept that there is a clear division of responsibility between management and workers, with management doing the goal setting, planning, and supervising, and workers executing the required tasks;
4. Establish the discipline whereby management sets the objectives and the workers cooperate in achieving them.

These became enormously popular, not only in industry but also in the management of all kinds of organizations, including the family. A bestseller of the 1950s, *Cheaper by the Dozen*, vividly recounts how "efficiency" invaded every corner of the family life of Frank B. Gilbreth, one of Taylor's closest colleagues and an expert on time-and-motion study. Taylor's "principles of scientific management" were aimed primarily at lowering the unit cost of factory production, although he and his followers claimed that these principles could be applied universally;[3] they became almost an obsession in the press and throughout our society.[4] In practice, Taylor's ideas led to time-and-motion studies, rigid discipline on the job, concentration on the tasks to be performed with minimal interpersonal contacts between workers, and strict application of incentive pay systems.[5]

At the same time that Taylor's ideas and their application were having such enormous impact on American life, a French industrialist was working out some powerful ideas of his own. Henri Fayol had a background quite different from Taylor's, which helps to account for some of the differences in perception of the two men. Whereas Taylor was essentially a technician whose first concern was the middle-management level of industry, Fayol had the background of a top-management executive. It would be useful to mention briefly some of the ideas Fayol advanced, to give us a better perspective of what he contributed to the growth of thought in administration:

1. Unlike Taylor, who tended to view workers as extensions of factory machinery, Fayol focused his attention on the manager rather than on the worker;
2. He clearly separated the processes of administration from other operations in the organization, such as production;
3. He emphasized the common elements of the process of administration in different organizations.

Fayol believed that a trained administrative group was essential to improving the operations of organizations, which were becoming increasingly complex. As early as 1916, Fayol wrote that administrative ability "can and should be acquired in the same way as technical ability, first at school, later in the workshop."[6] He added that we find good and bad administrative methods existing side by side "with a persistence only to be explained by lack of theory."[7]

In his most notable work, *General and Industrial Management,*[8] Fayol established himself as the first modern organizational theorist. It was Fayol who defined administration in terms of five functions: (1) planning, (2) organizing, (3) commanding, (4) coordinating, and (5) controlling. It should be noted that, in the sense that he used these terms, commanding and controlling mean what are now called leading and evaluating results. More than sixty years after its initial publication, many still find this insightful approach to administration practical and useful.

Fayol went further by identifying a list of fourteen "principles," among which were: (1) unity of command, (2) authority, (3) initiative, and (4) morale. Avoiding a rigid and dogmatic application of his ideas to the administration of organizations, Fayol emphasized that flexibility and a sense of proportion were essential to managers who adapted principles and definitions to particular situations—quite a different interpretation from that of Taylor, who held firmly to the uniform, emphatic application of principles.

By the time of Fayol and Taylor, it was clear that the Western world was becoming an "organizational society." As giant industrial organizations grew in the early 1900s, so did government and other organizational aspects of life grow. The relatively simple social and political structures of the preindustrial era seemed inherently inadequate in an urban industrial society. Life was not always completely happy in this new social setting, and a great deal of friction—social, political, and economic—resulted. The increasing sense of conflict between people and organizations became a major factor in the struggle of learning to live successfully with this new kind of world, this industrial world in which the individual was, at every turn, a part of some organization. The years before World War I were punctuated by frequent outbursts of this conflict, such as labor unrest, revolution, and the rise of Communism. In this setting, a German sociologist, Max Weber, produced some of the most useful, durable, and brilliant work on an administrative system; it seemed promising at that time and has since proved indispensable: *bureaucracy.*

At a period when people and organizations were dominated by the whims of authoritarian industrialists and entrenched political systems, Weber saw hope in bureaucracy. Essentially, the hope was that well-run bureaucracies would become fairer, more impartial, and more predictable—in general, more rational—than organizations subject to the caprices of powerful individuals. Weber felt that well-run bureaucracies would be efficient, in fact, would be the most efficient form of organization yet invented. Such a viewpoint may not reflect modern experiences with bureaucracies, but Weber was convinced that a *well-run* bureaucracy would be very efficient for a number of reasons, one of which was that bureaucrats are highly trained technical specialists, each skilled in a specific, limited portion of an administrative task.

According to Weber, the bureaucratic apparatus would be very impersonal, minimizing irrational personal and emotional factors and leaving bureaucratic personnel free to work with a minimum of friction or confusion. This, he concluded, would result in expert, impartial, and unbiased service to the organization's clients. In the ideal bureaucracy Weber envisioned certain characteristics that are, in a sense, principles of administration:

1. A division of labor based on functional specialization;
2. A well-defined hierarchy of authority;
3. A system of rules covering the rights and duties of employees;
4. A system of procedures for dealing with work situations;
5. Impersonality of interpersonal relations;
6. Selection and promotion based only on technical competence.[9]

Part of Weber's genius lay in his sensitivity to the dangers of bureaucracy, while at the same time he recognized the merits of bureaucracy in *ideal* circumstances. He emphasized very strongly the dangers of bureaucracy, even so far as to warn that massive, uncontrollable bureaucracy could very well be the greatest threat to both Communism and free enterprise capitalism.[10] It is helpful, in trying to understand the flow of ideas that guided the development of administration, to be aware that—although he produced his work at about the same time that Taylor and Fayol did (that is, from about 1910 to 1920)—Weber was almost unknown in the English-speaking world until translations of his work began to appear in the 1940s. This helps to explain why his systematic work on bureaucracy did not receive widespread attention in educational administration until after World War II.

We have, thus far, considered three people of ideas who represent many others, as well, and a prodigious field of effort in their time. Each pointed to the need for the principles and the theories that, by 1900, were generally regarded as essential if the administration of our growing organizations was to become more rational and more effective. The American, Taylor, emphasized the principles that viewed administration as management—the coordination of many small tasks so as to accomplish the overall job as efficiently as possible. Efficiency was interpreted to mean the cheapest net-dollar cost to produce the finished article. Taylor assumed that labor was a commodity to be bought and sold, as one buys oil or electricity, and that by "scientific management" the manager could reduce to a minimum the amount of labor that must be purchased.

The Frenchman, Fayol, emphasized broader preparation of administrators so that they would perform their unique functions in the organization more effectively. He felt that the tasks that administrators perform are, presumably, different from those that engineers perform, but equally as important.

Germany's Max Weber held that bureaucracy is a theory of organization especially suited to the needs of large and complex enterprises that perform services for large numbers of clients. For Weber, the bureaucratic concept was an attempt to minimize the frustrations and irrationality of large organizations in which the relationships between management and workers were based on traditions of class privilege.

THE RISE OF CLASSICAL ORGANIZATIONAL THEORY, 1910–1935

These three individuals—Taylor, Fayol, and Weber—were giants in the pre–World War I years and led the way in the early efforts to master the problems of managing modern organizations. There is no precise and universally agreed-upon beginning or end of this era; however, the period from 1910 to 1935 generally can be thought of as the era of scientific management. "Scientific management" had a profound and long-lasting impact upon the ways in which schools were organized and administered. Raymond E. Callahan, in *Education and the Cult of Efficiency*, vividly portrays how school superintendents in the United States quickly adopted the values and practices of business and industrial managers of that time.[11] Emphasis was on efficiency (that is, low per-unit cost), rigid application of detailed, uniform work procedures (often calling for minute-by-minute, standard operating procedures for teachers to use each day throughout a school system), and detailed accounting procedures. Though some educational administrators harbored doubts about all of this, there was a rush among school superintendents to get aboard the bandwagon of the day by adopting the jargon and practices of those with high status in the society—business executives. Typifying this, Ellwood Cubberley—long one of the leading scholars in American education—took the clear position in 1916 in a landmark textbook that schools were "factories in which the raw materials are to be shaped and fashioned into products to meet the various demands of life."[12]

This view was widely held over the span of years running roughly from before World War I until very close to the outbreak of World War II. Since the concept of scientific management called for the scientific study of jobs to be performed, professors of educational administration undertook to describe and analyze what school superintendents did on the job. Fred Ayer, at the University of Texas, for example, surveyed superintendents to find out what kind of work they did in 1926–1927. Nearly all reported "attending board meetings, making reports, and supervising teachers, 80 percent…reported that they went to the post office daily; and each week half of them operated the mimeograph machine, …93 percent inspected toilets, and 93 percent inspected the janitor's work."[13] To prepare individuals to become school superintendents, therefore, programs of study often featured courses in budgeting, heating and ventilating, methods for performing janitorial services and sanitation tasks, writing publicity releases, and record keeping. Professors of educational administration, in turn, commonly conducted studies to determine (for example) the cheapest methods of maintaining floors—such as the most efficient techniques for mopping or sweeping, oiling and/or waxing—in order that they could provide prospective school superintendents with the skills necessary to train janitorial workers.

As the study of the problems of organization, management, and administration became established more and more firmly in the universities—just as Wilson and Fayol had predicted—the "principles" of scientific management received increased attention and also challenge from scholars and practitioners. New ideas were becoming apparent to those who were attentive. Students of administration, finding the concepts then available inadequate to deal with such significant problems as the conflict arising from the demands of the organization, on the one hand, and the need of individuals to obtain a reasonable sense of satisfaction and reward from their participation, on the other hand, were already exploring new ideas by the 1920s.

Luther Gulick and Lyndall Urwick stand out among the many scholars who attempted to synthesize what is now known as the "classical" formulation of principles, which would be useful in developing good, functional organizations. Central to the work of these two men was the idea that elements of the organization could be grouped and related according to function, geographic location, or similar criteria. They emphasized the drawing up of formal charts of organizations that showed the precise ways in which various offices and divisions were related. Gulick and Urwick published a widely acclaimed book in 1937[14] and were still highly influential after World War II.[15] Many school administrators are familiar with some of the organizational concepts that were popularized by such classical writers.

Organizational concepts of classical theory.   Classical organizational theorists have sought to identify and describe some set of fixed "principles" (in the sense of "rules") that would establish the basis for management. The best known of these dealt with organizational structure. For example, central to the classical view of organization is the concept of hierarchy, which, in the jargon of classical theorists, is the *scalar principle*. (In practice it is usually referred to as "line and staff.") The contention is that authority and responsibility should flow in as direct and unbroken a path as possible, from the top policy level down through the organization to the lowest member. This general principle is rather widely accepted by organizational theorists today, being most often attacked because of the rigid insistence with which many classical thinkers tend to apply the concept in practice, limiting lateral relationships between parts of the organization. It is, thus, no accident that organizational charts of American school districts today frequently show vertical lines of authority and responsibility with little or no interconnection between operating divisions of the organization.

Another central classical principle of organization is *"unity of command"*: essentially, that no one in an organization should receive orders from more than one superordinate. Fayol, a strict interpreter of this point, was sharply critical of Taylor because the latter favored something called "functional foremanship," which permitted a worker to receive orders from as many as eight bosses (each being a specialist). As organizations and work became more complex over time, this principle has been greatly weakened by the need to modify it so often to meet changing conditions. The organizational charts of school districts frequently reflect this principle, while, in actual operation, the concept is routinely ignored.

The *"exception principle"* holds that when the need for a decision recurs frequently, the decision should be established as a routine that can be delegated to subordinates (in the form of rules, standard operating procedures, administrative manuals). This frees those in higher positions from routine detail to deal with the exceptions to the rules. This principle, too, has received wide acceptance: it underlies the delegation of authority and the concept that all decisions should be made at the lowest possible level in the organization. This has proved to be the most generally applicable principle of classical theory.

"*Span of control*" is the most discussed of the major ideas from classical organizational theory. The essence of the concept is to prescribe (and thereby limit) the number of people reporting to a supervisor or administrator. Much of the thinking about this principle arose from military organizations, which—under highly stressful, unstable, emergency conditions—need a dependable system of control and coordination. The problems in applying the concept to other kinds of organizations have led to more controversy than understanding. Whereas many theorists suggest having a small number of people reporting to an administrator (usually somewhere between three and six), many firms deliberately put executives in charge of larger numbers of people so as to force them to delegate more decision making to their subordinates.

The ideas of Mary Parker Follett. The work of Mary Parker Follett was unique in the development of management thought. Her ideas were rooted in the classical traditions of organizational theory but matured in such a way that she, in effect, spanned the gap between scientific management and the early industrial psychologists. Starting as a Boston social worker, Follett became active in the growing field of management. Following the stock market crash of October 1929, and the resultant Great Depression, her work—more than many others'—reflected the slowly growing realization that large business corporations had become social institutions whose concentration of power called into question the American tradition of unrestrained corporate action.

Her ideas were instrumental in modifying the trend toward rigidly structuralist views in classical management theory, provided a rationale that was helpful in ushering in the human relations movement, and pioneered conceptualizing about what today is called contingency theory.

Follett, first, viewed management as a social process and, second, saw it inextricably enmeshed in the particular situation. She did not see authority as flowing from the top of the organization's hierarchy to be parceled out among those in lower ranks. It was better practice, in her view, that orders should not be given by one person; rather, all should seek to take orders from the situation itself. She saw that the administrator has three choices of ways to handle conflict: (1) by the exercise of power, (2) by compromise, or (3) by "integration" (that is, bringing the conflict into the open and seeking a mutually acceptable, win-win resolution).

In 1932, Follett sought to summarize her views by developing four principles of sound administration. The first two were *Coordination by direct contact of the responsible people concerned* and *Coordination in the early stages*. These clashed with the typical classical preoccupation with hierarchical communication and control: she advocated placing control in the hands of those in the lower levels of the organization, which requires opening up communication horizontally across the organization as well as down the hierarchy. The third principle was *Coordination as the reciprocal relating of all the factors in the situation* (which laid the basis of the "law of the situation"). This emphasized the importance of linking departments in ways that enabled them to self-adjust to the organization's needs at lower levels of the organization. Finally, *Coordination as a continuing process* recognized that management is an ever-changing, dynamic process in response to emerging situations—a sharp contrast to traditional, static, classical views that sought to codify universal principles of action.

Classical and neoclassical administrative concepts. Though classical concepts of organization and administration—that is, the concepts associated with bureaucracy and "scientific management"—were developed early in this century and stood for a time unchallenged by competing concepts, it would be an error to view the classical approach as something that once flourished and is now gone from the scene. Nothing could be further from actuality.

Bureaucracies flourish among us today, of course: government bureaucracies, such as the Internal Revenue Service and state departments of motor vehicles, are among obvious examples encountered every day. Even in the case of nonbureaucratic organizations, however, many scholars as well as administrators essentially believe that the classical views are the best basis for administrative practice.

Many contemporary advocates of accountability programs, competency-based programs, and management by objectives operate from classical organizational concepts. These newer manifestations of the older classical concepts are often referred to as *neoclassical* or, in some cases, *neoscientific*.

Numerous federal interventions in public schooling—such as the Elementary and Secondary Education Act (ESEA), P.L. 93-380, the Emergency School Assistance Act (ESAA), P.L. 92-318, and the Comprehensive Employment and Training Act (CETA), P.L. 93-203—are organized and administered in conformity with classical concepts of bureaucracy. Planning, Programming, and Budgeting Systems (PPBS) and Zero-Based Budgeting Systems (ZBBS) are designed to implement the basic ideas of classic bureaucratic organizational strategies (as are most so-called rational planning and management systems). They are examples that are widely called *neoclassical* today.

THE HUMAN RELATIONS MOVEMENT, 1935–1950

In time, as the principles of scientific management were applied to industry with greater care, a need to be more precise about the effect of human factors on production efficiency was felt. The Western Electric Company was one of the more enlightened industrial employers of the time and, in routine fashion, cooperated with the National Research Council in a relatively simple experiment designed to determine the optimum level of illumination in a shop for maximum production efficiency. Western Electric's Hawthorne plant near Chicago was selected for the experiment. Before the research was over, an impressive team of researchers was involved; of its members, Elton Mayo is probably the best known to educators.

The original experiment was very well designed and executed, and it revealed that there was no direct, simple relationship between the illumination level and the production output of the workers. Since one of Taylor's "principles" suggested strongly that there would be such a relationship, this study raised more questions than it answered.

After pondering the surprising results from their initial experiment, the investigators sought to answer six questions that they hoped would explain their findings:

1. Do employees actually become tired?
2. Are pauses for rest desirable?

3. Is a shorter working day desirable?
4. What is the attitude of employees toward their work and toward the company?
5. What is the effect of changing the type of working equipment?
6. Why does production decrease in the afternoon?

These were rather simple, straightforward questions, but it is obvious that the answers to a number of them would be psychological, rather than physical, in nature. These questions triggered one of the most far-reaching series of experiments in the history of administration, which became known as the Western Electric studies and which led to discoveries that are not yet fully understood. However unexpected it may have been, one major finding of these studies was the realization that human variability is an important determinant of productivity. Thus, in the 1920s, the basis for the human relations movement was established.[16]

New concepts were now available to the administrator to use in practice. Among them were (1) morale, (2) group dynamics, (3) democratic supervision, (4) personnel relations, and (5) behavioral concepts of motivation. The human relations movement emphasized human and interpersonal factors in administering the affairs of organizations. Supervisors, in particular, drew heavily on human relations concepts, placing stress on such notions as "democratic" procedures, "involvement," motivational techniques, and the sociometry of leadership.

The human relations movement attracted social and behavioral scientists, particularly group dynamicists who had already been studying the phenomena of human behavior of individuals interacting with one another in dyads and in groups. Numerous studies carried out in group and organizational settings laid the groundwork for better understanding the nature of human groups and how they function. Illustrative of the better early work of group dynamicists is that of Jacob Moreno, who developed and refined the techniques of sociometric analysis. Moreno sensed that within groups there are informal subgroups—identifiable clusters of people that form essentially on the basis of how much they like or dislike one another.[17] Moreno developed techniques of gathering information from members of organizations as to the attraction they had for one another; the data were often gathered by interview, but other techniques (such as simple questionnaires) also were used. From such information, *sociograms* were developed which portrayed the dynamics of the *informal social structure* of human groups. A typical sociogram of a group of five people might look like Figure 1–1, for example. By asking the members of the group simple questions (such as with whom they would be most willing to work), it is possible to ascertain a great deal about the informal social structure of the group.

Another fruitful line of investigation emanating from the human relations approach was the work of Robert Bales. He developed a systematic technique for analyzing the patterns of interaction between the members of a group. Essentially, Bales's interaction analysis technique consisted of recording key facts about the discussions that occurred between individuals: how many took place between specific individuals, who initiated them, which of these were between two individuals and which were addressed to the group as a whole, and so on.[18] Bales's work not only provided a workable technique that others could use to study the interaction

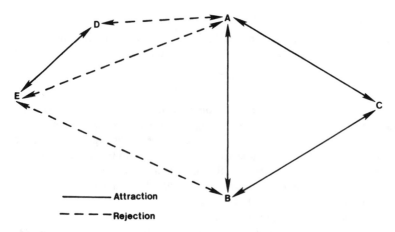

FIGURE 1–1.   Simple sociogram of five-person group.

patterns of groups, but also permitted him to draw some generalizations about groups that have proved to be useful.

For example, Bales was the first to document that successful groups tend to have people in them who play two key roles: it is necessary for someone (or, perhaps, several individuals in a group) to keep the group focused on *accomplishing its task,* and, at the same time, it is necessary for every successful group to have someone to see that the group pays attention to *maintaining productive human relations* within the group. These two dimensions of group behavior—task orientation and maintenance orientation—have proved to be of lasting value in understanding the dynamics of group functioning.

Leadership has long been a subject of great interest to those concerned with organizations, and social scientists were not long in realizing that—unlike the classical view—leadership is not something that "great people" or individuals with formal legal authority do to their subordinates, but, rather, is a process involving dynamic interaction with subordinates. Benjamin Wolman, for example, found that members of groups tend to elect to leadership positions individuals who are perceived to have the ability (or "power") to satisfy the needs of the group and who are, at the same time, perceived as ready to accept the responsibility.[19] Bales noted that groups tend to confer leadership on individuals, not so much on the basis of how well they are liked as on the basis of the ideas that the individuals contribute to the groups and the help that they give the groups in carrying out the ideas.[20] Helen Jennings found that dominant, aggressive people are not likely to be perceived by group members as leaders but, in fact, are likely to be rejected and isolated by the group.[21]

These few examples may serve in this discussion to illustrate some of the kinds of sociological, psychological, and social psychological investigations that were undertaken in large numbers during the human relations era. This was a time when, in fact, social psychology began to mature as a scientific and academic discipline. Kurt Lewin contributed richly to studies of organizational behavior during this period, especially in the area of group decision making.[22] More importantly, Lewin early developed crucial insights and theoretic views that were of great help to those who came after him. His work and that of his students, for example, inspired the laboratory method of personal growth training (that is, T-Groups or sensitivity training) which, in turn, laid the basis for the contemporary practice of organization development, discussed in Chapter 8.

Muzafer Sherif, whose studies of street gangs as human social systems became landmarks of insight and research methodology, went on to produce one of the early textbooks in social psychology.[23] George Homans (*The Human Group,* 1950), Felix Roethlisberger (*Management and Morale,* 1950), William Foote Whyte ("Human Relations in the Restaurant Industry," 1948), Fritz Redl ("Group Emotion and Leadership," 1942), Philip Selznick ("The Leader as the Agent of the Led," 1951), and Alvin W. Gouldner (*Studies in Leadership,* 1950) are only a few of the more famous contributors to the outpouring of theory and research during this period that was to establish an irreversible trend in thought and understanding about behavior in human organizations.

In American education, the human relations movement had relatively little impact upon school district administrators (for example, superintendents of schools), as compared with rather a substantial impact upon supervisory levels (for example, supervisors, elementary school principals). Superintendents, in general, continued to emphasize such classical concepts as hierarchical control, authority, and formal organization, while supervisors emphasized to a much greater extent such human relations concepts as morale, group cohesiveness, collaboration, and the dynamics of informal organization. A review of the proceedings and publications of representative organizations, such as the American Association of School Administrators (AASA) and the Association for Supervision and Curriculum Development (ASCD) readily reveals that, for the most part, those who saw their roles as educational administrators tended to emphasize attention to budgets, politics, control, and the asymmetrical exercise of power from the top downward, while those who were primarily concerned with instruction and curriculum placed much more emphasis on participation, communication, and de-emphasis on status-power relationships. This difference in emphasis persisted at least into the 1980s, though administrators moved somewhat to embrace human relations ideas.

THE ORGANIZATIONAL BEHAVIOR MOVEMENT, 1950–1975

Classical or bureaucratic concepts of organizations are sometimes said to focus on organizations without people. There is such great emphasis on *formal* organizational structure and the highly rational logic of hierarchical control that people are often viewed as fitting into that structure on the organization's terms.

Human relations concepts, on the other hand, are often said to deal with people without organizations. This is, in large measure, because early students of the dynamics of human behavior in groups often conducted their research in small groups rather than in work-oriented organizations. In the formative years of attempts to apply human relations concepts to well-structured organizations, a great deal of attention was devoted to *informal* aspects of the organization, and there was relatively little impact upon the formal (that is, "official") organization.

In the five-year span between 1937 and 1942, however, three significant books appeared that laid the groundwork for what was to develop during the post–World War II era into a new, major influence on thought and practice in administration. The first of these landmark books was Chester Barnard's *The Functions of the Executive*, which appeared in 1938. Barnard, a vice president of the New Jersey Bell Telephone Company, selected and integrated concepts from the many schools of thought that had appeared since Wilson's essay, and he introduced a number of new insights of his own. Barnard was in close communication with the scientists who conducted the Western Electric studies. One of his most important contributions, and one that is germane to this discussion, was to illuminate the crucial importance of better understanding the relationship between the *formal organization* and the *informal organization*. In this pioneer work Barnard made it clear (1) that it was illusory to focus exclusively on the formal, official, structural facets of administering organizations, and (2) that the effective executive must attend to the interaction between the needs and aspirations of the workers, on the one hand, and the needs and purposes of the organization, on the other hand.

In the very next year, 1939, the second of these three significant books appeared: *Management and the Worker*, by Felix J. Roethlisberger and William J. Dickson. These two scholars presented a new view of the dynamic mutual interaction between the formal organization and the informal organization (the latter being the informal social structure that exists among workers). Based upon evidence gathered from the Western Electric Company research, the authors described and documented, for example, the surprising sophistication of the informal organization and its power to exercise control over not only the behavior of workers but also (without their realizing it) over the behavior of supervisors and managers who thought that they were exercising the control. Their emphasis on "individual needs, informal groups, and social relationships was quickly endorsed by other social scientists and led to a 'philosophy of management' concerned primarily with human relationships in formal organizations."[24]

Finally, the third of this triumvirate of early books was Herbert A. Simon's *Administrative Behavior*, which was published in 1947. Even the title, with its emphasis on behavior, foreshadowed a fresh approach to understanding administrative practice. In his book, Simon—a professor with a strong background in political science, psychology, and business administration—sought to illuminate the importance of human behavior in such critical administrative processes as making decisions. This book, more than any other, established a fresh new concept of administration and set the pace for social and behavioral scientists who sensed in that post–World War II era that there was great promise in this new approach.

Although the adherents of classical and human relations approaches did not vanish in the years that followed, the most vigorous administrative research was in the areas of extending and developing the newer behavioral concepts. Scientists from a number of disciplines, or traditions, were to publish a steady stream of research and theory during the ensuing years. A listing of a few of the better-known books published in the 1950s through the 1960s, roughly classified by the academic tradition of their authors, presents a rather clear overview of the way the field developed:

PSYCHOLOGY AND SOCIAL PSYCHOLOGY

CHRIS ARGYRIS, *Personality and Organization* (1958)
BERNARD M. BASS, *Leadership, Psychology, and Organizational Behavior* (1960)
ALVIN W. GOULDNER, ED., *Studies in Leadership* (1950)
MUZAFIR SHERIF, ED., *Intergroup Relations and Leadership* (1962)
RENSIS LIKERT, *The Human Organization: Its Management and Value* (1967)

SOCIOLOGY

PETER M. BLAU AND W. RICHARD SCOTT, *Formal Organizations* (1962)
AMITAI ETZIONI, *A Comparative Analysis of Complex Organizations* (1961)
CHARLES PERROW, *Organizational Analysis: A Sociological View* (1970)

ANTHROPOLOGY

WILLIAM FOOTE WHYTE, *Men at Work* (1961)
ELIOT DISMORE CHAPPLE AND LEONARD R. SAYLES, *The Measure of Management* (1961)
HARRY F. WOLCOTT, *The Man in the Principal's Office* (1973)

POLITICAL SCIENCE

VICTOR A. THOMPSON, *Modern Organization* (1961)
ROBERT V. PRESTHUS, *The Organizational Society* (1962)
MARILYN GITTEL, *Participants and Participation: A Study of School Policy in New York City* (1967)

MANAGEMENT

DOUGLAS MCGREGOR, *The Human Side of Enterprise* (1960)
RENSIS LIKERT, *New Patterns of Management* (1961)
ALFRED J. MARROW, DAVID G. BOWERS, AND STANLEY E. SEASHORE, *Management by Participation* (1967)

Human relations and organizational behavior. The term "human relations" is a broad one that refers to the interactions between people in all kinds of situations in which they seek, through mutual action, to achieve some purpose. Thus, it can properly be applied to two people seeking to develop a happy and productive life together, a social club, a business firm, schools, and, indeed, entire governments and even whole societies. The social structure that regulates the human interactions that are the subject of human relations may be formal, clear, and readily apparent (for example, a government, a firm), or it may be informal, even diffuse, and therefore difficult to describe accurately (for example, the power structure of a group of prison inmates, the social system of a school faculty, or a neighborhood).

"Organizational behavior" is a narrower, more precise term that falls under the broader, more general meaning of human relations. Organizational behavior is a discipline that seeks to describe, understand, and predict human behavior in the environment of formal organizations. A distinctive contribution and characteristic of organizational behavior as a discipline is the explicit recognition that (a) organizations create internal contextual settings, or environments, that have great influence on the behavior of people in them, and (b) to some extent the internal environment of an organization is influenced by the larger context in which the organization itself exists (for example, the social, political, economic, and technological systems that support the organization). Moreover, the internal environment or context of the organization (which is so influential in eliciting and shaping human behavior) is not merely physical and tangible but also includes the social and psychological characteristics of the living human system.

Because management/administrative science has effective performance of goal-seeking formal organizations as its central focus, organizational behavior is closely linked with that science also. Management and administration necessarily must bear responsibility for establishing internal arrangements of the organization, so as to achieve maximum effectiveness. In the early years of human relations it was common for managers and administrators to speak of the human relations of employees or human relations of the firm as though the organization and the wellsprings of its employees' behavior were separate though related. Contemporary administrative science, on the other hand, views goal-directed organizational behavior as essential to results-oriented, cooperative endeavor that cannot be teased out from the management policies and administrative practices of the system.

EDUCATIONAL ADMINISTRATION STIRS

Educational administration was affected very little by the evolution of administration as a field of study until the middle of this century, largely because the teaching of educational administration was sequestered from the current mainstream of scholarly thought and research. Schools of education in even the most prestigious universities tended to have almost no contact with the business schools and the behavioral science departments on their own campuses. Traditionally, educational administration had been taught by former school superintendents whose knowledge of their subject came largely from years of hard-earned experience in the "front lines." Courses in educational administration tended to focus on practical, "how-to-do-it" problems, drawing on the past experience of practicing administrators. Emphasis was typically given to sharing the techniques of these administrators for solving problems—techniques that had been tried in school districts such as the ones with which the students were familiar.

Research in educational administration during the first half of this century consisted principally of status studies of current problems or the gathering of opinion. With rare exceptions, little research in educational administration dealt with the testing of theoretical propositions, and virtually none of it involved the insights and research methods that had been developed by behavioral scientists. As Van Miller has observed:

> A lot of the study of administration has been a matter of looking backward or sideways at what was done or what is being done. It is striking to contemplate how much administrative experience has been exchanged and how little it has been studied scientifically. The current excitement arises from the fact that within recent years educational administration has become a field of study and of development as well as a vocation.[25]

By the mid-1950s a new concept of organization was gaining wide acceptance among students of educational administration. This new concept recognized the dynamic interrelationships between (1) the structural characteristics of the organization and (2) the personal characteristics of the individual. It sought to understand the behavior of people at work in terms of the dynamic interrelationships between the organizational structure and the people who populated it.

Using this insight, students of organization began to conceptualize organizations—such as school systems and schools—as *social systems*. Although it is true that nearly any human group[26] constitutes a human social system (including such diverse groups as street gangs, hobby clubs, and church congregations), the concept that began to emerge in this post–World War II era was that *organizations* constitute a *particular kind* of social system: essentially, it is characterized by a clear and relatively strong *formal* structure. For example, unlike such informal human social systems as the office bowling team or the secretaries who eat lunch together, school systems and schools (and, indeed, all formal organizations) may be characterized as follows:[27]

1. They are specifically goal-oriented;

2. The work to be done so as to achieve goals is divided into subtasks and assigned as official duties to established positions in the organization;

3. These positions are arranged hierarchically in the formal organization, and authority relationships are clearly established;

4. General and impersonal organizational rules govern, to a large extent, what people do in their official capacity and also, to a large extent, shape and delimit the interpersonal interactions of people in the organization.

Beginning in the mid-1950s, increasing attention was devoted to efforts to better understand the relationships among (1) these characteristics of organizational structure, (2) the personality (and consequent "needs") of individuals in the organization, and (3) behavior on the job. For example, numerous studies of leader behavior conducted in the 1950s and 1960s revealed remarkable agreement on the point that leadership can be best understood in terms of two specific kinds of behaviors: (1) behavior that gives structure to the work of the group (for example, how the work is to be done, when, by whom, and so forth), and (2) behavior that is perceived by subordinates as showing consideration for the subordinates as human beings. These empirically derived insights were widely applied to business, industry, the military, and many other kinds of organizations, as well as to school systems and schools.[28]

The generalization that seemed to arise from empirical tests of this view was that there was one leadership style that promised to be more effective than any other: namely, a style characterized by behavior that emphasized *both* initiating structure *and* consideration for people. In this way, of course, both the demands of the organization and the needs of individuals to deal with the organization would be met. One study typical of this period, using the popular social systems model, found that school principals who displayed a style that emphasized concern for people tended to view teachers as professionals to a greater extent than did principals who stressed the role of initiating structure in the work group.[29]

In the years from roughly 1955 to 1970, there was a great outpouring of theorizing and research in educational administration which explored the basic concepts of social system (either explicitly or implicitly) as applied to public school systems and schools. Neal Gross, using sociological methods of inquiry, sought to illuminate the reasons why school board members and school superintendents in New England made the decisions that they did.[30] Daniel Griffiths initiated landmark work on decision making in educational administration which added considerably to our understanding of the importance of the decision-making behavior of administrators.[31] One of many studies based on Griffiths's work, for example, suggests that if the administrator confines himself or herself to establishing clear processes and procedures for making decisions (rather than actually making the final decisions), the administrator's behavior will be more acceptable to subordinates.[32]

A team of researchers, who were especially interested in understanding the processes of curriculum change in schools, conducted a study to explore the question, "To what extent do administrators and teachers in a given school system tend to agree or disagree in their perceptions of decision-making roles and responsibilities?" Among the many findings arising from this complex and comprehensive study, one of the most outstanding—according to Griffiths—was that consideration for subordinates is more valuable behavior for the superintendent to exhibit than behavior intended to initiate structure in the group.[33]

University graduate programs of study for educational administrators soon reflected the influence of social and behavioral science views of organizational behavior. In many cases, courses featuring some of the newer behavioral views—such as leadership, motivation, decision making, organizational climate, conflict management, and organizational change—took their place alongside courses on budgeting, financing, law, and school plant, site, and facilities. It soon became standard practice for writers of textbooks on the school principalship, general administration, and personnel administration to attempt to establish the relevance of organizational behavior research and concepts to the specific areas that the book addressed. Many professors, in their research and consulting activities, used these new ideas in their analysis of practical problems in the "field," as well as in the design of in-service training activities.

EMERGING DEVELOPMENTS IN ORGANIZATIONAL THOUGHT, 1975–PRESENT

The problem that this book addresses is to understand the behavior of people at work in educational organizations. This is the central problem confronting educational administrators because administration is defined as "working with and through other people, individually and in groups, to achieve organizational goals." In terms of administrative practice, then, we need to know which are the best and most effective ways of working with and through other people.

This is no arcane academic question. How you answer it goes to the heart of how you go about the work of school administration, whether as a department chairperson, a school principal, a superintendent of schools, or any position in-between. Nor is it a simple question. Teachers know, from working with children and their parents, that people are complex, idiosyncratic, full of contradictions, and that their behavior often seems baffling and difficult to grasp.

Moreover, we understand now much better than we did twenty years ago that schools, as organizations, are complex and confusing places that are—at their best—filled with contradiction, ambivalence, ambiguity, and uncertainty. These understandings help us realize that many of the most important problems confronting school administrators are neither clear-cut nor amenable to technical solutions. This is not a problem peculiar to school administration nor is it limited to schools as organizations. It is a problem that is generally shared by all professions and all organizations. Listen to Donald Schön as he describes what he calls a "crisis of confidence in professional knowledge":

> In the varied topography of professional practice, there is a high, hard ground overlooking a swamp. On the high ground, manageable problems lend themselves to solutions through the application of research-based theory and technique. In the swampy lowland, messy, confusing problems defy technical solution. The irony of this situation is that the problems of the high ground tend to be relatively unimportant to individuals or society at large, however great their technical interest may be, while in the swamp lie the problems of greatest human concern. The practitioner must choose. Shall he remain on the high ground where he can solve relatively unimportant problems according to prevailing standards of rigor, or shall he descend to the swamp of important problems...?[34]

For many years now, educational administrators have been urged to concentrate on technical solutions to the problems of education, and we have heard a lot about needs assessments; management by objectives; diagnostic-prescriptive teaching; planning-programming-budgeting systems; formalized approaches to teaching (such as the Hunter Model), and have been obsessed with the development of "programs" to meet every conceivable problem confronting the schools.

But important educational problems (those that are in the swampland that Donald Schön describes) are typically messy problems: ill-defined, ill-understood, complicated. Messy problems tend to be understood, or framed, in terms of the things about them that we are apt to notice. What you may notice, though, comes mainly from your own background, values, and perspectives. As Schön observes,

> A nutritionist, for example, may convert a vague worry about malnourishment among children in developing countries into the problem of selecting an optimal diet. But agronomists may frame the problem in terms of food production; epidemiologists may frame it in terms of diseases that increase the demand for nutrients or prevent their absorption; demographers tend to see it in terms of a rate of population growth that has outstripped agricultural activity; engineers, in terms of inadequate food storage and distribution; economists, in terms of insufficient purchasing power or the inequitable distribution of land or wealth.[35]

Similarly, as administrators seek to deal with the problems of education, their approach depends primarily on how they conceptualize their options, how they frame the problems. And as in the case of malnutrition of children, there are many ways of framing a response. But people are limited in their ability to make sense of problems, to frame them, by the number and variety of frames that they are familiar with and that they can draw upon to give them insight and perspective on the messy, ill-defined problems that every professional encounters in the swampy lowlands.

As I have described, for the last half-century, one single perspective has dominated thinking about educational organizations: the structural perspective. This is the familiar notion of hierarchical control, bureaucratic offices, the familiar organization chart, and rules and regulations such as "standard operating procedures."

After 1975, organizational thought took a major turn away from such formal theorizing that emphasized the machinelike characteristics that many scholars believed underlay the ways in which they worked toward a markedly increased emphasis on the human dimensions of organization. This shift was caused by a combination of several forces that came together simultaneously. One of these forces was intellectual: the development of a new analysis of the fundamental concept of what an organization actually is.

COLLAPSE OF TRADITIONAL ORGANIZATIONAL THEORY

As I have described, the period from the early 1950s into the mid-1970s produced a great outpouring of theory and research in educational administration, so much so that in retrospect the period is often called the era of The Theory Movement in educational administration. However, by the 1970s concern was being increasingly expressed that the theories and the research that had been spawned did not fully describe schools as they were experienced by people in them. Research, and indeed the academic establishment in leading universities at that time, was dominated by those who accepted logical-positivist assumptions about schools as organizations and about ways of understanding them. In other words, they assumed that there was some rational, logical, systematic order underlying the organizational realities of schools that must be discovered. Further, they thought that the means of discovery must be the approach to inquiry that emphasizes measurement, sampling, quasi-experimental methods, and quantification. Moreover, it was believed that these assumptions and these methods of discovery were the only way to improve the training of educational practitioners. Wayne Hoy and Cecil Miskel claimed, for example, that "The road to generalized knowledge can lie only in tough-minded scientific research, not in introspection and subjective experience."[36]

However, by 1974, T. Barr Greenfield articulated serious concerns about then-existing organizational theory that had been developing among both practitioners and a growing number of scholars. The crux of the concerns was that academicians, in their search to understand educational organizations and the behavior of people in them—to make sense of the "swamp" that Donald Schön spoke of—had become transfixed with the wish to be objective, to emphasize mathematical descriptions, and, worst of all, they had come to think of organizations as tangible, concrete entities that exist independently and that are governed by systematic laws and principles. "In common parlance," Greenfield said, "we speak of organizations as if they were real."[37] But they are not real, he went on to explain: "they are invented social realities"[38] that actually exist only in the minds of people, rather than as tangible, independent realities. Thus, the argument runs, we anthropomorphize when we speak of organizations as imposing themselves on people or of organizational systems "behaving" in certain ways. The essence of organization is human beings who populate the organization; it is they who choose, act, and behave, even if in their own minds they reify the organization as they do so.

Nevertheless, we are continually confronted by evidence that academic assumptions often contrast remarkably with the experiences of individuals engaged in the work of school administration. This pervasive discrepancy between the academic view of the world and that of the practitioner may well explain the lack of enthusiasm that practitioners chronically express toward the preparation that they have received at the university.[39] For example, striking differences exist between academic literature on the principalship and the principals' written reflections on their own practice:[40]

- Principals describe concrete everyday experiences while academics emphasize theory and abstract relationships;
- Principals communicate through metaphors, examples, and stories while academics use models and the language of science;
- Principals are aware of limits on rationality while academics stress rationality and defining problems in formal terms;
- Principals describe schools in human and emotional terms wherein school personnel agonize over and celebrate their daily ups and downs while academics describe them in terms of detached abstraction;
- Principals see schools as ambiguous and even chaotic places while academics describe an image of rationality and orderliness.

RISE IN QUALITATIVE RESEARCH METHODS

By the 1980s many students of education, who were well aware of these discrepancies, began to eschew traditional formal theorizing and the limitations of traditional quasi-experimental research methods and to find better ways of studying human behavior in schools. They began to go into the schools, instead of sending questionnaires and compiling statistics, to see what was going on and to talk to school individuals in order to understand how they were experiencing their lives. The results of such inquiries produced lively, rich narrative descriptions of life in present-day schools that illuminated the confusions, inconsistencies, ambiguities, and general messiness so characteristic of schools' organizational life.

Indeed, studies using these research methods, called *qualitative* or *ethnographic methods,* became the intellectual backbone of the educational reform movement of the 1980s. Gone were the spare statistical studies, so often elegant in style but yielding "no significant difference," replaced by lively, richly documented accounts of human beings at work that yielded insight and understanding of what was happening to people and how they were responding to their experiences.

This was a major shift in ways of thinking about and studying organizational behavior, and it directly arose from abandoning the old certainties of logical positivism in favor of significant new directions in understanding organizational behavior in schools. To get some flavor of the newer thinking, we turn now to a brief examination of some of the ideas about organization that began to emerge as traditional organizational theory collapsed.

The concept of middle-range theories. The state of the art in organizational behavior by the mid-1980s was that, although there was no single, overall explanation for organizational behavior, scientists were working with a group of what may be called "middle-range theories."[41] As Karl Weick has pointed out in discussing this concept of using middle-range theories in studying organization, there have been a number of attempts in the first two decades of the organizational behavior era (that is, from about 1955 to about 1975) to use social systems concepts as an overarching explanation of organization under which other concepts (such as motivation and organizational culture) are subsumed. He went on to suggest that a more useful approach might be to treat social systems theory as *one* important way to describe crucial aspects of organization, while recognizing that there are a number of other, related, middle-range theories that also have great power to describe and explain behavior in organizations. That is the approach being used in this book.

The ideas of James D. Thompson. In 1967, James D. Thompson described many new insights into the nature of organizations that laid the basis for a new impetus in organizational theorizing in the 1970s.[42] He saw that the fundamental problem confronting organizations was uncertainty and consequently described coping with uncertainty as the foundation of administration. An important aspect of uncertainty is our inability to foresee problems, changes, and unpredictable emerging events that the organization will encounter. Thus goals may be set, plans developed, programs and standard operating procedures implemented but inevitably those at the operating level (for example, in the classroom) will encounter situations in which the requirements of the "official" program (such as a curriculum or an administrative procedure) are inappropriate or unworkable. It is critically important for the organization to provide means for dealing with these problems. Those who lean toward traditional classical views of organization would favor passing such problems up the line of authority for decision at the appropriate level in the hierarchy. Another approach, however, might be to authorize greater decision-making latitude at lower levels in the organization. Each approach has advantages and disadvantages in terms of such issues as maintaining standards, control, and flexibility.

Thompson described the organization as having a "technical core" in which the actual work activities (such as teaching) are performed, plus "boundary spanning units." These boundary spanning units are in direct contact with the organization's external environment and their critical function is to deal with the uncertainties in that environment. The boundary spanning units, in the case of schools and school districts, are those that attend to such matters as placating hostile groups of parents and community members, obtaining needed financial resources, and predicting future political and social shifts. In so doing, the boundary spanning units of the organization protect the technical core by insulating it from the short swings of uncertainty in the external environment.

A third major concept that Thompson developed had to do with the nature of the interdependencies between people in the organization. He used the term *coupling* to describe the three possible ways in which to relate people and work. *Reciprocal coupling* refers to the situation in which workers pass their work back and forth. An example might be that in which the nurse prepares the patient for the dentist, the dentist works on the patient, and then the nurse finishes up. *Sequential coupling* is the situation in which the workers perform their work tasks one after the other in serial fashion over time. *Pooled coupling* is the situation in which organization members share resources in common but otherwise work independently. It is a situation frequently found in schools, where teachers typically share the building and facilities but generally work alone in their classrooms.

The fact that schools are characterized by pooled coupling is useful in understanding organizational behavior in them. It means, for example, that there is characteristically low interdependence among the members of educative organizations. Therefore, as long as the facilities and resources remain relatively stable, anyone can be taken out, replaced, or can perform poorly with little impact on the functioning of the organization. In reciprocal coupling and especially sequential coupling it matters very much whether the others are there and how well they are doing their work.

The concept of organized anarchies.   Traditional structuralist approaches of classical theory emphasize the logic and order of human social systems, viewing the decision-making processes as a highly integrated sequence of logical processes. In education, neoclassical (or neoscientific) approaches to organization and management that emerged in the 1960s sought to apply these concepts in newer, more sophisticated ways. There was great emphasis on stating objectives in explicit behavioral terms, formal detailed assessments of educational need, systems analysis, cost-benefit analysis, and rational planning systems such as Management by Objectives (MBO) and Planning Programming Budgeting Systems (PPBS). The approach generally envisioned (1) explicit definition of organizational goals (and sub-goals), (2) the systematic selection of the least costly plan from among alternative possibilities to achieve the goals, and (3) the development of programs, sub-programs, program elements and sub-elements (all rationally ordered and related) required to carry out the plan.

The problem with all of this is that educational organizations do not function this way in the "real world." Classical and neoclassical organizational theorists would, of course, contend that they *should* and strenuous efforts have been undertaken to correct the apparent deficiencies of educational organizations in this regard. However in the 1970s the discrepancy between what classical views posited "ought" to be and views commonly found in schools and institutions of higher education was so great that some social scientists began to reexamine the organizational characteristics of schools and institutions of higher education.

Michael Cohen, James March, and Johan Olsen identified three distinctive features of educational organizations that are troublesome in applying classical organizational concepts:[43]

1.   Their goals are not specific and clear. Indeed, the goals of educational organizations seem to shift often, are frequently in conflict with one another, are different for different groups of participants, and are difficult to translate into clear-cut programs of action.
2.   Their technology is unclear and in important ways not well understood. As I shall describe more fully in Chapter 3, considerably more technology is used in organizing

educational organizations than is generally realized. But we are unable to specify in more than rather general ways the impact of educational technology on learners. A common dilemma in public schools, for example, is for teachers and supervisors to find methods and materials that will assure that students who are not learning well can be "reached."

3. Participation in them is fluid. Students move in and out, teachers and administrators come and go, parents become involved sporadically, and others in the community take interest in the schools when the spirit moves them.

Organizations manifesting these characteristics have been called "organized anarchies" so as to clearly distinguish them as a distinctive type or class of organization quite different from that usually envisioned in traditional classical organizational thought.

Because they are different, new concepts for thinking about them must be developed. It should be emphasized here, however, that even very recently developed views are set upon the basic conceptualization that organizational behavior can be understood best in the context of a dynamic interrelationship between the *organization,* on the one hand, and the *human beings* who populate it, on the other hand. In the decade of the 1980s, the most promising new ideas appeared to focus on improving our understanding of the *organization* side of the equation. Many assumptions about the nature of organizations and the ways in which they are structured were being reexamined. This raised the distinct possibility that perhaps we have, for too long, been uncritical in accepting certain traditional ideas about the hierarchical, rational nature of organizations that in fact do not describe what organizations are actually like.

The garbage can model of organizational choice. Cohen, March, and Olsen, for example, attracted considerable attention in their effort to understand the decision-making processes found in organized anarchies. Whereas it has been popular for years to think of decision making as highly rational and systematic in organizations, they suggest that some organizations "can be described better as a loose collection of ideas than as a coherent structure; [the organization] discovers preferences through action more than it acts on the basis of preferences."[44] This, they believe, is especially true in organizations with goals that are not consistent or that are not fully shared by the participants.

And in some cases, "although the organization manages to survive and even produce, its own processes are not understood by its members. It operates on the basis of simple trial-and-error procedures, the residue of learning from the accidents of past experience, and pragmatic inventions of necessity."[45] Organizations in which the goals are hazy, the technology ill-defined, and the participation relatively fluid are not likely to solve problems in an orderly, rational manner. The conventional view of organizational choice, of course, is that some alternative solutions are generated; these are examined for likely consequences; then the alternatives are evaluated in terms of potential payoff in achieving the best solution to the problem; and, finally, a decision is reached. This model may be a poor description of what actually happens.

Instead, Cohen and his colleagues have described a much more complex and unstructured process, shifting combinations of problems, potential solutions, people, and opportunities to make choices that intermesh in complicated ways. It may not be the optimum way for organizations to solve problems, they admit, but in fact "when the organization is plagued with goal ambiguity and conflict, with poorly understood problems that wander in and out of the system, with a variable environment, and with decision-makers who have other things on their minds"[46] it may well describe the way in which many organizations do in fact make decisions. Although the research from which these ideas were developed was conducted in a university setting, the concepts—strongly at odds with previously held views of formal organization—may well lead to a more accurate description of how educational organizations actually do function.

Educational organizations as loosely coupled systems. Commonly, we are apt to think of and describe a school system or a school in classical structural terms: for example, as a hierarchically linked pyramid of units subject to strong central control and command (as bureaucracies and military organizations are usually described). Students of organization have recognized for quite some time, however, that school systems and schools are in fact characterized by structural looseness: schools in a district have considerable autonomy and latitude, and teachers in their classrooms are under only very general control and direction of the principal. As Charles Bidwell has pointed out,[47] this is a functionally necessary arrangement, given the nature of the school's task, clients, and technology. Karl Weick captures this reality with vivid imagery, which he credits to James G. March:

> Imagine that you're either the referee, coach, player or spectator in an unconventional soccer match: the field for the game is round; there are several goals scattered haphazardly around the circular field; people can enter or leave the game whenever they want to; they can throw balls in whenever they want; they can say "that's my goal" whenever they want to, as many times as they want to, and for as many goals as they want to; the entire game takes place on a sloped field; and the game is played as if it makes sense. And if you now substitute in that example principals for referees, teachers for coaches, students for players, parents for spectators, and schooling for soccer, you have an equally unconventional depiction of school organizations. The beauty of this depiction is that it captures a different set of realities within educational organizations than are caught when these same organizations are viewed through the tenets of bureaucratic theory.[48]

We can contrast this image of reality with the conventional explanation of how schools go about doing things: namely by planning, goal setting, and applying such rational processes as cost-benefit analyses, division of labor, job descriptions, authority vested in official office, and consistent evaluation and reward systems. The only problem with this latter, conventional view is that it is rare to find schools that actually work that way; more often than not, people in educational organizations find that rational concepts such as these simply do not explain the way the system functions.

Because so much of educational organization defies explanation by existing rational concepts, the suggestion is that we give serious thought to newer, more unconventional ideas that may lead us to more accurate understanding, such as the notion of "loose coupling." In general, the term, loose coupling, means that, although subsystems of the organization (and the activities that they carry out) are related to one another, each preserves its own identity and individuality. In a high school, for example, the guidance office is usually shown on an organization chart as reporting to the principal's office; yet the linkage is usually loose, with relatively infrequent interaction and typically slow responses of one to the other; the linkage is, in short, relatively weak and unimportant. The coupling—the very glue that holds the organization together—may be described as, at best, "loose."

Educational organizations as dual systems. The concept of loose coupling as a distinctive characteristic of schools and other educational organizations has been powerful in explaining aspects of their organization that were previously ill-understood. It does not, however, explain them fully: an observer can easily find much in schools that smacks of bureaucratic or classical organization as well as much that is loosely coupled.

By the mid-1980s there was general agreement among students of organizations that educational organizations are loosely coupled in some significant ways and are highly bureaucratic in other ways, and that this is important in understanding them and the behavior of people in them. For example, in reporting the results of a study of one hundred eighty-eight elementary schools in thirty-four school districts in the San Francisco area, John Meyer and Brian Rowan showed that

> ...the inspection of instructional activity is delegated to the local school and takes place infrequently. For example, only one of the thirty-four superintendents interviewed reported that the district office evaluates teachers directly. Nor does it appear that principals and peers have the opportunity to inspect and discuss teachers' work: Of the principals surveyed, 85 percent reported that they and their teachers do not work together on a daily basis. Further, there is little evidence of interaction among teachers: A majority of the principals report that there are no day-to-day working relations among teachers within the same grade level, and 83 percent report no daily work relations among teachers of different grades. Teachers reaffirm this view of segmented teaching. Two-thirds report that their teaching is observed by other teachers infrequently (once a month or less), and half report a similar infrequency of observation by their principals.[49]

Considerable other research evidence corroborates the observation that supervision by school administrators is rather infrequent.[50]

Of course, control may be exerted by means other than direct inspection (which public school people usually call supervision). For example, evaluation of student learning, close and detailed specification of the curriculum, and ensuring that students have mastered the work of a previous grade before being promoted to the next are among the many ways that schools may exercise strong control over teaching. However, the San Francisco area research and other studies reported by Meyer and Rowan provide evidence that these techniques are little used in meaningful ways.

Thus the central core activity of the school—instruction—is viewed as being loosely coupled to the extent that it is not directly controlled under the authority of administrators. While administrators bear general responsibility for the instructional programs of schools, their authority to control the instructional behavior of teachers is rather limited and, since the advent of collective bargaining, appears to be declining. For example, Meyer and Rowan report that only 12 percent of the principals they studied indicated that they have real decision power over the methods that teachers use, and a mere 4 percent said that they are extremely influential in determining the instructional methods used by teachers.[51]

Administrators, however, do have access to bureaucratic means by which to structure the work of teachers and, thereby, have indirect means of influencing the instructional behavior in the school. *The control of time* is one means: time schedules, the frequency with which students are pulled out for special classes and other activities, the frequency of interruptions of classroom instruction, and the burden of paperwork required of teachers all mold the teaching behavior of teachers and all are influenced by the administrator as a key actor. *The assignment of students to classes* (how many and what kind) is also considerably influenced by administrators and constrains the teachers' work behavior. *Grouping* is another way in which administrators can influence instruction—for example, students may be grouped heterogeneously or homogeneously; teachers may work alone in self-contained classrooms, on teaching teams, or in departments. Principals also influence instructional behavior of teachers through their *control of resources*: teaching space, the availability of equipment, access to the copying machine, and even the availability of such mundane basic supplies as paper and pencils. Yet, while these bureaucratic means are powerful in some ways in influencing the instructional behavior of teachers, they are relatively indirect. Further, as teachers have come to realize the power of these mechanisms, they have increasingly sought to gain some share in controlling them through collective bargaining. Thus, principals are increasingly constrained in their ability to dictate teaching schedules and class sizes, and even in their ability to impose paperwork on teachers.

While the core technical activity of the school is, thus, loosely coupled (as contrasted with what one would expect from a classic bureaucratic organization), noninstructional activities are often tightly coupled. The issuing of paychecks in timely fashion, the deployment of buses, the management of money, and pupil accounting (attendance, for example) are among the numerous noninstructional activities that are closely controlled by administrators and therefore may be described as tightly coupled. In contrast to the nebulous authority that administrators reported over the instructional activities of teachers in their research, Meyer and Rowan reported that 82 percent of the principals surveyed claim to make decisions about scheduling, 75 percent about the assignment of pupils to classes, and 88 percent (either alone or in consultation with other school administrators in the district) about hiring new personnel. These activities may be said to be tightly coupled inasmuch as they are carefully controlled by direct administrative oversight.

One may conclude that looseness in controlling the instructional behavior of teachers is somehow "wrong" and insist—in the tradition of classic bureaucratic thought—that it be tightened up. Indeed, many contemporary observers take such a view, and this explains many political initiatives undertaken in recent years by governors, legislatures, and a few state departments of education to "toughen up" standards and educational requirements by imposing new requirements and limitations on schools. These often include adding required instruction to the curriculum, increased testing of both students and teachers, and more detailed specification of teaching methods. However, the issue being raised here is not whether schools "ought" to be loosely coupled or tightly coupled. Our interest is in better understanding the organizational characteristics of educational organizations *as they exist* (rather than as someone may wish they are) so that we may better understand the management of people in them.

Indeed, recent studies strongly suggest that there are powerful mechanisms through which the organization exerts considerable control over the instructional activities of teachers that have heretofore been largely unseen and unrecognized. These mechanisms are in contrast with the hierarchical line of authority embodied in classical bureaucratic thought. Whereas we traditionally think of organizations exercising control exclusively through such formal mechanisms as supervision down the line of authority, a useful newer perspective is that, in educational organizations at least, powerful control is exercised through the use of far more subtle and indirect means: the development of organizational culture. Understanding this can be a powerful insight in understanding schools and universities and how to lead them effectively.

Organizational culture as a bearer of authority. Like all workplaces, an educational organization—each school and each university—is characterized by a distinctive organizational culture. By "organizational culture" is meant the *norms* that inform people what is acceptable and what is not, the dominant *values* that the organization cherishes above others, the *basic assumptions and beliefs* that are shared by members of the organization, the *"rules"* of the game that must be observed if one is to get along and be accepted as a member, the *philosophy* that guides the organization in dealing with its employees and its clients. These elements of organizational culture are developed over a period of time by the people in the organization, working together. They evolve during the history of the organization and are shared and subscribed to by those who are a part of that history.

The culture of the educational organization shapes and molds assumptions and perceptions that are basic to understanding what it means to be a teacher. The culture informs the teachers as to what it means to teach, what teaching methods are available and approved for use, what the pupils or students are like—what is possible, and what is not. The culture also plays a large role in defining for teachers their commitment to the task: it evokes the energy of the teachers to perform the task, loyalty and commitment to the organization and what it stands for, emotional bonds of attachment to the organization and its ideals. These give rise to teachers' willingness not only to follow the rules and norms governing their behavior in the organization but, more than that, to accept the ideals of the organization as their own personal values and, therefore, to work energetically to achieve the espoused goals of the organization.[52]

Do certain, specific kinds of organizational cultures promote greater effectiveness in educational organizations? The evidence is fragmentary at present. However, considerable evidence for the idea that certain kinds of organizational cultures create improved organizational performance is emerging from studies on business corporations. For example, Terrence E. Deal and his associates have contended that it is strong organizational culture that distinguishes high-performing companies from less successful companies in competitive markets.[53] In a highly popular and best-selling book, Thomas J. Peters and Robert H. Waterman, Jr., have argued that successful American corporations are characterized by the presence of specific, describable cultures that clearly differentiate them from others that would seek to compete with them.[54] Similarly, Rosabeth Moss Kanter has argued persuasively that companies that have what she calls an "open culture" are more innovative and more successful than those that do not.[55] Edgar Schein has described the relationship between organizational culture and the ability of administrators to exercise leadership.[56] A growing body of literature concerning the role of organizational culture in educational organizations (discussed in later chapters of this book) strongly suggests that organizational culture is as powerful in creating effective educational organizations as it is in creating profit-making corporations.

Contingency approaches. There is little likelihood that the hope, nurtured for many years among students of administration, of discovering a set of related concepts that will lead us to the one best way of organizing, leading, motivating, and administering will be realized in the near future. Many variables seem to create contextual settings that preclude applying overly broad generalizations. One of the powerful emerging ideas in understanding organizations and the behavior of people in them is the notion of *contingency.*

Should an organization be highly structured in the formal (bureaucratic) sense? Or is it better to use less rigid, more loosely coupled forms of organization? We are less certain that there is a general single answer to such questions today because it seems clear that it depends, is *contingent,* upon specific circumstances.

For example, organizations that manufacture a high volume of standardized products (such as mass-production factories) or provide standardized services in high volume (for example, the registrar's office in a university) seem to require organizations that are hierarchical in form and bureaucratic in style. On the other hand, organizations that must respond quickly to rapid and unexpected change, and organizations that require the collaborative integration of a number of specialists to get the work done, seem to require a less bureaucratic structure that is readily adaptable, flexible, and responsive to unforseen events.

The generalization seems to be that organizations whose purpose is to perform routinized tasks in relatively predictable environments can use effectively the highly formalized bureaucratic structure of classical tradition. Organizations that are expected to respond and adapt to emerging problems in an environment of change can use more effectively the more flexibly structured organization that emphasizes teamwork, collaboration, participation, and integrated effort.

But there are contingencies other than the mission of the organization. Numerous studies conducted in industry suggest that the nature of the technology that an organization uses goes a long way in shaping the kind of organizational structure that is most effective. Manufacturing firms that use sophisticated technology to produce products in small batches, such as custom tailors, makers of deep-sea oil drilling rigs, and producers of large turbines for hydroelectric dams, tend to have fewer administrative layers in their organizations than do mass-production firms, such as those who make refrigerators, automobiles, and television sets. But continuous-process producers, such as oil refiners and chemical producers, appear to do well with a type of organization that falls, in terms of formalism and layers of authority in the structure, somewhere between the small-batch producers and the mass-production firms.

The conclusion is that there is no one best way to organize, but this does not mean that any way of organizing is as good as any other: the optimum form of organizational structure will depend on a number of contingencies. The goals of the organization, the type of tasks to be done, the extent and nature of the technology required, the relative stability of the environment in which the organization functions, and the kinds of people employed are among the contingencies that must be reckoned with when designing and administering an organization.

The contingency approach to organization has effectively raised doubts about the now long-standing practice of transplanting management practices from business and industry to education, with little or no analysis of the critically different contingencies with which the two kinds of organizations very probably contend. This book reflects the belief that effective management of organizational behavior in schools must be set upon critical analysis of the organizational realities of schools.

NONTHEORETICAL INFLUENCES ON ORGANIZATIONAL THOUGHT

Academic theorizing is hardly the only force that develops our understanding of educational organizations and behavior in them. Two powerful and highly pragmatic emerging influences have largely ignored traditional organizational theory yet have substantially buttressed the kinds of thinking just described. One of these is the *effective schools research;* the other is the much larger, broader *school reform movement* that gathered momentum in the 1980s.

Effective schools research.   The now-substantial body of research literature on effective schools had its origins in despair. In the 1970s, big-city high schools were generally perceived as performing so badly that some were beginning to wonder, "Can big-city high schools be made to work for their poor, ethnic minority students? Do any big-city high schools exist in which student achievement levels are satisfactory? And, if they do, what can we learn from them that will help us to improve other schools?" An analysis of the reading-achievement test scores of big-city high schools quickly revealed that, at least on the basis of those scores, some—albeit, at the time, a few—inner-city high schools were clearly performing better than others.

Researchers began visiting these apparently effective schools to see what they were like, to observe what went on in them, to write case studies describing them. Over the years, this body of qualitative research has grown not merely in volume but also in scope and sophistication. It has powerfully influenced our understanding of the organizational characteristics and the work behaviors of people in effective schools and how they differ from those in their less-effective counterparts.

Findings of the effective schools research.   First, a word of caution. Ever since the first research on effective schools began to appear in the literature in the 1970s, there have been repeated efforts to synthesize the findings and extract the essence of what it tells us. The differences between early efforts to synthesize the work and those that were done later, when the research literature was more substantial and more sophisticated, are striking. Perhaps premature, the earlier efforts now appear to be relatively simplistic and somewhat misleading. By the late 1980s, considerable agreement had emerged among students of effective schools research as to what the key findings were.

Five basic assumptions of effective schools. First, let us look at five basic assumptions that underlie the concept of effective schools:[57]

1. Whatever else a school can and should do, its central purpose is to teach: success is measured by students' progress in knowledge, skills, and attitudes;
2. The school is responsible for providing the overall environment in which teaching and learning occur;
3. Schools must be treated holistically: partial efforts to make improvements that deal with the needs of only some of the students and break up the unity of the instructional program are likely to fail;
4. The most crucial characteristics of a school are the attitudes and behaviors of the teachers and other staff, not material things such as the size of its library or the age of the physical plant;[58]
5. Perhaps most important, the school accepts responsibility for the success or failure of the academic performance of the students. Students are firmly regarded as capable of learning regardless of their ethnicity, sex, home or cultural background, or family income. "Pupils from poor families do not need a different curriculum, nor does their poverty excuse failure to learn basic skills," Stewart Purkey and Marshall Smith assert, adding, "Differences among schools do have an impact on student achievement, and those differences are controllable by the school staff."[59]

Thus, the effective schools concept turns 180 degrees from traditional educational thought that tends to blame the victim, namely the student, for low academic achievement. Though one of the outstanding characteristics of effective schools is that they take responsibility for meeting the educational needs of students to a greater degree than their less-successful counterparts, this is still a concept that many educational practitioners find difficult to accept. Especially in those schools seemingly overwhelmed, as many inner-city and not a few suburban schools are, by poor children, children from diverse cultural backgrounds, and children from nontraditional families, it is not easy to focus the responsibility for the motivation and achievement of students on the school rather than on the students or forces outside the school. Nevertheless, this is the essential lesson from the effective schools research.

The question remains: what is it, specifically, that the schools do in order to fulfil this responsibility? Listen to Purkey and Smith, who developed a penetrating analysis of the effective schools research literature in the mid-1980s:

The most persuasive research suggests that student academic performance is strongly affected by school culture. This culture is composed of values, norms, and roles existing within institutionally distinct structures of governance, communication, educational practices and policies and so on. Successful schools are found to have cultures that produce a climate or "ethos" conducive to teaching and learning...efforts to change schools have been most productive and most enduring when directed toward influencing the entire school culture via a strategy involving collaborative planning, shared decision making, and collegial work in an atmosphere friendly to experimentation and evaluation.[60]

Thus the effective schools research suggests "increased involvement of teachers and other staff members in decision making, expanded opportunities for collaborative planning, and flexible change strategies that can reflect the unique 'personality' of each school. The goal is to change the school culture; the means requires staff members to assume responsibility for school improvement, which in turn is predicated on their having the authority and support necessary..."[61] to create instructional programs that meet the educational needs of their students.

Seeking an effective schools formula. The early effective schools research was quickly seized upon as the basis for developing programs for improving the performance of schools. Regrettably, some of the early popularizers of the effective schools research emphasized interpretations that consisted of a rather simple five- or six-factor formula. Effective schools, ran that early message, share the following characteristics:

- Strong leadership by the principal,
- High expectations for student achievement on the part of teachers and other staff members,
- An emphasis on basic skills,
- An orderly environment,
- Frequent and systematic evaluation of students, and
- Increased time on teaching and learning tasks.[62]

Many major-city school systems—including Chicago, New York, Minneapolis, Milwaukee, St. Louis, San Diego, and Washington, D.C.—and also several states established school-improvement projects based on a list of variables such as the one above. The secretary of education embraced the concept in 1987, and a bill was introduced into the U.S. Congress, although not passed, for the federal funding of school-improvement projects based on this notion.

Recent examination of the effective schools research continues to support the belief that we can identify and describe the essential organizational characteristics of effective schools and the behavior of people in them. However, installing in schools these five or six "correlates," as they soon came to be called, is not in itself sufficient to improve the effectiveness of schools.

Emerging approach to effective schools. Purkey and Smith have identified thirteen characteristics of effective schools from the reported research.[63] They fall into two groups. The first group of nine characteristics can be implemented quickly at minimal cost by administrative action. They are:

1. School-site management and democratic decision making, in which individual schools are encouraged to take greater responsibility for, and are given greater latitude for, educational problem solving;
2. Support from the district for increasing the capacity of schools to identify and solve significant educational problems; this includes reducing the inspection and management roles of central office people while increasing support and encouragement of school-level leadership and collaborative problem solving;

3. Strong leadership, which may be provided by administrators but also may be provided by integrated teams of administrators, teachers, and perhaps others;

4. Staff stability, to facilitate the development of a strong cohesive school culture;

5. A planned, coordinated curriculum that treats the students' educational needs holistically and increases time spent on academic learning;

6. Schoolwide staff development that links the school's organizational and instructional needs with the needs that teachers themselves perceive should be addressed;

7. Parental involvement particularly in support of homework, attendance, and discipline;

8. Schoolwide recognition of academic success, both in terms of improving academic performance and achieving standards of excellence;

9. Emphasize time on teaching and learning; for example, reduce interruptions and disruptions, stress the primacy of focused efforts to learn, and restructure teaching activities.

But these are not the only characteristics of effective schools and certainly they are not the most crucial. However, they are relatively easy and inexpensive to implement quickly and they set the stage for the development of a second group of four characteristics that have great power to renew and increase the school's capacity to continue to solve problems and increase effectiveness over time. These four school characteristics are:

10. Collaborative planning and collegial relationships that promote feelings of unity, encourage sharing of knowledge and ideas, and foster consensus among those in the school;

11. Sense of community, in which alienation—of both teachers and students—is reduced and a sense of mutual sharing is strengthened;

12. Shared clear goals and high achievable expectations, which arise from collaboration, collegiality, and a sense of community and which serve to unify those in the organization through their common purposes;

13. Order and discipline that bespeak the seriousness and purposefulness of the school as a community of people, students, teachers and staff, and other adults, that is cohered by mutual agreement on shared goals, collaboration, and consensus.

Clearly, the critical school characteristics listed in the second group are more complex than those in the first group, more difficult to achieve and sustain over time, yet they combine to produce great power to establish the improvement of educational effectiveness as a central focus of life within the school. The power, of course, lies in developing within the school a culture—norms, values, beliefs—that unites those in the school in their unending quest of seeking increased educational effectiveness. Many if not most school-improvement plans can be faulted precisely for seeking to "install" the relatively simpler first-order characteristics and falling short of seriously engaging in the culture-rebuilding suggested by the more complex second-order characteristics cited here.

THE SCHOOL REFORM MOVEMENT

The school reform movement, which got under way in the early 1980s with the publication of *A Nation at Risk: The Imperative for Educational Reform*,[64] had at the outset little connection with either the new developments in organizational thought or the effective schools research. It has, however, spawned a large number of studies of schools. Many of these studies were qualitative and describe the need to change schools drastically in ways that are highly compatible with the findings of the effective schools research literature.

The first wave of school reform.   Many observers describe the school reform movement of the 1980s as unfolding in two "waves." The so-called first wave of reform—the initial reaction to the outpouring of critiques of schooling that began with the publication of *A Nation at Risk* in 1983—was comprised largely of an astonishing increase in regulatory mandates imposed upon the schools by the states. Such regulations facilitated the reach of governmental bureaucracies directly into the classroom—a reach that was mimicked at the local level by many school district central office organizations—by specifying, for example, what textbooks must be used, how many minutes of time should be devoted to instruction, what teaching techniques were to be used, and by establishing elaborate systems of examinations and reporting through which compliance could be audited by governmental agencies.

By the 1990s, however, many thoughtful observers were expressing alarm that such regulatory approaches with their requisite detailed top-down bureaucratic administration of regulations were, in fact, counterproductive in two major ways.

First, regulatory approaches were driving schools to new heights of mindless rigidity that often failed to take into account the specific individual educational needs of students and the specific circumstances of the schools that they attended. Heightening the bureaucratic control of schools, it was argued, hampered teachers in making the professional judgments about the curriculum and teaching that a particular child needed—decisions that are best made not by the fiat of some faceless distant bureaucratic office but by today's highly qualified teachers who in face-to-face interaction with the student can bring their professional insights to bear on the problem.

Second, a growing body of research made clear that teachers—highly qualified and motivated to do the best for their "clients," namely the students—were increasingly frustrated by their growing inability to exercise their professional judgments in a school environment that was becoming steadily bureaucratized. This was reflected not only in the then-growing teacher shortage, as people left the profession and others declined to enter it, but also in growing evidence of alienation and declining morale of the teachers who remained on the job.

The second wave of school reform.   These concerns ushered in what became known as the second wave of school reform, which recognized that the increased regulatory practices of the first wave of reform were, as Alvin Toffler had put it, "a classic response to a need for fundamental change—the initial tendency is to work the old system harder." Through the promulgation of ever-more regulations, more courses were required and fewer electives were permitted, more hours of classes required, more services made available, more pay offered to teachers, more equipment provided; but these only made the old system work harder and improved schooling only marginally, at best. Why? Because they failed to deal with the fundamental need for change itself: the need for more productive human relationships in schools; the need by students to assume greater responsibility for their own learning; and the need for greater professional autonomy for teachers in diagnosing and solving instructional problems that confront them both in the school and in the classroom.

The old system, which the first wave of reform had taken for granted, saw teachers as low-level functionaries of public hierarchical bureaucracies who were accountable to officials in the higher echelons "above" them in those bureaucracies, who, in turn, are accountable to the public through the political mechanisms of school boards, legislatures, and state boards of education. Indeed, this structure of American public schools is so generally taken for granted that we are not aware of how powerfully it influences the relationships of the players and in turn influences how people behave when they are at work in the schools. The omnipresence of this view has caused us to see public schooling as a function delegated to a government agency, and any other model is literally inconceivable. Thus, education became understood in the bureaucratic mind as the "delivery of educational services," rather than as the mutual striving of teachers and students working together to achieve shared goals of success.

The second wave of school reform took a remarkably different view: that the "front line" of schooling lies in the individual school rather than in some distant bureaucratic government agency and that it is there—in the individual school and in its classrooms—that educational problems can best be identified, puzzled over, and solved. The second wave of school reform recognizes the professional role of teachers, as contrasted with the bureaucratic role. This requires giving teachers sufficient professional autonomy and leeway to exercise their abilities to understand and solve educational problems at the school level, where they are closest to those problems and where they see the complex factors that may be involved in them, and to hold teachers responsible for the results of their decisions and actions.

This new approach to school reform calls for a restructuring of roles and relationships between people at work in the schools. Rather than teachers who passively await mandates to be handed down from above for them to implement, it calls for teachers who are actively involved in studying professional problems, making decisions as to what to do about them, and being committed to achieving results in implementing those decisions. The vision is of a collaborative school environment with teachers more fully engaged than in the past, more highly motivated because of their increased "ownership" of the action.

HUMAN RESOURCES DEVELOPMENT

In this book, the emerging perspective on organizational behavior in education is called Human Resources Development (HRD). In this perspective, educational organizations are characterized—not by the order, rationality, and system inherent in classical thinking—but by ambiguity and uncertainty in their fast-changing environments, unclear and conflicting goals, weak technology, fluid participation, and loose coupling of important activities and organizational units. Because of these characteristics, the core activity of educational organizations—that is, teaching—is not carried out under close surveillance of the administrative hierarchy, as classical thought would envision, but is coordinated and controlled more by the culture of the organization: its values, its traditions, and the norms of acceptable behavior established over time. However, noninstructional activities of educational organizations—such as financial accounting, pupil accounting, and the transportation system—are commonly managed using bureaucratic perspectives and techniques. Thus, in HRD, schools and other educational organizations are understood to be dual organizational systems.

SUMMARY

The essay "The Study of Administration," which Princeton's Assistant Professor Woodrow Wilson published in *Political Science Quarterly* in the summer of 1887, marked the beginning of serious study of administration. During the century that was to follow, students of organization struggled to do what had never before been done: to increase through systematic inquiry our understanding of organizations and the behavior of people who work in them. Two very clear long-term trends developed that, together, set the stage for where we are now and where we are going.

The effort to create an administrative science.   The search for deep and stable principles believed to be the foundations of administrative thought and practice led first to the quest for a science of administration. The effort was fueled by the conviction that some fundamental rational logic, system, and order must underlie organization. These were to be discovered through objective, value-free scientific research using measurement and expressing descriptions in mathematical terms.

Once these factors were discovered, it was thought, systematic principles for engaging in the practice of administration could be scientifically derived from them. By the middle of the twentieth century, though, many observers were having doubts, not merely about the assumptions of system and rationality in organizations that guided the processes of scientific discovery but doubts that the assumed order and logical system even existed at all. These doubts arose from two main observations. First, that practicing administrators saw little relationship between the reality of organizational life as they experienced it and the theories of organizational life that academicians espoused. Second, scant convincing evidence was generated to support the "scientific" assumptions as being more valid than other insightful, thoughtful views.

Formal challenges to this logical-positivist paradigm began to be published in 1974, the so-called theory movement collapsed, and today students of educational administration, at least, have coalesced around a new paradigm that is in the process of being developed at this time. The new paradigm rejects anthropomorphism, which can lead us to reify organizations and think of them as existing in some sort of free-standing way independent of human beings, when organizations actually are social inventions that exist only in the minds of people. We now think not so much of analyzing organizations in mathematical terms but of making sense of them in human terms. We accept that organizations do not "act" or "think"; people do.

Thus, at the dawn of the second century of organizational study, few seriously believe that the time is yet ripe to develop a science of administration if, indeed, such a science ever will be developed. This does not mean, however, that we have failed either to discover some basic principles of organizational behavior or to develop increased understanding of organizational life. Far from it. The patient theorizing and research carried out over the course of a century has produced a rich legacy of knowledge that administrators can use in practice. But it is not marked by the logical precision and mathematical certitude that the pioneer scholars had expected it to have.

Centrality of the human dimension of organization. Perhaps the most powerful learning to have arisen during the first century of organizational studies concerns what is now obvious: that the key to understanding organization lies in understanding the human and social dimensions. Early scholars emphasized organizational structure, chiefly as a hierarchy of power, and the discipline of inducing those of the lower ranks to submit to the power and authority, perceived as legitimate, of those in the higher ranks of the hierarchy. Toward the middle of the twentieth century, triggered by the Western Electric researches, students of organization began to grasp what Douglas McGregor was later to describe as "the human side of enterprise." This was the realization that human motivation, aspiration, beliefs, and values have wondrous power in determining the effectiveness of efforts to lead and develop organizations.

At first, still obeisant to the then widely held conviction of the legitimacy of hierarchical authority, this was interpreted as "human relations," meaning taking steps to ameliorate and reduce the resistance of workers to their powerlessness. "Human relations," as it was interpreted by administrators, typically became ameliorative inducements for people to submit to organizational authority. The inducements ranged from health insurance plans to simple civility in daily encounters; from providing pleasant working environments to legitimizing the feelings of employees about their work. But through the human relations era, administrators clung to the notion that—while they might act civilly, even kindly, to subordinates— power in the organization is hierarchical and, of a right, ought to be exercised asymmetrically from top down.

But the "battle of the century," both in organizational studies and in the larger world, has been the struggle between centralized authority and individual freedom, between entrenched power elites and ordinary people. Organizations of all kinds, often once revered, are now suspect, viewed with hostility, and often described as oppressive. The ability to establish and maintain organizational discipline through traditional top-downward hierarchical exercise of power has been rapidly eroding in all kinds of organizations from nation-states to school districts. The larger canvas, the backdrop, is of course revealed in the collapse of traditional political hegemonies that began to unfold in the late 1980s in Eastern Europe, the USSR, and South Africa as people around the world demanded greater power and freedom from centralized organizational constraints, greater control over their own lives and destinies.

In the world of American education this theme is insistently echoed, if in muted tones, in oft-repeated themes that call for efforts to improve the performance of schools by restructuring them so as to increase the power of teachers to make critical educational decisions, facilitate collaborative decision making, and create collegial growth-enhancing school cultures. This is, of course, a marked departure from traditional thinking and is based on the conviction that overemphasis on bureaucratic structures, top-downward exercise of power, and centralized control have demonstrably failed to produce the organizational results that advocates of traditional organizational theory had claimed it would.

Where we are and where we are going.   At the present time, traditional bureaucratic approaches to organization and the newer approaches that emphasize the human dimensions of organization exist side by side and often compete for the attention and loyalty of educational administrators. Bureaucracy is far from dead in educational organizations, and many people are confident that centralized direction is the most effective way to reform them. On the other hand, nonbureaucratic approaches to organizing and administering have been rapidly gaining support in recent years. These two approaches will continue to compete in the marketplace of ideas for years to come with the newer, emerging, behavioral approach continuing to gain ground because it so well meets contemporary conditions.

SUGGESTED READING

BOLMAN, LEE G., AND TERRENCE E. DEAL, *Modern Approaches to Understanding and Managing Organizations*. San Francisco: Jossey-Bass, 1984.
An excellent survey and synthesis of contemporary theory and research, this volume describes four ways to analyze organizations: as structures, as cultures, as human resource systems, and as political systems.

MEYER, MARSHALL W., AND ASSOCIATES, *Environments and Organizations*. San Francisco: Jossey-Bass, 1978.
Structuralism, in the classical bureaucratic tradition, has long dominated thinking about organizations in sociology. This important book marks a sharp departure from that tradition and introduces the newer organizational theorizing that is emerging in that discipline. Excellent chapter on "The Structure of Educational Organizations." Highly recommended.

MINTZBERG, HENRY, *The Structuring of Organizations*. Englewood Cliffs, N.J.: Prentice-Hall, 1979.
A well-organized, comprehensive, and lucid discussion of contemporary problems of designing and building organizations. Describes the characteristics of five specific kinds of organizations and their implication for administration.

PETERS, THOMAS J., AND ROBERT H. WATERMAN, JR., *In Search of Excellence: Lessons from America's Best-Run Companies*. New York: Harper & Row, 1982.
Long on the best-seller lists, this is a "must" for those who want to find out how modern organizational theory is being used in the competitive corporate world. Though it focuses on business and industry, it contains a great deal of food for thought for educators.

SPROULL, LEE, STEPHEN WEINER, AND DAVID WOLF, *Organizing an Anarchy: Belief, Bureaucracy, and Politics in the National Institute of Education*. Chicago: University of Chicago Press, 1978.
This case study shows how an organization dedicated to rational procedures, excellence, and the use of intelligence came to be indecisive, incompetent, and disorganized. In the "Introduction," pp. 1–8, the authors provide a cogent explanation of the difference between the conventional view that organizations are rational models for decision making and the view that organizations are "organized anarchies."

NOTES

[1]Douglas McGregor, *The Human Side of Enterprise* (New York: McGraw-Hill Book Company, 1960), p. 3.
[2]Woodrow Wilson, "The Study of Administration," *Political Science Quarterly*, 2, no. 2 (June 1887), 197–222.

Mainstreams of Organizational Thought   39

[3]Frederick Taylor, *The Principles of Scientific Management* (New York: Harper & Row, Publishers, Inc., 1911), p. 8.

[4]For a vivid description of this period and the power of business and industrial leaders to force their values on school administrators, see Raymond E. Callahan, *Education and the Cult of Efficiency* (Chicago: University of Chicago Press, 1962).

[5]Amitai Etzioni, *Modern Organizations* (Englewood Cliffs, NJ: Prentice-Hall, 1964), p. 21.

[6]Henri Fayol, *General and Industrial Management*, trans. Constance Storrs (London: Sir Isaac Pitman & Sons, 1949), p. 14.

[7]Ibid., p. 15.

[8]Fayol's work was published in French in 1916 (when he was chief executive of a mining firm) and immediately received wide acclaim in Europe. His views swept into a dominant position (and remained there well into the 1940s) following their appearance in English translation, in *Papers on the Science of Administration*, ed. Luther Gulick and L. Urwick (New York: Columbia University, Institute of Public Administration, 1937).

[9]Richard H. Hall, "The Concept of Bureaucracy: An Empirical Assessment," *The American Journal of Sociology*, 69, no. 1 (July 1963), 33.

[10]J. P. Mayer, *Max Weber and German Politics* (London: Faber & Faber, Ltd., 1943), p. 128.

[11]Raymond E. Callahan, *Education and the Cult of Efficiency* (Chicago: University of Chicago Press, 1962).

[12]Ellwood P. Cubberley, *Public School Administration: A Statement of the Fundamental Principles Underlying the Organization and Administration of Public Education* (Boston: Houghton Mifflin, 1916), pp. 337–38.

[13]David B. Tyack and Robert Cummings, "Leadership in American Public Schools before 1954: Historical Configurations and Conjectures," in *Educational Administration: The Developing Decades*, ed. Luvern L. Cunningham, Walter G. Hack, and Raphael O. Nystrand (Berkeley, CA: McCutchan Publishing Corporation, 1977), p. 61.

[14]Luther Gulick and L. Urwick, eds., *Papers on the Science of Administration* (New York: Institute of Public Administration, Columbia University, 1937).

[15]Luther Gulick, *Administrative Reflection on World War II* (University, AL: University of Alabama Press, 1948).

[16]These studies, often called the Western Electric studies, may be known to the reader for another reason: they led also to identification of the so-called Hawthorne Effect, which became important in improving techniques of behavioral research. These studies are summarized in Fritz J. Roethlisberger and William J. Dickson, *Management and the Worker* (Cambridge, MA: Harvard University Press, 1939).

[17]Jacob L. Moreno, "Contributions of Sociometry to Research Methodology in Sociology," *American Sociological Review*, 12 (June 1947), 287–92.

[18]Robert F. Bales, *Interaction-Process Analysis: A Method for the Study of Small Groups* (Reading, MA: Addison-Wesley, 1950).

[19]Benjamin Wolman, "Leadership and Group Dynamics," *Journal of Social Psychology*, 43 (February 1956), 11–25.

[20]Robert F. Bales, "The Equilibrium Problem in Small Groups," in *Working Papers in the Theory of Action*, ed. Talcott Parsons, Robert F. Bales, and Edward A. Shils (Glencoe, IL: The Free Press, 1953).

[21]Helen H. Jennings, *Leadership and Isolation*, 2nd ed. (New York: Longman, Inc., 1950).

[22]Lewin, who defined *field theory* in social psychology, is often thought of as the father of social psychology. See his "Field Theory and Experiment in Social Psychology: Concepts and Methods," *American Journal of Sociology*, 44 (1939), 868–96, and "Group Decision and Social Change," in *Readings in Social Psychology*, eds. Theodore M. Newcomb and Eugene L. Hartley (New York: Holt, Rinehart & Winston, 1947), pp. 330–44.

[23]Muzafer Sherif, *An Outline of Social Psychology* (New York: Harper & Row, Publishers, Inc., 1948).

[24]Dorwin Cartwright, "Influence, Leadership, Control," in *Handbook of Organizations*, ed. James G. March (Chicago: Rand McNally & Company, 1965), p. 2.

[25]Van Miller, *The Public Administration of American School Systems* (New York: Macmillan, Inc., 1965), pp. 544–45.

[26]As distinguished from a collection of individuals.

[27]This discussion follows that of Max G. Abbott, "Intervening Variables in Organizational Behavior," *Educational Administration Quarterly*, 1, no. 1 (Winter 1966), 1–14.

[28]See, for example, John K. Hemphill and Alvin E. Coons, *Leader Behavior Description* (Columbus: Ohio State University Press, 1950). For later research using their concept, see Andrew W. Halpin and

B. J. Winer, *The Leadership Behavior of the Airplane Commander* (Columbus: Ohio State University Press, 1952); and Andrew W. Halpin, "The Behavior of Leaders," *Educational Leadership*, 14 (1956), 172–76.

[29]Daniel Griffiths, "Administrative Theory," *Encyclopedia of Educational Research*, ed. R. L. Ebel (Toronto: Macmillan, Inc., 1969), p. 18.

[30]Neal Gross, *Who Runs Our Schools?* (New York: John Wiley & Sons, Inc., 1958).

[31]Daniel E. Griffiths, *Administrative Theory* (New York: Appleton-Century-Crofts, 1959).

[32]Leon A. Panttaja, "Subordinates' Perceptions of the Decision-Making Behavior of Their Chief School Administrator" (unpublished doctoral dissertation, University of Southern California, 1966).

[33]Daniel Griffiths, "Administrative Theory," in *Encyclopedia of Educational Research, p. 20*.

[34]Donald A. Schön, *Educating the Reflective Practitioner* (San Francisco: Jossey-Bass, 1987), p. 3.

[35]Ibid., pp. 4–5.

[36]Wayne K. Hoy and Cecil G. Miskel, *Educational Administration*, 2nd. ed. (New York: Random House, 1982), p. 82.

[37]T. Barr Greenfield, "Theory About Organization: A New Perspective and Its Implication for Schools," in *Administering Education: International Challenge* ed. M.G. Hughes (London: Athlone, 1975), p. 71.

[38]Ibid., p. 81.

[39]Robert W. Heller, James A. Conway, and S.L. Jacobson, "Here's Your Blunt Critique of Administrative Preparation," *The Executive Educator* (September 1988), 18–30.

[40]Roland S. Barth and Terrence E. Deal, *The Effective Principal: A Research Summary* (Reston, VA: Association of Secondary School Principals, 1982).

[41]Karl E. Weick, "Middle-Range Theories of Social Systems," *Behavioral Science*, 19, no. 6 (November 1974), 357–67.

[42]James D. Thompson, *Organizations in Action* (New York: McGraw-Hill Book Company, 1967).

[43]Michael D. Cohen, James G. March, and Johan P. Olsen, "A Garbage Can Model of Organizational Choice," *Administrative Science Quarterly*, 17, no. 1 (1972), 1.

[44]Ibid., p. 1.

[45]Ibid.

[46]Ibid., p. 16.

[47]Charles E. Bidwell, "The School as a Formal Organization," in *Handbook of Organizations*, ed. James G. March (Chicago: Rand McNally & Company, 1965).

[48]Karl E. Weick, "Educational Organizations as Loosely Coupled Systems," *Administrative Science Quarterly*, 21 (March 1976), 1.

[49]John W. Meyer and Brian Rowan, "The Structure of Educational Organizations," in *Organizational Environments: Ritual and Rationality*, eds. John W. Meyer and W. Richard Scott (Beverly Hills, CA: Sage Publications, Inc., 1983), p. 74.

[50]For examples see Van Cleve Morris, Robert L. Crowson, Emanuel Hurwitz, Jr., and Cynthia Porter-Gehrie, *The Urban Principal: Discretionary Decision Making in a Large Educational Organization* (Chicago: College of Education, University of Illinois at Chicago Circle, 1981); and N. A. Newberg and A. G. Glatthorn, *Instructional Leadership: Four Ethnographic Studies of Junior High School Principals* (final report of grant number NIE G-81-0088, 1983).

[51]Meyer and Rowan, "The Structure of Educational Organizations," p. 75.

[52]William A. Firestone and Bruce L. Wilson, *Using Bureaucratic and Cultural Linkages to Improve Instruction: The High School Principal's Contribution* (Eugene: Center for Educational Policy and Management, College of Education, University of Oregon, 1983), pp. 14–15.

[53]Terrence E. Deal and A. Kennedy, *Corporate Cultures: The Rites and Rituals of Corporate Life* (Reading, MA: Addison-Wesley, 1982); and Lee G. Bolman and Terrence E. Deal, *Modern Approaches to Understanding and Managing Organizations* (San Francisco: Jossey-Bass, 1984).

[54]Thomas J. Peters and Robert H. Waterman, Jr., *In Search of Excellence: Lessons from America's Best-Run Companies* (New York: Harper & Row, Publishers, Inc., 1982).

[55]Rosabeth Moss Kanter, *The Change Masters: Innovation and Entrepreneurship in the American Corporation* (New York: Simon & Schuster, Inc., 1983).

[56]Edgar H. Schein, *Organizational Culture and Leadership* (San Francisco: Jossey-Bass, 1985).

[57]S. C. Purkey and M. S. Smith, "School Reform: The District Policy Implications of the Effective Schools Literature," *The Elementary School Journal*, 85 (December 1985), 353–89.

[58]Ibid., p. 355.

[59]Ibid., p. 355.

[60]Ibid., p. 357.

[61]Ibid., p. 357.

[62]L. C. Stedman, "It's Time We Changed the Effective Schools Formula," *Phi Delta Kappan* (November 1987), 215–24.

[63]This discussion follows the analysis of Purkey and Smith, "School Reform," pp. 358–59.

[64]National Commission on Excellence in Education (Washington, D.C.: Government Printing Office, 1983).

2

ORGANIZATIONAL
THEORY

"There is nothing impractical about good theory....Action divorced from theory is the random scurrying of a rat in a new maze. Good theory is the power to find the way to the goal with a minimum of lost motion and electric shock."

—*Paul R. Mort and Donald H. Ross*[1]

The previous chapter provided a historical perspective on contemporary mainstreams of organizational thought and concluded with the observation that, by the mid-1980s, students of educational organization recognized that schools had evolved into essentially dual systems: partly bureaucratic and partly nonbureaucratic. That is, contemporary observers of schools generally find that, regardless of conventional rhetoric among educational administrators and governing officials to the contrary, instructional activities at the classroom level are typically controlled and coordinated by nonbureaucratic means whereas noninstructional activities are typically controlled and coordinated by traditional bureaucratic means. This was made clear in early entries in the literature of the 1960s and 1970s that laid the conceptual groundwork for understanding schools as loosely coupled systems.[2] Until the 1980s, however, the novelty of the loose coupling analysis had so captured the attention of many observers that the fact that schools exhibit bureaucratic characteristics as well has frequently been overlooked.

This should not be interpreted to suggest that many school administrators do not seriously try to exercise bureaucratic control and coordination of the instructional behavior of teachers, or that they do not seek to convey the impression that they do in fact exercise such control. It does suggest, however, that until recently we have underestimated the organizational complexity that characterizes the seemingly simple public school.

ORGANIZATIONAL THEORY

Discussion of different perspectives that may be used in thinking about organizations—such as bureaucratic and nonbureaucratic—is really discussion of organizational theory. Many practicing administrators are skeptical of theory, often thinking

42

of it as some ideal state or idle notion (commonly associated with the pejorative "ivory tower"), whereas they—administrators—must deal with the tough practicalities of daily life. The position taken here is that, far from being removed from daily life, theory is crucial in the shaping of our everyday perception and the understanding of commonplace events.

Theory defined and described. Theory, as used in this book, is systematically organized knowledge thought to explain observed phenomena. A given theory is a statement intended to describe and explain phenomena and events in the world around us. It is comprised of a system of assumptions and accepted principles accompanied by recognized rules of procedure by which events may be analyzed and explained.

Utility of theory. Theory is useful insofar as it provides a basis for thinking systematically about complex problems, such as understanding the nature of educational organizations. It is useful because it enables us to *describe* what is going on, *explain* it, *predict* future events under given circumstances, and—essential to the professional practitioner—it helps in thinking about ways in which to exercise *control* over events.

Theory is informed by experience. To the scholar or scientist, research is considered to be an especially powerful ally of theory building inasmuch as research is a highly systematic form of inquiry. Much research, for example, seeks to examine systematically explicit assumptions embodied in formal theory as a means of refining or revising those assumptions.

However, pondering human experience in a less formally systematic, yet thoughtful, manner—as, for example, Chester Barnard did of his experiences in running New Jersey Bell Telephone, Robert Townsend did of his experiences running Avis Rent A Car, and Warren Bennis did of his experiences as an administrator in the State University of New York at Buffalo[3]—also constitutes a useful way of examining our assumptions. Indeed, Barnard's observations have proven to be so astute that they still remain an important source of insight for contemporary organizational theorists fifty years after their original publication.

TWO MAJOR THEORETIC ORIENTATIONS TO ORGANIZATION

Organizations, and particularly educational organizations, are so ubiquitous—so commonplace—that we frequently deal with them with scant examination of the assumptions about them that we often take virtually for granted. A major concern of contemporary organizational theory is to clarify and differentiate between the assumptions that underlie the two major competing theoretic views of what organizations are all about: classical (or bureaucratic) theory on the one hand and the newer perspectives, often called human resources development, on the other hand. Consider, for example, two contrasting approaches to the problem of coordinating and controlling the cooperative behavior of people to achieve the goals of the organization.

BUREAUCRATIC THEORY

As was discussed in Chapter 1, assumptions of bureaucratic theory are important in organizational thought today and have been for some time. The bureaucratic approach tends to emphasize the following five mechanisms in dealing with issues of controlling and coordinating the behavior of people in the organization:

1. *Maintain firm hierarchical control of authority and close supervision of those in the lower ranks.* The role of the administrator as inspector and evaluator is stressed in this concept.
2. *Establish and maintain adequate vertical communication.* This helps to assure that good information will be transmitted to the decision makers and orders will be clearly and quickly transmitted down the line for implementation. Because the decision makers must have accurate information concerning the operating level in order to make high-quality decisions, the processing and communicating of information up the line is particularly important but often not especially effective. The use of computers to facilitate this communication is highly attractive to adherants of this concept.
3. *Develop clear written rules and procedures to set standards and guide actions.* These include curriculum guides, policy handbooks, instructions, standard forms, duty rosters, rules and regulations, and standard operating procedures.
4. *Promulgate clear plans and schedules for participants to follow.* These include teachers' lesson plans, bell schedules, duty rosters, pull-out schedules, meeting schedules, budgets, lunch schedules, special teacher schedules, bus schedules, and many others.
5. *Add supervisory and administrative positions to the hierarchy of the organization as necessary to meet problems that arise from changing conditions confronted by the organization.* For example, as school districts and schools grew in size, such positions as assistant principal, chairperson, director, and coordinator appeared. As programs became more complex, positions for specialists appeared; director of special education, coordinator of drug abuse programs, school psychologist, and school social worker are a few examples.

The overwhelmingly widespread acceptance of these as the preferred mechanisms for exercising control and coordination in schools is illustrated by the reform movement that burst upon the scene in the early 1980s. The effectiveness of schools arose as a major theme in the public agenda on education in the 1980s to join the linked duo that had been inherited from the 1970s—equality and access. While there had been a steadily-growing body of research literature on effective schools and what they were like, a virtually unrelated "reform movement" suddenly erupted in 1982 that—in the popular press and electronic media, at least—seized the center stage and strongly influenced numerous efforts to improve the functioning of schools. This is of interest to us here because it illustrates the very strong conviction of many educational leaders that bureaucratic theory is highly useful in thinking about schools and how to improve them.

During the biennium of 1982–1983, led by *A Nation at Risk,* issued by the National Commission on Excellence in Education, no less than ten major reports were published on the state of public education in the United States.[4] Each of these cataloged various deficiencies perceived by the reporters and proffered an array of corrective measures to deal with them. If nothing else, they stand as testimony to the widespread concern about the effectiveness of public schooling at the time and they were the source of considerable popular discussion of the shortcomings of public schooling in the press and electronic media. Indeed, for the first time in the history of the Republic—thanks in large part to the interest stimulated by these reports (and approximately twenty others that were to appear by mid-1985)—the president of the United States chose to elevate the discussion of the condition of public schools in the nation to the level of presidential discourse and politics. The Educational Commission of the States counted not less than 175 state-level, active task forces on education that were issuing recommendations in 1983.[5] By 1985, a total of some thirty reports and calls for reform had appeared in print. It was an extraordinary outpouring of concern for the effectiveness of public schools in America that resulted in a dazzling array of observations and recommendations for improvement, and an unprecedented, broad-scale discussion of what became known as the movement for public school "reform." One veteran observer called it "the best opportunity for school renewal we will get in this century." Considering that a mere sixteen years then remained in the century, that seemed like a hardly overoptimistic assessment.

The profusion of recommendations emanating from this body of work was preponderantly based on traditional assumptions about the nature of schools held by at least some of those who conducted the studies and certainly of many who read them. Of course, there were many variations and differences among the recommendations of the reports, some being partially in conflict with one another. Essentially, however, the gist of the major recommendations in them ran as follows:

Somehow, goals of the schools (then described by John Goodlad as being mired in a conceptual swamp) should be simplified, clarified, and limited; all students should be required to complete some sort of core curriculum (bereft of "soft, nonessential courses" as the Education Commission of the States put it); mastery of the English language should be emphasized, but greater stress should also be given to math, the sciences, and computer technology; teachers should be paid more, trained better, and provided with better working conditions; schools should be more effectively linked to outside leadership groups—principally partnerships with business, and more effective relationships with the state and federal governments; the school day and school year should be extended and reorganized with a keen eye to time on task, and more homework should be assigned to students; the status of teaching and teachers should be enhanced by such means as improving compensation, creating career ladders so as to reward superior teachers for superior teaching performance, and professionalizing the working environment of teachers; and stronger educational leadership should be developed, chiefly at the level of the school principalship.

In sum, the recommendations emanating from these reports on the state of education in America have been described as barren in terms of large-scale influence, containing few fresh ideas and few promising initiatives, and offering essentially warmed-over ideas of modest conceptual strength.[6] In response to the stimulus of the various reports every state and numerous local school districts sought quickly to implement some of the recommendations. Predictably, the manner of implementation has weighed heavily on the side of traditional bureaucratic mandates intended to compel schools to effect change (described in Chapter 8 as power-coercive methods).

For example, many states issued new rules, regulations, and mandates to "toughen-up" the curriculum in local schools. Frequently, these were aimed at such things as reducing the number of elective courses and increasing the number of required courses, as well as dictating the assignment of homework by teachers. The impact of such efforts at reform in effecting improved instructional effectiveness of schools remains problematic.

This is well-illustrated by the effort to extend both the school year and the school day. At the time of its appearance in 1983, one of the popular recommendations of *A Nation at Risk* was that "school districts and state legislatures should consider the seven-hour school day and the 200 or 220 day school year" as a means of providing more time for instruction. This would appear to be a relatively simple change to effect, requiring only a clear mandate from the state. And, though several states did mandate additional days to be added to the minimum pupil-teacher contact days, the net effect nationwide was simply to move some states closer to the already-existing national average of 180 days of instruction per year. Arkansas, for example, decided to move from its 175-day school year to a 180-day year by 1989. Colorado went from 172 school days per year to 176 in 1984. Several other states extended the work year *for teachers* while holding the number of instructional days *for students*. Thus Florida, Tennessee, and North Carolina each requires 180 days of student-teacher contact time while permitting the employment of teachers for additional days to cover emergency closings, inservice training programs, and other administrative purposes. The net effect has been scant change nationally. In 1985 the school year ranged from a high of 184 days in Washington, D.C., to a low of 173 days in North Dakota with 29 states clustered at the national average of 180 school days. Viewing the resistance to a longer school calendar from employers in agriculture and the travel industry as well as from the general public the Education Commission of the States concluded in 1985 that the 200 or 220 day school year was "not realistic" and that "there may be a bigger payoff in wringing more honest instruction time out of the regular day, and this may be the only acceptable solution as far as parents and the public are concerned."[7] In other words, it does not appear likely that schools will move much beyond the "time on task" concept that had been widely implemented in schools long before the appearance of the report.

Virtually all of the "reform" proposals have assumed a "top-down" strategy similar to this; that is, decisions are made in the legislature or another place high in the hierarchy, such as the state education department, and handed down to be implemented by teachers in their classrooms. For example, the California Business Roundtable—comprised of large business corporations in the state—managed to get the legislature to enact (and the governor to sign) a new major education law for California that was funded for $2.7 billion over a two-year period—money that was desperately needed by the schools in the wake of the stringent cutbacks that had been imposed as a result of Proposition 13. The new law—150 pages long—prescribed in detail things that were to be done in the classrooms (for example, what textbooks to use, how many minutes of instruction would be given in a particular subject), and specified how the state education bureaucracy would audit and verify compliance with all these complex provisions. Similarly, the New York State Board of Regents developed an Action Plan accompanied by the "Part 100 Regulations" that enabled the Regents to reach into virtually every public school classroom in the state to direct, implement, and verify compliance with a comprehensive set of highly detailed directives for changes in school practice. These specify not only policy directions (such as the goals or intent desired), but also, by directives, such things as requiring certain remedial instruction to be carried on in rooms separate from regular classrooms, specifying the types of instruction to be used, and indicating the periods of time. In the 1980s, every state developed and implemented plans similar to these—more or less comprehensive, perhaps, but virtually all using bureaucratic assumptions as the basis for change strategy. The federal government continued its now long-established tradition of direct top-down mandates to the public schools of the nation. The Hatch Act, for example, went so far—in establishing open and equal access to the schools for certain religious groups—as to specify the permissible actions of children, teachers, administrators, and other adults in its mandate to encourage before-school and after-school voluntary assemblies of students who were interested in religion.

Clearly, there is a strong tendency for contemporary educational reformers to have in mind a set of assumptions—which reflect a theory—about the nature of schools on which the logic of their efforts pivots. That theory resembles nothing so much as the old-fashioned factory, in which management decided what was to be done, directed the workers to do it, then supervised them closely to be sure that the directives were followed in full. Denis Doyle and Terry Hartle observed:

> It simply doesn't work that way. The impulse to reform the schools from the top down is understandable: it is consistent with the history of management science. The explicit model for such reform was the factory; Frederick Taylor's scientific management revolution did for the schools the same thing that it did for business and industry—created an environment whose principal characteristics were pyramidal organization....The teacher was the worker on the assembly line of education; the student, the product; the superintendent, the chief executive officer; the school trustees, the board of directors; and the taxpayer, the shareholder.[8]

HUMAN RESOURCES DEVELOPMENT THEORY

But, Doyle and Hartle go on to present a different set of assumptions about the organizational characteristics of schools and the behavior of teachers in their classrooms: a view that places the teacher foremost in creating instructional change and, therefore, that questions the wisdom of any change strategy that seeks to force change upon the teacher arbitrarily and without his or her participation in the processes of deciding what should be done. As discussed in Chapter 1, this is far from a new theory of organization. But recent failures of bureaucratic methods to rectify severe organizational difficulties—especially in the corporate world—coupled with the emergence of such newer organizational perspectives as loose coupling and the power of organizational cultures to influence behavior has brought human resources development concepts to the fore as a major new way to think about organizational problems.

While bureaucratic theory stresses primacy of the organization's officially prescribed rules, and their enforcement, as a means of influencing individual participants to perform dependably in predictable ways, human resources development emphasizes using the conscious thinking of individual persons about what they are doing as a means of involving their commitment, their abilities, and their energies in achieving the goals for which the organization stands. The central mechanism through which the organization exercises coordination and control is the socialization of participants to the values and goals of the organization, rather than through written rules and close supervision. Through this intense socialization the participant identifies personally with the values and purposes of the organization and is motivated to see the organization's goals and needs as being closely congruent with his or her own. Thus, the culture of the organization epitomizes not only what the organization stands for but also the aspirations of the individual participants themselves.

The culture of an organization makes clear what the organization stands for—its values, its beliefs, its true (as distinguished from its publicly stated) goals—and provides tangible ways in which individuals in the organization may personally identify with that culture. The culture of an organization is communicated through symbols: typically stories, myths, legends, and rituals which establish, nourish, and keep alive the enduring values and beliefs that give meaning to the organization and make clear how individuals become and continue to be part of the saga of the organization as it develops through time.

In this view, close inspection and supervision are far from the only means of assuring the predictable performance of participants. Personal identification with the values of the organization's culture can provide powerful motivation for dependable performance even under conditions of great uncertainty and stress. Consider, for example, what it is that causes an individual to join an organization, stay in it, and work toward that organization's goals. In contemporary organizational theory, a response to this fundamental question is facilitated by Douglas McGregor's Theory X and Theory Y.[9]

THEORY X AND THEORY Y

Theory X rests on four assumptions that may be held by the administrator:

1. The average person inherently dislikes work and will avoid it whenever possible.
2. Since people dislike work, they must be supervised closely, directed, coerced, or threatened with punishment in order for them to put forth adequate effort toward the achievement of organizational objectives.
3. The average worker will shirk responsibility and seek formal direction from those in charge.
4. Most workers value job security above other job-related factors and have little ambition.

Administrators who—tacitly or explicitly—accept the assumptions underlying this explanation of humankind will, of course, use them as a guide to action in dealing with employees in the organization. Theory Y, however, embraces some very different assumptions about the nature of people at work:

1. If it is satisfying to them, employees will view work as natural and as acceptable as play.
2. People at work will exercise initiative, self-direction, and self-control on the job if they are committed to the objectives of the organization.

3. The average person, under proper conditions, learns not only to accept responsibility on the job but to seek it.
4. The average employee values creativity—that is, the ability to make good decisions—and seeks opportunities to be creative at work.

Administrators who—tacitly or explicitly—favor this explanation of the nature of human beings at work could reasonably be expected to deal with subordinates in ways that are quite different from those who hold Theory X views.

These theories are not presented here as something for the reader to accept or reject; they are merely proffered as a classically simple illustration of how theory is actually used by practitioners of educational administration in viewing the world—a guide to rational decisions and actions "on the firing line." Theory is as essential to administrative practice as it is to scholarship and research.

Theory X and Theory Y are, obviously, two different, contrasting explanations of real-world conditions. They are clearly based upon differing assumptions about people. Those of us with administrative, management, or leadership responsibilities tend to believe that one or the other of these theoretic statements is more accurately representative of the nature of human beings than the other. Those of us whose behavior is congruent with our beliefs and perceptions will act in ways that are harmonious with the theoretic statement that we think is "true." Those who tend to hold a Theory X view of people, for example, will tend to believe that motivation is basically a matter of the carrot and the stick; they will tend to accept readily the necessity for close, detailed supervision of subordinates, and they will tend to accept the inevitability of the need to exercise down-the-line hierarchical control in the organization. Collaborative, participative decision making will tend to be viewed as perhaps a nice ideal in the abstract but really not very practical in the "real" world.

As Chris Argyris put it, Theory X views give rise to Behavior Pattern A on the part of leaders.[10] This pattern of behavior may take one or the other of two principal forms:

1. Behavior Pattern A, *hard*, is characterized by no-nonsense, strongly directive leadership, tight controls, and close supervision;
2. Behavior Pattern A, *soft*, involves a good deal of persuading, "buying" compliance from subordinates, benevolent paternalism, or so-called good (that is, manipulative) human relations.

In either case, Behavior Pattern A, whether acted out in its hard or its soft form, has the clear intention of manipulating, controlling, and managing in the classical sense. It is based upon Theory X assumptions about the nature of human beings at work.

Argyris goes on to explain that Theory Y assumptions about people give rise to Behavior Pattern B. This is characterized by commitment to mutually shared objectives, high levels of trust, respect, satisfaction from work, and authentic, open relationships. Pattern B leadership may well be demanding, explicit, and thoroughly realistic, but it is essentially collaborative. It is a pattern of leader behavior that is intended to be more effective and productive than Pattern A, because it is thought to reflect a more accurate understanding of what people at work are "really" like.

In this discussion of the relationship between theory and understanding organizational behavior in schools, it should be emphasized—as Argyris cautions—

that Behavior Pattern *A, soft,* is often superficially mistaken for Behavior Pattern *B*. This ambiguity, as Thomas Sergiovanni points out, has caused considerable confusion among those trying to apply these theoretic ideas to schools:

> Behavior associated with Theory *Y* assumptions...is basically developmental. Here supervisors focus on building identification of and commitment to worthwhile objectives in the work context and upon building mutual trust and respect in the interpersonal context. Success in the work and the interpersonal contexts are assumed interdependent, with important satisfactions for individuals being achieved within the context of accomplishing important work.[11]

The important differences in the assumptions that underlie Behavior Pattern *A, soft,* and Behavior Pattern *B* are compared and contrasted in Figure 2–1.

FIGURE 2–1. Comparison of assumptions underlying Argyris's behavior pattern *A, soft,* and behavior pattern *B*. Adapted from Thomas J. Sergiovanni, "Beyond Human Relations," in *Professional Supervision for Professional Teachers*, ed. Thomas J. Sergiovanni (Washington, D.C.: Association for Supervision and Curriculum Development, 1975), pp. 12–13.

Assumptions Underlying Behavior Pattern *A, soft*	Assumptions Underlying Behavior Pattern *B*
(Theory *X, soft*)	(Theory *Y*)

With Regard to People

1. People in our culture, teachers among them, share a common set of needs—to belong, to be liked, to be respected.	1. In addition to sharing common needs for belonging and respect, most people in our culture, teachers among them, desire to contribute effectively and creatively to the accomplishment of worthwhile objectives.
2. Although teachers desire individual recognition, they, more importantly, want to *feel* useful to the school.	2. The majority of teachers are capable of exercising far more initiative, responsibility, and creativity than their present job or work circumstances require or allow.
3. They tend to cooperate willingly and to comply with school, department, and unit goals if these important needs are fulfilled.	3. These capabilities represent untapped resources which are currently being wasted.

With Regard to Participation

1. The administrator's basic task is to make each teacher *believe* that he or she is a useful and an important part of the team.	1. The administrator's basic task is to create an environment in which teachers can contribute their full range of talents to the accomplishment of school goals. The administrator works to uncover the creative resources of the teachers.

(continued)

(Theory X, soft)	(Theory Y)
2. The administrator is willing to explain *his* or *her* decisions and to discuss teachers' objections to his or her plans. On routine matters, teachers are encouraged in planning and in decision making.	2. The administrator allows and encourages teachers to participate in important as well as routine decisions. In fact, the more important a decision is to the school, the greater are the administrator's efforts to tap faculty resources.
3. Within *narrow* limits, the faculty unit or individual teachers who comprise the faculty unit should be allowed to exercise self-direction and self-control.	3. Administrators work continually to expand the areas over which teachers exercise self-direction and self-control as they develop and demonstrate greater insight and ability.

With Regard to Expectations

1. Sharing information with teachers and involving them in school decision making will help satisfy their basic needs for *belonging* and for individual recognition.	1. The overall quality of decision making and performance will improve as administrators and teachers make use of the full range of experience, insight, and creative ability that exists in their schools.
2. Satisfying these needs will improve teacher morale and will *reduce* resistance to formal authority.	2. Teachers will exercise responsible self-direction and self-control in the accomplishment of worthwhile objectives that they understand and have helped establish.

But the Behavior Pattern *A, soft,* approach often used by supervisors to manipulate teachers into compliance with what is basically highly directive leadership—in the guise of "good human relations"—has done much in American education to discredit the plausibility of Theory *Y* as applicable to the "real" world of schools and school systems. "By treating teachers in a kindly way," Sergiovanni observes, "it is assumed that they will become sufficiently satisfied and sufficiently passive so that supervisors and administrators can run the school with little resistance."[12]

The utility of theorizing in this way is illustrated by the work of Rensis Likert. In over thirty years of research in schools as well as in industrial organizations, Likert has identified a range of management styles, called Systems 1, 2, 3, and 4. Further, his studies support the hypothesis that the crucial variable that differentiates more effective from less effective organizations is human behavior in the organization:

> The main causal factors [of organizational effectiveness or ineffectiveness] are the organizational climate and the leadership behavior which significantly affect how subordinates deal with each other individually and in work groups in order to produce the end results. These variables can be used to define consistent patterns of management....The range of management styles begins with System 1 which is a punitive authoritarian model and extends to System 4, a participative or group interaction model. In between is System 2, a paternalistic authoritarian style that emphasizes [person-to-

person] supervision in a competitive (or isolative) environment, and System 3, which is a [person-to-person] consultative pattern of operation.[13]

Essentially, these four categories of "management systems" are theoretic descriptions of conditions that may be found in schools and school systems. By the 1970s, Likert and others were conducting a number of studies in school settings to ascertain whether these same factors of organizational behavior are applicable to the unique characteristics of effective school systems. Early results seem to support the view that "the more effective schools are those with a participative environment more toward System 4, while the less effective are much more authoritarian, toward a System 1 pattern of operation."[14]

Figure 2–2 shows that there is a remarkable compatibility between Douglas McGregor's work and that of Likert. Both were basically concerned, not with being nice to people or making work pleasant, but with understanding how to make work organizations more effective, which is as pressing a need in business and industry as it is in education. This general point of view is widely and strongly supported by a vast amount of organizational research. Robert R. Blake's and Jane Srygley

FIGURE 2–2. Likert's Management Systems Theory related to McGregor's Theory *X* and Theory *Y*.

Theory X | System 1 *Management is seen as having no trust in subordinates.*
a. Decision imposed—made at the top.
b. Subordinates motivated by fear, threats, punishment.
c. Control centered on top management.
d. Little superior-subordinate interaction.
e. People informally opposed to goal by management.

System 2 *Management has condescending confidence and trust in subordinates.*
a. Subordinate seldom involved in decision making.
b. Rewards and punishment used to motivate.
c. Interaction used with condescension.
d. Fear and caution displayed by subordinates.
e. Control centered on top management but some delegation.

System 3 *Management seen as having substantial but not complete trust in subordinates.*
a. Subordinates make specific decisions at lower level.
b. Communication flows up and down hierarchy.
c. Rewards, occasional punishment, and some involvement are used to motivate.
d. Moderate interaction and fair trust exist.
e. Control is delegated downward.

Theory Y | System 4 *Management is seen as having complete trust and confidence in subordinates.*
a. Decision making is widely dispersed.
b. Communication flows up and down and laterally.
c. Motivation is by participation and rewards.
d. Extensive, friendly, superior-subordinate interaction exists.
e. High degree of confidence and trust exists.
f. Widespread responsibility for the control process exists.

Mouton's organizational grid research,[15] Gordon Lippitt's studies of organizational renewal,[16] Paul Berman's and Milbrey McLaughlin's extensive studies of change in American schools[17]—these are only a few of the many studies that support the general theoretic position that pioneers such as McGregor and Likert held.

Traditional classical organizational theory would indicate the opposite point of view: tighten up, exercise stronger discipline and tougher leadership, and demand more work from subordinates. In the parlance of neoclassical theory, it is: teacher accountability, specified performance objectives, and cost-benefit analysis. Yet much of the best theory and research in organizational behavior strongly suggests that this latter approach would be, at best, self-defeating. But we must not forget that classical and neoclassical views are—themselves—theoretic. The essential point of this discussion is that theory, far from being impractical and irrelevant daydreaming, is the stuff that guides administrators in their quest for more effective ways to plan, lead, and decide—ways that will, in fact, be more effective in producing the improved results that are sought. The utility of theory to the administrator lies in the help it can provide in planning, selecting strategies, and developing a management style that will be most effective.

SUMMARY

Organizational theory provides a systematic body of knowledge upon which we base assumptions about the nature of organizations and the behavior of people in them. Far from being the impractical plaything of scholars, theory is used constantly by administrators—albeit often in an intuitive and unexamined way—as a basis for the professional work they do every day.

Bureaucratic theory has long been, by an overwhelming margin, the most widely used perspective in developing assumptions about educational organizations. Human resources theory has, however, been steadily developing and gaining greater acceptance as research following the tradition of the Western Electric studies has been pushed forward and as bureaucratic responses to the problems of schools have failed to work as well as had been expected. Since the 1960s human resources development theory has been considerably strengthened by the emergence of such newer perspectives as concepts of loose coupling.

It is recognized today that, as a broad generalization, schools characteristically tend to use human resources approaches in the management of the instructional behavior of teachers and to use bureaucratic approaches in the management of other, more routine aspects of the enterprise. Each of these two theoretic approaches gives rise to different assumptions about the nature of people and, therefore, of effective ways of managing them—Theory *X* and Theory *Y*.

A word of caution to the reader is in order here. Bureaucratic and human resources perspectives have been compared and contrasted as ideal cases for the purpose of clarifying and delineating the very real, basic differences between them. In the "real world" of educational administration, of course, one rarely encounters ideal cases, which is not to suggest that organizations cannot properly be classified as being bureaucratic or nonbureaucratic. Indeed, they can be and often are. However, it does not mean, either, that to be described as nonbureaucratic an organization must be totally devoid of policies, regulations, standard operating procedures, or hierarchical organization; or that to be described as bureaucratic an organization must be totally devoid of sensitivity to or respect for people. This is particularly true of schools, which have been described here as being dual organizations: bureaucratic in some ways and nonbureaucratic in some very important ways. What it does suggest is that organizations may be properly described as *relatively* bureaucratic or nonbureaucratic. It also suggests that schools are undoubtedly far more organizationally complex than has been traditionally understood prior to the mid-1980s.

SUGGESTED READING

FIRESTONE, WILLIAM A., AND BRUCE L. WILSON, "Using Bureaucratic and Cultural Linkages to Improve Instruction: The Principal's Contribution." *Educational Administration Quarterly*, 21 (Spring 1985), 7–30.
Discusses the two kinds of "linkages" available for principals to use in influencing the instructional behavior of teachers: bureaucratic and cultural. An excellent source of references to the literature for those who wish to probe this topic more fully.

MEYER, JOHN W., AND BRIAN ROWAN, "The Structure of Educational Organizations." In John W. Meyer and W. Richard Scott, eds., *Organizational Environments: Ritual and Rationality*. Beverly Hills, CA.: Sage Publications, Inc., 1983.
A provocative analysis of schools from a sociological perspective that challenges the conventional tradition of bureaucratic logic and order. The entire book, of which this chapter is part, will be of great interest to the serious student.

MEYER, MARSHALL W., *Theory of Organizational Structure*. Indianapolis: Bobbs-Merrill Educational Publishing, 1977.
In this seventy-eight-page book, sociologist Meyer first discusses the various functions of organizational theory. He then goes on to describe a theory of organizational structure that departs from traditional bureaucratic concepts. Much in this book is directly related to the emerging new perspectives on the structure of educational organizations.

WEICK, KARL E., "Educational Organizations as Loosely Coupled Systems." *Educational Administration Quarterly*, 21 (1976), 1–19.
While Weick did not invent the concept of loosely coupled systems, in this article he did lay the foundation for a major shift in the theory of schools as organizations. This is a classic that should be read in the original.

NOTES

[1]Paul R. Mort and Donald H. Ross, *Principles of School Administration* (New York: McGraw-Hill Book Company, 1957), p. 4.
[2]For examples, see Charles E. Bidwell, "The School as a Formal Organization," in *Handbook of Organization*, ed. James G. March (Skokie, IL: Rand-McNally, 1965); and Karl E. Weick, "Educational Organizations as Loosely Coupled Systems," *Administrative Science Quarterly*, 21 (1976), 1–19.
[3]Chester I. Barnard, *The Functions of the Executive* (Cambridge, MA: Harvard University Press, 1938); Robert Townsend, *Up the Organization* (New York: Alfred A. Knopf, Inc., 1970); Warren G. Bennis, *The Leaning Ivory Tower* (San Francisco: Jossey-Bass, 1973).
[4]Mortimer Jerome Adler, *The Paideia Proposal* (New York: Macmillan Publishing Company, 1982); Ernest L. Boyer, *High School: A Report on Secondary Education in America* (New York: Harper & Row Publishers, Inc., 1983); Business-Higher Education Forum, *America's Competitive Challenge: The Need for a National Response* (Washington, D.C.: The Forum, 1983); College Entrance Examination Board, *Academic Preparation for College: What Students Need to Know and Be Able to Do* (New York: The Board, 1983); John I. Goodlad, *A Place Called School: Prospects for the Future* (St. Louis: McGraw-Hill, 1983); National Commission on Excellence in Education, *A Nation at Risk: The Imperative*

for Educational Reform (Washington, D.C.: Government Printing Office, 1983); National Science Board Commission on Precollege Education in Mathematics, Science, and Technology, *Educating Americans for the 21st Century* (Washington, D.C.: National Science Foundation, 1983); Southern Regional Education Board, *Meeting the Need for Quality: Action in the South* (Atlanta: The Board, 1983); Task Force on Education for Economic Growth, *Action for Excellence: A Comprehensive Plan to Improve Our Nation's Schools* (Denver: Education Commission of the States, 1983). Twentieth Century Fund, *Report of the Twentieth Century Fund Task Force on Federal Elementary and Secondary Education Policy* (New York: The Fund, 1983).

[5]Education Commission of the States, *A Summary of Major Reports on Education* (Denver: The Commission, 1983), p. 11.

[6]Luvern L. Cunningham, "Leaders and Leadership: 1985 and Beyond," *Phi Delta Kappan,* 67 (September 1985), 20.

[7]Education Commission of the States, "Tracking the Reforms," *Education Week* (September 18, 1985), 18.

[8]Denis P. Doyle and Terry W. Hartle, "Leadership in Education: Governors, Legislators, and Teachers," *Phi Delta Kappan,* 67 (September 1985), 24.

[9]Douglas M. McGregor, *The Human Side of Enterprise* (New York: McGraw-Hill Book Company, 1960), pp. 37–57.

[10]Chris Argyris, *Management and Organizational Development* (New York: McGraw-Hill Book Company, 1971), pp. 1–26.

[11]Thomas J. Sergiovanni, "Beyond Human Relations," in *Professional Supervision for Professional Teachers,* ed. Thomas J. Sergiovanni (Washington, D.C.: Association for Supervision and Curriculum Development, 1975), p. 11.

[12]Ibid.

[13]Albert F. Siepert and Rensis Likert, "The Likert School Profile Measurements of the Human Organization" (paper presented at the American Educational Research Association National Convention, February 27, 1973), p. 3.

[14]Ibid., p. 4.

[15]Robert R. Blake and Jane Srygley Mouton, *Building a Dynamic Corporation through Grid Organization Development* (Reading, MA.: Addison-Wesley, 1969).

[16]Gordon L. Lippitt, *Organizational Renewal: Achieving Viability in a Changing World* (New York: Appleton-Century-Crofts, 1969).

[17]Paul Berman and Milbrey Wallen McLaughlin, *Federal Programs Supporting Educational Change, Volume VIII: Implementing and Sustaining Innovations* (Santa Monica, CA.: Rand Corporation, 1978).

3

SYSTEMS THEORY
AND ORGANIZATIONAL
BEHAVIOR

"Modern society is a network of social systems growing increasingly complex, overlapping, competitive, sometimes cooperative, in which as individuals we find ourselves enmeshed."

—*F. Kenneth Berrien*[1]

A major theme, perhaps the dominant one, in organizational theory for at least a half-century has been the interaction between organizational structure and people. It can be argued, for example, that the structure of an organization is the prime determinant of the behavior of people in the organization. Charles Perrow points out that

> ...one of the persistent complaints in the field of penology, or juvenile correctional institutions, or mental hospitals, or any of the "people-changing" institutions is the need for better workers. Their problems, we hear, stem from the lack of high-quality personnel. More specifically, the types of individuals they can recruit as guards, or cottage parents, or orderlies typically have too little education, hold over-simplified views about people, tend to be punitive, and believe that order and discipline can solve all problems. [2]

He goes on to describe a study in which applicants for positions in a juvenile correction institution were, when tested, found to be quite enlightened and permissive, whereas after they had worked in the institution for a while they had become less permissive and took a punitive, unenlightened view regarding the causes of delinquency and the care and handling of delinquents. Perrow offers this as an illustration of the power of organizations to shape the views and attitudes—and, thus, behavior—of participants.

On the other hand, much of the literature of organizational theory is devoted to the view that the people in the organization tend to shape the structure of the organization. Much attention is given to the impact of the behavior of people in the processes of making decisions, leading, and dealing with conflict, upon the structure, values, and customs of organizations. Much attention has been devoted to the possibilities of improving organizations by means, not of changing their structures as a way of inducing more effective organizational behavior, but of training participants in more effective group processes as a way of bringing about desirable changes in organizational structure.

GENERAL SYSTEMS THEORY

Contemporary attempts to describe, explain, and predict organizational behavior generally depend—as does much of modern scientific thought—upon systems theory. A biologist, Ludwig von Bertalanffy, is generally credited with having first outlined, in 1950, the notion of what is now known as general systems theory.[3] The nature of his work and its significance to the science of biology is suggested by the following statement:

> An organism is an integrated system of interdependent structures and functions. An organism is constituted of cells and a cell consists of molecules which must work in harmony. Each molecule must know what the others are doing. Each one must be capable of receiving messages and must be sufficiently disciplined to obey. You are familiar with the laws that control regulation. You know how our ideas have developed and how the most harmonious and sound of them have been fused into a conceptual whole which is the very foundation of biology and confers on it its unity.[4]

This statement captures the basic ideas of a way of considering and analyzing complex situations that have come to be preeminent in both the physical and the social sciences.

If we substitute *organization* for organism, *group* for cell, and *person* for molecule in the above statement about biology, it has relevance for thinking about organizations:

> An *organization* is an integrated system of interdependent structures and functions. An *organization* is constituted of *groups* and a *group* consists of *persons* who must work in harmony. Each *person* must know what the others are doing. Each one must be capable of receiving messages and must be sufficiently disciplined to obey....[5]

Two basic concepts of system. The system approach to understanding and describing phenomena is well established in both the physical sciences and the social sciences. Social scientists tend to draw their illustrations and analogues from the biological sciences.

A young child, for example, might think of a nearby pond as a wonderful playground, away from the ever-watchful eyes of grownups. A fisherman might see it as a great place in which to fill his creel. A farmer might think of it as a good source of water for irrigating his crops. A biologist, however, would tend to view the pond as a system of living things, all of which are interdependent in many ways and all of which are dependent in some ways on the larger environment in which the pond exists (for example, the air and sunlight). In terms of understanding the pond and being able to describe it, it is obvious that we are dealing with different levels of insight. However, in terms of being able to predict more accurately the consequences of things that might be done to the pond—such as pumping a large volume of water from it or removing large numbers of its fish—the biologist clearly has the advantage.

It is this advantage in dealing with cause and effect that has made systems theory so attractive to those concerned with organizational behavior. There is a strong tendency in our culture to ascribe single causes to events; in fact, the causes of even relatively simple organizational events are often very complex. We may be unwilling to accept this fact and, as a way of rejecting it, choose to apply simplistic cause-and-effect logic to our problems.

This was illustrated by congressional interest in reducing automobile accidents in this country, which started out by concentrating on the automobile as a primary "cause" of accidents. From this flowed a logical line of thought: if we require automobile manufacturers to improve the design of their cars and install certain mechanical safety features, the result would be a reduction in the appalling carnage on our highways.

In fact, however, more careful study seemed to show that automobile accidents are "caused" by an enormously complex, interrelated set of variables. Automobile design is clearly one, but others include road conditions and such relatively intangible factors as social mores and the psychological state of the driver. As we dig behind each of these conditions (for example, why was the road built that way? Why was the driver drunk? Why didn't the driver yield the right of way?) we find that each is part of a complex set of interrelated factors of its own. Clearly, significant reduction in automobile accidents must eventually require analysis of the interrelated factors of these complex subsystems of causative factors.

Systems theory, then, puts us on guard against the strong tendency to ascribe phenomena to a single causative factor. Similarly, if our car is not running well, we often take what is, in effect, a systems approach to the problem: we get a tune-up from someone who understands the functions and interrelatedness of the subsystems (for example, the ignition system, the fuel system, the exhaust system) that comprise the engine.

These two concepts—the concept of subsystems and the concept of multiple causation—are central to systems theory.

SOCIAL SYSTEMS THEORY

Systems can be divided into two main classes: "open" systems, which interact with their environments, and "closed" systems, which do not interact with their environments. Social systems theory generally deals with so-called open systems, because it is virtually impossible to envisage a social system, such as a school, that is not interactive with its environment. When observers describe certain schools or school systems as "closed systems," they generally mean that those organizations tend to try to limit the influence of the community and tend to proceed as though unrelated to the larger real world in which they exist. Thus, in the late 1960s and into the 1970s, it was popular to describe unresponsive school systems that resisted constructive change as "closed systems." Though the calumny has a certain ring of scientific credibility, it is in fact technically impossible. The input-output relationship of the school to its larger environment is an endless cyclical interaction between the school and its larger environment.

In Figure 3–1 we show schooling as a process involving (1) *inputs* from the larger societal environment (for example, knowledge that exists in that society, values that are held, goals that are desired, and money), (2) *process* that occurs within the social system we call a school (involving subsystems of organizational structure, people, technology, and work tasks), and—resulting from that process—(3) *outputs* to society (in the form of changed individuals). In this sense it is impossible for a school to be, in fact, a closed system. Indeed, in recent years professional educators have become increasingly aware of the extent and importance of the interaction between the school and its environment—which is, conceptually, the basis for much of what goes on under the rubrics of accountability and community relations.

A contextual approach.   The input-output concept is often called a "linear model"; it is, in effect, a theory that attempts to explain how things can be described in the "real world." It is a seductive concept—seemingly logical, rational, and orderly. It lends itself well to concepts of efficiency, such as cost effectiveness; one can relate the value of inputs to the value of outputs and arrive at relative cost efficiency. It has been extremely popular in analyzing the apparent relative effectiveness of competing programs and technologies. By the late 1970s, however, it was becoming increasingly apparent that this theoretical model contributed little to our understanding of the ways in which educative organizations function. For

FIGURE 3–1.   Schooling as an input-process-output system.

INPUTS
FROM   OUTPUTS
SOCIETY ⟶ EDUCATIONAL PROCESS ⟶ TO SOCIETY

| Knowledge
Values
Goals
Money | *Structure* (for example, grade levels, classes, school levels, departments, organizational hierarchy)
People (for example, teachers, bus drivers, counselors, coaches, custodians, supervisors, dieticians, administrators, nurses)
Technology (for example, buildings, class schedules, curricula, laboratories, libraries, chalkboards, books, audio-visual equipment, buses)
Tasks (for example, teach classes; serve food; run buses; administer tests; account for funds, stewardship; supervise personnel, conduct extracurricular program. | *Individuals more able to serve themselves and society because of improved*
* Intellectual and manual skills
* Powers of reason and analysis
* Values, attitudes, motivation
* Creativity and inventiveness
* Communication skills
* Cultural appreciation
* Understanding of the world
* Sense of social responsibility |

example, it presupposes that when students and teachers go to school each day, their dominant concerns are to achieve the formal, official goals of the school. Even a casual observer soon learns, however, that actually these people bring to school with them a host of their own beliefs, goals, hopes, and concerns that are more significant and more powerful to them. Clearly, the many subtle ways in which teachers, administrators, and students accommodate to the rules, regulations, and discipline of the school have more to do with the need to "survive" in a frustrating, crowded environment than with commitment to the achievement of some remote and often ambiguous educational goals.

A more useful approach to understanding educative organizations and the behavior of people in them is to focus our attention on what actually goes on in them. Thus, our attention is centered on examining the inner workings of that system we call an organization. This requires us to see the organization as a whole system which creates the setting, the context in which the whole pattern of human behavior that characterizes the organization occurs. With this approach we seek to study organizations as systems that create and maintain environments in which complex sets of human interactions (both group and individual) occur with some regularity and predictability. In this view, our understanding of educative organizations requires us to examine the relationships between human behavior and the context (environment, ecology) that are characteristic of the organization. Thus, as I shall discuss in detail in Chapter 7, the organizational culture (climate, ecology, ethos) of the system we call an organization becomes critical to our understanding.

The realm of organizational behavior tends to focus primarily on the school district or on the school as a system. Some scientists, in studying organizational behavior, have unwittingly encouraged the illusion that a school can, in fact, be a closed social system. Andrew Halpin and Don Croft, for example, in their highly influential study of the organizational climate of schools "concentrated on internal organizational characteristics as though they function independently from external influences"[6] and, further, used the terms "open" and "closed" to describe the profiles of schools that represented selected characteristics of what they chose to call organizational climate.[7] This was, to some extent, a convenience for the researchers: it is, indeed, difficult to study and discuss the behavior of people in a system without assuming (implicitly or otherwise) that the organization is separate from its environment. Many studies of organizational behavior in schools have, in fact, focused on the internal functioning of schools—that is, have treated the schools as "closed systems"—as though they function independently of influences from their larger, outside environments.[8]

In the physical realm, a burning candle has become a classic illustration of an open system: it affects its environment and is affected by it, yet it is self-regulating and retains its own identity. If a door is opened, the candle may flicker in the draft, but it will adjust to it and return to normal at the first opportunity—provided, of course, that the environmental change (the draft) was not so overwhelming as to destroy the system (that is, to extinguish the flame).

It is not so simple to describe *social* systems on even this superficial level. Daniel Griffiths speaks of the organization (the system) as existing in an environment (the suprasystem) and having within it a subsystem (the administrative apparatus of the organization). He diagrams it in Figure 3–2. The boundaries of the

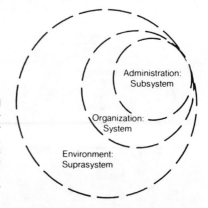

FIGURE 3–2. An organization viewed as an open social system. From Daniel E. Griffiths, "Administrative Theory and Change in Organizations," in *Innovation in Education*, ed. Matthew B. Miles (New York: Teachers College Press, 1964), p. 430. © 1964 by Teachers College, Columbia University. Reproduced by permission of the publisher.

various systems and subsystems are suggested in the figure by the tangential circles; however, we must bear in mind that these boundaries are permeable, permitting interaction between the systems and their environments. One application of this viewpoint can be illustrated by labeling the figure, as in Figure 3–3. It then becomes obvious that factors that interfere with the interactive and adaptive relationships between the components of the interrelated parts of the system could pose a threat to the functioning of the whole. One form of interference would be a loss of permeability of one or more of the boundaries, thus tending to make the system "closed" and less sensitive to environmental change.

Where does the individual fit into all of this? This becomes clearer if we modify the original model, as in Figure 3–4. Here, again, a relabeling of the diagram can specify—a little more clearly, at least—one way in which the view would apply to people working in schools. The individual is functioning in the organization not only as an individual but also as one who occupies a certain *role* within the social system in the organization. In the hypothetical case illustrated in Figure 3–5, the person occupies the role of "teacher" in the chemistry department of John F. Kennedy Senior High School, a situation possessing a number of useful implications for anyone interested in analyzing, predicting, and perhaps controlling organizational behavior.

When we consider the individual person carrying out a unique role in an organization, we become concerned with the complex web of human involvement

FIGURE 3–3. A social systems view of the school.

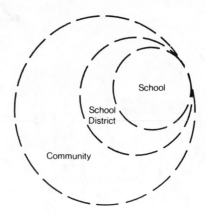

FIGURE 3–4.   Levels of interaction of the individual and the organization. From Richard C. Lonsdale, "Maintaining the Organization in Dynamic Equilibrium," in *Behavioral Science and Educational Administration*, ed. Daniel E. Griffiths. The Sixty-Third Yearbook of the National Society for the Study of Education, Part II (Chicago: National Society for the Study of Education, 1964), p. 143.

and its attendant behavior in organizational life. As the individual, with all the needs, drives, and talents that human beings have, assumes an official role, he or she shapes that role to some extent and is also shaped by it. The dynamic interaction of people with varying psychological makeups in the organizational setting is the domain of role theory.

ROLE THEORY

In attempting to analyze face-to-face, interpersonal behavior of people in organizations, Erving Goffman, in *The Preservation of Self in Everyday Life,*[9] drew a useful analogy between "real-life" situations and the unfolding of a play on the stage. People in organizations have definite roles to perform, and many interactive factors help to determine precisely what kind of "performance" each role will receive. Each "actor" must interpret his or her role, and this interpretation depends to some extent on what the individual brings to the role. But behavior in a role as part of an organization—no less than for an actor on the stage—will be influenced to some extent by dynamic interplay with other people: other actors and the audience. Role performances are also shaped by the expectations of the director and others attempting to control the situation. Presumably, each actor attempts, to some degree, to

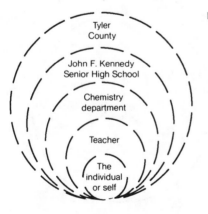

FIGURE 3–5.   A social systems view of the individual in a hypothetical school organization.

behave in conformity with these expectations—and the expectations of colleagues and other referent groups as well. Goffman describes the actors in an organization as being on stage when they are formally carrying out their roles, but he points out that backstage there is a different behavioral standard. Those of us connected with schools, for example, know that a certain kind of behavior is exhibited by teachers in the presence of students and their parents, which differs from their behavior in the teachers' cafeteria.

Role theory has been used extensively by observers and researchers in many kinds of organizations, in efforts to better understand and predict organizational behavior. A vocabulary of generally understood terms is fairly well established in the literature. Some of the more commonly used terms are described below.

Role. Role[10] is a psychological concept dealing with behavior enactment arising from interaction with other human beings. The various offices or positions in an organization carry with them certain expectations of behavior held by both onlookers and by the person occupying the role. These expectations generally define role, with some additional expectation that the individual will exhibit some idiosyncratic personality in role behavior.

Role description. This refers to the actual behavior of an individual performing a role or, more accurately, one's perception of that behavior.

Role prescription. This is the relatively abstract idea of what the general norm in the culture is for the role. What kind of role behavior is expected of a teacher in this country, for example?

Role expectation. This refers to the expectation that one person has of the role behavior of another. Teachers, for example, expect certain behaviors from a principal, and the principal has expectations of behaviors for teachers. Thus, as teacher and principal interact in their roles in the school, they have complementary role expectations.

Role perception. This is used to describe the perception that one has of the role expectation that another person holds for him or her. In dealing with the P.T.A. president, for example, the principal knows that the president has some role expectation of the principal. The principal's estimate of that expectation is role perception.

Manifest and latent roles. Naturally, a person plays more than one role in life; indeed, an individual may well play more than one in an organization. In the case of multiple roles, the term *manifest role* is used in referring to the obvious role that one is performing, but one also occupies *latent roles*. For example, in the classroom, a teacher's manifest role is "teacher"; but the teacher may also be the building chairperson for the teachers' union and that role—while he or she is teaching—is a latent role. A history teacher may also be an activist in a consumers' rights organization and thus holds a latent, as well as a manifest, role.

Role conflict. This is commonly thought to be a source of less-than-satisfactory performance in organizations. There are many sources of role conflict, all of which inhibit optimum performance by the role incumbent. An obvious role conflict is a situation in which two persons are unable to establish a satisfactory complementary, or reciprocal, role relationship, which can result from a wide variety of causes and—not infrequently—may involve a complex set of conflict behaviors. Confusion over role expectation and role perception is commonly observed.

Moreover, role conflict frequently exists within a single individual. The role expectation may well clash with the individual personality needs of the role incumbent. A case in point is that of a school principal who was employed by a school district largely because of his innovative skill and strong leadership qualities; when a taxpayers' revolt in the school district suddenly caused a sharp reversal of school board policy, the superintendent was dismissed, and the school board put strong emphasis on economy of operation and conformity to mediocre educational standards. The school principal was plunged into a role conflict situation in which he could not perform to his, or anyone else's, satisfaction and ended up seeking another job with a more manageable amount of conflict.

A common source of tension from role conflict is the expectation that the incumbent, perhaps an administrator, will be empathetic and understanding in dealing with his or her subordinates and will still enforce the rules of the organization and strongly support the school board in dealing with teachers as members of a collective bargaining unit. Many administrators feel this sort of conflict when they zealously attempt to build trust, confidence, and high morale in the teaching staff and then are required to conduct a formal evaluation or to participate in a grievance procedure that seems to be in conflict with those goals.

Role ambiguity. This arises when the role prescription contains contradictory elements or is vague. Role ambiguity is rather commonly observed in the attempt to preserve the distinction between administration and supervision: the first is generally seen as a "line" authority, whereas the other is thought to be a "staff" responsibility. Yet supervisors are often perceived as being in hierarchical authority over teachers; not infrequently, supervisors feel that they are being maneuvered, against the spirit of their role, into the exercise of authority over teachers, which threatens their more appropriate, collegial relationship with them.

Role conflicts—some of which have been described above—produce tensions and uncertainties that are commonly associated with inconsistent organizational behavior. In turn, this inconsistent behavior, being unpredictable and unanticipated, often evokes further tension and interpersonal conflict between holders of complementary roles. Frequently, those who must perform their roles under the conditions of ambiguity and tension outlined here develop dysfunctional ways of coping with the situation.

Thus, while we may find such socially acceptable avoidance behavior as joking about the conflict or ambiguity, in organizations in which this kind of avoidance is not acceptable rather elaborate and mutually understood avoidance patterns may exist. These can include a studied avoidance of any discussion of the problem or substituting any kind of "small talk" instead. A common avoidance technique is found in ritualistic behavior which permits parties to get through their role performances with a minimum of actual conflict. Vagueness, pomposity, complex structure, clichés, and overly obscure vocabulary in communication are popular avoidance techniques.[11]

Role set. The notion of *role set* is helpful in clarifying some of the concepts of role theory as they are found to be operational in organizations. If we were to observe a work group, we would, of course, find it possible to sort out the participants into subgroups in a variety of ways. And one way would be in terms of role. In the case of the role set that will be used here as an illustration, the pivotal role player may be thought of as an administrator.[12] Naturally, he or she has superordinates in the hierarchy of the organization, people to whom he or she reports (see Figure 3–6). These are key people in the individual's referent group, and they convey their role expectations in many ways. But the administrator not only has superordinates, he or she also has subordinates, or people who report to him or her. As shown in Figure 3–7, subordinates also are significant persons in the administrator's group, and they, too, communicate role expectations to the administrator. Thus, the role player's position becomes pivotal, and it is obvious that the role expectations being communicated are likely to be somewhat in conflict.

The role set is incomplete, however, until a third group of referents is added: the role player's colleagues. With their addition to the role set, as in Figure 3–8, we see the administrator in a pivotal position in relationship to subordinates and superordinates. When we realize that, in this example, twelve persons—two superordinates, four subordinates, and six colleagues—are acting as *role senders* (that is, they are communicating role expectations to the administrator) it is evident that the interpersonal dynamics of the role set are complex.

There undoubtedly will be some role conflict present in such a situation, as well as some role ambiguity. Robert Kahn and his colleagues have used this operational concept of role theory to describe and measure role conflict and role ambiguity and to correlate their presence with attitudes that members of the set have toward their work situation and to the behavioral functioning of these people in the

FIGURE 3–6. Relationship of role player to superordinates in the work group. Adapted from Warren G. Bennis, *Changing Organizations* (New York: McGraw-Hill Book Company, 1966), p. 193.

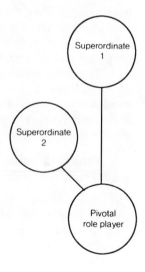

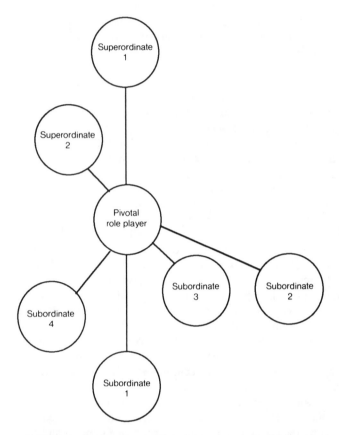

FIGURE 3–7.   Relationship of pivotal role player to superordinates and subordinates in the work group. Adapted from Warren G. Bennis, *Changing Organizations* (New York; McGraw-Hill Book Company, 1966), p. 193.

work group.[13] Thus, the role set is an important concept in a consideration of the ecology of the social setting in which the individual makes his or her contribution to the organization. It is a useful way of conceptualizing the connection between the person and the organization.

To possess knowledge of role theory and some of its concepts is, in itself, of little use. However, the construct can be useful in analyzing some of the interpersonal behavior that we encounter in the work groups of organizations. For example, leaders are concerned with facilitating the acceptance, development, and allocation of roles that are necessary for the group to function well.

Functional roles in the group.   Kenneth Benne and Paul Sheats have pointed out that a group has three types of roles that must be filled.[14]

1. *Group task roles*. These are roles that help the group to select the problems to be worked on, to define these problems, and to seek solutions to these problems.
2. *Group building and maintenance roles*. These roles facilitate the development of the group and its maintenance over time.

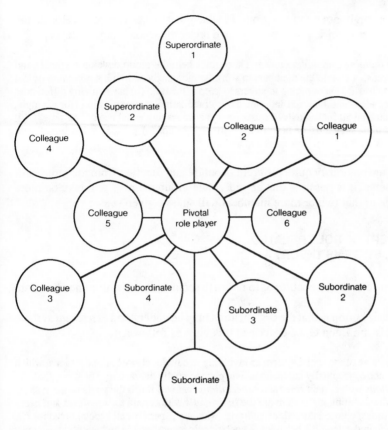

FIGURE 3-8. Illustration of role set. Adapted from Warren G. Bennis, *Changing Organizations* (New York: McGraw-Hill Book Company, 1966), p. 193.

3. *Individual roles.* These are the roles that enable group members to satisfy their own idiosyncratic needs as individuals.

Although we must be wary of too much labeling, let us consider Benne's and Sheats's further description of possible specific roles that are available to group members in meeting two critical needs of a group.

> *Group task roles:* These are roles that help the group to achieve its tasks. They include the roles of (a) initiating action and contributing ideas, (b) seeking information, (c) seeking opinions from the group, (d) giving information, (e) giving one's opinion, (f) coordinating the work of group members, (g) helping to keep the group focused on goals, (h) the evaluator-critic, (i) the energizer who prods the group to action, (j) the procedural technician who attends to routine "house-keeping" tasks of the group, and (k) the recorder.[15]

Benne and Sheats stress that each of these roles must be played by someone in the group; the leader must either assume these essential roles or see that they are allocated to other members of the group. Part of the leader's responsibility is to provide for the creation of an environment in the group in which these roles can be developed and carried out. Other specific roles are suggested under the second major category:

> *Group building and maintenance:* These roles help the group develop a climate and processes that enable the members to work harmoniously and with a minimum of lost time, such as (a) encouraging members to keep at the task, (b) harmonizing differences between ideas and between individuals, (c) facilitating communication (for example, by helping silent individuals to speak up and encouraging equal use of "air time"), (d) setting high standards of performance for the group, (e) providing the group with feedback as to its own processes and actions.[16]

These roles are obviously quite different in nature and function from the group task roles. Of course, it is possible that an individual group member will take on more than one role or that two or more members will share a given role.

THE CONCEPT OF ROLE RELATED
TO SOCIAL SYSTEMS THEORY

The foregoing discussion enables us to return to social systems with somewhat more insight.

The basic notion is that the organization may be understood as a *social system.* Jacob Getzels and Egon Guba described this view as follows:

> We conceive of the social system as involving two major classes of phenomena, which are at once conceptually independent and phenomenally interactive. There are, first, the *institutions* with certain *roles* and *expectations* that will fulfill the goals of the system. Second, inhabiting the system are the *individuals* with certain *personalities* and *need-dispositions,* whose interactions comprise what we generally call "social behavior."...
> ...[T]o understand the behavior of specific role incumbents in an institution, we must know both the role expectations and the need-dispositions. Indeed, needs and expectations may both be thought of as motives for behavior, the one deriving from personal propensities, the other from institutional requirements. What we call social behavior may be conceived as ultimately deriving from the interaction between the two sets of motives.
> The general model we have been describing may be represented pictorially as indicated [in Figure 3–9]. The nomothetic [organizational] axis is shown at the top of the diagram and consists of the institution, role, and role expectations, each term being

FIGURE 3–9. Model of the organization as a social system (the so-called "Getzels-Guba model"). Adapted from Jacob W. Getzels and Egon G. Guba, "Social Behavior and the Administrative Process," *The School Review,* 65 (Winter 1957), 423–41.

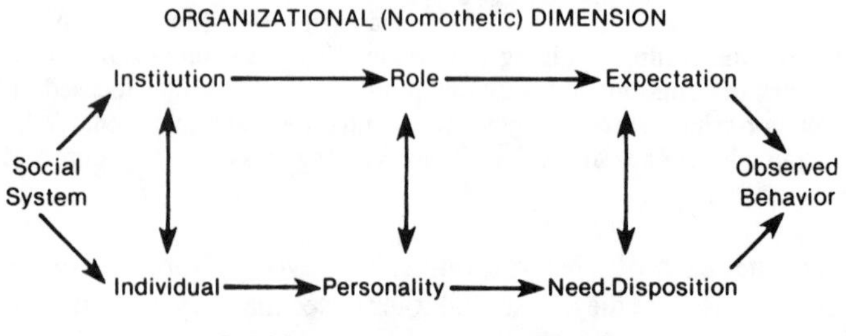

ORGANIZATIONAL (Nomothetic) DIMENSION

Institution ——————→ Role ——————→ Expectation

Social System ... Observed Behavior

Individual ——————→ Personality ——————→ Need-Disposition

PERSONAL (Idiographic) DIMENSION

the analytic unit for the term next preceding it....Similarly, the idiographic [individual] axis, shown at the lower portion of the diagram, consists of individual, personality, and need-dispositions, each term again serving as the analytic unit for the term next preceding it. A given act is conceived as deriving simultaneously from both the nomothetic and the idiographic dimensions. That is to say, social behavior results as the individual attempts to cope with the environment composed of patterns of expectations for his behavior in ways consistent with his own independent pattern of needs.[17]

Viewed in this way, each behavioral act is seen as stemming simultaneously from the nomothetic and the idiographic dimensions. But how do these dimensions interact? What proportion of each dimension is present in organizational behavior? That depends, of course, on the individual and on the institutional role and is best expressed as a function of the interplay between the two dimensions. Getzels gives us this general equation to express it:

$$B = f\,(R \times P),$$

where B = observed behavior,
R = institutional role, and
P = personality of the role incumbent.[18]

Thus the school, as an organization, creates certain offices and positions that are occupied by individuals. The offices and positions represent the nomothetic dimension of the organization and role expectations held by the organization for incumbents are specified in a number of ways. These may range from elaborate written job descriptions to the more subtle (and usually more powerful) group norms established by custom and tradition. By this means, the organization establishes not merely some formal, minimal level of job performance that would be acceptable but also communicates rather elaborate specifications of behavior in role that may well extend to the kinds of clothes worn on the job, the manner of speech used, and so on.

But the individuals who are incumbent in the offices and positions have their own personality structures and needs, which represent the idiographic dimensions of the organization. To some extent, even in highly formal organizations, the role incumbents mold and shape the offices in some ways in order to better fulfil some of their own expectations of their role.

The mechanism by which the needs of the institution and the needs of the individual are modified so as to come together is the work group. There is a dynamic interrelationship in the work group, then, not only of an interpersonal nature but also between institutional requirements and the idiosyncratic needs of individual participants. The shaping of the institutional role, the development of a climate within the social system, and the very personality of the participants all dynamically interact with one another. Organizational behavior can be viewed as the product of this interaction.

How much organizational behavior can be ascribed to role expectation and role prescription, and how much is traceable to the personality needs of the role incumbent? In other words, if $B = f\,(R \times P)$, what values can be assigned to R and P, respectively? A useful way of picturing the problem is shown in Figure 3–10. We can see that, for some people, a role can have far greater influence in prescribing behavior than for others.

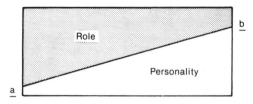

FIGURE 3–10. The interplay of role and personality in organizational behavior. Behavior is a function of organizational role and personality, or B = f (R × P). Adapted from Jacob W. Getzels, "Administration as a Social Process," in *Administrative Theory in Education*, ed. Andrew W. Halpin (Chicago: Midwest Administration Center, University of Chicago, 1958), p. 158.

For example, there has been considerable study of individuals who exhibit an authoritarian personality syndrome and of their impact on others.[19] Such an individual possesses a combination of personality characteristics that are stable, describable, and go far in shaping his or her view of the world. Typically the authoritarian individual tends to think in terms of relatively simple dichotomies: things are seen in black-or-white terms (with few shades of gray); concrete ideas are typical (with little patience for abstract thinking or ambiguity); and he or she identifies strongly with the "in" group (and particularly with authority figures). Authoritarian individuals, being insecure in ambiguous circumstances, place little trust in others and seek to control as much of the environment as possible (including the people around them). Such a person tends to seek a role in which he or she is seen as strong and in which control can be exercised. Behavior in that role tends to be relatively consistent: dogmatic, seeking absolute solutions to complex problems, and exercising power for personal gratification.

Mary Crow and Merl Bonney describe the impact of such people when they take on the leadership roles of a school district:

> Picture a moderate-sized urban school system in Middle America. The clean-cut, conservatively dressed superintendent has made it clear who is on his side and who isn't. Among his supporters are the building principals, men who are much more like the superintendent: wanting to be tough disciplinarians, yet subservient to the boss. Of these principals, teachers will tell you that more competent candidates were often passed over for principalships in favor of these supporters who would be no threat to the superintendent's job....At the first faculty meeting of the year, the superintendent comes across forcefully. He stresses how important it is that his teachers be honest, upstanding citizens, maintain good discipline in their classes, and work hard if they wish to be successful in his system....Students are afraid of teachers; teachers are afraid of principals; principals are afraid of the superintendent; and the superintendent is afraid of the board.[20]

Though this is admittedly a stereotype of one kind of personality frequently found in leadership roles in American school districts, everyone shapes his or her own role to *some* extent; hence, as shown in Figure 3–10, point *a* would not ordinarily be at zero; on the other hand, in any organization everyone plays some sort of institutional role and, therefore, point *b* is somewhat below the 100 percent mark. The line *ab*, however, suggests the possible range of variation of the function of role and personality that normally would be encountered in organizations.

Different kinds of roles in different kinds of organizations do suggest that some role players will be closer to point *a* (that is, will permit very little infusion of personality into the role). Conversely, we know that some kinds of roles demand greater personality involvement, as illustrated in Figure 3–11. One generally supposes that the role of an army private is very largely prescribed and clearly limits the extent to which the private can meet his or her individual personality needs. Closer to the other extreme would be an artist who exhibits highly creative behavior, with a minimum of organizational constraint, and who expresses personal idiosyncratic needs to a great degree.

Equilibrium. People participate in organizations in order to satisfy certain needs. Presumably, the organization has needs of its own which are fulfilled by the participants who function in its various roles. This is illustrated by the Getzels-Guba social systems model, with its stress on the interplay between the nomothetic (organizational) needs and the idiographic (personal) needs of the "actors" who fill the various roles. There is obviously a *quid pro quo* relationship between the role player and the organization, the maintenance of which can be thought of as a state of *equilibrium* between the needs of the organization and those of the individual. As long as this state of equilibrium exists, the relationship presumably will be satisfactory, enduring, and relatively productive.

On a very rudimentary level, the notion of equilibrium between the needs of the organization and its participants is illustrated by the well-known case of Schmidt at Bethlehem Steel. Schmidt, as he was called in Fredrick W. Taylor's description,[21] was a pig-iron handler, who picked up, carried, and loaded pig iron—12.5 tons in a ten-hour day for $1.15 per day. Obviously, the company needed men to do the pig-iron handling, and this need was satisfied by the men whose role was that of "handler." Presumably, as long as the needs and satisfactions exchange was in a state of balance or equilibrium, the organization functioned adequately. In his account Taylor described how he applied his "scientific principles" to the task of rigorously training Schmidt to increase Schmidt's daily work-load to 47.5 tons. The needs-inducements balance was maintained by boosting the pay by 60 percent, to $1.85 per day. Schmidt and the company apparently found the needs-inducements arrangements mutually satisfactory, because Schmidt was described as staying on the job for "some years."

FIGURE 3–11. Personality and role factors in organizational behavior of army private and artist (proportions are approximate). Adapted from Jacob W. Getzels, "Administration as a Social Process," in *Administrative Theory in Education*, ed. Andrew W. Halpin (Chicago: Midwest Administration Center, University of Chicago, 1958), p. 158.

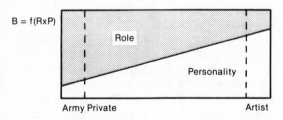

$B = f(R \times P)$

Role

Personality

Army Private   Artist

Chester Barnard discussed equilibrium as "the balancing of burdens by satisfactions which results in continuance"[22] of participation of both the individual and the organization in a mutual relationship. In his lexicon, the term "effectiveness" was the "accomplishment of the recognized objectives of cooperative action."[23] "Efficiency" referred to the ability of the organization to sustain the continued participation of individuals by offering adequate satisfactions to them.

Barnard described the organization as inducing cooperation by distributing its "*productive* results" to individuals. "These productive results," he wrote, "are either material or social, or both. As to some individuals, material is required for satisfaction; as to others, social benefits are required. As to most individuals, both material and social benefits are required in different proportions."[24] Barnard points out—and this is familiar to us all—that the definition of what constitutes "adequate satisfactions" to individuals in the organization varies, depending in great measure on the makeup and circumstances of the individual involved. Some people certainly find great satisfaction in material reward, especially money, and in order to get it will accept an organizational role that may be insecure, unpleasant, or strenuous. Regardless of the many possible negative aspects of such a role, as long as there is enough material reward, such people may well find the inducement satisfying. Others, for whatever reasons, might find a higher income not worth the price that must be paid.

In the recent history of educational administration this can be seen in connection with the role of the superintendent of schools and, to a lesser degree, with that of the high school principal. Although the salaries being offered to superintendents are reaching very high levels, many qualified people are not attracted to these roles, and many incumbents have shifted to university teaching or to other fields altogether. Long working hours, arduous demands, and enormous pressures are some of the drawbacks of the superintendency; in many cases there is little reward in terms of achievement or self-fulfillment. In order to attract and hold capable people as superintendents, school districts must proffer a combination of material and psychological rewards that incumbents will find attractive.

Similarly, not many years ago in the United States, an important problem was attracting good teachers to rural areas and keeping them there in spite of the low pay, inadequate school facilities, and limited cultural opportunities which made teaching in such areas relatively unrewarding to many. Today, of course, the situation is reversed; other careers and schools in nonurban areas offer considerable reward to many teachers, whereas the bleak, hostile, frustrating environment of the teacher in the urban ghetto school is barely adequate—both in terms of money and a sense of fulfillment—for many capable teachers.

In discussing organizational equilibrium from the systems-theory point of view, we must remember that there is not only a needs-inducements relationship between the individual participant and the organization; the organization itself is part of a larger system. Further, if the system is "open"—as in the case of schools and school systems—the organization will interact actively with the external systems that comprise its environment. An expanded version of the Getzels-Guba social system model, shown in Figure 3–12, depicts this interaction of school with its larger environment. Presumably, changes in the environment will stimulate a reaction by the organization, either *static* or *dynamic*. If the reaction is static, the system responds so as to keep relationships in their original state, that is, the *status quo* is maintained. Dynamic

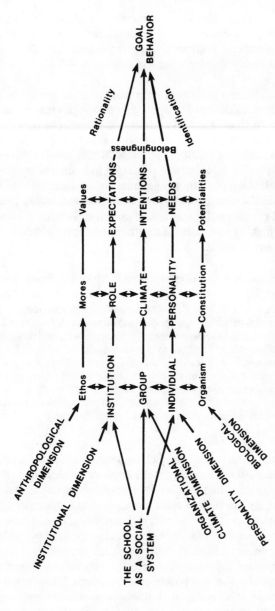

FIGURE 3–12. Dimensions of the school as a social system. Adapted from Jacob W. Getzels and Herbert A. Thelen, "The Classroom Group as a Unique Social System," in *The Dynamics of Instructional Groups: Sociopsychological Aspects of Teaching and Learning*, ed. Nelson B. Henry. N.S.S.E. Yearbook LIX, Part II (Chicago: National Society for the Study of Education, 1960), p. 80.

equilibrium, however, is characterized by a rearrangement of the internal subsystems of the organization or by a change in its goals in order to adjust to changing circumstances in its external environment. Dynamic equilibrium, in other words, helps to keep the system in a steady state by being adaptable.

Homeostasis.   This is a biological term that has been applied to organizations and that refers to the tendency of an open system to regulate itself so as to stay constantly in balance. The biological organism tends to retain its own characteristics, to maintain itself and to preserve its identity, but, at the same time, it has compensatory mechanisms that enable it to adapt to and survive environmental changes within certain limits. Homeostatic processes in human beings include the body's tendency to maintain a constant temperature and to maintain blood pressure by repairing a break in the circulatory system through coagulation. Homeostatic mechanisms in school systems and schools, such as well-developed communication systems and decision-making processes, enable them to adapt to and deal effectively with changes in their environment.

Feedback.   Feedback is described by John Pfiffner and Frank Sherwood:

> In its simplest form, feedback is the kind of communication an actor receives from a live audience. If the crowd is enthusiastic, the performer reacts with similar enthusiasm. There is in a way a closed circuit between performer and audience with continuing interchange of information....Essential to feedback is the notion that the flow of information is actually having a reciprocating effect on behavior. This is why the term loop is frequently associated with feedback. This circular pattern involves a flow of information to the point of action, a flow back to the point of decision with information on the action, and then a return to the point of action with new information and perhaps instructions. A primary element in this process is the sensory organ, the instrument through which information is obtained.[25]

Systems that do not have sensitive antennae picking up accurate feedback information, or—perhaps worse—that do not provide for the accurate transmission of feedback information to decision makers, find it difficult to react appropriately to environmental changes. Such systems tend to be in a static, rather than in a dynamic, equilibrium with their environments. They tend to lack the self-correcting, homeostatic processes essential to maintaining themselves in environments characterized by change.

We have, then, in the social systems view, an organization that is—by definition—an open system. This means, in part, not only that the organization has internal subsystems but also that it is part of a suprasystem. Moreover, the organization is in an interactive relationship with this suprasystem: it exchanges inputs and outputs with it. And, to some extent, the organization affects its environment (the suprasystem) and is also affected by changes that occur in the suprasystem.

It can resist and deny changes in the suprasystem or environment by ignoring or fighting them or by attempting to insulate itself from them (that is, by becoming more "closed"). It can attempt to accommodate to environmental change by homeostatic adaptation—"business as usual." Or, finally, the organization can adapt to environmental changes by developing a new balance, a new equilibrium. In a world such as ours, dominated by rapid and extensive change, it would appear that the organization with poor feedback mechanisms or weak homeostatic characteristics would show declining performance and increasing evidence of disorganization.

It is important to remember that essential to systems theory is the concept that *systems are composed of subsystems that are highly interactive and mutually interdependent.* It would seem clear from the Getzels-Guba model of the school as an open social system, which has already been described, that at least two subsystems can be identified and their interaction at least suggested: (1) the organizational or institutional system and (2) the human system. However, useful as this model was in early attempts to understand the dynamics of organizational behavior, it is incomplete. By the mid-1980s it was clear that organizations possess more than these two subsystems and that analysis of organizational behavior requires us to use more complex concepts. One of the more currently useful approaches is to conceptualize organizations—for example, the school system and the school—as *sociotechnical systems.*

SOCIOTECHNICAL SYSTEM THEORY

By definition, an organization exists for the purpose of achieving something: reaching some goal or set of goals. It seeks to do this by accomplishing certain *tasks.*[26] Rationally, of course, the organization is structured, equipped, and staffed appropriately to accomplish its mission. The main goal of a school district, for example, requires it to operate schools, a transportation system, and food services. The district must employ people, provide legally mandated services, and perhaps engage in collective bargaining. There are numerous tasks that the school district must organize internally in order to achieve its goals.

In order to achieve an assigned task—that may include a large number of subtasks and operationally necessary tasks—we build an organization: that is, we give it *structure.* It is the structure that gives an organization order, system, and many of its distinctive characteristics. The structure establishes a pattern of authority and collegiality, thus defining role: there are top-management executives and middle-management supervisors, bosses and workers, each of whom attempts to know the extent of his or her own legitimate authority as well as that of others. Structure dictates, in large measure, the patterns of communication networks that are basic to information flow and, therefore, to decision making. Structure also determines the system of work flow that is, presumably, focused on achieving the organization's tasks.

The organization must have *technological resources* or, in other words, the "tools of its trade." Technology, used in this sense, does not only include such typical hardware items as computers, milling machines, textbooks and chalk, and electron microscopes. Technology may also include program inventions: systematic procedures, the sequencing of activities, or other procedural inventions designed to solve problems that stand in the way of organizational task achievement. Thus the teacher's daily lesson plan, the high school class schedule, and the district's curriculum guides are illustrative of technology in educational organizations.

Finally, of course, the organization must have *people.* Their contribution to the task achievement of the organization is ultimately visible in their acts—that is, their organizational behavior. It is this behavior that selects, directs, communicates, and decides.

These four internal organization factors—*task, structure, technology,* and *people*[27] (Figure 3–13)—are variables that differ from time to time and from one organization to the next. Within a given organization these four factors are highly interactive, each tending to shape and mold the others. As in any system, the interdependence of the variable factors means that a significant change in one will result in some adaptation on the part of the other factors. Important in determining the nature and interrelationship of these internal organizational arrangements in a school district or school is the response of the organization to changes occurring in the larger system in which it exists.

Suppose, for example, there is an academically oriented high school that admits limited numbers of talented students by competitive examination for the express purpose of preparing them for college. If the board of education rules that the school be converted into a comprehensive high school to meet the needs of the total youth population (which, of course, would be a change in the organization's goal), it is apparent that a number of internal adjustments would be necessary for the school to achieve its new goal reasonably well. Many of these changes would be compensatory in nature. For example, in order to accommodate those students interested in a business career it would be necessary to teach courses in business (task). To do this, business education equipment would have to be installed (technology), business education teachers would have to be employed (people), and a department of business education might be created (structure). However, some of the changes flowing from the board's directive might be retaliatory rather than compensatory. For example, some people in the school might seek to resist these changes, with the result that their former cooperative, and productive, behavior would be replaced by alienation and conflict. This, in turn, could disrupt the normal communications patterns in the school, thereby producing a structural change.

A technological change, such as the introduction of a comprehensive, computer-related instructional system in a high school, could bring about important side effects: it could change the goals of the school by making it possible to achieve new things

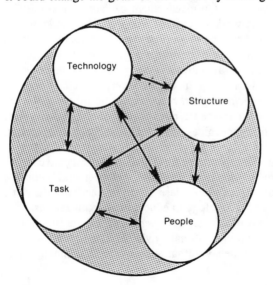

FIGURE 3–13. Interacting subsystems in complex organization. Adapted from Harold J. Leavitt, "Applied Organizational Change in Industry: Structural, Technological and Humanistic Approaches," in *Handbook of Organizations,* ed. James G. March © 1965 by Rand McNally & Company, Chicago, Figure 1, p. 1145.

and, simultaneously, by rendering certain traditional tasks obsolete. A change in people would include the employment of new personnel with technical skills, affecting the work activities of others in the school by making some activities unnecessary and requiring certain new activities to be introduced. Finally, the introduction of new departments and changes in those involved in the decision-making processes would be structural changes flowing out of the technical change originally initiated.

Thus, in coordinating the internal processes of the school district or school, it is necessary to attend to the dynamic interaction of the four subsystems—people, structure, technology, and task. However, if it is proposed to introduce a significant change through primarily one of the target variables, it is clear that the other variables soon will be affected. Change efforts that are basically technological in nature result in some compensatory or retaliatory behavior on the part of people and in some structural adjustments within the organization. Those who seek to bring about significant structural rearrangements in the school—such as differentiated staffing plans— must reckon with the people involved and the way they will react to the change.

Although it is easy to speak of different administrative strategies and to categorize various tactics and procedures as "belonging" to one strategy or another, we must recognize the symbiotic interrelationship that exists among the internal organizational subsystems with which we are concerned: task, technological, structural, and behavioral.

The schematic diagram in Figure 3–14 illustrates the key internal and external relationships of a school system or school. In the figure I have provided only a few illustrative examples of the many things that are normally included in the task, technology, and structure subsystems. In conceptualizing the human subsystem, the reader is cautioned to note that it is insufficient to name or label the occupational roles of participants (such as teachers, nurses, and custodians). In terms of the dynamics of internal organizational functioning, the values, beliefs, and knowledge possessed by individuals in the human system are fully as important as the facts that the individuals are present and that the organization has formalized ways of dealing with them (such as rules, grievance procedures, and personnel policies). It should be obvious that the human subsystem is the only one that has nonrational (that is, affective, not irrational) capability.

CONTINGENCY THEORY

Theorizing, thinking, research, and experience with organizations have been accompanied by an observable tendency for individuals (whether theorists or practitioners) to adopt advocacy positions. Those who favor classical approaches to organization, for example, have consistently supported the notion that a hierarchy of authority based upon rank in the organization is essential to the very concept of organization. Human relations adherents may differ on many points but are almost unanimous in espousing supportive, collaborative, people-centered leadership and highly participative management styles as superior to other approaches. Behavioral adherents have, with a fair degree of consistency, sought to find the one best way to integrate, in the most productive manner, the key elements of the classical and human relations approaches. The result, for many years, was the development of

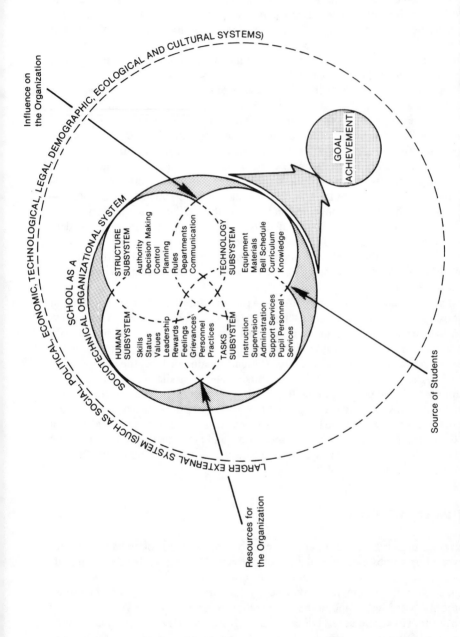

FIGURE 3-14. Four primary organizational subsystems characterize the internal arrangements of school systems and schools. Adapted from Robert G. Owens and Carl R. Steinhoff, *Administering Change in Schools* (Englewood Cliffs, NJ: Prentice-Hall, 1976), p. 143.

78

competing advocacy positions, with very mixed results when attempts were made to apply any one of the positions to organizations: none of the three approaches is demonstrably superior in *all* situations.

Traditional (classical or neoclassical) approaches to the administration of school systems and schools have tended not only to use a hierarchical model of organization (drawn from the tradition of the military and large corporations) but also to emphasize the importance of rational, logical, and potentially powerful control systems, whereby decisions are made at the top of the hierarchy and implemented at the bottom. As a conceptually ideal state, at least, the whole is characterized by hierarchically maintained order, system, and discipline. Remember, as in the discussion of Douglas McGregor's Theory X in Chapter 2, classical concepts may be used in either hard (coercive) or soft (manipulative) form.

Rational planning models. These models, such as Planning, Programming, and Budgeting Systems (PPBS), Program Evaluation and Review Technique (PERT), Management by Objectives (MBO), and Zero-Based Budgeting (ZBB) are adapted from massive, military-industrial enterprises that had been created for such purposes as building and maintaining huge fleets of enormous, technologically complex systems of weapons, such as intercontinental ballistics missiles, atomic-powered submarines, and giant aircraft, and, lest we forget, for carrying out vast space exploration programs.

The approach, characterized by use of modern rational systems concepts and technology (as differentiated from *social* systems concepts), is traditional, classical in viewpoint, and *mechanical* in operation. Organizations are said to be mechanical when the primary basis for managing the system features:

1. Highly differentiated and specialized tasks with precise specification of rights, responsibilities, and methods;
2. Coordination and control through hierarchical supervision;
3. Communication with the external environment controlled by the top offices of the hierarchy;
4. Strong, downward-oriented line of command;
5. One-to-one leadership style emphasizing authority-obedience relationships;
6. Decision-making authority reserved for top levels of the hierarchy.

The concepts of *mechanical* and *organic* systems are widely discussed in the literature of organizational theory.[28] These concepts help us to discuss and analyze specific organizational situations without resorting to such potentially pejorative dichotomies as the bureaucratic-humanistic or democratic-authoritarian ones, which, in our culture, are obviously value-laden. Organic organizational systems are recognizable by the fact that they emphasize a different approach to managing the system:

1. Continuous reassessment of tasks and responsibilities through interaction of those involved, with functional change being easy to arrange at the working level;
2. Coordination and control through interaction of those involved, requiring considerable shared responsibility and interdependence;

3. Communication with external environment relatively extensive and open at all levels of the organization;

4. Emphasis on mutual confidence, consultation, and information sharing—up and down, laterally, and diagonally across the organization—as the basis of organizational authority;

5. Team leadership style, featuring high levels of trust and group problem solving;

6. Wide sharing of responsibility for decision making at all levels in the organization.

These two views of organization in public education have long represented what John Goodlad describes as two irreconcilable modes of thought that have struggled for dominance.

> They have been with us for a long time. William James characterized them as "the hard and the tough" and the "soft and the tender"....So far as the rhetoric of schooling is concerned, these two themes rise and fall like tides, one usually flooding as the other ebbs. Each during its high [tide] deposits its share of debris on the beach and occasionally changes the shoreline a little. But the vast interior of schooling is disturbed scarcely at all.
>
> During the 1960s, both modes of thought struggled for attention. But the avant garde was represented by the soft and tender. Teachers were exhorted to open up their classrooms; open-space schools were the work of an enlightened school district. But all of this [was] replaced [in the late 1970s] with the rhetoric of "back to the basics."...The cry is picked up in the daily press, on radio and television, and at P.T.A. meetings. There is a flurry of activity—more of it outside the schools than within. Hundreds of conventions carry the theme; legislative bills are enacted—for accountability by objectives, competency-based teacher education and, of course, proficiency tests for high school students. This activity builds up for two or three years, is intense for from three to five years, but then...falls from its own weight....What bothers me most is that educators contribute so significantly to these excesses. Indeed, they pick them up and, for a brief while, make dubious reputations out of them. Usually, too, they are just a little late so that they are swinging exuberantly to one drumbeat at about the time an alternate drumbeat is coming on strong.[29]

The ebb and flow of the tides of rhetoric and viewpoint, alternately bringing a mechanical-bureaucratic-hierarchical emphasis to the fore, then a soft human relations-humanistic sweep followed, perhaps, by a more manipulative, "soft" mechanical emphasis, historically has been painfully evident in the administration of American public schooling. Many school superintendents, principals, and others, having witnessed this reality, have decided to eschew any theoretical or analytical approach, but have elected what is generally described by practitioners as an eclectic or pragmatic approach: to go out into the "real world" of school districts and to do whatever seems to "work." After all, the argument goes, "theory doesn't make any difference." This is not only a gross misreading of what organizational studies have to teach us, but it also offers no hope whatever of setting educational administration on a solid foundation of knowledge from which systematic administrative practice may be developed.

A contingency approach to organization takes a different view: although there is no one best way to organize and manage people in all circumstances, there are certain designs of organizational structure and describable management methods that can be identified as being most effective under specific situational contingencies. The key to understanding and dealing effectively with organizational behavior, from a contingency point of view, lies in being able to *analyze* the critical variables in a given situation. Effective administrator behavior (that is, behavior likely to increase achievement of the organization in attaining its goals, to improve the culture for working and learning, and to deal as productively as possible with conflict) is not seen as characterized by a universal fixed style (for example, "nomothetic" or "idiographic") but reveals a repertoire of behavioral styles tailored to the contingencies of the situation. In sum, three basic propositions underlie the contingency approach to organizational behavior in schools:

1. There is no one best universal way to organize and administer school districts and/or schools;
2. Not all ways of organizing and administering are equally effective in a given situation: effectiveness is contingent upon appropriateness of the design or style to the situation;
3. The selection of organizational design and administrative style should be based upon careful analysis of significant contingencies in the situation.

Open system related to contingency theory. As I have described, contingency theory represents "a middle ground between (a) the view that there are universal principles of organization and management and (b) the view that each organization is unique and that each situation must be analyzed separately."[30] Contingency approaches represent a rather sensible theoretical development that seems to have value in dealing with the theory-practice gap.[31] The basic contribution of contingency thinking lies not in providing ready-made, pat answers to complex problems or easy recipes for "how to do it"; it lies, rather, in providing us with new ways of analyzing the interrelationships within and among the interacting parts of the organizational system.[32] One critical set of relationships arises from the interaction of the organization (which, remember, is an open system) with its environment.

One of the early influential attempts along this line was the work of Paul Lawrence and Jay Lorsch,[33] who viewed organizations as open systems that are capable of differentiating their internal subsystems in response to a variety of environmental contingencies. Organizations that deal successfully with uncertain environments (that is, environments that are apt to call for relatively sudden change in the organization) tend to differentiate internally more than less successful organizations do; yet they are able to maintain high levels of integration between the various subunits. Such organizations are characterized by joint decision making, clear interdepartmental linkages, and well-developed means of dealing with conflict between units of the organization. Organizations that function in environments characterized by change and instability must, to be effective, organize differently to meet the need for planning, decision making, and conflict management than do those organizations that deal with relatively stable environments.

As environmental conditions change, the organization needs to adapt by responding with an appropriate structure and administrative system. Stable technologies and stable environmental conditions call for mechanistic organizations, characterized by rigidity and by explicitly defined tasks, methods, and job descriptions. In contrast, organizations facing unstable or changing technologies and environments require relatively flexible structures, with emphasis on lateral rather than on vertical communications, expert power (rather than hierarchical power) as the predominant base of influence, loosely defined responsibilities, and emphasis on exchanges of information rather than on giving direction.[34]

Response to technological change. Critics who fault American schools for failing to make full use of modern technology often have "hardware" technologies in mind (such as computers, television and videotape, and other machines) and have a limited grasp of the extensive "software" technology which is widely used in American education. The term "technology" properly includes such "software" as procedures for sequencing instruction; scheduling the interface of time, people, and material resources; specialized programs and curriculum guides; and techniques for generating and managing information. Thus the term—when applied to school organizations—must include such diverse forms as curriculum guides, the high school schedule, biology laboratories and band rooms, the testing program, and methods for classifying, grouping, and promoting students. The array of technology utilized in schooling has considerable power to affect behavior in the entire sociotechnical system, as was suggested earlier.

But, again, technology is usually developed outside of the school system or school; its impact is a result of the interaction of the open sociotechnical system with its environment. New technological developments of every description tend to alter the contingencies that affect the internal arrangements of the school. They are, in effect, one aspect of the large environment in which school systems or schools as organizations exist.

Interaction with external environment. The school system or school, as a sociotechnical system, is in constant dynamic interaction with the larger external environment in which it exists. As used here, environment refers to the suprasystem in which the school district or school exists: the social, political, and economic systems of our culture. Thus, demographic shifts resulting in declining enrollments and increasing percentages of older people in the population, changing attitudes toward individual freedom, emphasis on women's rights to equality, shifting patterns of social mobility, dissatisfaction with the performance of schools, massive changes in legal-judicial philosophy, increased taxpayer resistance, organization of teachers into labor unions, and even mounting distrust of authority and institutions in our society in general are among the many environmental contingencies to which public school organizations have had to adapt in recent years.

Internal arrangements of the organization are largely contingent upon circumstances in that environment. Changes in the environment cause the organizational system to respond with changes in its internal arrangements. Those internal arrangements are best understood as containing four dynamically interactive subsystems: *tasks* to be performed, *structure* of the organization, *technology* utilized to perform the tasks, and the *human* social system.

One way that the social, political, and cultural environment of the school district or school has an impact is in setting goals to be achieved. Although educators play a part in establishing the goals of schooling, the process is ultimately in the political realm: state legislatures representing the body politic, for example, are normally instrumental in formalizing important aspects of the goals of schooling. Legislation of minimum competency standards for graduation and/or promotion can have a powerful impact on what schools seek to achieve. At the federal level, P.L. 94-142 has had a widespread, direct effect on school goals—not only for youngsters with special educational needs but also on virtually all other students as well.

Other political processes, such as approving budgets and levying taxes or electing school board members, also serve as means for influencing the goals of schools. Frequently, a display of potential political power is sufficient to effect reassessment and revision of organizational goals. Not infrequently, of course, judicial intervention is a means of implementing goal changes in schooling. This is readily observable in situations in which federal district courts not only have ordered the desegregation of school districts but also have specified the means by which this is to be achieved (for example, intradistrict transportation and inter-district transportation). Courts also have not infrequently required changes in curricula, testing procedures, and methods of selecting and assigning staff. All of these represent some of the ways that the environment of the school organization affects the internal functioning of the organization; and the organization will either adapt smoothly and easily, or it may tend to resist.

Thus, a groundswell of popular support for "back to basics" might appear in a local school district that motivates the board of education and the administrative staff to initiate a goal-setting and educational planning project with community involvement. As a result, the schools would likely revise their curricula, shift their teaching style, perhaps reorganize their grade structure, and adopt new textbooks—that is, make internal rearrangements in response to changes in the organization's environment.

Not infrequently, however, schools will seek to resist external changes and maintain the *status quo,* almost regardless of the degree or power of the new environmental contingencies. Our history with regard to desegregation, equal rights, and nondiscriminatory practices—even in the face of concentrated, massive, statutory, judicial, and political action—makes it clear that there are many occasions when schools attempt to close off the organizational system in order to deflect the impact of changes in the larger environment, rather than seek ways of making appropriate internal rearrangements so as to adapt to them. From a contingency point of view, this tends to put the school or school system out of touch with the real-world contingencies in which these organizations exist. In terms of organizational behavior, a negative result in such a case is likely to be the leadership and administrative styles that—in the long run—are not the most effective and may even be counterproductive.

Contingency theory and organizational behavior in schools.   Operationally, using the contingency approach in the practice of school administration does not necessarily have to be terribly exotic or to require highly sophisticated methods. It does, however, require the administrator to use some analysis of relevant contingencies in the situation at hand as a basis for selecting a way of dealing with them. Since *administration is working with and through individuals and groups to achieve organizational goals,* a fundamental contingency to consider is, "What will likely yield the most productive behavior (in terms of achieving organizational goals) from my subordinates in this situation?" An important assumption underlying this kind of question is, of course, that different administrative styles are likely to evoke predictably different responses from people.

For example, an issue that often confronts the administrator concerns leadership style: is a good leader one who sets goals, directs subordinates as to what to do, and checks closely to see that they do things as directed? Or is a good leader one who involves subordinates in setting goals, collaborates with them in deciding what to do and how to do it, and provides coordination of the group in evaluating progress and results? In the parlance of public school administrators, which is better: directive leadership or "democratic" leadership?

A contingency approach to this issue starts with clarifying what is meant by "good." Since the administrator's intent is to maximize the achievement of organizational goals, "good" is probably best redefined as "effective." The question then becomes: Which leadership style is most effective—that is, which will likely contribute most to the goal performance of the school system or school?

As I shall discuss more fully in Chapter 6, contemporary understanding of the dynamics of leader behavior makes it clear that there is apparently no one most effective style: effectiveness of leadership style clearly depends upon its appropriateness in terms of the critical contingencies in a given situation. The power of the leader, the quality of relationships with subordinates, the clarity of the structure of the task to be done, the degree of cooperation required to implement decisions, the levels of skill and motivation of subordinates—these are a few of the many contingencies that can be assessed by the administrator and related to predictable outcomes of various, specific, alternative ways to lead. In the contingency view, the effective leader is able to match leadership style to the contingencies of the situation in order to achieve the behavior on the part of subordinates that will contribute most to achieving the goals of the school district or school.

Similarly, a contingency orientation is helpful in dealing with issues of motivation, decision making, organizational change, organizational culture, and conflict management. The remaining chapters of this book explore these aspects of organizational behavior in schools.

SUMMARY

Open systems theory is the basis for contemporary analysis of organizational behavior. Social systems theory, such as the Getzels-Guba model, has provided a useful way of conceptualizing organizational behavior as a function of the interaction between the demands of organizational requirements and the needs-dispositions of individuals in the organization. Although the Getzels-Guba model often has been used to stress this internal dynamic relationship of the organization, the expanded version of the model clearly illustrates the dynamic relationship between the organizational system itself and its external larger environment, the suprasystem.

Role theory not only helps us to understand the idiographic-nomothetic relationship in greater detail but also illuminates many of the broader interpersonal relationships that exist in schools and school systems. Although role theory lacks the power to explain the organization in its entirety, it is useful as a framework for examining relationships between person and organization, as well as interpersonal behavior.

Sociotechnical concepts help us to understand the dynamic interrelationship among the structure, tasks, technology, and human aspects of educational organizations as a force in evoking and molding the behavior of people. In the typical high school, for example, people's daily lives are deeply affected by "the schedule" that governs all and often defines the possible. Architects design buildings that evoke psychological responses and shape behavior. The choice to equip a classroom with movable desks or "screwed-down" desks has an impact on behavior. A curriculum that mandates individually prescribed instruction also mandates behavior. The need to transport students to and from school on buses has an impressive impact on the school as an organization and on the behavior of people in it.

But the fact that educational organizations are *open* systems has additional behavioral consequences. A school, for example, is subject to two major external forces that define the very nature of its internal arrangements. One of these forces is the fact that the school *is* a school: it is probably more like other schools from coast to coast than different from them. Professional standards and expectations expressed through teacher training institutions, accrediting associations, the entrance requirements of colleges, the wares of the educational-industrial complex, and the speakers at annual conventions—all of these are but a representative few of the many "professional" influences that reach in from the outside and define what a school *is* in behavioral terms.

The *second* cluster of these forces represents the broader social-cultural influences that reach in from the outside and establish "norms" for behavior in the school. These include such diverse sources as community standards, tradition, judicial decisions, statutory law, and—not least, by any means—the broad generalizations embodied in such concepts as "Western culture." More specifically, perhaps, is the impact of the "youth subculture" that has become so influential in Western nations. Because the school is an open system, this facet of the school's environment has a powerful impact on its internal functioning. The fact that children watch television, are exposed to a "drug culture," and are developing new concepts of sex, marriage, and the family does shape the nature of life in schools. All of these, together, combine to create an *organizational* culture that is powerful in determining how people perceive things, value them, and react to them.

Thus, the concept of the educative organization as an open sociotechnical system enables one to see the internal arrangements of a particular organization as at once unique and part of an interaction with its larger suprasystem. This is the view of schools that people like Goodlad have when they speak of the "culture" of the school, and it is discussed again in Chapter 7, on organizational culture.

In contemporary organizational theory, this concept is coupled with contingency theory: the view that there is no one universal "best" way of dealing with organizational issues. Contingency approaches to organizational behavior require developing a systematic understanding of the dynamics of organizational behavior in order to be able to diagnose or analyze the specific situation that exists.

SUGGESTED READING

HELLRIEGEL, DONALD, and JOHN W. SLOCUM, JR., "A Framework for Understanding Behavior in Organizations," in *Organizational Behavior: Contingency Views*. St. Paul, MN: West Publishing Co., 1976.

An excellent eleven-page description of the contingency approach to organizational behavior and its usefulness in studying important management issues.

LEAVITT, HAROLD J., "Applied Organizational Change in Industry: Structural, Technological, and Humanistic Approaches," in *Handbook of Organizations*, ed. James G. March. Chicago: Rand McNally & Company, 1965.
A classic discussion of the relationship between organizational realities and three widely advocated strategies of planning and managing change. Though this early work was concerned with industry, it is helpful to educators who want an orientation to important perspectives in the literature. Also in this volume is the classic analysis of "The School as a Formal Organization," by Charles E. Bidwell.

LORTIE, DAN C., *School Teacher*. Chicago: University of Chicago Press, 1975.
This remarkably sensitive and readable report of a sociological study of teachers convincingly portrays much of the reality of working in schools and the consequences for teachers. Strongly recommended.

PASMORE, WILLIAM A., and JOHN J. SHERWOOD, eds., *Sociotechnical Systems: A Sourcebook*. La Jolla, CA: University Associates, Inc., 1978.
This book provides convenient access to twenty-four articles on theory, research, and practice in sociotechnical systems, heretofore available only as scattered publications in scientific journals, and includes classic works of British and European as well as American scholars. Though it is concerned solely with private-sector corporations (chiefly industrial firms), it discusses organizational concepts readily applicable to educational organizations.

SCOTT, W. RICHARD, "The Subject Is Organizations," in *Organizations: Rational, Natural, and Open Systems*, 2nd ed., ed. W. Richard Scott. Englewood Cliffs, N.J.: Prentice-Hall, 1987.
This compact chapter compares and contrasts three contemporary ways of thinking about organizations.

NOTES

[1]F. Kenneth Berrien, "A General Systems Approach to Organizations," in *Handbook of Industrial and Organizational Psychology*, ed. Marvin D. Dunnette (Chicago: Rand McNally & Company, 1976), p. 42.

[2]Charles B. Perrow, *Organizational Analysis: A Sociological View* (Monterey, CA: Brooks/Cole Publishing Co., 1970), pp. 3–4.

[3]Ludwig von Bertalanffy, "An Outline of General Systems Theory," *British Journal of Philosophical Science*, 1 (1950), 134–65. A more complete work, by the same author, is *General Systems Theory* (New York: George Braziller, Inc., 1968).

[4]Andre Lwoff, "Interaction among Virus, Cell and Organization," *Science*, 152 (1966), 1216.

[5]F. Kenneth Berrien, "A General Systems Approach to Organizations," in *Handbook of Industrial and Organizational Psychology*, ed. Marvin D. Dunnette (Chicago: Rand McNally & Company, 1976), p. 43.

[6]Ronald G. Corwin, "Models of Educational Organizations," in *Review of Research in Education*, ed. Fred N. Kerlinger and J. B. Carroll (Itasca, IL: F. E. Peacock, Publishers, Inc., 1974), p. 263.

[7]Andrew W. Halpin and Don B. Croft, *The Organizational Climate of Schools* (Washington, D.C.: Cooperative Research Report, U.S. Office of Education, 1962).

[8]Some examples are James G. Anderson, *Bureaucracy in Education* (Baltimore: The Johns Hopkins University Press, 1968); Neal Gross and Robert E. Herriott, *Staff Leadership in Public Schools: A Sociological Inquiry* (New York: John Wiley & Sons, Inc., 1965). These may be compared with later studies, such as the Rand investigations of educational change conducted by Berman and McLaughlin. See, for example, Paul Berman and Milbrey Wallin McLaughlin, *Federal Programs Supporting Educational Change, Volume VII: Factors Affecting Implementation and Continuation* (Santa Monica, CA: Rand Corporation, 1977), especially pp. 16–20.

[9]Erving Goffman, *The Presentation of Self in Everyday Life* (New York: Doubleday & Co., Inc., Anchor Books, 1959): A later study in a similar vein by the same author is *Encounters* (Indianapolis: The Bobbs-Merrill Co., Inc., 1961).

[10]The term, "role," is a highly useful metaphor that is widely used in human relations research and practice. Because there is such extensive literature on role theory in psychiatry, psychology, sociology, and education, not surprisingly there is some imprecision attached to the use of this metaphor. It should

be clear, however, that what is under discussion here is a psychological concept and not merely job titles or job descriptions. For discussion of the problem of definition, see Theodore R. Sarbin and Vernon L. Allen, "Role Theory," in *The Handbook of Social Psychology*, vol. 1, 2nd ed., eds. Gardner Lindzey and Elliot Aronson (Reading, MA: Addison-Wesley, 1968).

[11]Robert Boguslaw, *The New Utopians: A Study of System Design and Social Change* (Englewood Cliffs, N.J.: Prentice-Hall, 1965), pp. 170–77.

[12]The material presented here on role set is based on Warren G. Bennis, *Changing Organizations* (New York: McGraw-Hill Book Company, 1966), pp. 193–96.

[13]Robert L. Kahn, Donald M. Wolfe, Robert R. Quinn, and J. Diedrick Snoek, *Organizational Stress: Studies in Role Conflict and Ambiguity* (New York: John Wiley & Sons, Inc., 1964).

[14]The following discussion of role allocation is based on Kenneth D. Benne and Paul Sheats, "Functional Roles of Group Members," *Journal of Social Issues*, 4, no. 2 (Spring 1948), 41–49.

[15]Ibid., pp. 43–44.

[16]Ibid., pp. 44–45.

[17]Jacob W. Getzels and Egon G. Guba, "Social Behavior and the Administrative Process," *The School Review*, 65 (Winter 1957), 423–41. This version of the organization as a sociopsychological system is based upon the earlier work of Talcott Parsons and was first suggested by Getzels in 1952 in his "A Psycho-Sociological Framework for the Study of Educational Administration," *Harvard Educational Review*, 22, no. 4 (1952), 235–46. Later, in collaboration with Egon Guba, the model was developed to include *psychological* concepts (such as personality), *sociological* notions (for example, role expectation), *anthropological* concepts of culture, and *social-psychological* concepts (for example, group norms and organizational climate). This more elaborate model—the so-called Getzels-Guba model—is discussed later in this chapter (see Figure 3–12).

[18]Jacob W. Getzels, "Administration as a Social Process," in *Administrative Theory in Education*, ed. Andrew W. Halpin (Chicago: Midwest Administration Center, University of Chicago, 1958), p. 157.

[19]There is extensive literature on the authoritarian personality. Classic works are Theodore W. Adorno, Else Frenkel-Brunswik, Daniel J. Levinson, and R. N. Sanford, *The Authoritarian Personality* (New York: Harper & Row, Publishers, Inc., 1950); and Milton Rokeach, *The Open and Closed Mind* (New York: Basic Books, Inc., Publishers, 1960).

[20]Mary Lynn Crow and Merl E. Bonney, "Recognizing the Authoritarian Personality Syndrome in Educators," *Phi Delta Kappan*, 57, no. 1 (September 1975), 40.

[21]Frederick W. Taylor, *The Principles of Scientific Management* (New York: Harper & Row, Publishers, Inc., 1911), pp. 42–43.

[22]Chester I. Barnard, *The Functions of the Executive* (Cambridge, MA: Harvard University Press, 1938), p. 57.

[23]Ibid., p. 55.

[24]Ibid., p. 57.

[25]John M. Pfiffner and Frank P. Sherwood, *Administrative Organization* (Englewood Cliffs, N.J.: Prentice-Hall, 1960), p. 299.

[26]The following discussion is adapted from Robert G. Owens and Carl R. Steinhoff, *Administering Change in Schools* (Englewood Cliffs, NJ: Prentice-Hall, 1976), pp. 60–63 and 143 and is based on the concepts developed by Harold J. Leavitt cited below.

[27]This view is based upon the concepts developed by Harold J. Leavitt, *Managerial Psychology*, 2nd ed. (Chicago: University of Chicago Press, 1964). See also by the same author, "Applied Organizational Change in Industry: Structural, Technological, and Humanistic Approaches," in *Handbook of Organizations*, ed. James G. March (Chicago: Rand McNally & Company, 1965), pp. 1144–70.

[28]See, for example, Wendell L. French and Cecil H. Bell, Jr., *Organizational Development* (Englewood Cliffs, NJ: Prentice-Hall, 1973), pp. 183–85, whose description is reflected in this discussion.

[29]John I. Goodlad, "Educational Leadership: Toward the Third Era," *Educational Leadership*, 35, no. 4 (January 1978), 330.

[30]Fremont E. Kast and James E. Rosenzweig, *Contingency Views of Organization and Management* (Chicago: Science Research Associates, 1973), p. ix.

[31]Dennis Moberg and James L. Koch, "A Critical Appraisal of Integrated Treatments of Contingency Findings," *Academy of Management Journal*, 18, no. 1 (March-June 1975), 109–24.

[32]Donald Hellriegel and John W. Slocum, Jr., *Organizational Behavior: Contingency Views* (St. Paul: West Publishing Co., 1976), p. 6.

[33]Paul R. Lawrence and Jay W. Lorsch, *Organization and Environment* (Homewood, IL: Richard D. Irwin, Inc., 1967).

[34]Stephen P. Robbins, *The Administrative Process: Integrating Theory and Practice* (Englewood Cliffs, NJ: Prentice-Hall, 1976), pp. 272–73.

4

WOMEN'S ISSUES
IN ORGANIZATIONAL
BEHAVIOR

"...women do not want an advantage over their male peers, rather they seek only the chance to compete as equals for leadership roles in schools."

—*Sakre Kennington Edson*[1]

As we have seen, organizational behavior in education as we understand it today is the result of a century-long process of continuous inquiry and study. Knowledge of organizational behavior is slow to emerge for at least two reasons:

1. The behavior of people in educational workplaces is neither simple nor self-evident, and
2. Our basic assumptions about human nature, and the values about human beings that arise from these assumptions, are continually changing and developing. The relationship between our basic assumptions about human nature and the values that we derive from these assumptions is described more fully in Chapter 7 (see Figure 7–2).

These give rise to ambiguity, complexity, and the general messiness that is inherent in the study of organizational life. Thus, developing a body of knowledge in organizational behavior requires, as does the effort to understand any aspect of complex human experience, a process of repeated iterations of developing theory, research to test the theory, and criticism of resulting outcomes in a continuous effort to build and expand the body of knowledge. All of this is, of course, essential to the development of any body of scientific knowledge and scholarship.

By the 1980s it had become obvious to women scholars that educational administration has traditionally been a male bastion that has generally resisted women who seek admission. The preponderance of scholars who studied administration and organizational behavior in education have traditionally been men, as well. Moreover, despite the doubt that has been cast on the tradition of authoritarianism in school administration by emerging knowledge in organizational behavior and despite the enlightened views of schools advocated by many students of school reform who deplore the widespread alienation commonly found in them, many Americans still harbor the belief that the solution to seemingly intractable problems in schooling lies in the greater exercise of coercion from the top down. Because of this, given the gender stereotypes that are so prominent in our culture, doubt still lingers as to whether or not women are as able as men to be effective in school administration. For example, some doubt that women possess the toughness traditionally thought to be necessary to maintain discipline in high schools. Yet, as we shall see, the feminist critique posits that women possess abilities that suit them well to exercise leadership in schools that are much in need of change from the past. Women, runs the critique, not only can succeed in administrative work but they can excel at it. Moreover, schools would perhaps be better than they are if their organizational cultures more fully reflected the thinking, the values, and the perspectives of women than they traditionally have.

In the context of the general movement in recent years toward gender equity, these facts and ideas cried out for study and explanation. The result has been a recent critique of scholarship in organizational behavior, centered on gender issues.

This critique challenges the traditional ways in which we think about organizations, organizational behavior, organizational theory, and administration that has traditionally been done by men from the perspective of men. The literature in these areas of theory and research is described as having been androcentric, that is, male-centered. Because it is, the theories and the results of research based on those theories may well be biased and, therefore, flawed.

ANDROCENTRISM

All scientific inquiry, including inquiry into organizational behavior, reflects some basic assumptions and fundamental beliefs that the inquirer implicitly holds. As I explain more fully in Chapter 7, these include assumptions about human nature, the nature of human relationships, the nature of reality, and the nature of human activity.[2] A hazard for any scholar lies in the fact that many of these basic assumptions are so taken for granted by the scholar, so implicitly held, and so thoroughly internalized as to be virtually invisible to the individual who holds them. Each of us holds some assumptions that seem to be so obviously true, so commonplace, that "everyone" shares them. They are shared among colleagues, friends, and others in one's group or in one's culture. Because such assumptions are commonplace, they become invisible, and are not discussed because no one even thinks to raise the subject. When that happens, members of the group believe that any other premise is inconceivable. This is precisely the basis of the gender issues that have been raised about scholarship in organizational behavior.

The systematic development of knowledge in educational administration and in organizational behavior may be viewed as effectively describing the world as men have understood it, a description of the world as viewed through a "male prism"[3] or a "male lens."[4] Critics describe organizational behavior research as having been largely done by men who studied populations comprised mostly of men and who used the unexamined worldview of men in theorizing and carrying out the investigations. Women were virtually uninvolved in much of the research, either in conceptualizing it or as the subjects of the investigations. "The underlying assumption is that the experiences of males and females are the same, and thus research on males is appropriate for generalizing to the female experience. In developing theories of administration, researchers didn't look at the context in general and, therefore, were unable to document how the world was different for women. When female experience was different, it was ignored or diminished,"[5] according to one observer.

This dominance of the male worldview in research and knowledge, this "male-defined scholarship" has been called *androcentrism*.[6] Androcentrism in organizational behavior research is thought to introduce a bias into the study of organizational behavior in schools especially because schools are predominantly female workplaces while efforts to understand those workplaces are essentially derived from male-based scholarship.[7]

Androcentrism in scholarship and research methods should not be confused with prejudice or a particular bias against women as a class of people, which would be sexism.[8] Rather, androcentrism in organizational studies refers to the virtual overlooking of women, their absence from the scholarship itself, the unexamined assumption held by those who conducted the studies that men and women experience organizational life in essentially the same ways. Recent critiques, largely from women scholars, raise serious questions about this assumption.

The history of the development of the study of organizational behavior during this century as a linchpin of educational administration has largely coincided with the post–World War II entry of men into teaching and educational administration. Almost a century after Catharine Beecher popularized the notion of teaching as "woman's true profession,"[9] men returning from military service in World War II began to take women's places in teaching in large numbers with the help of education under the GI Bill. Early in the century, the majority of elementary school principals were women although high school principalships and superintendencies were largely held by men. Beginning in the 1930s, however, there was a trend toward selecting men for elementary school principalships as well. By the early 1950s, the dominance of women in administrative positions in the elementary schools had clearly given way to men. This ushered in the modern era in which administration has been largely a male preserve while teaching has been largely a woman's preserve.

The decades of the 1950s and 1960s were also, as I shall describe fully in later chapters of this book, marked by the profound development of research and theory in such aspects of organizational behavior as motivation, leadership, organizational climate, conflict management, and decision making. This body of organizational behavior knowledge quickly became, and still largely is, the foundation upon which modern concepts of educational administration stand. Virtually all research and teaching of educational administration in universities in the Western world draws upon organizational behavior as fundamental to understanding educational administration. However, the charge of androcentrism became a major challenge to traditional theorizing and study of organizational behavior from a feminocentric[10] perspective.

THE FEMINOCENTRIC CRITIQUE

The feminocentric critique posits that for a variety of reasons men and women understand and experience the world in significantly different ways. Women "see" things differently from men, hold different values, seek different goals, and have different priorities. For example, one reason given for this is the belief that men, from boyhood into adulthood, receive more direct feedback on their behavior, in the form of both criticism and praise, than do women. Some speculate that men are thus better able to learn appropriate work behaviors and deal effectively with the give-and-take that ordinarily occurs between supervisor and teacher.[11] Other reasons often given in the literature of the feminocentric critique include that women are more concerned about relationships and caring for others than are men, who are depicted as concerned about territoriality and justice.

Thus the educational workplace is described as having two cultures: a male culture and a female culture and these two overlap only partially; they are not coterminous. These differences have been little-recognized until now and, in the feminocentric view, that leads to errors in the body of literature that describes, interprets, and predicts organizational behavior. What differences are we talking about?

In summarizing the findings of the feminocentric literature, Charol Shakeshaft discussed five characteristics of the female world in educational organizations and how they contrast with what she perceives to be the misogynous[12] male world that exists in schools:

1. "Women spend more time with people, communicate more, care more about individual differences, are concerned more with teachers and marginal students, and motivate more." Consequently, "staffs of women administrators rate women higher, are more productive, and have higher morale. Students of schools with women principals also have higher morale and are more involved in student affairs. Further, parents are more favorable toward schools and districts run by women...."[13]

2. Women administrators exhibit greater knowledge of teaching methods and techniques, are more likely to help new teachers and supervise all teachers directly and create a climate more conducive to learning that is orderly, safer, and quieter. "Not surprisingly," Shakeshaft adds, "academic achievement is higher in schools and districts in which women are administrators."[14]

3. "...women exhibit a more democratic, participatory style...involve themselves more with staff and students, ask for and get higher participation, and maintain more closely knit organizations. Staffs of women principals have higher job satisfaction and are more engaged in their work than those of male administrators."[15]

4. The woman administrator is always on display and always vulnerable to attack in the misogynous male world of educational administration. Whether or not "the assault actually occurs is less important than the knowledge that it is always possible. Women perceive their token status...."[16]

5. Women are more likely than men to behave the same way in public as they do in private and this often results "in behavior that men often label inappropriate."[17]

Patricia Schmuck tells us that androcentrism, which takes men's experience as representative of all human experience and simply excludes women as a particular group to be studied, is merely the first of five stages of thinking about women in educational organizations.[18] The second stage she calls "compensatory thinking," in which the underrepresentation of women in the ranks of school administration is recognized and efforts are undertaken to recruit women to ameliorate that deficiency. The third stage she calls a "psychological deficiency model," in which the low number of women is explained away and interpreted in psychological terms.

The fourth stage of thinking generally conceptualizes women as being oppressed by organizational arrangements. The fifth and last stage of thinking about these issues is what Schmuck calls the "New Scholarship," in which gender becomes central in disciplined inquiry that seeks to describe, understand, and explain the deficiencies of traditional androcentric organizational research. Thus, in the fifth stage, "Research is modified to include women as well as men as the objects and subjects of study. This scholarship is corrective: it provides alternative points of view and transforms existing knowledge." This neat five-level model is problematic even from the feminine perspective[19] but it does illustrate the current struggle by feminocentric scholars to conceptualize serious reservations about which all students of organizational behavior in education, both men and women, are concerned and wish to eliminate.

Women scholars have generally used two different ways to modify administrative research so as to include women. As I shall explain below, one way has been to reexamine existing research and theory to show that it is androcentric and therefore seriously flawed methodologically. Another way has been to engage in new research using research methods that are thought to be more appropriate to understanding the organizational behavior of both women and men in educational administration.

Feminocentric critique of existing research.   In perhaps the most prominent feminocentric critique of existing research, Charol Shakeshaft and Irene Nowell selected five distinguished examples of scholarly work for careful examination.[20] They were:

1. The social systems model of organization created by Jacob Getzels in 1952[21] and elaborated with the assistance of Egon Guba in 1957.
2. The Leader Behavior Description Questionnaire (LBDQ) created by John Hemphill and Alvin Coons in 1950.
3. The Organizational Climate Description Questionnaire (OCDQ) created by Andrew W. Halpin and Don B. Croft in 1962.
4. The contingency theory of leadership developed by Fred E. Fiedler in the early 1960s.
5. The theory of human motivation created by Abraham H. Maslow in 1943.

The concepts and theories embodied in each of the above works are truly seminal. Each has spawned a substantial literature of research based upon their concepts and theories, and each is described in virtually every textbook on administrative theory. The present textbook describes each of them. Indeed, few individuals who have taken even an introductory course in school administration have failed to be exposed to them. They can be taken, therefore, as representative of the concepts and theories that have guided thinking about important aspects of organizational behavior in education.

Shakeshaft's critique makes a strong case that these theorists largely ignored women in their thinking and seem to assume that their theories and research illuminate the organizational behavior of men and women equally. She points out that, in describing their social systems model, Getzels and Guba simply ignored women and did not investigate their actual experience of role conflict as teachers, for example.

Although the Leader Behavior Description Questionnaire (LBDQ) was orig-inated in the research of Helen Jennings, in which she studied the leader behavior of girls in a New York State residential institution, much of the development work of the LBDQ instrument was done in military and corporate settings, which were then predominantly male.

In conducting extensive research to test his contingency theory of leader-ship, Fred Fiedler not only ignored the gender of the leader (though he had women in his research samples) but also engaged in some speculation about aspects of women's organizational behavior that Shakeshaft derides as "masculist" and "uninformed."

Finally, Maslow's approach to motivation is described by Shakeshaft as reflecting patronizing views toward women of one who believes that the work of women does not require intelligence, talent, or genius.[22]

In their pioneering study of organizational climate in schools, in which they developed and used the now-classic Organizational Climate Description Question-naire (OCDQ), Halpin and Croft described perceptions of principals by teachers as a major factor in organizational climate. Despite the high likelihood that virtually all principals in their research sample of elementary schools were men while undoubtedly virtually all teachers were women, Halpin and Croft completely ignored the possibility that gender may play some part, perhaps a very significant part, in molding these critical perceptions.

One might be tempted to dismiss the feminocentric critique as being merely another of a long series of criticisms, from various perspectives, which this body of venerable scholarly work has inevitably and properly endured during the many years that it has been in the central core of the marketplace of ideas about organizational behavior. However, the critique was given added significance by a study of the articles reporting administrative research that were published in a leading scholarly journal, *Educational Administration Quarterly,* over a span of ten years.[23] The study found that the majority of articles published in that distinguished journal could properly be described as exhibiting androcentric bias inasmuch as:

1. Reviews of research literature rarely examined how gender issues had been accounted-for in previous work;

2. The instruments and survey strategies used were often biased;

3. In articles describing the research samples used, 90 percent were samples of men only;

4. The research results were described as generalizable to the population as a whole with no discussion of possible limitations in terms of gender.

Remember that before articles are accepted for publication in such a journal each manuscript must be reviewed by a panel of reputable scholars to scrutinize it in terms of its intellectual and methodological rigor and significance. Because the scholarly standards are rigorous, most work submitted is rejected. However, the findings of this study clearly imply that the androcentric qualities of this ten-year body of work had gone unnoticed not only by a substantial group of scholars who served as reviewers but also by readers of the journal. It would seem apparent that the charge of androcentrism in this field of scholarship is strongly supported.

Feminocentric scholarship.   Over the years, many female scholars have written on educational administration and organizational behavior. Generally, their work is indistinguishable in the body of literature from the work authored by men. For example, Paula Silver's book, *Educational Administration: Theoretical Perspectives on Practice and Research*,[24] does not differ in terms of its treatment of theory, concepts, or topics covered from the many textbooks prepared by males that compete with it in the marketplace. "Taken as a whole," Daniel Griffiths tells us, "there appear to be no theoretical or methodological differences [in the work written by women] from the literature written by men."[25] However, in addition to the feminocentric critique that has been discussed, a new body of research literature that specifically addresses the concerns of women is emerging. This is what Patricia Schmuck alluded to as "the new scholarship." It is, at this point, a small but growing body of literature. Its central characteristic is that it addresses questions and issues of deep and personal concern to women.

Characteristics of "the new scholarship."   A central characteristic of the new scholarship is, of course, an avowed interest in gaining a better understanding of the experience of women in the organizational life of education. This interest has tended to focus the research on three main areas:

1. Studies of such things as the ways in which women fit into organizations, what motivates them, the ways in which they get satisfaction from their work, and how they move from teaching into administration.
2. Studies of attitudes toward women such as negative attitudes toward them that they encounter as they seek to become administrators and the general bias in favor of men that they encounter in their administrative careers.
3. Descriptions of women school administrators at work, their effectiveness in administrative positions, and comparisons of the behavior of administrative women with that of their male counterparts.

A second characteristic of this body of research is methodological. Increasingly, inquiries into women's issues in organizational life make use of a broader array of techniques for gathering data than had heretofore been customary. For example, many women investigators find it useful to collect data by going into educational organizations to observe the behavior of people in them and to conduct open-ended unstructured interviews. Such research methods are called *qualitative* (or *ethnographic*) and contrast markedly with the more impersonal questionnaires that were traditionally the principal means for gathering data in the survey research typical in administrative studies prior to the emergence of the feminocentric critique.

TWO STUDIES OF WOMEN'S ISSUES

Although the history of research on women administrators in educational organizations is relatively new, it has produced a growing and very diverse body of published literature. This, of course, indicates the intense and rising interest that the field of study has attracted. From that large body of research literature, I will describe two recent studies that are of particular interest to those concerned with organizational behavior in schools.

Women who aspire to school administration. Ever since the 1960s, the number of women enrolling in university courses in educational administration has risen dramatically. By the 1980s, women comprised over 50 percent of the students in such courses.[26] This, of course, indicates rising aspirations of women for administrative careers. However, although the number of females being appointed to administrative positions in the schools has increased over time, the rate of increase was disappointing to many women. Studies have sought to understand the barriers to women seeking to develop administrative careers in education. Gladys Johnston and her colleagues examined the patterns of the employment of women administrators in public education[27] and found that the perception that women do not fare well in the job market is well-founded. Another study examined prejudice against female school administrators by the public and explored the possibilities of changing what is considered to be an unfavorable situation.[28] Others have explored possible strategies and tactics for facilitating the appointment of women to administrative positions and their advancement through the ranks.[29] Flora Ortiz examined the problems and opportunities confronting a female administrator who sought to scale the hierarchy of a school system.[30] Numerous other studies relevant to women in administration cover topics as varied as women dealing with stress in administration,[31] networking for administrative women,[32] and ways of handling the combination of career and home responsibilities.[33]

While these early studies, and many others, suggest that men are part of the problem by being hostile or indifferent not only to the aspirations but also to the abilities of women, more recent research suggests that that traditional male view may be waning. Sakre Edson, for example, used qualitative research methods (principally interviews) to conduct a nationwide study in which she followed, for a period of five years, the careers of 142 women who wanted to get into educational administration.[34] One conclusion from that research was that the attitudes of male administrators toward women who wish to become administrators is becoming more supportive and helpful. Many of the women in the study credited men administrators with initiating their interest in administration, encouraging them, and being helpful colleagues and mentors. Edson reports,

> "Some men find it difficult to alter their long-held beliefs about female administrators; however, women appreciate the efforts of those men who earnestly try to change their perceptions about women's management abilities....[M]any aspirants sense a new openness towards women seeking school management positions. Although hiring statistics fail to document their optimism, many feel it is only a matter of time before genuine change will occur. Throughout the country, female aspirants admit that they might never have considered aspiring to administration except for the encouragement of those male colleagues who are changing their attitudes about women.[35]

Edson attributes the more favorable climate toward women administrators to "the women's movement" and to recent equity legislation.

Women superintendents and school boards. Although, as Edson's study shows, some women have high aspirations for administrative work and while enrollments of women in preparatory courses soar and those of men decline, the number of women being appointed to administrative positions has not risen appreciably. Indeed, the American Association of School Administrators reported that, whereas in 1981–1982 some 25 percent of American school administrators were female, by 1984–1985 the figure had risen to only 26 percent. Moreover, the higher the administrative position, the lower the proportion of women being appointed. While about 21 percent of the school principals in America were women in 1984–1985, only 16 percent were deputy, assistant, or associate superintendents, and fewer than 3 percent of superintendents of schools were female.[36] Colleen Bell and Susan Chase reported that a 1987 survey of state departments of education found that 2.8 percent of superintendents in American K-12 school districts were women.[37] This state of affairs has caused thoughtful investigators to seek to understand more fully how women experience the superintendency.

Bell and Chase examined the experiences of three women superintendents, including the procedures used to evaluate and select candidates when they were considered for appointment, as well as their experiences on the job.[38] Because a key aspect of the superintendency lies in the unique relationship between the members of the school board, collectively and individually, and the superintendent, this relationship became a focus of the study. The investigators used qualitative methods to conduct the study: they went to the school districts to

- observe the behavior of people on the scene,
- conduct lengthy unstructured interviews with the superintendents and also with members of the boards of education, and
- study documents ranging from newspaper stories to such official documents as minutes of school board meetings and copies of the school district budgets.

The women who were ultimately selected by the largely male school boards to be superintendents were described as being highly qualified: they were experienced administrators and, in most cases, had doctorates. Furthermore, the boards had considered not only women but also some male candidates. But many board members had acknowledged their discomfort and doubt about the ability of women to perform the tasks of the superintendency. In each case the school board had initially been inclined to favor male candidates even though school board members acknowledged that the credentials of the women were superior. As the selection process went forward, however imperfect as it was, each woman finally emerged as successful and got the job. But, Bell and Chase wondered, why would a school board be inclined to select a less-qualified man when these well-qualified women were in the running?

The answer, the researchers think, has to do with social conformity: this is the notion preferred by Rosabeth Moss Kanter [39] that organizations have many characteristics that create pressure for members to conform to accepted standards. School boards, for example, face a great deal of uncertainty, ambiguity, and not a little conflict in fulfilling their mandate to govern the schools. Naturally, in looking for a superintendent, board members want to reduce that uncertainty, yet they realize that the superintendent must exercise wide-ranging discretionary authority on their behalf. Therefore, board members want a superintendent on whom they feel they can rely, one whom they can trust, whose behavior they feel they can predict. In this situation they tend to look for someone whose values, experience, and language they share; someone like themselves and like other superintendents with whom they have worked. This is social homogeneity and it increases confidence, predictability, ease of communication, and trust that, as Kanter has pointed out, is essential in all effective organizations. When people who are "different" are brought into the inner circle of organizations it becomes difficult to preserve the culture of trust that homogeneity fosters. "Thus," Bell and Chase argue, "...what the preferred candidates [men] had going for them and what operated against the women who applied [for the job] was a social homogeneity factor; that is, male board members find it easier to communicate and interact with, and hence to trust, male candidates for the superintendency."[40]

SOME FINDINGS OF FEMINOCENTRIC RESEARCH

Men, and women as well, are often uncomfortable in thinking about and discussing gender issues. The sources of this discomfort run deep in the traditions of our cultural heritage and will not be readily assuaged, let alone eradicated. The need to deal with the issues, and the discomfort, also runs deep and is hardly new. George Bernard Shaw built a considerable reputation (and not inconsiderable fortune) by bringing wit and satire to bear on the battle of the sexes in such plays as *Man and Superman* and *Pygmalion,* which continue to draw audiences to this day. Noël Coward gained a sort of immortality by bringing his genius for song and sophisticated comedy to the discussion. And many people still remember Professor Higgins's puzzlement, in the Broadway musical, *My Fair Lady,* as to why a woman cannot be more like a man. If nothing else, the feminocentric critique of traditional administrative research and the contributions of what Patricia Schmuck calls "the new scholarship" have made it clear that, in organizational life of education at any rate, Professor Higgins's Question is not the one posed today.

Increased awareness of androcentrism in administrative thought. A major contribution of feminocentric criticism and research has been to increase the awareness of men and women alike to a serious shortcoming in our understanding of organizational behavior in education. The message, sometimes delivered in the measured dispassionate tones of traditional scholarly discourse and sometimes in rhetoric that is on the cusp of hostility, has been received and accepted at least by leading theoreticians and scholars. For example, the *Administrative Science Quarterly* not only printed the critique documenting its own contribution to androcentrism but has responded by including women more often and more centrally in its own decision-making processes. Moreover, its pages, as well as the pages of other scholarly journals, have since carried a number of articles further illuminating aspects of gender issues in organizational life. Indeed, it would be difficult today to have a manuscript accepted for publication in a major scholarly journal that ignored women's issues.

Another example is in the *Handbook of Research on Educational Administration,*[41] which appeared in 1988. This landmark scholarly tome included a number of women on its editorial advisory board and it features a chapter on women in educational administration and another on equity. Some other chapters also reveal awareness of, sensitivity to, and knowledge about the new scholarship in women's issues in organizational behavior. Regrettably, a number of other chapters—such as the one on motivation, work satisfaction, and organizational climate—ignore the topic altogether.

The American Educational Research Association, as a matter of policy, has for some years encouraged the participation of women, and their research has been well-represented among the presentations of papers and at seminars of its annual meetings. Progress in areas such as these seem to suggest that, at least at the level of awareness among scholars, a good deal of progress has been made. Because this progress is formalized and institutionalized it strongly suggests that the new direction will be enduring and increase in vigor and leverage as time goes on.

Better understanding of the differences between the ways that men and women do administrative work. Consider the description by Anne Wilson Schaef that the "world" of white males and the "world" of females and minority people are very different, in effect creating at least two different cultures.[42] Because the white male culture is dominant, everyone who would deal effectively with that world must learn its culture and how to deal with it. Women, however, and minority people as well, also live in a culture that excludes white males and about which white males know very little. However, recent studies of the world of women has done a great deal to help both women and men to better understand how they see and respond to things in different ways. More than that, these studies explain the ways in which the resulting differences in behavior of men and women administrators may well make women more effective in at least some kinds of administrative work.[43]

For example, the new scholarship raises the distinct possibility that women may, in fact, be better suited for the elementary school principalship than men.[44] But, then, this has been well-known for many years but little discussed. A large-scale landmark study of elementary school principals that was published in 1962 drew the following conclusions after analyzing massive nationwide data that had been collected:

"In considering the question, 'Should men be appointed as elementary school principals in preference to women?' it would appear that the answer is probably no.
    The study does not present evidence that a woman principal should always be preferred over the man who may also be a candidate. It does indicate, however, that as a class men are not overwhelmingly superior to women as elementary school principals. The evidence appears to favor women if the job of the principal is conceived in a way that values working with teachers and outsiders; being concerned with objectives of teaching, pupil participation, and the evaluation of learning; having knowledge of teaching methods and techniques; and gaining positive reactions from teachers and superiors."[45]

This is a startling finding from some of the most distinguished students of American public schooling who very properly went where the data took them. But it is a finding that was, in effect, buried in obfuscation. As Shakeshaft has drily pointed out, a question more consistent with the data provided by the researchers would be, "Should women be appointed as elementary school principals in preference to men? And that answer, based upon their findings, would be *probably yes.*"[46]

Feminocentric research has produced a much larger body of research literature than can be reviewed here. Broad and diverse in scope, it documents significant characteristics of women and their world and how these affect women's performance in the male world of administration. Moreover, it suggests that replacing much of the present dominant male culture of administration with female culture may well improve administrative practices and the effectiveness of schools as well.

SUMMARY

As an aspect of the older and larger women's movement, the feminocentric critique of administrative research and the rapid development of the new feminocentric scholarship has already caused reconsideration of many traditional male assumptions. Students of organizational behavior in education now readily concede that the behaviors of men and women school administrators differ in some crucial ways that we are now only beginning to understand. This body of knowledge and thought is in its early stages and it appears likely to endure, to continue to expand, and to develop growing impact over time. How much it will contribute to the breakdown of long-entrenched biases in educational organizations and in the public and also increase opportunities for women to move into positions of leadership in education remains to be seen.

SUGGESTED READING

EDSON, SAKRE KENNINGTON, *Pushing the Limits: The Female Administrative Aspirant*. Albany: State University of New York Press, 1988.
   A penetrating study that illuminates the world of the contemporary woman student of educational administration who aspires to that first administrative appointment. Rich in the actual language of those whose story it tells, this research transports the reader to the world of these women as they see it and understand it.

SCHMUCK, PATRICIA A., and W. W. CHARTERS, JR., eds., *Educational Policy and Management: Sex Differentials*. New York: Academic Press, 1981.
   A scholarly sourcebook on significant policy issues in sex equity in American public schooling.

SHAKESHAFT, CHAROL, *Women in Educational Administration*. Newbury Park, CA: Sage Publications, Inc., 1987.
   A briskly written, well-researched survey of the "state of the art" that has received a respectful and responsive hearing from the community of scholars in educational administration. This is "must" reading, especially for men, who should know the feminist view even though it may disconcert them.

NOTES

[1]Sakre Kennington Edson, *Pushing the Limits: The Female Administrative Aspirant*. Albany: State University of New York Press, 1988, p. 281.
   [2] Edgar H. Schein, *Organizational Culture and Leadership* (San Francisco: Jossey-Bass, 1985), p. 14.
   [3]J. Bernard, "Afterword," in J.A. Sherman and E.T. Beck, eds., *The Prism of Sex* (Madison: University of Wisconsin Press, 1979), 267–75.
   [4]Charol Shakeshaft, *Women in Educational Administration* (Newbury Park, CA: Sage Publications, Inc., 1987), p. 150.

[5]Ibid., p. 148.
[6]Ibid., p. 150.
[7]Ibid., p. 149.
[8]Dorothy E. Smith, "A Peculiar Eclipsing: Women's Exclusion from Man's Culture," *Women's Studies International Quarterly*, 1, no. 4, 281–95.
[9]Nancy Hoffman, *Woman's "True" Profession: Voices from the History of Teaching* (Old Westbury, NY: Feminist Press, 1981), 2–17, 35–56.
[10]If androcentrism is "the practice of viewing the world and shaping reality from a male lens" then, conversely, we can take feminocentrism to be the practice of viewing the world and shaping reality from a female lens. See Shakeshaft, *Women in Educational Administration*, p. 150, and Carol A. B. Warren, *Gender Issues in Field Research* (Newbury Park, CA: Sage Publications, Inc., 1988), p. 8.
[11]Charol Shakeshaft, "The Gender Gap in Research in Educational Administration," *Educational Administration Quarterly*, 25 (1989), 324–37.
[12]Misogyny means the hatred of women.
[13]Shakeshaft, *Women in Educational Administration*, p. 197.
[14]Ibid.
[15]Ibid.
[16]Ibid., p. 198.
[17]Ibid.
[18]Patricia A. Schmuck, ed., *Women Educators: Employees of Schools in Western Countries* (Albany: State University of New York Press, 1987).
[19]Gabrielle Lakomski, review of Patricia Schmuck, *Women Educators. The Journal of Educational Administration*, 26, no. 1, (March 1988), 117–20.
[20]Charol Shakeshaft and Irene Nowell, "Research on Theories, Concepts and Models of Behavior: The influence of gender," *Issues in Education*, 2 (Winter 1984), 186–206.
[21]J.W. Getzels, "A Psycho-Sociological Framework for the Study of Educational Administration," *Harvard Educational Review*, 22 (1952), 225–46.
[22]Shakeshaft, *Women in Educational Administration*, p. 158.
[23]Charol Shakeshaft and M. Hanson, "Androcentric Bias in the Educational Administration Quarterly," *Educational Administration Quarterly*, 22 (1986), 68–92.
[24]New York: Harper & Row, Publishers, Inc., 1983.
[25]Daniel E. Griffiths, "Administrative Theory," in Norman J. Boyan, ed., *Handbook of Research on Educational Administration* (New York: Longman, Inc., 1988), p. 47.
[26]Jill Y. Miller, "Lonely at the Top," *School & Community*, 72 (Summer 1986), 9–11; M.M. McCarthy, G. Kuh, and J. Beckman, "Characteristics and Attitudes of Doctoral Students in Educational Administration," *Phi Delta Kappan*, 61 (1979), 200–203; and Sakre Oller, "Female Doctoral Students in Educational Administration: Who Are They?," *Sex Equity in Educational Leadership Report 7* (Eugene, OR: Center for Educational Policy and Management, 1978).
[27]G.S. Johnston, C.C. Yeakey, and S.E. Moore, "An Analysis of the Employment of Women in Professional Administrative Positions in Public Education," *Planning and Changing*, 11 (1980), 115–32.
[28]J. Stockard, "Public Prejudice Against Women School Administrators: The Possibility of Change," *Educational Administration Quarterly* 15 (1979), 83–96.
[29]K.D. Lyman and J.J. Speizer, "Advancing in School Administration: A Pilot Project for Women," *Harvard Education Review*, 50 (1980), 25–35.
[30]F.I. Ortiz, "Scaling the Hierarchical System in School Administration: A Case Analysis," *Urban Review*, 11 (1979), 111–25.
[31]A.T. Elshof and E. Tomlinson, "Eliminating Stress for Women Administrators," *Journal of the National Association for Women Deans, Administrators, and Counselors*, 44 (1981), 37–41.
[32]A. Stent, "Academe's New Girl Network," *Change*, 10 (1978), 18–21.
[33]A.W. Villadsen, and M.W. Tack, "Combining Home and Career Responsibilities: The Methods Used by Women Executives in Higher Education." *Journal of the National Association of Women Deans, Administrators, and Counselors*, 45 (1981), 20–25.
[34]Edson, *Pushing the Limits*.
[35]Ibid., p. 146.
[36]E. Jones and X. Montenegro, *Women and Minorities in School Administration* (Arlington, VA: American Association of School Administrators, 1982), 5–15.
[37]Colleen S. Bell and Susan E. Chase, "Women Superintendents and School Boards: Their Experiences and Perceptions of Gender Issues." Paper presented at the annual meeting of the American Educational Research Association, 1988. A revised version of this paper, entitled "Organizational Influences on Women's Experience in the Superintendency," *Peabody Journal*, is in press.

[38]Ibid.

[39]Rosabeth Moss Kanter, *Men and Women of the Corporation* (New York: Basic Books, Inc., Publishers, 1977).

[40]Bell and Chase, "Women Superintendents," p. 10.

[41]Norman J. Boyan, ed., *Handbook of Research on Educational Administration* (New York: Longman, Inc., 1988).

[42]Anne Wilson Schaef, *Women's Reality: An Emerging Female System in the White Male Society* (Minneapolis: Winston Press, 1981).

[43]J.M. Frasher and R.S. Frasher, "Educational Administration: A Feminine Profession," *Educational Administration Quarterly*, 15 (1979), 1–15.

[44]A. Fishel and J. Pottker, "Performance of Women Principals: A Review of Behavioral and Attitudinal Studies," in J. Pottker and A. Fishel, eds., *Sex Bias in the Schools* (Cranbury, NJ: Associated University Presses, 1977).

[45]John K. Hemphill, Daniel E. Griffiths, and Norman Frederiksen, *Administrative Performance and Personality* (New York: Teachers College Press, 1962).

[46]Shakeshaft, *Women in Educational Administration*, p. 168.

5

MOTIVATION

"Managements have always looked at man as an animal to be manipulated with a carrot and a stick. They found that when man hurts, he will move to avoid pain—and they say, 'We're motivating the employees!' Hell, you're not motivating them, you're moving them."

—*Frederick Herzberg*[1]

INTRODUCTION

Motivation of subordinates and associates is a pivotal concern for virtually all supervisors, administrators, and managers. Motivation is not behavior: it is a complex internal state that we cannot observe directly but that affects behavior. Therefore, we must infer the motivation of individuals from their behavior (either verbal or nonverbal). Motivation is made up of "all those inner striving conditions described as wishes, desires, drives, etc....it is an inner state that activates or moves individuals."[2] Without motivation there would be no purposive, organized behavior by the individual—either at work or elsewhere.

Motivation is generally considered to be rooted in human needs: the individual responds to needs by *doing* something about them. But, although the close relationship between motivation and behavior is understandable in a general, global way, the nature of the precise relationship between needs and motivation is not at all clear. In other words, motivation is an intervening variable, as shown in Figure 5–1. Behavior is an attempt to satisfy the needs that motivate the individual: behavior is the means by which the individual seeks to satisfy needs. Not surprisingly, therefore, the basis for understanding motivation in organizations lies in understanding the needs that motivate the behavior of the people in those organizations. This has been the subject of intensive, persistent, and widespread research since the famous Western Electric researches began in the early 1920s to explode long-cherished, traditional (classical) management views.

The classical management view of motivation is, traditionally, quite simple: people need money, so if you pay them well, they will work. Such problems as laziness, goofing off, or poor work performance are best dealt with by devising pay schedules that provide the necessary incentives to keep individuals performing well.

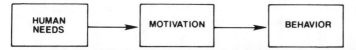

FIGURE 5-1. Motivation as an intervening variable between human needs and behavior.

For example, you might choose to pay a factory worker on a piece rate with some provision to penalize under-par performance, such as shoddy work. Better still, you might choose to pay the worker daily so that there is a close relationship between behavior on the job and take-home pay. So, what one really has are a carrot (pay) and a stick (penalties) to motivate the worker. Such a view of motivation is based upon the clear assumption that Theory X generally explains the nature of people: they are inherently lazy, will avoid work if possible, and must be coerced. Of course, this view does not necessarily have to take the "hard" form described here but can be applied equally as well in "softer" forms of Theory X that may tend to obscure its true nature. In practice, this often means that softer language and less direct practices are used to implement the concept.

Obviously, this classical view of motivation has not been implemented well in American public schools: there is a loose fit, indeed, between the reputation that a teacher has for excellence in teaching and his or her salary. Many people, of course, argue that the fit is *too* loose and that "accountability" schemes that tie "productivity" to such rewards as tenure and salaries should be instituted. In higher education, on the other hand, this approach to motivation has been widely (albeit imperfectly) applied. It is not at all uncommon to find that the rewards of the system (for example, tenure, promotion, salary) are tied to performance on the job. To the dismay of students, some institutions tend to reward published research more than teaching, and in those places young assistant professors soon learn to put their energies into these activities and pay scant attention to teaching or program development. There are other institutions of higher education, of course—usually undergraduate colleges—that emphasize and reward teaching ahead of knowledge generation. In these latter institutions, teachers may well devote considerable attention to developing their teaching skills, planning coursework, and developing a strong following of students.

The western electric studies. Most students of education have heard something about the "Hawthorne studies" or the "Western Electric research," if in no other way than to have learned about the so-called Hawthorne effect. This classic research has had such profound impact upon the understanding of motivation at work—and has been so widely misunderstood in educational circles—that we should take some time to review it here.

The Hawthorne works of the Western Electric Company (located near Chicago) was chosen as the site for an experimental study that was started in 1924 and concluded some ten years later.[3] The study was an important part of a large, complex research project that was undertaken to determine how much illumination was required to achieve the maximum output from workers.

Two groups of employees doing similar work under similar conditions were chosen, and records of output were kept for each group. The intensity of the light under which one group worked was varied, while that under which the other group worked was held constant. By this method, the investigators hoped to isolate from the effect of other variables, the effect of changes in the intensity of illumination on the rate of output.[4]

But, in the early stages of the research, the investigators were disappointed: it soon became obvious that there was no simple relationship between the intensity of illumination and the workers' rate of output. "The employees [reacted] to changes in light intensity in the way they assumed they were expected to react," George Homans reports, adding, "that is, when light intensity was increased, they were expected to produce more; when it was decreased, they were expected to produce less. A further experiment was designed to demonstrate this point...[5] in which the light bulbs were changed so that the workers were allowed to assume that there would be more light when, in fact, other bulbs of the same power had been installed. Of course, as we now know, each change of bulbs resulted in some increase in output by the workers, regardless of the level of illumination they provided. Clearly, the workers in the experimental group were responding to *their perceptions* of the expectations of the experimenters and not to the changes in their physical environment. Thus, the workers were responding to *psychological* factors that motivated their behavior at work, and, at the time of the experiments, the nature of these psychological factors was unknown to the investigators.

The significance of this study was not lost on the researchers. Whereas classical management theory would have posited that changes in the physical environment would have an impact on worker productivity, this experiment showed a direct relationship between productivity and *psychological* phenomena (for example, expectations of others and being the focus of attention). This is sometimes referred to as the "Hawthorne effect." At this point a new experimental study was organized involving workers who assembled telephone relays: a control group which worked in the regular shop and an experimental group which was set up in a separate area. To initiate the experiment:

> ...the operators who had been chosen to take part were called in for an interview in the office of the superintendent of the Inspection Branch [remember, this was in 1927, and the workers all were women]....The nature of the test was carefully explained to these girls and they readily consented to take part in it....They were assured that the object of the test was to determine the effect of certain changes in working conditions, such as rest periods, midmorning lunches, and shorter working hours. They were especially cautioned to work at a comfortable pace, and under no circumstances to try to make a race of the test. This conference was only the first of many that were to be held during the course of the experiment. Whenever any experimental change was planned, the girls were called in, the purpose of the change was explained to them, and their comments were requested. Certain suggested changes which did not meet with their approval were abandoned.[6]

Working methodically for over a year, the researchers kept careful production records while trying different experimental interventions: rest pauses, special lunch periods, a shorter working day, and a shorter working week. Throughout the experimental work, the output curve rose slowly and steadily. In each experimental period, output was higher than in the preceding period. Finally, the work conditions of the group were—with the consent of the workers—returned to the same as they had been prior to the start of the research (no rest periods, no special lunches, and a regular-length workday and workweek). The result: productivity *continued to rise.* In fact, "the output of the group continued to rise until it established itself on a high plateau from which there was no descent until the time of discouragement and deepening economic depression which preceded the end of the test" in 1933.[7] In sum, the group had (1) become more productive and (2) had maintained that high productivity even after the experimental interventions had been taken away. If rest periods and shorter working hours, plus the "special attention" of being in an experimental group, could not account for the change, what could?

It took a number of people some years to analyze all the data and begin reporting them, but gradually a picture of what had happened began to emerge:

1. The workers liked the experimental situation and considered it to be fun;

2. The new form of supervision (encouraging them to work at a normal pace and not to try to hurry) "made it possible for them to work freely without anxiety";[8]

3. The workers knew that what they did was important and that results were expected;

4. The workers were consulted about projected changes—often by the superintendent himself—and during that process were encouraged to express their views and were, in fact, permitted to veto some ideas before they were ever implemented;

5. The group itself—as a human social system—had undergone change and development during the course of the experiment. Though the last step of the experiment was an attempt to return the group to the original conditions of work (by taking away the rest periods, new hours, and the like), this was, in fact, impossible because the group itself had changed. It had become more cohesive, it had developed a distinctive esprit, and it was functioning at a significantly more mature level than it had been in the beginning.

In sum:

...the women were made to feel they were an important part of the company...they had become participating members of a congenial, cohesive work group...that elicited feelings of affiliation, competence, and achievement. These needs, which had long gone unsatisfied at work, were now being fulfilled. The women worked harder and more effectively than they had previously.[9]

This research set the stage for the human relations movement which sought (a) to better understand the nature and needs of human beings at work and (b) to apply this knowledge to the development of more effective organizations, administration, supervision, and other aspects of management. Although the early years of the human relations movement included a number of instances in which attempts to use this new knowledge were naive, it is now clear that sound management and administration draw from the knowledge generated from studies of human relations. We now realize, for example, that the experimental results were not caused merely by the usual concept of "Hawthorne effect," which has been interpreted by many to suggest that if you pay special attention to people (for example, put them into an experimental group, make them aware that they are getting "special" treatment) that it, in itself, will motivate them to higher levels of performance. *The higher productivity developed in the Western Electric research resulted from the fact that—under participative leadership—the groups of workers themselves developed cohesiveness, morale, and values that were highly motivating.*

Contemporary views of the Western Electric research. The series of studies that comprised the Hawthorne research stands as perhaps the most seminal research project of this century on organizational behavior in the workplace. It illumined a whole new approach to understanding the subject and paved the way for such modern notions as participative management, democracy in the workplace, power sharing or empowerment, and more. As one would expect with any major research study, however, a half-century of close study has revealed some weaknesses and oversights.

Recent critiques of the Western Electric research have pointed out that the research is marred by androcentric bias, which was probably inevitable given the historical time period in which the research was done. For example, I have pointed out that in one major phase of the research the workers were women and the managers were men. At the time that the studies were done, in the 1920s and early 1930s, the power relationships between managers and workers were far more unequal than they are today. This was heightened, of course, by the inequality of power that was socially sanctioned between men and women at that time. There seems to be little question that this fact, ignored at the time, may have been more influential in interpreting the results than has traditionally been imagined.

The fundamental importance of the Western Electric studies, however, should not be obscured by these valid criticisms: it drew attention to the psychological aspects of organizational behavior with such power and authority as to have literally changed the course of management and administration history.

SOME THEORETICAL APPROACHES TO MOTIVATION

Douglas McGregor made a brilliant and powerful contribution when—recognizing this fact—he proffered his Theory X and Theory Y, which was discussed in Chapter 2. These are not theories of human motivation, as they are sometimes thought to be, but instead describe the assumptions upon which individuals are likely to base their view of humankind and thus—of course—their behavior toward people in organizational settings.

Because the precise nature of the complex relationships between human needs and goal-seeking behavior is not easy to understand, some scientists have developed theoretic explanations in the course of their investigations of human motivation. No theoretic model or explanation is now universally accepted as being fully explanatory, but there are several major concepts of motivation in the workplace that have been fruitful sources of insight for practicing managers and administrators seeking ways to make organizations more effective. Three of these views of motivation will be described here:

1. The *hierarchy-of-needs theory,* which is based upon the work of Abraham Maslow;
2. The *two-factor theory,* originally called the motivation-hygiene theory by its developers, Frederick Herzberg and his associates, and;
3. *Expectancy theory* (sometimes called valence theory), which is often associated with the work of Victor H. Vroom.

MASLOW'S HIERARCHY-OF-NEEDS THEORY

Abraham Maslow suggested that the driving force that causes people to join an organization, stay in it, and work toward its goal, is actually a *hierarchy of needs*.[10] When the lowest order of needs in the hierarchy is satisfied, a higher-order need appears, and, since it has the greater potency at the time, this higher-order need causes the individual to attempt to satisfy it.

Basic physiological needs. The lowest order of human needs consists of the basic physiological necessities such as food, water, shelter, and the like. In the less complex societies of the past, it was possible for one to meet these needs individually or as a participant in relatively primitive organizations. The nomadic hunter or the peasant in a simple agrarian society spent much time and energy providing these necessities. In our modern, technologically oriented society, however, it is not possible for many of us to dig a well for water or to hunt for game when we are hungry. Rather, we must earn money to purchase necessities, such as paying the rent, purchasing food at the grocery store, and paying taxes. In modern society, the basic drives of human existence cause us to become enmeshed in organizational life—we become participants in the organization that employs us, as well as in the myriad government agencies and private companies that provide the essential goods and services on which we depend. Thus, at the simplest level of human need, we are motivated to join organizations, remain in them, and contribute to their objectives.

Security and safety. However, because of the nature of humankind, once the basic physiological needs are adequately met, a new level of need, which is one step higher in the hierarchy of needs, automatically appears: the need for safety or security. This need, according to Maslow, now has the greater potency, and the individual will seek to satisfy it. Security can, of course, mean many things to different people in different circumstances. For some, it means earning a high income to assure freedom from want in case of sickness or during old age. Thus, many people are motivated to work harder to seek "success," which frequently is measured in terms of income. Or security can be interpreted in terms of "job security," which is so important, for example, to many civil service employees and school teachers. To them, the assurance of life tenure and a guaranteed pension may be strong motivating factors in their participation in employing organizations.

Social affiliation. New levels of need unfold as the needs below them are met. Once the need for safety is satisfied, the individual is free to try to meet the need for social affiliation with others. Until the earlier needs are met, however—the basic physiological needs and the need for safety or security—the individual will be motivated more highly by them than by any psychological need. Thus, a person who is out of work and growing short of funds would probably find the promise of high pay a good reason for taking a job with a particular company. However, once the individual has enough income to get along reasonably well, he or she can begin to think in terms of security. Moving up the hierarchy of needs, once the basic levels are assured, the employee with a reasonably well-paying and secure job will begin to feel that belonging and approval are important motivators in his or her organizational behavior. One not only becomes aware of these needs but also tends to seek situations in which they can be met; moreover, individuals tend to behave in ways that are intended to produce the response in the organization that will best meet this need for belonging and affiliation.

Esteem.   Having satisfied the needs to belong and to be accepted, the individual—according to Maslow—has needs to be recognized, to be respected, and to have status and prestige. We deal here with self-image: the view that one holds of oneself. Thus, there is a dynamic interplay between one's own sense of satisfaction and self-confidence, on the one hand, and feedback from others in such diverse forms as being asked to chair a group, being elected to office, being asked for advice, and being included on the "right" invitation lists, on the other hand.

Self-actualization.   This, in Maslow's view, is the highest level of need in the hierarchy, and he described it as the desire to become more and more what one is, to become everything that one is capable of becoming. The self-actualized person is strongly inner-directed, seeks self-growth, and is highly motivated by loyalty to cherished values, ethics, and beliefs. Not everyone reaches the self-actualized state, of course, and—even then—Maslow estimated that these higher-level needs are met about 10 percent of the time (Fig. 5–2).

In the application of the hierarchy-of-needs concept to observations of people, it is helpful to keep four points in mind:

1. A need that has been satisfied is not a motivator. Once a need is satisfied, another (higher-order) need arises to take its place as a motivator. Thus, one is always motivated by striving to satisfy needs that have not yet been fully met. It is *unmet needs* that motivate people. This is the concept of prepotency.
2. The web of needs of an individual is very complex. Maslow's hierarchy is useful in helping us to conceptualize motivating forces, but, of course, reality is not that neat and simple: one is always subject to a variety of (often conflicting) needs at once. One may, for example, be motivated to remain in teaching because of the job security it offers and yet—at the same time—apply for a less secure administrative position because it will bring status and approval from others.
3. However, one will tend to behave in a way intended to satisfy motivating needs, once the lower-level needs are met, at least in a general way. The concept of hierarchy does not imply that there will never be ambivalence as to what a person wants to do.
4. There are usually many ways in which higher-order needs may be met but relatively fewer ways in which to satisfy lower-order needs.

It should be borne in mind that Maslow's theory of human motivation is a *general* theory. It was not developed in an effort to explain the motivation of people at work, which is the specific concern of the student of organizational behavior in schools. Maslow himself did not, in fact, publish anything about the application of the hierarchy-of-needs theory to human behavior in organizations until some twenty-five years after the original appearance of his work.[11] It has, however, been eagerly seized upon by practicing managers and teachers of management and administration. This has been, in part, because it is easy to understand and has

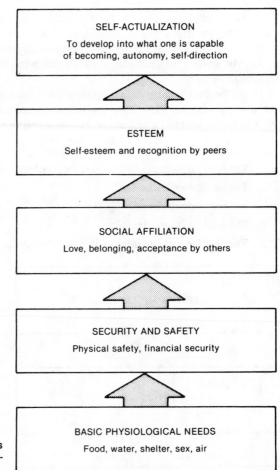

FIGURE 5–2. Hierarchy of Needs as used in Maslow's Theory of Motivation.

logical appeal. This widespread acceptance results, in no small measure, from the work of Douglas McGregor, which drew heavily upon Maslow's concepts of motivation and which—in its own right—has been extraordinarily influential in shaping management thought since mid-century.

Comments on Maslow's theory. In its long history, Maslow's concept of human motivation has frequently been subjected to intense criticism, as any such scholarly claim should be. Many point out that the theory was neither developed from controlled empirical studies nor has it been rigorously tested using such methods. As I have discussed in Chapter 4, it has also been severely criticized for its androcentric bias. A focus of that criticism has been on Maslow's clearly jaundiced views of what self-actualization means for men and what it means for women. But, then, the notion of self-actualization has been seen as problematic from many points of view.

Nevertheless, Maslow's understanding of motivation has had strong intuitive attraction: it seems and sounds sensible to a great many people. Imperfect as it is, it continues to be widely influential in illuminating the nature of motivation for many individuals. Some have, in fact, found the theory a very useful framework for studying links between organizations and behavior at work. Lyman W. Porter, for example, used it in studying the job satisfaction of nineteen hundred managers.

Porter first reformulated Maslow's original hierarchy. On the assumption that—in present-day America—few managers are motivated by such basic physiological needs as thirst and hunger, Porter identified a hierarchy of five prepotent needs that is a little different from Maslow's:

1. The need for *security* (the lowest in the hierarchy),
2. The need for *affiliation,*
3. The need for *self-esteem,*
4. The need for *autonomy,* and
5. The need for *self-actualization.*[12] (See Figure 5–3.)

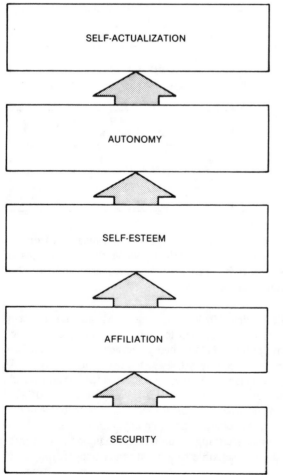

FIGURE 5–3.   Porter's concept of the hierarchy of needs that motivates managers.

The significant additional level that Porter saw in the hierarchy was *autonomy*. This refers to the individual's need to participate in making decisions that affect him or her, to exert influence in controlling the work situation, to have a voice in setting job-related goals, and to have authority to make decisions and latitude to work independently. Using Porter's concept of the needs hierarchy, it is relatively easy to see the ways in which work organizations, such as school districts, schools, and institutions of higher education, can be sources for fulfilling these motivating needs (Figure 5–4).

Porter went on to conduct research that is interesting because it is representative of a whole line of inquiry that followed. Among the characteristics he attempted to measure concerning the managers he studied were:

1. To what extent the need characteristic (of any level of the hierarchy) *was being met* by the manager's job, and
2. To what extent the manager thought the job *should* meet the need characteristic.

FIGURE 5–4. A hierarchy of work motivation, based on Porter's model.

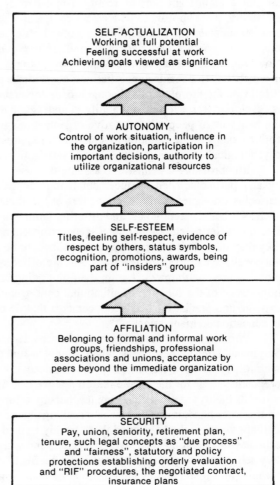

SELF-ACTUALIZATION
Working at full potential
Feeling successful at work
Achieving goals viewed as significant

AUTONOMY
Control of work situation, influence in
the organization, participation in
important decisions, authority to
utilize organizational resources

SELF-ESTEEM
Titles, feeling self-respect, evidence of
respect by others, status symbols,
recognition, promotions, awards, being
part of "insiders" group

AFFILIATION
Belonging to formal and informal work
groups, friendships, professional
associations and unions, acceptance by
peers beyond the immediate organization

SECURITY
Pay, union, seniority, retirement plan,
tenure, such legal concepts as "due process"
and "fairness", statutory and policy
protections establishing orderly evaluation
and "RIF" procedures, the negotiated contract,
insurance plans

The differences between the first question (to what extent need was being met) and the second question (to what extent the job should meet the need) provide a measure of either (1) the amount of *need satisfaction* the person is experiencing or (2) the perceived *need deficiency* that the person is experiencing. Research such as this has been conducted widely in an effort to understand the relationship between need satisfaction and/or need deficiency and the performance of people on the job.[13]

Since such studies "contend that human behavior is goal-directed toward fulfilling unsatisfied needs, an individual's need satisfaction should be related to his job performance. And, as Maslow's theory would predict, higher-order needs should be more closely linked to job performance than lower-order needs that can be readily satisfied."[14] One generalization that seems to arise from the substantial body of research of this kind is that it is situation-bound. That is, when or where times are good and jobs plentiful (such as public education in the United States in the decade of the 1950s), such research tends to pick up little concern for the lower-order needs (for example, security and physiological needs), because they are not a significant part of reality. But when or where there is employment instability, there appears to be a closer connection between the lower-order needs and job satisfaction. This admittedly general observation may be disconcerting to those who seek a broad, generally applicable explanation of human motivation. However, the fact that people at work respond to the realities of the circumstances in which they find themselves is harmonious with the notions of contingency theory. It follows, therefore, that until some broad, universal theory of human motivation is developed (if it ever is), our ability to understand the motivation that lies behind the behavior of people in educative organizations requires us to assess fully the contingencies in the situation as much as it requires us to understand the general psychological concepts of human needs satisfaction.

It is probably unrealistic to assume that teachers are, as a group, motivated by any particular needs inducement that is applicable only to that group; the variables among teachers are too great to expect that. There are personal variables, such as life and career goals, and differing family and financial obligations. There also are differing situational contingencies; teachers who work in schools where they may have their coats stolen, or be robbed, or be in danger of being raped may very well reveal needs dispositions that are different from those of teachers in a more secure environment. Again, the point being emphasized here is the critical importance of the function of situational contingencies in attempting to describe, explain, and predict the needs inducements that lie behind the behavior of people in educational organizations.

With this caveat in mind, we should consider the studies reported by Thomas Sergiovanni and his associates, which sought to find out "at what level teachers are with respect to the hierarchy [of prepotent needs]. We need to know their level of prepotency..."[15] for the simple reason that we cannot (according to the hierarchy-of-needs theory) motivate insecure teachers by offering them greater autonomy or, on the other hand, motivate teachers seeking autonomy by offering them security. Perhaps worse is the likelihood that "freshly trained school executives who over-estimate the operating need level of teachers and scare them off with ultraparticipatory self-actualizing administration are as ineffective as others who deny teachers meaningful satisfaction by underestimating operating need levels."[16] To shed light on what he calls the "operating need levels" of teachers, Sergiovanni and his colleagues conducted two studies: one of the teachers and administrators of an upstate New York suburban school district and the other of the teachers in thirty-six Illinois high schools.

These studies are of interest on two levels: (1) the data-gathering instruments and techniques for analyzing the data that were used demonstrate one way to study systematically important situational contingencies in the motivation of people in educative organizations; and (2) the results drawn from the populations they studied provide some useful insights.[17] In general, "esteem seems to be the level of need operation showing greatest need deficiency for these professionals. Large deficiencies are also reported for autonomy and self-actualization, and these gaps will continue to rise as teachers make gains in the esteem area."[18] In other words, these studies suggest that (in the populations studied and at the time of the study) the teachers—overall, as a group—(a) had satisfied the lower-order needs and (b) were generally ready to respond to higher-order needs. They felt reasonably secure and reasonably affiliated with their colleagues, and, therefore, more of these kinds of inducements were unlikely to be very motivating. But, were these teachers to be given opportunities to feel better about themselves and opportunities to have greater influence in the processes of making decisions, these would likely be highly motivating opportunities. But the groups of people studied were not monolithic: the researchers report (not surprisingly, to be sure) some differences related to age (in this case, age probably was an indicator of where individuals were in the development of their careers). They found, for example, that the younger teachers (that is, ages twenty to twenty-four) seemed to be the most concerned with esteem. Slightly older teachers (ages twenty-five to thirty-four), on the other hand, showed the most unmet motivational needs, across the board. One could speculate that this is the period in a teacher's career when he or she hits dead end: for most, there will be little opportunity for professional growth, advancement, and significant achievement in the years ahead. Perhaps even more disturbing, however, are some insights concerning older teachers (forty-five years or over). At first glance, the data seemed to indicate that older teachers had the smallest need deficiencies of all; this tends to suggest that, in the later years of their careers, teachers were finding their work rather highly motivating at all levels. When the researchers examined this phenomenon, however, there appeared to be quite a different explanation: older teachers "are not getting more in terms of need fulfillment as the years go by but, rather, are expecting less. Levels of aspiration seem to drop considerably with age. Teachers become more 'realistic' or resigned to things as they are."[19]

The significance of findings such as these looms very large, indeed, to those who are concerned with improving the effectiveness of public schools. There is strong support for believing that job security, salaries, and benefits—though far from being irrelevant to teachers—have little likelihood of motivating them. A greater motivational need, it seems clear, is for teachers to achieve feelings of professional self-worth, competence, and respect; to be seen increasingly as people of achievement, professionals who are influential in their workplaces, growing persons with opportunities ahead to develop even greater competence and a sense of accomplishment. But in an era in which public schools (and, increasingly, institutions of higher education) have been pervaded by a powerful sense of adversarial relationships between teachers and management, there appears to be little support from the organizational hierarchy of many schools to meet these needs. Indeed, the negotiating posture of most school districts has been highly defensive on this point, viewing every gain by teachers in opportunities to develop their autonomy and participation and to increase their scope of influence as a loss of jealously guarded management authority and prerogatives.

Similarly, the widespread loss of confidence in the effectiveness of schools has led to a rash of actions that have had a direct impact on the motivating environment of educative organizations. Reductions in force (RIF), slashed budgets, mandated competency programs, legislated school reforms, and massive federal interventions at the local school level all—of course—have laudable intent in terms of overall social policy. But in terms of Maslow's needs-hierarchy theory of motivation, as applied to the organizational behavior of people at work in schools, they tend to produce disastrous results in combination.

HERZBERG'S TWO-FACTOR THEORY OF MOTIVATION

The two-factor theory of motivation posits that motivation is not a single dimension describable as a hierarchy of needs but that it is composed of two separate, independent factors:

1. *Motivational factors,* which can lead to job satisfaction, and
2. *Maintenance factors,* which must be sufficiently present in order for motivational factors to come into play, and when not sufficiently present can block motivation and can lead to job dissatisfaction.

The work of Frederick Herzberg began to appear some twelve years after Maslow's and has become widely influential in management thought around the world, particularly in profit-making organizations. He started with systematic studies of people at work, thereby producing an empirically grounded theory, rather than using an "armchair" approach. In his research Herzberg asked people to recall the circumstances in which (1) they had, at specific times in the past, felt satisfaction with their jobs, and in which (2) they similarly had been dissatisfied with their jobs.[20] Analysis of the responses indicates that there is one specific, describable cluster or group of factors that is associated with motivation and satisfaction at work and another, equally specific, group of factors that is associated with dissatisfaction and apathy. Perhaps no other theory of motivation at work has been more extensively researched and argued about than this, and in all likelihood none has been as widely applied to complex organizations.

Traditionally, it had been believed that the opposite of job satisfaction is job dissatisfaction; thus, by eliminating the sources of dissatisfaction from work, the job would become motivating *and* satisfying. But Herzberg suggests that this is not so: that the opposite of satisfaction is no satisfaction (see Figure 5–5). Thus, by eliminating sources of dissatisfaction, one may placate, pacify, or reduce the dissatisfaction of a worker, but *this does not mean that such reduction either*

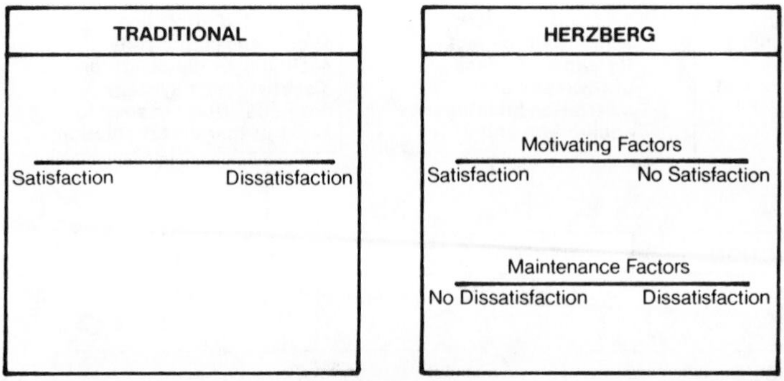

TRADITIONAL	HERZBERG
	Motivating Factors
Satisfaction Dissatisfaction	Satisfaction No Satisfaction
	Maintenance Factors
	No Dissatisfaction Dissatisfaction

FIGURE 5–5. Traditional concept of job satisfaction-dissatisfaction contrasted with Herzberg's concept.

motivates the worker or leads to job satisfaction. For example, salary, fringe benefits, type of supervision, working conditions, climate of the work group, and attitudes and policies of the administration can be sources of dissatisfaction. However, if one improves the salary-benefit "package" and working conditions, and develops a more humane, concerned administration, one can expect to reduce dissatisfaction, but one cannot expect to motivate the workers by such means. Such conditions as these, taken together, originally were called "hygiene" factors. That term was chosen because—to Herzberg, at least—they have a preventive quality. They are being called, increasingly, "*maintenance*" factors, however, and that is the appellation that is used in this book.

Motivation appears to arise from a separate cluster of conditions, different from and distinct from those related to the sources of dissatisfaction. For example, achievement, recognition, the challenge of the work itself, responsibility, advancement and promotion, and personal or professional growth appear to motivate people and are, therefore, associated with job satisfaction. They are called motivating factors or *motivators*.

The theory, which is shown schematically in Figure 5–6, suggests that it is not possible to motivate people at work through maintenance factors. Reducing class size, developing a more amiable atmosphere; and improving the fringe benefits may well do two things: (1) reduce or eliminate the dissatisfaction of teachers and (2) create conditions wherein they may be motivated. But these kinds of efforts, in themselves, are not motivating. It does not follow, however, that the maintenance factors are unimportant: minimum levels must be maintained if we are to avoid so much dissatisfaction that motivators will not have their expected effect. For example, failure to keep the salary schedule at a level that teachers think is reasonable or threats to job security can generate such dissatisfaction that teachers cannot respond to opportunities for professional growth, achievement, or recognition. Thus, although maintenance factors are not—in themselves—motivating (or do not lead to job satisfaction), they are prerequisite to motivation.

An important concept in the two-factor theory is that people tend to see job satisfaction as being related to such intrinsic factors as success, the challenge of the work, achievement, and recognition, while they tend to see dissatisfaction as being

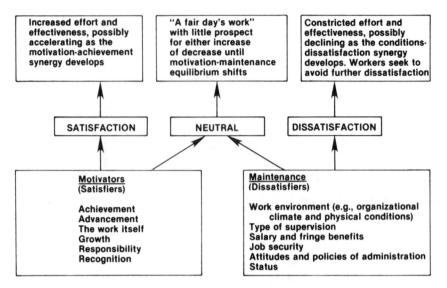

FIGURE 5–6. Model of Herzberg's motivator-maintenance theory.

related to such extrinsic factors as salary, supervision, and working conditions. In other words, they attribute motivational characteristics to themselves and attribute dissatisfaction to characteristics of the organization. In this context, Herzberg has suggested three main ideas for those who would practice his theory:

1. *Enrich the job,* which involves redesigning the work that people do in ways that will tap the motivation potential in each individual. This would include making the job more interesting, more challenging, and more rewarding.

2. *Increase autonomy* on the job. The reader is specifically cautioned to note here that it was not suggested that complete autonomy be somehow granted to workers but that autonomy be increased. This suggests more participation in making decisions as to how the work should be done.

3. *Expand personnel administration* beyond its traditional emphasis on maintenance factors. The focus of personnel administration should be on increasing the motivational factors present in the work. In this view, school districts in which personnel administration focuses almost exclusively on such things as contract administration, the routines of selection-assignment-evaluation-dismissal, and the details of teacher certification and pension plans are attending to important things but not to motivating things. Since 80 percent or more of the current operating budget of many school districts is allocated directly to salaries, wages, and related items, it would seem that the personnel function should be deeply involved in creating or redesigning jobs that motivate the incumbents and thus increase the effectiveness or productivity of the district's employees. This is the view that, for many, underlies the concept of "human resources administration" in contrast to more traditional views of personnel administration.

Herzberg's motivation-maintenance theory has been widely accepted and applied to the management of organizations, especially to American business and industrial corporations. It has, at the same time, provided the basis for considerable academic debate. The four principal criticisms that crop up in that debate are often expressed as follows:

1. Herzberg's basic research methods tended to foreshadow the responses he got. When things went well and people felt satisfied, they tended to take the credit for it; but when things went badly on the job and the respondents were not satisfied, they tended to project the fault onto other people or onto management.

2. The reliability of his research methods is also open to question. The research design required a number of trained individuals to score and interpret the responses from the respondents. Obviously, there may be some differences in the way individuals do the rating, with one rater scoring a response in one way and another rater scoring a similar response in another way (so-called interrater reliability).

3. There is no provision in the research to cover the likely possibility that a person may get satisfaction from part of his or her job and not from another part.

4. The theory assumes that there is a direct relationship between effectiveness and job satisfaction; yet the research studies only satisfaction and dissatisfaction and does not relate either of them to the effectiveness (or productivity) of the respondents.

The first three of these criticisms are easily dealt with as merely representing typical problems of designing research that requires us to infer *causes* of behavior from observations of the behavior itself. They make the basis for nice arguments, but in fact, Herzberg's research—after exhaustive review in the literature over a period of two decades—must be accepted as representing the state of the art. The fourth criticism, however, is not so simple.

There is a chicken-or-the-egg aspect to the research literature on job satisfaction and its presumed link to effectiveness on the job. Roughly, investigators with a human relations orientation tend to think that satisfied workers are likely to be productive. Herzberg, however, is among those scholars who tend to think that satisfaction at work arises from the work itself or, more precisely, that job satisfaction comes from achievement. There is a massive body of research literature in this area; because of methodological problems as well as ideological conflicts, the overall results are inconclusive. Conversely, scant support exists for the notion that dissatisfied workers are likely to be more effective than those who report a higher level of satisfaction; the question, then, revolves around the *sources* of satisfaction (that is, maintenance factors or motivating factors). The Herzberg theory has been tested numerous times in school situations and—in this organizational setting, at least—appears to be well supported.

Ralph Savage, using interviews to obtain data from Georgia teachers, reports that Herzberg's theory was generally supported,[21] as did Rodney Wickstrom in reporting a study of teachers in the Province of Saskatchewan, Canada.[22] Gene Schmidt studied 132 high school principals in districts in the Chicago suburbs and found that, again, the two-factor theory appeared to be strongly supported by these school administrators, indicating that "recognition, achievement, and advancement are major forces in motivating them to lift their performance to approach their maximum potential."[23] In operational terms, this investigator concluded that "encouragement and support for administrators who desire to be creative, to experiment with new educational programs, and to delve into different educational endeavors are needed to allow more opportunities for achievement."[24]

Thomas Sergiovanni, in the late 1960s, after replicating Herzberg's work among teachers, reports that the theory appears to be supported.[25] His findings are that achievement and recognition were very important motivators for teachers, along with the work itself, responsibility, and the possibility of growth. Among the dissatisfiers reported were (not surprisingly) routine housekeeping, taking attendance, paper work, lunch duty, insensitive or inappropriate supervision, irritating administrative policies, and poor relationships with colleagues and/or parents. Sergiovanni makes the point that *advancement*, frequently an important motivator in studies conducted in private-sector corporations, was missing in the study of teachers. On this significant point, he observes that "advancement was simply not mentioned by teachers because teaching as an occupation offers so little opportunity for advancement. If one wishes to advance in teaching, he must leave teaching for a related education profession such as administration, supervision, and counseling."[26]

Comments on Herzberg's two-factor theory.   The Herzberg two-factor theory of motivation was developed through research, in which people were asked to describe critical incidents in their work lives that involved motivation and job satisfaction. Subsequently, it has been strongly supported by additional research carried out by a number of investigators using similar techniques. Together, these provide strong support for the concept. However, some investigators find it troubling that studies that use other research techniques generally fail to support the theory.

Herzberg's theory has been widely influential, however, and commonly appears in the literature of business and industry as well as that in education. While some advocate abandoning it in favor of the newer and more complex expectancy theory, the two-factor theory remains a powerful explanation of motivation in the workplace.

INTEGRATING HERZBERG'S AND MASLOW'S THEORIES

Some of the essential differences between Maslow's hierarchy-of-needs theory and Herzberg's motivation-maintenance theory have already been pointed out. The central difference is that Maslow thought of every need as a potential motivator, with the range of human needs in a prepotent hierarchical order, whereas Herzberg argued that only the higher-order needs are truly motivating (the lower-order needs being conceptualized as maintenance factors). Another difference—not quickly apparent, perhaps—is that Maslow's was a *general* theory of human motivation, concerned, as Stephen Robbins puts it, "with the person's needs 24 hours a day,"[27] whereas Herzberg tried specifically to illuminate motivational issues *in the workplace*.

Nevertheless, a comparison of the two theories, as shown in Figure 5–7, reveals that they are basically highly compatible and, in fact, support one another. I feel (as Figure 5–7 shows) that the Porter version of the hierarchy-of-needs model lends itself to such a comparison, for the simple reason that such basic physiological drives as the need for food, water, and air have little relevance for motivating behavior at work in American educational organizations. Even so, I agree with Robbins:

> The lower-order needs on Maslow's hierarchy tend to closely approximate the maintenance factors as outlined by Herzberg. Salary, working conditions, job security, [school district] policy and administration, and supervision are generally physiological and safety-oriented needs. In contrast, the intrinsic motivational factors of recognition, advancement, responsibility, growth, achievement, and the work itself tend to be closely

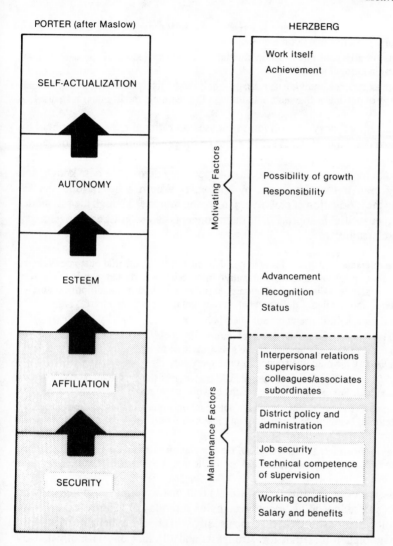

PORTER (after Maslow)

SELF-ACTUALIZATION

AUTONOMY

ESTEEM

AFFILIATION

SECURITY

HERZBERG

Work itself
Achievement

Possibility of growth
Responsibility

Advancement
Recognition
Status

Interpersonal relations
supervisors
colleagues/associates
subordinates

District policy and
administration

Job security
Technical competence
of supervision

Working conditions
Salary and benefits

Motivating Factors

Maintenance Factors

FIGURE 5–7. Need-priority model compared with motivation-maintenance model.

related to the desire for esteem and self-actualization. The integrated model would also suggest that organizations have traditionally emphasized lower-order needs. If workers are to become motivated on their jobs, it will be necessary for administrators to make the alterations necessary to stimulate the motivational factors in the [jobs themselves].[28]

EXPECTANCY MODELS OF MOTIVATION

Expectancy theory is based upon three assumptions:

1. People do not just respond to events after they occur; they anticipate (or *expect*) that things will occur and that certain behaviors in response to those events will probably

produce predictable consequences. Expectancy theory suggests, then, that individuals are highly proactive and not merely reactive.

2. Humans usually confront possible alternative behaviors (and their probable consequences) in rational ways.

3. Through experience, individuals learn to anticipate the likely consequences of alternative ways of dealing with events and, through this learning, modify their responses.

In sum, expectancy theory of motivation focuses on rational expectations held by the worker that desirable rewards are likely to be the predictable outcome of certain behaviors.

Although there are various models of expectancy theory, the best-known and most widely used is that developed by Victor H. Vroom, whose work focused especially on the motivation of employees in organizations.[29] Though the full model is a complex, quantifiable approach, its main concepts can be grasped *if* several key words are understood:

Valence refers to the degree of preference that one has for a potential outcome. Valence can be either positive (desired) or negative (not desired). Different people will assign different valence values to such things as income, working conditions, status, or security. In short, valence defines what an individual wants from a job.

Outcome means the consequence of one's behavior.

First-level outcome means the direct, or immediate, consequence of one's behavior. For example, the first-level outcome of one's acts might be to achieve better results at work. This is usually the outcome sought by the supervisor.

Second-level outcome refers to the personal impact that the first-level outcome has on the individual. For example, better results at work might result in gaining tenure.

Expectancy is the belief that a behavior will result in a predictable, first-level outcome. For example, being more demanding and less permissive might be expected to result in higher test scores in the class.

Instrumentality refers to the strength of the correlation between the first-level outcome (improved test scores) and the second-level outcome (being granted tenure).

The basic notions of this theory are (1) that one experiences motivations in varying intensities, depending upon the complex interplay of valence-expectancy-instrumentality relationships, (2) that one usually will choose to behave in response to the motivational forces that are strongest, and (3) that one is motivated by *expected* events and likely outcomes of alternative ways of dealing with them. Many models have been developed from this theory, the best-known of them seeking to quantify the various forces through complex and often sophisticated mathematical modeling techniques.

One of the vexing central issues in expectancy theory is whether to focus on intrinsic rewards or on extrinsic rewards. John W. Atkinson has proposed an expectancy model based on intrinsic motivation, specifically achievement.[30] Lyman Porter and Edward Lawler have produced a later expectancy model that is more complete and therefore more complex.[31] As in any expectancy model of motivation, they suggest that the effort one puts into work depends upon (1) the value one places on the expected reward and (2) the likelihood that the reward actually will be received if the effort is made. This immediately raises the need for the individual to possess (1) the necessary abilities and traits, and (2) an accurate perception of his or her role, in order to back up the effort and to produce the results intended. Porter and Lawler also recognize in their model that *both* intrinsic and extrinsic rewards play an important role in expectancy motivation.

The simple diagram of the Porter-Lawler expectancy model in Figure 5–8 is helpful in following the broad-stroke outline of the main concepts of expectancy motivation theory. First, the worker assigns some value to the possible reward for performing work [1]. He or she also has some subjective judgment as to the likelihood that the proposed effort on the job actually will result in receiving the reward [2]. The combination of wanting the reward plus the perceived chances of actually getting the reward leads to a certain level of effort [3].

Of course, effort alone does not produce results: as the model shows, effort is mediated by a combination of the worker's abilities and traits [4] and the perception that he or she has of the role on the job [5]. The interplay of these three—effort, abilities, and role perception—is seen as yielding certain results (that is, actual accomplishment from the performed behavior) [6].

Based upon his or her performance, the individual expects to receive a fair reward [8] and is, in fact, rewarded. Rewards can be intrinsic [7A] (for example, satisfaction) or extrinsic (for example, pay, recognition) [7B]. At this point, these rewards are perceived to be equitable to some degree or another, in terms of the individual's own subjective values and expectations, and it is this complex interplay that leads to some level of satisfaction [9].

The model is completed with two feedback loops: one shapes the individual's perception of the likelihood that effort *will actually yield the expected reward*. The other feedback loop shapes the individual's judgment as to the *value of the rewards* obtained. In short, the Porter-Lawler model suggests (1) that performance leads to satisfaction and (2) that the level of satisfaction obtained shapes future effort to perform.

FIGURE 5–8. The Porter-Lawler model of motivation to work. From Lyman W. Porter and Edward E. Lawler, III, *Managerial Attitudes and Performance* (Homewood, IL: Richard D. Irwin, Inc., 1968), p. 165.

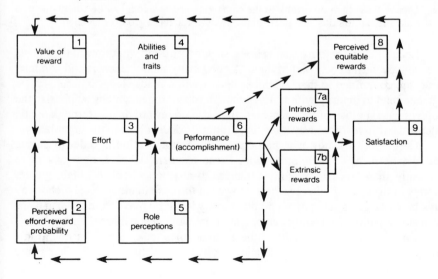

Comments on expectancy theory of motivation. This approach to understanding motivation tends to find support among those who are attracted to the idea
of finding mathematical solutions to the complexities of human experience. However, expectancy theory has encountered serious difficulties owing to the methodological difficulties of assigning numerical values to the intricacies of the processes
of human behavior. In general, expectancy theory tends to hold a certain amount of
fascination for technically oriented research methodologists but has drawn little
serious attention from those concerned with administrative practice.

STYLES OF ORGANIZATIONAL BEHAVIOR

These concepts of motivation in work organizations are more than mere abstract
explanations of human behavior: numerous students of organization have used them
(intuitively or intentionally) as the basis of systematic descriptions of various *styles*
of organizational behavior. For example, Alvin W. Gouldner described people as
being motivated by their "cosmopolitan" or "local" orientation toward their work
and the organization.[32]

Cosmopolitans and locals. Gouldner has pointed out that individuals in
organizations occupy certain latent roles that center around the personal loyalty or
attachment they feel toward the organization. "Cosmopolitans" may be described
as those whose commitment is essentially to their profession, whereas "locals" are
those whose prime loyalty is to the organization. Orientation in the latent role is
associated with organizational behaviors that we can easily observe. The organizational behavior of "locals" is quite different from that of "cosmopolitans."
Gouldner's definitions are:

1. *Cosmopolitans:* those low on loyalty to the employing organization, high on commitment to specialized role skills, and likely to use an outer reference group orientation.
2. *Locals:* those high on loyalty to the employing organization, low on commitment to
   specialized role skills, and likely to use an inner reference group orientation.[33]

Locals generally join organizations, stay in them, and work toward their goals
because they wish to be a part of them. A good many school teachers and administrators are committed to their school system, want to render long, faithful service
to it, and tend to identify with it. Even though school organizations emphasize the
professional expertise of their teachers, they also do reward them—through public
statements, if in no other way—for long, faithful "dedication" to the organization.
Cosmopolitans, however, participate in the organization in order to pursue
their commitment to their profession. Some teachers, who change jobs more
frequently than "locals," willingly transfer to another school to obtain greater
prestige in the eyes of other teachers. However, the cosmopolitan-local dichotomy
is *not* based on geography; in our mobile society locals do move from place to place
and a cosmopolitan frequently can operate from a rather fixed base.
Gouldner's original study of these latent roles took place in a liberal arts
college that he called "Co-op College": it had 1,000 students and 130 faculty

members and was located in a community with a population of about 5,000. Gouldner found that the labels "cosmopolitan" and "local" were not fully descriptive of types of latent roles; rather, he discovered that these terms identified clusters of types, within which clusters were four kinds of locals and two kinds of cosmopolitans. His description may be summarized as follows:

1. *Locals*
   a. *The dedicated.* These are the "true believers" who attach much importance to the goals and philosophy of a specific organization. They stress commitment to the institution, rather than to the technical competence of colleagues; they tend to see themselves primarily as members of the faculty and only secondarily as professional specialists; they stress consensus and internal harmony; and they comprise an inner reference group in the organization—the loyal and reliable group.
   b. *The true bureaucrats.* They resist "outside" control of the institution, and their loyalty is not so much to the ideals of the school as it is to the idea of the school, or the place itself. Sensitive to external criticism, true bureaucrats are willing to make changes in traditional institutions in order to ameliorate it. They generally recommend their school to young teachers as a place to start their careers. They do not favor lighter work loads to provide more time for research and writing. Finally, as "true bureaucrats," they tend to favor formal regulations.
   c. *The homeguard.* In the college studied, these tended to be second-echelon administrators, mostly women. They have the least professional specialization and attend few professional conventions. They are not committed to the distinctive values of the organization, nor to its community. Many of the "homeguard" in Gouldner's study were people who had graduated from the college they worked for.
   d. *The elders.* These are the oldest locals and have been with the organization for the longest time. Generally in their fifties or sixties, elders are deeply rooted in the informal organization; they look forward to retirement and tend to evaluate the present situation in the organization in terms of past events they have experienced.

2. *Cosmopolitans*
   a. *The outsiders.* They have very little involvement in either the formal or informal structure of the organization, little influence in the faculty—and do not want more—and are not likely to stay with the organization permanently. Such cosmopolitans are highly committed, not to the institution, but to their specialized professions. Their outer-reference orientation is expressed in their feeling that they do not get much intellectual stimulation from their colleagues. They read many journals and meet with fellow specialists at meetings and conventions, which they often attend in various locations.
   b. *The empire builders.* These cosmopolitans are similar to outsiders but are integrated into the formal structure of the organization (although not into its informal structure). Their affiliation to their department is strong, and they favor strong departmental autonomy. Like the outsiders, the empire builders feel they can easily find jobs outside the institution—they are economically and professionally quite independent. And they would quickly accept an appointment at an institution which would accord them higher professional prestige.[34]

The implications of this kind of analysis of behavioral style are clear. Locals and cosmopolitans view their organizations differently and interpret their relationship to them differently; moreover, their behavior style can be influenced by this differing orientation in both formal and informal relationships. In most public school organizations, locals will tend to exercise greater influence in the organization and will achieve greater acceptance in the social system than cosmopolitans.

The local–cosmopolitan orientation of staff members can be a very real source of conflict with regard to such issues as views held by teachers concerning the need for rules, the importance of loyalty to the organization, and the question of professional outer-reference orientation versus the value of local longevity of service.

Upward mobiles and indifferents. The individual who participates in an organization is not merely an inanimate object being molded by forces and events, and he or she does not merely react to events that occur as a consequence of being in the organization. One's own values, goals, aspirations, and the needs that one wishes to fulfill are important factors that shape not only one's manifest role but also one's latent role.

Schools are largely staffed by people from so-called middle-class backgrounds; their home life and education have imbued them with a life-style that, for the most part, emphasizes success and/or security. We can say that cosmopolitans are generally success-oriented and locals are generally security-oriented. However, in schools both are likely to have middle-class backgrounds and to accept the behavioral standards implied by that fact: discipline and avoidance of open aggression in interpersonal contacts. They will also have a certain amount of anxiety about their "image." In their own organizational settings, both teachers and administrators tend to "stay in role," that is, to look, act, and talk as they "should."

Conflict that is considered "bad" is camouflaged: fistfights and strong verbal language are rarities—and are virtually never condoned. Even ambition is restrained and carefully revealed only in forms that the individual thinks are acceptable to role-referents. Over a period of years, the author of this text has asked many graduate students in educational administration what their goals were. The typical response is usually something like this: "Well, I hope that some day, if an opening occurs, maybe I will be considered for an assistant principalship in my district—or something." When asked, "Why do you want to become a school principal?" the typical response, accompanied by visible discomfiture, tends to be, "Well, I think that I've been a good teacher—my supervisors have told me so—and maybe I can make a contribution as a leader. I believe in the importance of education, and I want to do what I can to contribute to improving what we have." Although the trend today is toward greater openness and frankness, it is still rare to hear a teacher say, "I'd like to get to the top in this profession. I think I've got the stuff and I'm looking for opportunities to get ahead." Such an admission would generally not be well accepted by either a teacher's colleagues or his or her superordinates. In the social system of the school, laden with prohibitions and proscriptions imposed by its class structure, the administrator must look carefully at behavior through a variety of "lenses" in order to comprehend fully why individuals tend to mold their roles as they do—and how to deal with them effectively.

Robert Presthus has suggested that people view ambition in three different ways.[35] Each type can be identified, not necessarily by spoken declarations but by how organizational roles are shaped, particularly with regard to attitudes toward their superordinates in the hierarchy:

1. *Upward mobiles* generally accept "the system"—its goals and values, its authority and demands. This acceptance is genuine and, which is significant, the upward mobile sees his or her superordinates in a good light—as friendly and sympathetic.

2. *Indifferents* largely ignore the organization and find their satisfactions away from the job. They work to "make a living," but they rarely are involved in the organization more than is necessary.

3. *Ambivalents* are tempted by the power, authority, and prestige that accompany promotion; but they are not "organization persons," for they value their own individuality and their friendships more than the rewards that the organization can offer. Presthus feels that there are relatively few ambivalents.

This additional set of dimensions, which can help us to understand the interpersonal behavior of people in the structured roles of an organization, is composed of ideal types, of course, and will not necessarily be so easily identifiable in the "real" world of schools. But if we think of the ideal types as points on a continuum (see Figure 5–9), the concept is helpful for understanding and predicting organizational behavior. We have recently observed an increase in the number of teachers who are, organizationally speaking, ambivalent, and who have challenged well-established practices such as the primacy of administrators, the status traditionally associated with "promotion" from teaching to administration, and the rewards customarily reserved for administration. These teachers no longer see the foregoing organizational values as relevant to them or to their personal goals. Such an attitude, which is bewildering to some administrators, is reflected in requests for election of principals by teachers, for removing or reducing pay differentials between administrators and teachers, and for increasing the emphasis on the central importance of the teacher as opposed to the conventional tendency to view him or her at the bottom of the hierarchy.

In terms of administrative practice in the schools, the upward-mobile concept suggests the following especially appropriate ideas:

1. Administrators tend to show considerable drive for achievement, are strongly inclined toward mobility, are favorably inclined toward control from above, and tend to identify with their superordinates rather than with their subordinates. Even though the realities of organizational life may preclude further promotion for principals, they still tend to associate themselves with the central office and the values held there.[36]

2. Because of the sharply pyramidal structure of the school organization, it is inevitable that many upward-mobile persons are passed over for promotion and will never have their upward-mobility needs met.[37] In recent years—with declining enrollments and attendant reductions in force—this problem has been sharply exacerbated, undoubtedly affecting large percentages of teachers. The consequences—in terms of frustration and discouragement—pose serious motivational problems in school districts and schools.

FIGURE 5–9. Upward-mobile—indifferent continuum of attitudes toward ambition.

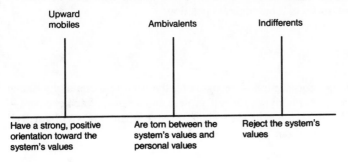

Upward mobiles	Ambivalents	Indifferents
Have a strong, positive orientation toward the system's values	Are torn between the system's values and personal values	Reject the system's values

Career-bound and place-bound administrators.   "An organization," Victor
A. Thompson has pointed out, "is a structure made up of positions and roles that people
move in and out of without destroying the organization."[38] But the newly arrived role
incumbents *do*, to some extent, shape their roles and, consequently, the organizations
to fit their own behavioral style. Richard O. Carlson studied this problem at what is
probably its most powerful level in school systems: the superintendency.[39] In so doing
he has provided some useful insights into organizational behavior style that can, at
least in general terms, be applied to other positions in the organization.

In studying the circumstances surrounding the employment of school superintendents, Carlson identified two distinct types of administrators:

1. One type is an insider who, having moved up through the school system's hierarchy,
    has waited for the superintendency to become vacant. If he or she eventually does
    become superintendent, that person usually retires on the job and probably does not
    become superintendent in another district. This type is described by Carlson as being
    place-bound.
2. Another type does not wait, but seeks the jobs he or she wants and does not hesitate to
    move from one district to another for advancement. This person is an outsider and may
    make a career of the superintendency, probably holding a position in more than one
    district before retirement. This type is said to be *career-bound.*

The essential difference between these two types is the importance attached
to career and place. The insider stays in the organization by choice and attains the
superintendency only if he or she can do so in that organization, but the outsider
places great stress on career objectives and is mobile in the course of his or her
career development. The parallel between these career types and Gouldner's cosmopolitan–local typology is clear. For example, the place-bound person who longs
for promotion—perhaps covertly—can be described as an upward mobile. It is
significant that the data that Carlson used to develop his classifications were taken
from actual career histories of a number of school superintendents.

Not surprisingly, Carlson noted a systematic difference in the organizational
behavior of place-bound and career-bound administrators. The latter, who had other
job offers available, were in a stronger bargaining position with the board of
education than were the former; thus, they had a freer hand and tended to make
more and earlier changes in the system. However, these superintendents are not
necessarily "steamroller" types. In a somewhat similar study, Melvin Seeman[40]
found that the job-mobile superintendents were high on consideration; they probably relied heavily on a professional-collegial relationship to gain influence and get
things accomplished, as differentiated from the place-bound person's emphasis on
the rules and the authority of a hierarchical position.

JOB ENRICHMENT

A number of industrial corporations—recognizing the need to focus motivational
attempts on the needs of employees for self-growth and a sense of achievement—
have implemented *job enrichment* (JE) plans. Fred Luthans and William Reif
provide an excellent definition:

Job enrichment is concerned with designing jobs that include a greater variety of work content; require a higher level of knowledge and skill; give the worker more autonomy and responsibility for planning, directing, and controlling his own performance; and provide the opportunity for personal growth and meaningful work experience.[41]

One of the best-known applications of job enrichment to the management of an organization was the work, which began in the 1960s, of M. Scott Myers at Texas Instruments.

Shortly after identifying the satisfiers and dissatisfiers, the company began to investigate means of redesigning jobs of technicians, assemblers, and foremen, most of whom were performing repetitive jobs. A job-enrichment program was initiated which permitted the employees to plan and control their jobs in conjunction with their foremen. While the workers were planning, controlling, and doing their jobs, the foremen had the opportunity to mediate interpersonal conflicts, measure individual and group production, plan for future projects, and provide the performance feedback and recognition that were viewed as integral parts of the motivation process. In mid-1965, the company had 3,200 direct-labor workers who were producing 26 million germanium transistors per month...at the end of [an] 18-month period, there were only 1,800 employees and they were performing at the rate of the original 3,200. Texas Instrument's management attributed the higher productivity to job enrichment, because throughout that period of time, there had been no major mechanical changes or automation of operations, no changes in processes, materials, or product mix.[42]

This is illustrative of job enrichment, which is intended to redesign the work not for the purpose of making it easier but, rather, to make it more challenging, a source of personal growth, and a source of a sense of achieving something worthwhile. The emphasis in supervision shifts from close, detailed monitoring of activities, to focus on achieving mutually set goals. The worker participates more in setting goals and controlling the job, performs more of the complete job, and accepts greater responsibility. Some experts insist that this should be called *vertical* job enrichment, because it calls for bringing higher motivational needs satisfactions into play. It specifically does *not* call for merely adding more low-level tasks to the worker's job, which, clearly, can be *demotivating*.[43] Don Hellriegel and John Slocum report that IBM uses the following four criteria in deciding whether or not a job is to be enlarged (enriched): "Any addition to the job should (1) increase responsibility, (2) increase worker autonomy, (3) permit the worker to do the complete task, and (4) provide feedback (performance appraisal) to the worker. Unless all four criteria can be satisfied, IBM recommends that the job not be enlarged."[44] In education, it is the latter criterion (that is, the provision of feedback) that often poses problems in job enrichment: all too often, valid, reliable, and objective criteria as to the effectiveness of a teacher's work (in terms of student learning) are not easily obtainable.

By the late 1970s, among large American corporations reporting the use of job-enrichment programs, in addition to IBM and Texas Instruments, were Traveler's Insurance Company, Corning Glass Works, Imperial Chemical Industries (now ICI), Polaroid, Gaines Pet Food Manufacturing Corporation, American Telephone and Telegraph Company, Donnelly Mirrors, and United Airlines. The total list represented about 20 percent of the list of the five hundred largest corporations regularly compiled by *Fortune* magazine. There were indications that the concept also was being widely used by somewhat smaller firms, as well as by a rapidly growing number of European and Japanese companies.

SUMMARY

The development of the mainstreams of organizational thought during the course of this century has been intertwined with increasing understanding of the motivation of people at work. If there is a single overarching trend in the study of motivation at work, it is the growing awareness of the importance of such intrinsic factors as a sense of achievement and pride arising from doing the work as contrasted with such extrinsic factors as reward and punishment. By the mid-1980s, therefore, business and industry—hard-pressed by foreign competition—were aggressively seeking to find ways to apply this insight in practice.

All widely accepted contemporary theories of motivation agree on one point: extrinsic rewards have, at best, limited power to motivate people and intrinsic rewards are essential in order to develop highly motivated workers. This view is at odds with classical organizational thinking wherein motivation is seen as being closely tied to compensation, on the one hand, and coercion by management on the other.

Herzberg's work, widely applied in business and industry, has emphasized the role of intrinsic factors as motivators whereas such extrinsic factors as compensation serve merely to inhibit or enhance (depending upon their adequacy) the likelihood that the intrinsic motivational needs of individuals may be tapped. By the mid-1980s both the popular press and the scientific literature abounded with case studies, research reports, and other descriptions of attempts to apply intrinsic motivation concepts to the management of business and industrial firms as a major part of the effort to "turn them around" in their competition with Japanese firms. Generally these included some form of job enrichment, such as quality circles, which was intended to tap such higher levels of motivation as the need for affiliation, and the need for self-esteem. At the same time there were reports of only scattered similar efforts to implement such ideas in public school organizations even though polls repeatedly made clear that teachers were experiencing high levels of dissatisfaction on the job and were increasingly reluctant to recommend teaching as a career to others.

While at that time some efforts were being made to increase the salaries of teachers as a means of inducing more (and supposedly better-qualified) people to enter the profession, it remained questionable as to the extent to which teachers would find their work motivating. In view of the research on motivation discussed in this chapter, the outcome would seem to depend greatly on the extent to which management style in the schools shifted to one that rewarded teachers with an increasing intrinsic sense of achievement at work.

SUGGESTED READING

ARGYRIS, CHRIS, *Integrating the Individual and the Organization*. New York: John Wiley & Sons, Inc., 1964.
    Argyris' studies, done mostly in industrial settings, focus on the apathy and low level of effort so widely found among workers. He notes that workers are generally encouraged or required to be

submissive, passive, and dependent—in short, to behave in immature ways rather than as mature adults. Most organizations (that is, organizations managed in classical or bureaucratic ways) intentionally create situations to maintain this kind of behavior (because they are based on Theory *X* assumptions). This does not have to be, he argues, and suggests how organizations can facilitate mature and more highly motivated behavior by applying Theory *Y* assumptions. Highly relevant to public school organizations, many of which still heavily reinforce immature conformity on the part of the faculty as well as the children.

HERZBERG, FREDERICK, *The Managerial Choice: To Be Efficient and to Be Human.* Homewood, IL: Dow Jones-Irwin, 1976.
In this, his fourth book on the psychology of people at work, Herzberg emphasizes the practical applications of his theory (although Chapter 2 does describe the theory). He draws from cases, research, and his own anecdotes, as well as from many of his monographs and articles that have appeared in widely scattered sources from 1952 through 1975. In Chapter 5 he responds to criticisms of motivation-hygiene theory and in Chapter 6 answers a number of questions about the theory and its application.

LORTIE, DAN C., "Career and Work Rewards," Chapter 4 in *Schoolteacher.* Chicago: University of Chicago Press, 1975.
A vivid, sensitive description of the extrinsic and intrinsic rewards of teaching as interpreted by a sociologist from teachers' own descriptions. Chapter 5, in the same book, entitled "Perspectives on Purpose," and Chapter 6, "Endemic Uncertainties," continue this probe of the rewards and motivations in teaching as an occupation. Strongly recommended.

MCCLELLAND, DAVID C., "Toward a Theory of Motive Acquisition," *American Psychologist,* 20 (1965), 321–33.
Noting that people seem to vary greatly in their need to achieve (*n ach*)—hence vary greatly in the extent to which they are motivated by *n ach*—McClelland has studied the personality characteristics of those who seek success and prestige. In this article he describes the high *n* achiever and methods by which low *n* achievers may be developed into high *n* achievers. Provocative reading for those who are interested in developing the achievement motive in educators. McClelland's work has received widespread interest, especially among entrepreneurs.

MITCHELL, DOUGLAS E., ORTIZ, FLORA IDA, and MITCHELL, TEDI K., *Work Orientation and Job Performance: The Cultural Basis of Teaching Rewards and Incentives.* Albany: State University of New York Press, 1987.
Reporting the results of case studies in a meticulous program of research, this monograph illuminates the relationships between the ways that classrooms are organized and managed, the leadership style of principals, and the organizational culture of the school. The authors describe four kinds of teachers—helpers, coaches, instructors, and master teachers—and four kinds of principals—administrators, supervisors, leaders, and managers—and discusses how they interact to create school cultures. An insightful and challenging analysis.

U.S. CONGRESS, SENATE COMMITTEE ON LABOR AND WELFARE, *Work in America.* Washington, D.C.: Government Printing Office, 1973.
The report of a task force appointed by the United States Secretary of Health, Education and Welfare to study problems of improving the quality of life at work. It explores sources of dissatisfaction and alienation, demographics and characteristics of the work force, and devotes particular attention to job enrichment (JE) as a way of stimulating greater job satisfaction. Excellent bibliography and a very informative table summarizing thirty-four case studies of humanizing work. Although not focused on problems of educative organizations, this book is helpful to the educator in placing in perspective the motivation-alienation problems of schools.

NOTES

[1]Quoted in William Dowling, ed., *Effective Management and the Behavioral Sciences* (New York: AMACOM, 1978), p. 44.
[2]Bernard Berelson and Gary A. Steiner, *Human Behavior: An Inventory of Scientific Findings* (New York: Harcourt, Brace & World, 1964).
[3]I alluded briefly to this study and its importance in Chapter 2.
[4]George C. Homans, "The Western Electric Researches," in *Human Factors in Management,* ed. Schuyler Dean Hoslett (New York: Harper and Brothers, Publishers, 1951), p. 211.

⁵Ibid.

⁶Ibid., pp. 214–15.

ᴵIbid., p. 217.

⁸Ibid.

⁹Paul Hersey and Kenneth H. Blanchard, *Management of Organizational Behavior: Utilizing Human Resources*, 3rd ed. (Englewood Cliffs, NJ: Prentice-Hall, 1977).

¹⁰Abraham H. Maslow, *Motivation and Personality*, 2nd ed. (New York: Harper & Row, Publishers, Inc., 1970).

¹¹Abraham H. Maslow, *Eupsychian Management* (Homewood, IL: Richard D. Irwin, Inc., and The Dorsey Press, 1965).

¹²Lyman W. Porter, "A Study of Perceived Need Satisfaction in Bottom and Middle-Management Jobs," *Journal of Applied Psychology*, 45 (1961), 1–10.

¹³Exemplary of such research are Edward E. Lawler III, and Lyman W. Porter, "The Effect of Job Performance on Job Satisfaction," *Industrial Relations*, 6 (1967), 20–28; and David G. Kuhn, John W. Slocum, and Richard B. Chase, "Does Job Performance Affect Employee Satisfaction?" *Personnel Journal*, 50 (1971), 455–60.

¹⁴Don Hellriegel and John W. Slocum, Jr., *Management: A Contingency Approach* (Reading, MA: Addison-Wesley, 1974), p. 308.

¹⁵Thomas J. Sergiovanni and Fred D. Carver, *The New School Executive: A Theory of Administration* (New York: Dodd, Mead & Company, 1973), pp. 58–59.

¹⁶Ibid., p. 59.

¹⁷This research is summarized and the sources fully documented in ibid., pp. 56–63.

¹⁸Ibid., p. 59.

¹⁹Ibid., p. 61.

²⁰Frederick Herzberg, *Work and the Nature of Man* (Cleveland: World Publishing Co., Inc., 1966), p. 56.

²¹Ralph M. Savage, "A Study of Teacher Satisfaction and Attitudes: Causes and Effects" (unpublished doctoral dissertation, Auburn University, 1967).

²²Rodney A. Wickstrom, "An Investigation into Job Satisfaction among Teachers" (unpublished doctoral dissertation, University of Oregon, 1971).

²³Gene L. Schmidt, "Job Satisfaction among Secondary School Administrators," *Educational Administration Quarterly*, 12 (1976), 81.

²⁴Ibid.

²⁵Thomas J. Sergiovanni and Fred D. Carver, *The New School Executive: A Theory of Administration* (New York: Dodd, Mead & Company, 1973), pp. 75–78.

²⁶Ibid., p. 77.

²⁷Stephen P. Robbins, *The Administrative Process: Integrating Theory and Practice* (Englewood Cliffs, NJ: Prentice-Hall, 1976), p. 312.

²⁸Ibid.

²⁹Victor H. Vroom, *Work and Motivation* (New York: John Wiley & Sons, Inc., 1964).

³⁰John W. Atkinson, *An Introduction to Motivation* (Princeton, NJ: Van Nostrand, 1964).

³¹Lyman W. Porter and Edward E. Lawler III, *Managerial Attitudes and Performance* (Homewood, IL: Richard D. Irwin, Inc., 1968).

³²Alvin W. Gouldner, "Cosmopolitans and Locals: Toward an Analysis of Latent Social Roles," *Administrative Science Quarterly*, 2 (December 1957, March 1958), 281–306. и d 440–80.

³³Ibid., p. 290.

³⁴This description is based on ibid., pp. 446–50.

³⁵Robert Presthus, *The Organizational Society*, rev. ed. (New York: St. Martin's Press, Inc., 1978).

³⁶William E. Henry, "The Business Executive: The Psychodynamics of a Social Role," *American Journal of Sociology*, 54, no. 4 (January 1949), 286–91.

³⁷For one approach to a solution to this problem, see Thomas E. Powers, "Administrative Behavior and Upward Mobility," *Administrators Notebook*, 15, no. 1 (September 1966), 1–4.

³⁸Victor A. Thompson, *Modern Organization* (New York: Alfred A. Knopf, Inc., 1961), p. 113.

³⁹See Richard O. Carlson, *Executive Succession and Organizational Change: Place-Bound and Career-Bound Superintendents of Schools* (Chicago: Midwest Administration Center, University of Chicago, 1962).

⁴⁰Melvin Seeman, "Social Mobility and Administrative Behavior," *American Sociological Review*, 23, no. 6 (December 1958), 633–42.

⁴¹Fred Luthans and William E. Reif, "Job Enrichment: Long on Theory, Short on Practice," *Organizational Dynamics*, (1977), 91.

[42]Don Hellriegel and John W. Slocum, Jr., *Management: A Contingency Approach* (Reading, MA: Addison-Wesley, 1974), p. 317.

[43]Richard Walton, "How to Counter Alienation in the Plant," *Harvard Business Review*, 50 (1972), 70–81.

[44]Hellriegel and Slocum, *Management*, pp. 316–17.

6

LEADERSHIP

"Of course educational organizations are much too complex for effectiveness to be attributed to any single dimension. Nevertheless, leadership quality owns a fair share of responsibility for effectiveness. Unlike other factors beyond the control of the school...the nature and quality of leadership seem readily [amenable] to...improvement."

—*Thomas J. Sergiovanni* [1]

DEFINITION

Recent emphasis on school reform in America has stressed the need for more effective leadership in education. However, leadership is one of the most fascinating topics in organizational behavior and, at the same time, a notoriously slippery concept that has produced literally hundreds of definitions in the literature. Among those definitions, however, two things are agreed on:

1. Leadership is a function of groups, not individuals. We speak, of course, of individuals as being leaders but leadership occurs only in the processes of two or more people interacting. In the interaction process, one person is able to induce others to think and behave in certain desired ways. That brings up the second key point, which is *influence*.
2. Leadership involves intentionally exercising influence on the behavior of other people.

Thus, any concept of leadership deals with exercising influence on others through social interaction.

Leadership and management. A major criticism of American school administration in recent years is the contention that administrators have emphasized management at the expense of leadership. This suggests that there is not only a difference between management and leadership but that, moreover, they may be mutually exclusive. The demand for stronger leadership makes it more urgent than ever for those in education to clearly understand the issues that are involved.

Some contend that managers deal with *things*, while leaders deal with *people*. We can *manage* finances, inventories, and programs, for example, but we *lead* people. Others contend that managing and leading are qualitatively different from each other and, moreover, mutually exclusive. Warren Bennis and Burt Nanus, for example, tell us that "managers are people who do things right and leaders are people who do the right thing."[2] However that may be, leadership is complex and not easy to understand.

Many ways of describing leadership and unlocking its mysteries have been developed. No one of these has yet emerged at the single best way. Therefore, in this chapter you will read about a number of approaches that have been influential in thinking about leadership in order to deepen your understanding of this difficult but important topic. We begin with a consideration of the most time-honored approach, which is that leadership is some sort of innate characteristic of people who are gifted with certain traits.

Trait theory of leadership. A popular concept of leaders, supported by years of philosophical speculation and research effort, is that they are people who are endowed with certain traits or characteristics that especially fit them for their leadership roles. It has been popularly believed that such traits as intelligence, imagination, perseverance, and emotional stability characterize the individual qualified to exercise leadership. This concept, of course, suggests that those who possess these traits must be sought out for their leadership potential.

Extensive research has been conducted by numerous investigators in efforts to discover whether or not leadership is associated with personal traits of individuals. Leaders in all kinds of settings have been studied, from nursery schools to armies and from detention homes to churches. Every imaginable trait seems to have been examined, including height, weight, state of health, intelligence, emotional adjustment, self-confidence, authoritarianism, and many more. As early as 1948, Ralph Stogdill, after a thorough survey of the psychological literature then in print, concluded that there was little to support the belief that traits and the capacity to lead effectively are systematically related.[3] Richard Mann reported a similar view in 1959,[4] and Bernard Bass echoed the conclusion in 1960.[5] It is safe to say three things about the scientific evidence concerning the relationship between personal traits and leadership:

1. *No systematic relationship between personal traits and leadership has been established.* Although one study may reveal that tall people are chosen as leaders more frequently than short people, other studies in the literature will refute this. Although authoritarianism may correlate positively with perceived leadership in one group of studies, another group of studies finds no support for such a view. And so on, so that the body of scientific evidence (despite what a single study here or there might conclude) fails to support the widely held notion that leaders are individuals possessing certain traits.

2. *At least a part of the inability to establish a clearer body of evidence lies in problems of research methodology.* One problem lies in the inherent difficulties of developing accurate, reliable, and valid measures of psychological attributes, such as emotional integration, interpersonal sensitivity, group characteristics, and group perceptions. Another lies in the difficulty of designing appropriately sensitive psychological research procedures. Reviews of the literature suggest that results of studies are often biased by the methods used to conduct the studies.

3. *The situation in which leadership is attempted is probably at least as influential as the personal traits of the leader.* The characteristics of the group being led (for example, maturity level, level of trust, cohesiveness), the nature of the group's tasks or mission

(for example, clarity of goals, complexity of tasks), and the psychological environment in which leadership is attempted (for example, levels of ambiguity, uncertainty, threat, and conflict), are illustrative of variables that differ from situation to situation and that have an impact on the ability of individuals to lead effectively. What is being talked about here is a *contingency approach* that, as we shall see in this chapter, is central to contemporary understanding of leadership. Contingency views of leadership hold, briefly, that although there is no one best, universally applicable way to lead, there are describable situational contingencies that call for different specific leadership styles and methods.

It should be clear from these statements that leadership is a highly complex activity that is not reducible to simple statements or definitions. Indeed, Warren Bennis and Burt Nanus reported in 1985 that they had located over 350 definitions of leadership in the literature.[6] There is, however, considerable agreement among students of the subject that the essence of leadership is in the distinctive relationships between leaders and followers.

THE LEADER AND THE GROUP

Leadership occurs in some kind of group, and the leader functions, necessarily, in relationship to the members of the group. Viewing leadership as an interactive process between the leader and the group requires that we clarify three commonly used terms in discussing leadership: *group, leader,* and *leader behavior.*

Group.   In dealing with leadership it is necessary to keep in mind the difference between an aggregation of people, on the one hand, and a group, on the other hand. A group may be defined (and differentiated from an aggregation of people) by the presence—to a greater or lesser degree—of at least three characteristics:

1. *Members of a group are interdependent:* they share with each other certain values, beliefs, attitudes, knowledge, fears, or whatever. This interdependence is expressed through interactions between and among members of the group, such as communicating, sharing, engaging in rituals, and so on.
2. *Members of a group derive satisfaction of individual needs from being part of the group.* These needs will include those discussed in Chapter 5, such as safety, security, belonging, esteem, and so on.
3. *Members of a group share goals.* A group, as a unit, seeks to achieve some specific objectives or goals. In order to achieve these goals the members of the group must interact and must derive some needs satisfaction from the interaction processes, as well as from the goal achievement itself.

Groups differ from one another in ways that are describable in terms of specific characteristics, such as size, homogeneity, flexibility, and stability. These characteristics were called "group dimensions" by John Hemphill.[7] Not all characteristics of a group are associated with leadership in the group (for example, size of the group). Hemphill pointed out, however, that leadership is closely related to (1) the cohesiveness that group members feel and (2) the feeling of satisfaction that individuals receive from being members of the group. Thus, the sense of unity and pride that is so often observed in seemingly effective groups (and often called *morale*) is closely linked to the leadership present.

Leader. Initially, it may seem obvious that the leader of a group is the individual incumbent in an official position, such as principal or chairperson. In a highly structured organization with strong traditions supporting hierarchical authority—such as a school—it may appear that leadership is, in fact, synonymous with official position. However, the criticism of "poor leadership" has been so frequently leveled at school superintendents and principals that one must pause before accepting this view. Robert Starratt has argued that "the public...should be disabused of their expectations that everyone who occupies a principal's or superintendent's position will somehow be a great leader. They should be thankful enough that the people occupying these positions are competent administrators".[8]

The leader of a group may well be an official officeholder in the organization's hierarchy, or he or she also may be unofficial. A strong element in identifying the leader of a group is the nature of the power that is exercised: a leader is voluntarily granted considerable power by the members of the group, and they accept his or her influence and direction by shared agreement (no matter how informally the agreement is arrived at). This is quite different from vested authority (which is the legitimate right to command). Vested authority rests upon legal power that is customarily granted to official positions in the hierarchy (such as dean, superintendent, or principal). These two are not necessarily mutually exclusive: a university dean, for example, may have considerable legal "clout" in making decisions regarding reappointment and tenure, and yet, at the same time, have strong support as a leader by the faculty. But it is important to distinguish between administrative authority and the power of a leader.

Although an important source of power for the leader is the group, the leader has influence on the group itself. One influence is on the way the group functions internally: that is, how people interact, communicate, conduct their business, and—in general—function as an interdependent group. A second influence is on the performance of the group in achieving its purposes. A leader, then (whether or not he or she is an official of the formal organization), is a member of the group who helps it to develop ways of interacting that facilitate achieving the goals that the individuals share.[9]

These concepts are central to many modern definitions of leadership. For example, James MacGregor Burns points out that:

> Some define leadership as leaders making followers do what followers would not otherwise do, or as leaders making followers do what the leaders want them to do; I define leadership as leaders inducing followers to act for certain goals that represent the values and the motivations—the wants and needs, the aspirations and expectations—*of both leaders and followers*....Leadership, unlike naked power wielding, is thus inseparable from the followers' needs and goals. The essence of the leader-follower relation is the interaction of persons with different levels of motives and of power potential, including skill, in pursuit of a common or at least joint purpose.[10]

Finally, it should be emphasized that most groups have more than a single leader. Although it is common in schools and other educative organizations to speak as though the administrator in charge were the leader, and the only leader, the fact is that a number of individuals may act as leaders at different times. Contemporary views of leadership tend to focus less upon the behavior of the officially designated head of the group and more upon the behavior of any individuals in the group who engage in leader behavior. In this sense, *leadership* is a term that refers to the exercise of leader behavior in the group rather than to any sets of traits or personal attributes of individuals who may happen to be incumbent in official positions of authority.

Leader behavior. The remainder of this chapter will focus on theories of leadership that concentrate on describing and analyzing *leader behavior.* The focus, then, is not on what leaders are like (that is, what traits or characteristics they possess) or on the broad general concept called leadership, but on what leaders *do* to help groups (1) develop appropriate internal arrangements for productive interaction and (2) accomplish their tasks.

TWO-DIMENSIONAL LEADERSHIP THEORY

Leadership may be viewed as a process through which others are influenced to achieve goals in a specific situation. Thus, the important elements of leadership are (1) the behavior of the leader, (2) the behavior of the followers, and (3) the environment of the situation.

Although a wide range of possible leader behaviors exist, for the purpose of simplifying the discussion, the choice can be thought of in polarized terms:

1. The leader can decide what to do and tell followers how to do it, or
2. The leader can permit followers to operate freely within limits dictated by things over which he or she has no control.

Obviously, the authoritarian leader (the one who decides and tells) has a Theory X orientation toward followers, whereas the participative leader (the one who permits followers to operate freely) holds a Theory Y point of view. Oversimplified, these two leadership styles can be differentiated as being either *task-oriented* or *people-oriented.* Figure 6–1 gives some indication of the range of leadership styles that lie between these polar positions.

Leadership style evidenced by a specific leader is a combination of task-oriented behavior and people-oriented behavior. Some leaders are very task-oriented, whereas others are much more concerned about human relationships. Most leaders show a balance of behavior somewhere in between. These *two dimensions of leadership* have been identified, time and time again, in research on leader behavior. According to Dorwin Cartwright and Alvin Zander, *one dimension is concerned with the achievement of some specific group goal, and the other is concerned with the maintenance or strengthening of the group itself.*[11] Daniel Katz referred to the dimensions of leadership as *employee-orientation* and *production-orientation.*[12] Rensis Likert used the term *employee-centered* to describe the attention given to the human aspects of group members, and the term

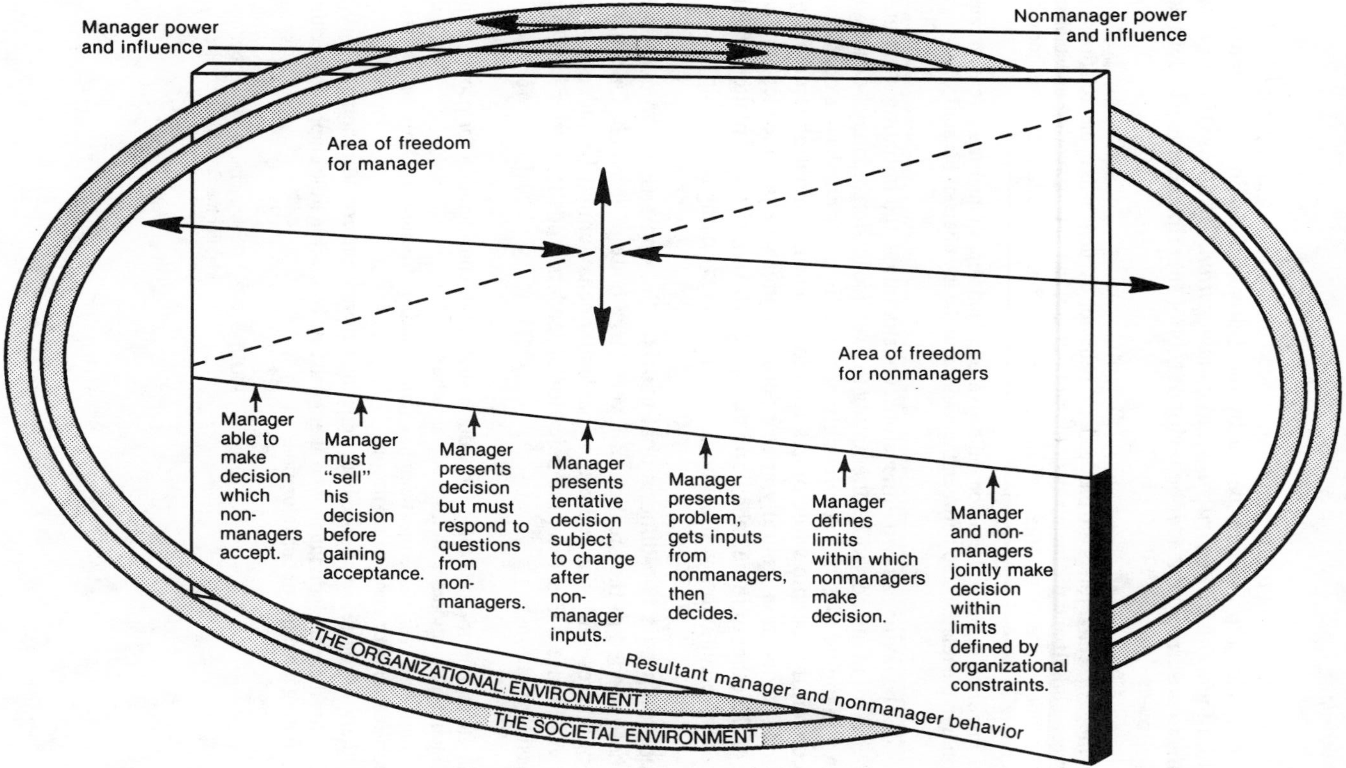
Manager power and influence
Nonmanager power and influence
Area of freedom for manager
Area of freedom for nonmanagers
Manager able to make decision which non-managers accept.
Manager must "sell" his decision before gaining acceptance.
Manager presents decision but must respond to questions from non-managers.
Manager presents tentative decision subject to change after non-manager inputs.
Manager presents problem, gets inputs from nonmanagers, then decides.
Manager defines limits within which nonmanagers make decision.
Manager and non-managers jointly make decision within limits defined by organizational constraints.
Resultant manager and nonmanager behavior
THE ORGANIZATIONAL ENVIRONMENT
THE SOCIETAL ENVIRONMENT

FIGURE 6–1. Leadership style is evident in a range of possible behaviors. From Robert Tannenbaum and Warren H. Schmidt, "How to Choose a Leadership Pattern," *Harvard Business Review*, 51 (May–June 1973), p. 167. Copyright © 1973 by the President and Fellows of Harvard College; all rights reserved.

job-centered in referring to the emphasis placed on achieving group goals.[13] The Ohio State Leadership Studies, begun by the Bureau of Business Research in 1945, called them *initiating structure* and *consideration*.[14] Andrew Halpin used these terms to describe the leader behavior of school superintendents. He defined them as follows:

1. *Initiating structure* refers to the leader's behavior in delineating the relationship between himself and the members of his work group, and in endeavoring to establish well-defined patterns of organization, channels of communication, and methods of procedure.
2. *Consideration* refers to behavior indicative of friendship, mutual trust, respect, and warmth in the relationship between the leader and the members of his staff.[15]

If leader behavior has two dimensions, consideration and initiating structure, then the behavior of an individual attempting to exercise leadership may be thought of as shown in Figure 6–2. Not surprisingly, some individuals emphasize consideration or concern for people while others tend to emphasize initiating structure or production. The question naturally arises: does it matter whether a leader emphasizes one or the other of these behavioral dimensions? And, if it does matter, which mix of these two behaviors will be more effective in exercising leadership?

Leadership as a two-dimensional matrix.   Seeking answers to questions such as these has led to the creation of a very large body of research. One major outcome of that research was realization that leader behavior may be understood as a matrix. As Figure 6–3 shows, the behavior of leaders tends to cluster into four major possible patterns:

- In attempting to lead, some individuals show high consideration for people while placing little emphasis on initiating structure.
- Others, however, place great emphasis on initiating structure and little emphasis on consideration or concern for people.
- Others, of course, emphasize both initiating structure and consideration.
- Finally, there are individuals who attempt to lead by placing little emphasis on either initiating structure or consideration.

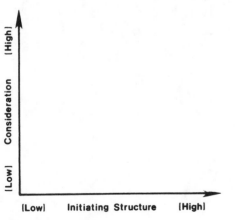

FIGURE 6–2. Dimensions of leader behavior (after the Ohio State studies).

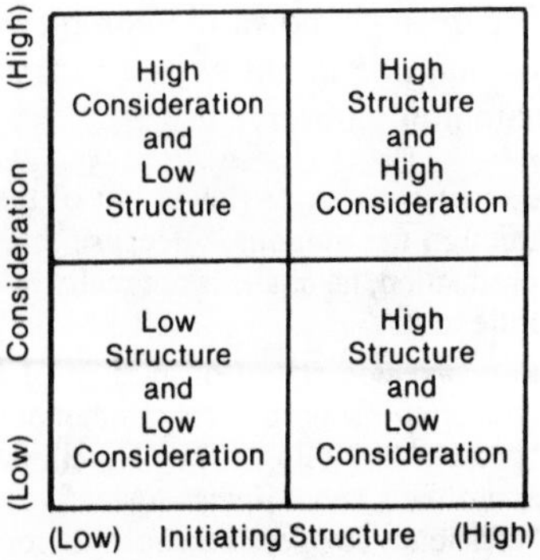

	High Consideration and Low Structure	High Structure and High Consideration
(Low) ← Consideration → (High)	Low Structure and Low Consideration	High Structure and Low Consideration

FIGURE 6–3. The Ohio State Leadership Quadrants.   (Low)   Initiating Structure   (High)

This knowledge, which arises from numerous studies of leadership, raises some interesting questions. Does it matter? Are any of these patterns of leader behavior more effective than the others? The answer, according to extensive research such as the Ohio State Leadership studies, seems to be, yes, it does matter. This view is strongly supported by the research of Robert Blake and Jane Srygley Mouton who developed the Managerial Grid.®

The managerial grid.®   The Managerial Grid®, developed by Robert Blake and Jane Mouton,[16] has been widely popular in clarifying the dynamics of the dimensions of organizational leadership. Its use is helpful in identifying the alternatives available to an administrator for improving effectiveness as a leader. It is sometimes used as the basis for self-diagnosis by those participating in leadership training.

The grid has two axes: one indicates *concern for people* and the other *concern for production* (Figure 6–4). For the administrator, these two concerns do not remain isolated but interact with one another as he or she works with others. This interaction of concern for people, on the one hand, and concern for production (for example, achievement of the organization's goals), on the other hand, very much influences the leader's thinking, feelings, and actions—whether he or she is aware of it or not—in the course of attempting to lead.

FIGURE 6–4. The two axes of the Managerial Grid represent the interaction of two concerns of the leader.

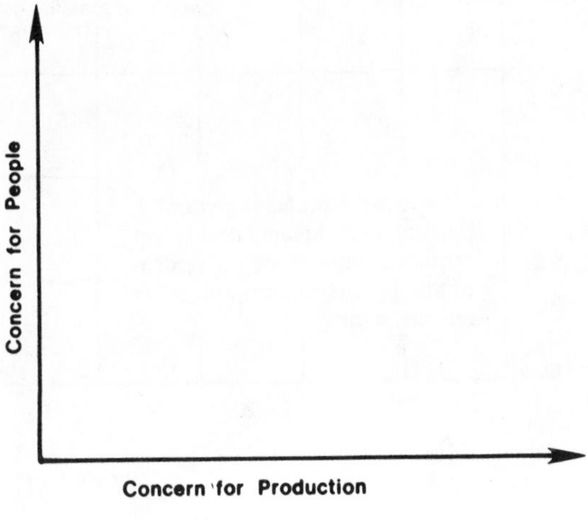

Concern for People

Concern for Production

Figure 6–5 shows the complete Managerial Grid. Of the array of possible patterns that one might expect to find administrators using, five stand out as the most commonly observed:

> *1, 1 oriented style* (lower left of the grid) is that of the administrator who is "going through the motions." Because this individual has little concern for either people or production, he or she is not really involved in the organization's affairs and contributes little to it.

> *9, 1 oriented style* (lower right of the grid) depicts the administrator with (a) little concern for subordinates or other people in the organization but (b) intense concern for "getting things done." In all likelihood, this administrator "knows" what has to be done and directs subordinates toward goals that he or she has set. In such an organization, "efficiency in operations results from arranging conditions of work in such a way that human elements interfere to a minimum degree."[17]

FIGURE 6–5.   The Managerial Grid figure. From the Managerial Grid III: The Key to Leadership Excellence Robert R. Blake and Jane Srygley Mouton, Houston,: Gulf Publishing Company, Copyright © 1985, p. 12. Reproduced by permission.

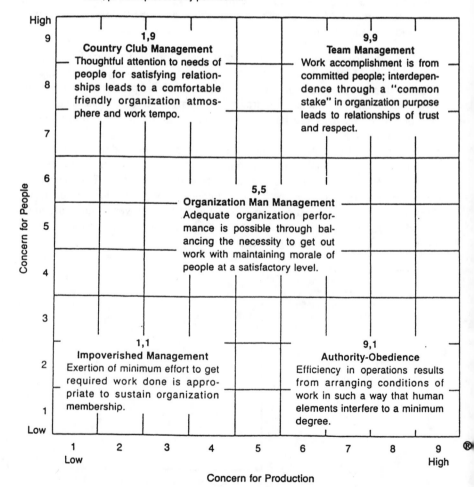

5, 5 oriented style is that of the person (a) moderately concerned with production and (b) also somewhat concerned with maintaining a reasonable level of morale. By sticking to the middle of the road such an individual helps to keep the organization stable; thus "adequate organization performance is possible through balancing the necessity to get work out with maintaining morale of people at a satisfactory level."[18]

1, 9 oriented style (upper left of the grid) is that of a leader who probably believes that a happy group will be productive. Therefore, this leader is little concerned with production directly and devotes much attention to maintaining satisfying relationships in the group. In this situation, "thoughtful attention to needs of people for satisfying relationships leads to comfortable friendly organization atmosphere and work tempo.[19]

9, 9 oriented style (upper right) strongly reflects Douglas McGregor's Theory Y orientation: people can be highly involved and enjoy their work, and the demands of production can coincide nicely with the needs that people have for satisfaction and recognition from their work. "Work accomplishment is from committed people; interdependence through a 'common stake' in organization purpose leads to relationships of trust and respect."[20]

Blake and Mouton have made it clear that, in their view, the 9, 9 pattern of leadership is likely to yield optimum results in most organizations. "Results" mean the effectiveness of the organization in (1) achieving its goals and (2) maintaining a high level of morale. Goal achievement might be measured by such indicators as test scores, rate of dropouts, percent of graduates going on to further education, employee-management relations, community support for bond issues, and feedback from employers on the performance of graduates. Morale may be indicated by such things as absenteeism, number of grievances, employee-management relations, and cohesiveness of the group.

Rensis Likert's large-scale research firmly supports a similar view. After numerous studies carried out over a span of thirty years and involving more than 220,000 managers and employees in industrial organizations, Likert concluded that participative patterns of leadership can achieve higher performance (as much as 20 to 40 percent higher) than the average business operation. The causal variables (that is, things that leaders can modify) are described by Likert as (1) organizational climate, (2) supervisory leadership, and (3) structure of the organization. These shape the internal state of the organization: such factors as "the loyalties, attitudes, and motivations of all members and their collective capacity for effective interaction, lateral communication, sharing of influence, and decision making.[21] The causal variables determine the quality or state of these intervening variables, and these, in the end, determine the results that the school achieves (for example, dropout rate, educational achievement levels, teacher satisfaction, absence rate, cost-benefit relationship). Substantial early data strongly suggest that the relationship between leadership style and organizational effectiveness holds for schools as well as for nonschool organizations.

This view, strongly supported by extensive research, calls for two comments at this point:

1. In attempting to decide which style of leader behavior is best, it is insufficient to use a philosophical criterion (for example, one "ought" to be a participative leader). The significant criterion is *effectiveness:* what leader behavior will produce the best results in terms of the overall performance of the organization (for example, the achievement of the organization's goals or performance of its tasks).

2. If one leadership style is most effective (that is, a highly participative or team style), how does that square with contingency theory, which posits that there is no one best way of leading but that effectiveness depends upon using a leadership style appropriate to the contingencies in a specific situation? The point here is that research shows that effective organizations are characterized by having participative team leadership and that less effective organizations are not. But moving an organization from a state of low effectiveness to a state of higher performance cannot be achieved instantly: it requires the skillful use of intermediate (often highly task-oriented) leader behavior to develop the working group to the point at which participative methods will succeed. A significant contingency that leaders must contend with is the readiness and ability of the members of the group to function well under participative leadership conditions. In short, the *goal* is to develop a highly effective organization, and that will be characterized by an appropriately participative, team-leadership style. But to arrive at that desirable organizational state may require the use of less participative leadership methods at various stages of the organization's development.

CONTINGENCY THEORIES OF LEADERSHIP

Generally accepted, contemporary efforts to describe and understand leadership share four assumptions:

1. Leadership is describable in terms of styles of behavior that leaders use in relating to groups.
2. A key issue is the extent to which leader behavior should be directive (authoritarian), on the one hand, or participative (democratic), on the other hand (see Figure 6–1).
3. There is no one universal, best way to exercise leadership under all conditions; it is necessary, therefore, to use some system for assessing the situational contingencies in selecting a style of leader behavior.
4. In choosing a leadership style (for example, to be directive or participative), the appropriate criterion is effectiveness (for example, which style produces the greatest organizational effectiveness?).

The issue of effectiveness versus success.[22] The term "leadership" connotes patterns of interpersonal behavior that help a group to achieve its needs. Remember that every task-oriented group has two fundamental needs: (1) to achieve its goals (for example, to accomplish its tasks or mission) and (2) to maintain itself. Leaders, then, interact with groups in ways intended to elicit behaviors from group members that contribute to these group needs.

Attempted leadership refers to actions by the leader that are intended to elicit such behaviors. Attempted leadership may or may not be *successful:* that is, it may or may not elicit the behaviors from followers that were intended.

When one attempts to lead and the intended behaviors are in fact elicited from members of the group, we speak of successful leadership. However, although successful leadership may produce the intended behaviors in the group, it does not necessarily follow that they actually help the group either to achieve its tasks or to strengthen itself as a group. One could, for example, try to improve the effectiveness of a group by emphasizing orderly standard operating procedures. A leader who was able to get these procedures developed and installed so that people implemented them, could be described as *successful.* If, however, the processes of establishing the new procedures produced a great deal of dissatisfaction among members of the group and—in the end—the organization did not seem to be any more effective in achieving its goals, then the leadership could hardly be termed *effective*.

The concept of effectiveness in leadership has much to do with the motivation of followers. If a school principal, by acting in a manner that he or she considers to be forceful and dynamic, can get teachers to perform in ways that conform to the principal's expectations—but does so at the expense of arousing resentment within the teachers—then the leadership is, at best, only partially effective, inasmuch as the maintenance needs of the group are weakened. Such a leader is operating from position power alone, and is foregoing the development of power conferred by the followers. Effective leadership is marked by followers being *motivated* to do what the leader indicates. Although successful leaders can undoubtedly move people, effective leaders motivate people to *want* to move in the desired ways because they find it rewarding and satisfying to do so.

Success in leadership, then, refers to the way in which followers behave. Effectiveness refers to the internal motivational state of followers. Those who emphasize success in leadership tend to emphasize the official power of their position in the organization and feel that it is important to supervise closely to be sure that things are done as they should be. Such leaders emphasize control and feel the need to be everywhere at once, either personally or in the form of some supervisory or reporting system. On the other hand, effective leaders tend to combine the authority of position with the power conferred by the group—which is evoked by leaders who identify with the followers' needs and expectations—and typically use more general supervisory methods that tend to be focused on results rather than activities. The terms "successful" and "effective" have important meanings in the study of leadership.

Four contingency theories of leadership that are frequently mentioned in the literature of educational administration will be described below. Each of these initially assumes the two dimensions of leader behavior that have been discussed thus far.

FIEDLER'S CONTINGENCY THEORY OF LEADERSHIP

In discussing leader behavior, Fred Fiedler comments:

> Leaders affect group performance by means of verbal or gestural behavior which communicates the leader's directions, evaluations, and attitudes to the group members. Many recent leadership theories have therefore attempted to relate leader behavior directly to group performance. They have tried to show that certain types of behavior are conducive and others are detrimental to effective group performance, on the assumption that this will then permit us to teach leaders how to behave in a way that will ensure effective group performance.
>
> These theories have held, for example, that considerate (human relations-oriented) leader behavior is found in effective groups, that effective leaders invite member participation in the planning and decision-making process....[23]

Antithetically, other theories have held that effective leaders need to use highly structured and directive behavior in their relationships with the group. However,

Fiedler points out that reviews of the research literature have shown that neither the considerate leader nor the structuring leader is consistently more effective and that participative management has been effective in some situations but not in others.[24]

Further, Fiedler reminds us that it is commonplace for individuals to hold certain views about leadership as a general, abstract concept, whereas they do not always behave in conformity with those concepts in "real-world" situations. He illustrates this by reporting research in which he

> ...asked seasoned school administrators to indicate how they thought they ought to handle a variety of personnel matters. They could be very considerate by showing only disapproval or trying to persuade, or they could be more directive by making new rules or disciplining the offending individual. We then assigned these same school administrators to leadership positions in small experimentally assembled groups and obtained behavior observations from group members and observers. Thus, the same individuals were asked how they should behave and were then observed in two different situations to determine how they actually behaved.
>
> The results of this study indicated that the behavior of these experienced administrators varied considerably more with the characteristics of the situation than with either the way they felt they should behave or the way they expressly intended to behave.
>
> Thus, while there were some who said that they would only show disapproval as a means for dealing with a variety of personnel problems—a very considerate leader behavior—they were in fact seen as quite inconsiderate by their group members and by the observer. Those who said they would actively discipline were rated quite considerate in one condition, but as inconsiderate in another condition. Since we must assume that people really intend to behave as they say they do, it appears that the situation must play a substantial role in shaping behavior, while the intent to behave in a certain way plays a lesser part.[25]

Fiedler thus takes us back to a basic concept of the forces that shape and mold *all* behavior, and that is, of course, the classic view that behavior (including the behavior of leaders) arises from an interaction between personality (needs, motives, drives) and the situation (environment). His research, therefore, depends upon (1) an assessment of the leader's motivational structure (for example, what goals are most important to him or her?) and (2) an assessment of how favorable the situation is to achieving those goals.

Least preferred co-worker scale.   To measure the leader's motivation, Fiedler developed the Least Preferred Co-worker (LPC) Scale (Figure 6–6). As the directions on the scale itself indicate, it asks a person to describe certain attributes of the one individual with whom he or she has been able to work least well in getting a job done. As Fiedler puts it:

> An individual who describes his or her least preferred co-worker in very negative and rejecting terms (a low LPC) in effect shows a strong emotional reaction to people with whom he or she cannot work—in effect, "If I can't work with you, you are no damn good!" This is the typical pattern of a person who, when forced to make a choice, opts first for getting on with the task and worries about his interpersonal relations later. Someone who describes even his least preferred co-worker in relatively more positive terms in effect looks at the individual not only as a co-worker but also as a person who might otherwise have some acceptable, if not admirable, traits. The "high LPC" leader sees close interpersonal relations as a requirement for task accomplishment.[26]

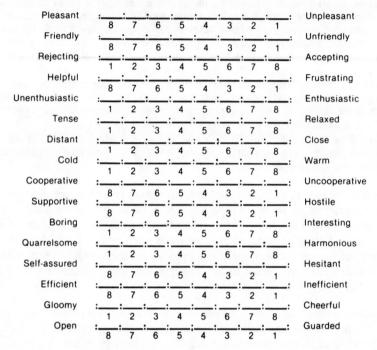

LEAST PREFERRED CO-WORKER SCALE

Think of the person with whom you can work least well. He may be someone you work with now, or someone you knew in the past. He does not have to be the person you like least well, but should be the person with whom you had the most difficulty in getting a job done. Describe this person as he appears to you.

FIGURE 6–6. Least Preferred Co-worker Scale. From Fred E. Fiedler, *A Theory of Leadership Effectiveness* (New York: McGraw-Hill Book Company, 1967), p. 41.

Many individuals are neither high LPC nor low LPC people but fall somewhere nearer the center of the LPC scale. Fiedler describes the intermediate LPC leader as being:

> …cognitively more complex, less authoritarian or acquiescent, less concerned with socially desirable responses, and more critical and task-oriented than either the high or low LPC person. He seems also to be somewhat more concerned with personal competence and somewhat less concerned with personal warmth and industriousness in the selection of his work partners, hence less interested in team work.[27]

Thus, LPC appears to give an indication of the complexity of the thinking of individuals, as well as an indication of the personal goals that motivate them to lead.[28]

Assessing contingencies in the situation. The other element in Fiedler's contingency model of leadership is the critical factors in the situation in which leadership is attempted. Since some leaders seem to be able to perform in one situation and some perform best in another, Fiedler's research specifically sought to classify different situations in terms of *favorableness to the leader.* The extent to which a situation may be classified as favorable or unfavorable to the leader (that is, *situational favorableness*) is seen as related to three key factors:

1. *The quality of relations between leader and followers.* When relations are good (for example, leader is trusted, respected, liked), the leader finds it easier to exercise influence and authority than if relations are not good (for example, leader is disliked and mistrusted). Fiedler has said that "research has shown that this is by far the most important single dimension"[29] in assessing the favorableness of a situation to a leader.

2. *The degree to which the task is well structured.* In some cases, the goals are specific, the steps in the task are clear-cut, and the proper way to proceed is a matter of technical knowledge. In many cases, however, the tasks are ambiguous, one may not be sure how to organize the work, and proper procedure is problematical. In schools, for example, there is the difference between organizing an emergency evacuation plan for the building and improving discipline in the school.

3. *Power of the leader's position.* This refers to the extent to which the leader is vested with such prerogatives as the right to hire, fire, give or withhold pay increases, promote, reassign, and punish or reprimand.

These three factors of "situational favorableness" can be arranged in eight possible combinations, as shown in Figure 6–7, and, for the sake of simplicity, can be regrouped into "very favorable," "intermediate in favorableness," and "unfavorable" categories. Extensive research supports the contention that Fiedler's method of assessing the favorableness of the situation to the leader is useful in suggesting the leadership style most likely to be effective in various situations. This is summarized in Figure 6–8.

Effective leadership style.   As Figure 6–8 shows, both a favorable situation and an unfavorable one generally call for a task-oriented (directive, low LPC) leader. The logic of this generalization becomes clearer if we follow a couple of situations. For example, when the leader enjoys good relations with the group, possesses strong position power, and the task is well-structured, the leader using a participative style runs the risk of weakening his or her position. After all, he or she already has the trust and support of the group, as well as the power to do what is necessary, and the task is clear-cut. The followers are likely to expect the leader to act without needless ado and to get the job done. On the other extreme, though— when the situation is highly unfavorable to the leader—a task orientation is also required. With his or her power already weak, little support from the group, and an ill-structured task at hand, only directive, task-oriented behavior seems likely to get

FIGURE 6–7. Categories of "Situational favorableness" in Fiedler's model of leadership. Based on Fred E. Fiedler, *A Theory of Leadership Effectiveness* (New York: McGraw-Hill Book Company, 1967), p. 146.

	Very Favorable			Intermediate in Favorableness			Unfavorable	
	1	2	3	4	5	6	7	8
Leader-member relations	Good	Good	Good	Good	Poor	Poor	Poor	Poor
Task structure	High	High	Low	Low	High	High	Low	Low
Position power	Strong	Weak	Strong	Weak	Strong	Weak	Strong	Weak

CONTINGENCIES IN THE SITUATION | FAVORABLENESS ⟶ | MOST EFFECTIVE LEADER STYLE

	POSITION POWER OF LEADER A	RELATIVE STRUCTURE OF TASK B	LEADER-MEMBER RELATIONS C	FAVORABLENESS OF SITUATION TO LEADER	EFFECTIVE LEADER STYLE
1.	STRONG	STRUCTURED	GOOD	FAVORABLE	TASK ORIENTED (low LPC score)
2.	WEAK	STRUCTURED	GOOD	FAVORABLE	TASK ORIENTED (low LPC score)
3.	STRONG	UNSTRUCTURED	GOOD	FAVORABLE	TASK ORIENTED (low LPC score)
4.	WEAK	UNSTRUCTURED	GOOD	FAVORABLE	RELATIONS ORIENTED (high LPC score)
5.	STRONG	STRUCTURED	POOR	INTERMEDIATE	RELATIONS ORIENTED (high LPC score)
6.	WEAK	STRUCTURED	POOR	INTERMEDIATE	RELATIONS ORIENTED (high LPC score)
7.	STRONG	UNSTRUCTURED	POOR	INTERMEDIATE	RELATIONS ORIENTED (high LPC score)
8.	WEAK	UNSTRUCTURED	POOR	UNFAVORABLE	TASK ORIENTED (low LPC score)

FIGURE 6-8. Fiedler's contingency model uses an analysis of situational variables to suggest which leader style is likely to be most effective.

the group moving and—if successful—likely to lay the groundwork for better relations with the group. But in moderately favorable circumstances, especially when good relationships with the group will strengthen the leader's effectiveness, the relationships-oriented style is indicated. A situation commonly encountered in elementary schools is shown in line 4 of Figure 6–8. Possessing weak official position power, yet maintaining good relations with the teachers in the school, and confronted with an array of ill-structured problems (for example, how do we improve pupil performance on the math achievement tests?), the effective principal tends to nurture and strengthen his or her strongest leadership asset—the support of the teachers and parents—by using a relationship-oriented style.

Fiedler tells us:

> Leadership performance depends then as much upon the organization as it depends upon the leader's own attributes. Except perhaps for the unusual case, it is simply not meaningful to speak of an effective leader or an ineffective leader; we can only speak of a leader who tends to be effective in one situation and ineffective in another. If we wish to increase organizational and group effectiveness we must learn not only how to train leaders more effectively but also how to build an organizational environment in which the leader can perform well.[30]

Leadership training. Because the LPC measures certain aspects of the motivational structure of individuals that are, like other personality characteristics, stable and difficult to change through training, Fiedler thinks that leadership training must be given a fresh look. The goal of training would not be to change the basic LPC orientation of individuals but, rather, to provide them with the skills that enable them to increase the favorableness of situations in terms of their leadership style. Such programs should teach (1) ways of getting along better with subordinates, (2) ways of handling administrative routines more effectively, (3) technical knowledge needed for decision making, and—not least important—(4) how to assess the favorableness of various situations.[31] The intent of such training would be to supplement experience as an important factor in helping the leader to control the favorableness of situations in terms of his or her own style. For example, a low LPC (that is, high task-oriented) principal could be taught to see that his or her "natural," highly directive leadership style is unlikely to be productive in situations in which position power is weak and the task is ill-structured. One possibility for being more effective might be to shift to a more participative style to deal with these contingencies, but Fiedler's model would suggest, instead, seeking ways of either increasing position power or restructuring the task so as to make the situation more favorable to the low LPC style of leadership. High LPC principals might need to learn that when the situation is unfavorable to their style, they must change the situation in favor of their style. In the situation in which (1) leader-member relations are poor, (2) the task is unstructured, and (3) the position power of the principal is weak, the considerate, permissive person might find that asking too many questions about what to do is likely to lead to no decision at all and, consequently, to poor performance by the group. This may be a time to restructure the task into highly structured segments that can be achieved relatively easily and, at the same time, to seek increased position power from the organization; achievement of these changes would shift the situation in favor of the principal's participative team style.

Research on Fiedler's model in public schools.   Efforts to test the applicability of Fiedler's model to public schools tend to encounter the traditional difficulty of assessing the effectiveness of schools. In one study of Canadian elementary schools, the criterion was the ratings of school performance by superintendents and their staffs.[32] A study of Canadian high schools used achievement test results,[33] while another study of Canadian high schools by Parnell Garland and Robert O'Reilly—perhaps, to date, the best research using the Fiedler model in schools—related LPC of principals to the organizational climate in the schools.[34] The rationale for the latter approach is based largely on the belief that school staffs do not directly cause achievement but that their responsibility is to develop environments in which high levels of learning and student development may occur.

But the researchers reporting various studies in which Fiedler's model is tested in schools are also in disagreement as to (1) the position power of principals and (2) the degree of structure in the tasks that confront principals and teachers. Fiedler reasons that the principal, by virtue of his or her official position in the school district, has high position power and that—since curriculum is decided upon outside the school—the tasks are highly structured. It follows then, in his view, that (for the experienced principal, at least) the situation is one of very favorable leadership and calls for task motivation. Vincent McNamara, however, found that the position power of principals is high and that the tasks confronting school staffs are unstructured,[35] suggesting that a relations-oriented leadership style would be most effective. Parnell Garland's and Robert O'Reilly's assessment was similar to that of McNamara's: that the empirical evidence and the judgments of school people support the view that principals have high position power but that the tasks confronting schools are characteristically ill-structured. This has held true in the past. However, with the advent of collective bargaining by organized teachers, as well as a host of laws and court decisions concerning constitutional rights and fairness doctrine, it is believed by many that there was a sharp reduction in the position power of school principals during the decade of the 1970s.

Although those inexperienced in managing schools may believe that the challenge to leadership in them arises largely in providing the routine, ongoing programs of instruction, the fact is that such questions as "How do we offer instruction in the least restrictive environment for every child?" "How do we reduce alcohol abuse, crime, and vandalism among students?" and "How do we develop and maintain public support for the school budget?" are more typical of the kinds of issues on which the effectiveness of principals and school staffs are often judged in America. It is my view, therefore, that, contrary to Fiedler's perception, the tasks for which American school principals must provide leadership are frequently ill-structured and that the critical tasks are nearly always ill-structured. This phenomenon appears to be increasing over time.

VROOM'S AND YETTON'S NORMATIVE CONTINGENCY THEORY

Victor Vroom's and Philip Yetton's contingency model points up with remarkable clarity that the central issue in contemporary leadership is participation in the process of making decisions. The issue is often confused by value-laden arguments over the relative merits of hard-nosed, directive administrative style, as contrasted with a more consultative style. Even the eminent Peter Drucker lapses occasionally into contrasting "democratic management," "participatory democracy," and "permissiveness" with the supposed successes of autocratic, tyrannical management that makes decisions by fiat.[36] Clearly, the complexities of modern organizations require—as Fiedler has suggested—decision-making processes carefully selected with an eye to the probability of effectiveness in view of the contingencies in the situation. There may be situations in which an autocratic style is most effective and other situations that call for highly participatory methods for greatest effectiveness. The problem for the leader is to analyze the contingencies in each situation and then behave in the most effective manner.

Whereas Fiedler's model of leadership suggests the appropriateness of different leadership styles in the context of various situational contingencies, Vroom and Yetton go further and try to specify how leaders "ought" to behave in order to be effective in view of specific contingencies. The Vroom and Yetton model is not prescriptive, as Blake's and Mouton's is (that is, team-leadership style is most effective), but it can be described as a normative model because it tries to tie appropriate leader behavior to specific contingencies.[37]

Five leadership styles. Vroom and Yetton have developed a taxonomy of five leadership styles, as follows:

AUTOCRATIC PROCESS

AI. Leader (manager, administrator) makes the decision using whatever information is available.
AII. Leader secures necessary information from members of the group, then makes the decision. In obtaining the information, the leader may or may not tell followers what the problem is.

CONSULTATIVE PROCESS

CI. Leader shares the problem with relevant members of the group on a one-to-one basis, getting their ideas and suggestions individually without bringing them together as a group; then the leader makes the decision.
CII. Leader shares the problem with members as a group at a meeting, then decides.

GROUP PROCESS

GII. Leader, acting as chairperson at a meeting of the group, shares the problem with the group and facilitates efforts of the group to reach consensus on a group decision. Leader may give information and express opinion but does not try to "sell" a particular decision or manipulate the group through covert means.

Notice that Vroom and Yetton have described these leadership styles in behavioral terms (for example, "leader decides" or "leader shares the problem with the group") rather than in general terms (for example, "directive style" or "participative style"). There is no implied judgment that one style is more highly valued than others; that issue must be addressed in terms of which behavior "works" in the specific situation.

Seven situation issues. Analysis of the situation begins with "yes" or "no" answers to the following questions:

A. *Does the problem possess a quality requirement?* One quality might be time: is this a decision that must be made now, with no time to consult others? Other quality factors might be the desirability of stimulating team development or keeping people informed through participation.

B. *Does the leader have sufficient information to make a good decision?*

C. *Is the problem structured?*

D. *Is it necessary for others to accept the decision in order for it to be implemented?*

E. *If the leader makes the decision alone, how certain is it that others will accept it?*

F. *Do others share the organizational goals that will be attained by solving this problem?*

G. *Are the preferred solutions to the problem likely to create conflict among others in the group?*

Decision-process flowchart. The leader can quickly diagnose the situation contingencies by answering yes or no to each of these seven questions as they are arrayed on the decision-process flowchart (Figure 6–9). As the flowchart shows, it is possible to identify fourteen types of problems in this way, and the preferred way of dealing with each becomes evident as one follows the chart from left to right.

Given a problem, the first question is, "Does the problem possess a quality requirement?" In effect the question is "Is one decision preferable to or more rational than another?" If not, then questions B and C are irrelevant, and one follows the flowchart to question D, "Is acceptance of the decision by others important to implementing it?" If not, then it makes little difference as to which of the five leadership styles is utilized: AI, AII, CI, CII, or GII. However, the flowchart clearly suggests that there is a logical basis for utilizing various leadership styles for maximum effectiveness under specific, describable circumstances.

REDDIN'S 3-D THEORY OF LEADERSHIP

Earlier in this chapter, the two dimensions that have been used so widely in efforts to understand leadership (that is, relationships dimension and task dimension) were described. The person generally credited with adding the "effectiveness" dimension was William J. Reddin, who developed a "3-D Theory of Leadership" (see Figure 6–10).

The three dimensions of leadership. In analyzing leadership style, Reddin described task orientation (TO) as "the extent to which a manager is likely to direct his own and subordinates' efforts toward goal attainment" and relationship orientation (RO) as "the extent to which a manager is likely to have highly personal job relationships characterized by mutual trust, respect for subordinates' ideas and consideration of their feelings."[38] Effectiveness, Reddin argued, cannot be defined in such terms as the leader's behavior or activity but can be understood only in terms of the extent to which the manager achieves the goals for which his or her position is responsible. Like the other two dimensions of leadership, the effectiveness dimension of leadership is not "either-or" but, rather, is a continuous scale.

In a fashion similar to the Ohio State Leadership Studies and Blake's and Mouton's Managerial Grid, Reddin's 3-D model identifies four basic leadership

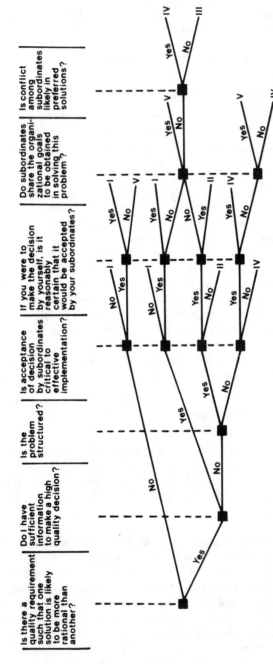

Is there a quality requirement such that one solution is likely to be more rational than another? | Do I have sufficient information to make a high quality decision? | Is the problem structured? | Is acceptance of decision by subordinates critical to effective implementation? | If you were to make the decision by yourself, is it reasonably certain that it would be accepted by your subordinates? | Do subordinates share the organizational goals to be obtained in solving this problem? | Is conflict among subordinates likely in preferred solutions?

I You solve the problem or make the decision yourself, using information available to you at the time. II You obtain the necessary information from your subordinate(s), then decide on the solution to the problem yourself. You may or may not tell your subordinates what the problem is in getting the information from them. The role played by your subordinates in making the decision is clearly one of providing the necessary information to you, rather that generating or evaluating alternative solutions. III You share the problem with relevant subordinates individually, getting their ideas and suggestions without bringing them together as a group. Then you make the decision that may or may not reflect your subordinates' influence. IV You share the problem with your subordinates as a group, collectively obtaining their ideas and suggestions. Then you make the decision that may or may not reflect your subordinates' influence. V You share a problem with your subordinates as a group. Together you generate and evaluate alternatives and attempt to reach agreement (consensus) on a solution. Your role is much like that of a chairperson. You do not try to influence the group to adopt "your" solution and you are willing to accept and implement any solution that has the support of the entire group.

FIGURE 6–9. Vroom-Yetton normative leadership model. From Fred Luthans, *Organizational Behavior*, 2nd ed. (New York: McGraw-Hill Book Company, 1977), p. 458.

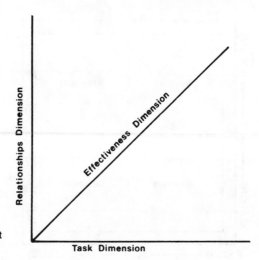

FIGURE 6–10. Three-dimensional concept of leadership.

styles: (1) low task and low relationships, (2) low task and high relationships, (3) high task and low relationships, and (4) high task and high relationships.

Situational factors. Reddin defined the situation in terms of five factors in addition to the leader's style: (1) the psychological climate in the organization (for example, "the way we do things around here"), (2) the technology used to do the work (for example, kind of work performed, the tools and equipment used), (3) relationships with superiors, (4) relationships with co-workers, and (5) relationships with subordinates. It is especially important to note the emphasis that Reddin gave to the profound influence of technology on organizational behavior. He makes the point that managing an assembly line is quite different from managing a laboratory, because the nature of the work in these two situations is different, as are the tools and processes. This is a crucial point to bear in mind when we seek to apply to schools those leadership concepts that have been developed in organizations that have notably different tasks and technology.

Leadership styles. Reddin identified four basic leadership styles, which are essentially the same as those identified by Blake and Mouton in the Managerial Grid. As shown in Figure 6–11, Reddin's "Separated" style corresponds to 1, 1 on the Managerial Grid; "Related" style corresponds to 1, 9 style; "Integrated" to 9, 9; and "Dedicated" to 9, 1.[39]

But Reddin went beyond the grid approach by building in the concept that different situations require different styles and that the effectiveness of a style depends upon the situation in which it is used (see Figure 6–12). The four effective and four ineffective styles of leadership have been nicely summarized by Fred Luthans as follows:

EFFECTIVE STYLES

1. *Executive.* This style gives a great deal of concern to both task (TO) and people (RO). A manager using this style is a good motivator, sets high standards, recognizes individual differences, and utilizes team management.

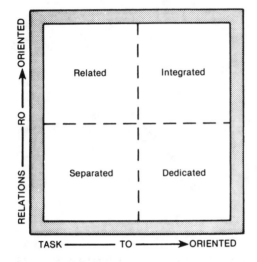

FIGURE 6–11. Basic leadership styles identified by Reddin. Adapted from William J. Reddin, *Managerial Effectiveness* (New York: McGraw-Hill Book Company, 1970), p. 27.

2. *Developer.* This style gives maximum concern to people (RO) and minimum concern to the task (TO). A manager using this style has implicit trust in people and is mainly concerned with developing them as individuals.

3. *Benevolent Autocrat.* This style gives maximum concern to the task (TO) and minimum concern to people (RO). A manager using this style knows exactly what he or she wants and how to get it without causing resentment.

4. *Bureaucrat.* This style gives minimum concern to both task (TO) and people (RO). A manager using this style is mainly interested in the rules and wants to maintain and control the situation by their use but is seen as conscientious.

FIGURE 6–12. Reddin's 3-D model of leadership effectiveness. From Fred Luthans, *Organizational Behavior* (New York: McGraw-Hill Book Company, 1977), p. 451.

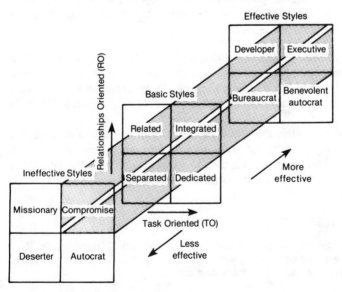

INEFFECTIVE STYLES

1. *Compromiser.* This style gives a great deal of concern to both task (TO) and people (RO) in a situation that requires only emphasis on one or neither. This style of manager is a poor decision maker; the pressures affect him or her too much.
2. *Missionary.* This style gives maximum concern to people (RO) and minimum concern to the task (TO) where such behavior is inappropriate. This manager is typically the "do gooder" who values harmony as an end in itself.
3. *Autocrat.* This styles gives maximum concern to the task (TO) and minimum concern to the people (RO) where such behavior is inappropriate. This manager has no confidence in others, is unpleasant, and is interested only in the immediate job.
4. *Deserter.* This style gives minimum concern to task (TO) and people (RO) in a situation where such behavior is inappropriate. This manager is uninvolved and passive.[40]

HERSEY'S AND BLANCHARD'S SITUATIONAL THEORY OF LEADERSHIP.

The Tri-Dimensional Leader Effectiveness Model of Leadership developed by Paul Hersey and Kenneth Blanchard is essentially similar to Reddin's model, with some relabeling of major components. Their Life Cycle Theory of Leadership (which they later renamed Situational Theory of Leadership), however, is helpful in emphasizing the importance of characteristics of subordinates in selecting a leadership style.

An important contribution of Hersey and Blanchard to understanding leadership is that the level of maturity of group members is a critical factor in the situation that determines the effectiveness of a leadership style. Maturity, as they use the term, does not refer to a general, overall characterization of individuals or groups. In the first place, maturity—as used here—is seen only in terms of a specific task to be performed. The question is not, "Is this group mature or immature?" but, rather, "In terms of what is to be done here, what is the maturity level of this group?"

Further, the leader has to assess not only the maturity of the group as a unit but also the maturity of individuals. Hersey and Blanchard illustrate this by pointing out that "a teacher may find that a class as a group may be at one level of maturity in a particular area, but a student within that group may be at a different level. When the teacher is working one-to-one with that student, he or she may have to behave quite differently from when working with the class as a group."[41] Thus, they point out, with the weak student whose work is characteristically disorganized, the teacher may structure tasks very carefully and supervise the student very closely. When working with a more able student who is insecure and shy, the teacher may use a more relationships-oriented style, emphasizing not only developing good interaction with the student but also helping the student to develop useful relationships with others in the group.[42]

As Hersey and Blanchard use the term, maturity in performing work-related tasks is composed of two interrelated factors:

1. *The skill and willingness to set high but realistic goals.* This factor was derived by Hersey and Blanchard from David McClelland's achievement motivation (see suggested reading in Chapter 5). People high in need for achievement (*n ach*) want to know how well they are succeeding in achieving their goals, while those low in *n ach* are more concerned with how well they are liked or accepted.

2. *The skill and willingness to take responsibility for the achievement of goals.* Skill, in this factor, includes possessing the technical knowledge and abilities necessary to do the work itself. Technical skill may well include the abilities to work productively with others in a group effort (for example, communicating effectively, dealing productively with conflict, developing trust).

Essentially, Situational Leadership Theory contends that (1) the maturity level of organizational participants can be increased over time and (2) as the maturity level of participants increases, the effective leadership style will be characterized by a reduction in task-oriented behavior and by an increase in relationships-oriented behavior.

The theory, depicted in Figure 6–13, is built upon the two-dimensional concept (that is, relationships-oriented behavior and task-oriented behavior), with the added dimension of the maturity level of followers. When the maturity level of followers is low (MI), the effective leadership style will emphasize task and place less emphasis on relationships (QI). At the lowest level of maturity, the followers have little capacity either to set goals or to take responsibility for their own work. The leader in this situation must set the goals (tell followers what to do and how to do it) and supervise the work closely.

But growth (increased maturity) is possible. The bell-shaped curve indicates that even within QI (high task–low relationship), there is a *range* of leader behavior; one can shift, for instance, from very low emphasis on relationships-oriented behavior to moderate emphasis. The shift of leadership behavior style from right to left (along the bell-shaped curve) would match any shift in the maturity level of followers, from low (immature) to high (mature), in order to be maximally effective.

Suppose, for example, a superintendent finds that a school principal is constantly late in sending in his or her reports and other paperwork, and, perhaps, it often must be sent back to be corrected. He or she might rate the maturity level of that principal quite low (Figure 6–14). To be effective, the superintendent would

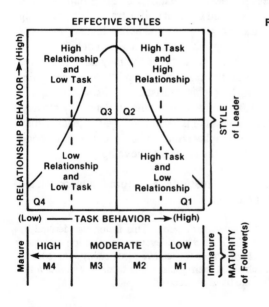

FIGURE 6–13. Situational Leadership Theory, showing that effective leadership styles are related to the maturity of followers. From Paul Hersey and Kenneth H. Blanchard, *Management of Organizational Behavior: Utilizing Human Resources* (Englewood Cliffs, NJ: Prentice-Hall, 1977), p. 167.

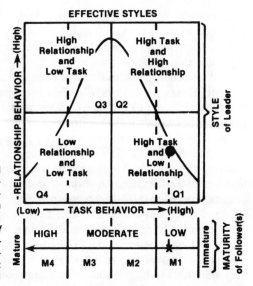

EFFECTIVE STYLES

FIGURE 6–14. Low maturity level of school principal requires highly directive behavior from superintendent of schools. From Paul Hersey and Kenneth H. Blanchard, *Management of Organizational Behavior: Utilizing Human Resources* (Englewood Cliffs, NJ: Prentice-Hall, 1977), p. 194.

tell the principal explicitly what he or she expects in terms of performance in filing reports next month and then would closely monitor the principal's work.[43] The superintendent's behavior in doing this need not be uncivil or threatening, but it should be highly directive and explicit. As the performance of the principal improves (reports in on time and properly done), the superintendent can shift a bit to a more relationships-oriented style but still emphasize the task, as shown in Figure 6–15. In essence, the superintendent—through appropriate leader behavior—is helping the principal to acquire the technical competence to do the work and, as soon as success permits, will shift to helping him or her to develop the motivation to work more independently. Through a steady developmental process over time, it

FIGURE 6–15. As school principal's skill and motivation (that is, maturity) improve, superintendent's behavior shifts to concern for relationships as well as to concern for task. Based on Paul Hersey and Kenneth H. Blanchard, *Management of Organizational Behavior: Utilizing Human Resources* (Englewood Cliffs, NJ: Prentice-Hall, 1977), p. 167.

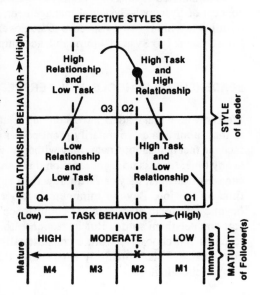

EFFECTIVE STYLES

is conceivable that the task of filing reports with the central office would be fully delegated to the school principal, with only a general monitoring of results (Q4). The superintendent would have very little interaction with the principal at that point, *regarding this particular task.*

A common problem that this theory illuminates is the immaturity enforced upon followers by leaders who feel the need constantly to direct others. The superintendent, for example, who does not train principals when they need it and who does not allow them opportunities to set their own goals and standards will, in all likelihood, never have high-maturity principals to lead.

On the other hand, it also illustrates the problem of the leader who thrusts responsibilities on followers who are not ready—either in terms of skill or motivation—to deal with them. An all-too-common example of this is the superintendent of a traditional school district who assembles the principals and other administrators in the district and announces that from now on they will be operating as an administrative team with everyone sharing and participating in decision making. But, with long experience in a well-structured, hierarchical way of operating, these administrators have only rudimentary skills in collaborative team behavior (besides, they want only to be left alone). As team meetings come and go, with little being done (except wrangling, political intrigue, and one-upmanship), the superintendent becomes alarmed and "takes charge" (engaging in more "telling" than "delegating"). In other words, the superintendent has attempted to shift from Style 1 leader behavior to Style 4, which will almost surely fail. When the leader reverts to Style 1, the followers are likely to perceive that the whole participative gambit was only a phony show. Hersey and Blanchard make it clear that development from Style 1 through Styles 2 and 3 and (perhaps), ultimately, to Style 4 must occur in an incremental sequence of steps over time. When the group flounders or experiences frustration, the effective leader reverts in style only far back enough to restart the group's learning and maturation process at its highest level.

Situational Leadership Theory is conceptually very close to Likert's earlier concept of System 1–System 4 management, which has been discussed. Much of its utility lies in suggesting specific strategies and tactics for moving an organization from System 1 to System 4 through leadership.

LEADERSHIP IN SCHOOLS: NEW PERSPECTIVES

We know now that leaders have a unique relationship with subordinates—unique, in that subordinates voluntarily grant power and authority to the leader. Leaders face the fact that subordinates may withdraw their support, their grant of authority, at any time; there is no legal sanction that can change this. Teachers can quit; they can seek transfers; they can withdraw their support by reducing their effort and/or time on the job. Beyond minimum legal or contractual requirements—that is, beyond minimum standards of "competence"—there is little that administrators can compel them to do. But in response to leadership to which they resonate, teachers can choose to work enthusiastically far beyond any minimal notion of competence. This is precisely what sparks the present-day calls for leadership in public schooling.

The evidence (from the annual Gallup Poll on Education, for example) is strong that America has an abundance of well-managed "competent" schools.[44] They are, for the most part, well-run: buses roll on time, order is maintained and schedules observed, meal service may not be grand but everyone gets fed, and classes are taught. But some schools are exceptional: more than merely "competent," more effective in the instruction of their students and pupils. What sets them apart from others? We do not know all the answers yet, but it is clear that the presence of leadership is a central causal factor.

As I have described, for the first three-quarters of this century research has emphasized two crucial factors in leader behavior. The first is emphasis on the things that Fayol taught us to attend to so long ago: planning, organizing, coordinating, commanding, and controlling. Many have learned to think of these as initiating structure or task orientation. On the job, that means attending to scheduling, organizing, supervising, and monitoring; all of which are absolutely essential to running schools well.

The second of the two crucial factors in leader behavior is rooted in things that Mayo taught us: consideration for subordinates, attention to human factors. Therefore, we attend to such things as morale, motivation, group processes, conflict management, and decision making. On the job, we try to use participative methods and couch our demands in ways thought to be humane.

But there is more to leadership than that. For instance, exemplary educational leaders (as distinguished from competent school managers) have long been known to be skilled instructional leaders. That is, they do well at diagnosing educational problems, counselling teachers, developing curriculum, developing staff, and evaluating and remediating the pedagogical work of teachers. On the job, such leaders emphasize their role as instructional leaders and tend to be "teachers of teachers."

Sergiovanni argues that these three types of leadership—which he calls "technical," "human," and "educational"—are essential if we are to have "competent" schools. The presence of these kinds of leadership is a precondition, but insufficient in itself, for the development of "excellent" schools.[45]

Leadership for excellent schools. In order to move from competence to excellence in schools, we must provide two other forms of leadership: symbolic leadership and the leadership that can build organizational culture.

Through symbolic leadership, administrators signal and demonstrate to others what is important, what is valued, what is wanted, what goals override all others. Symbolic leaders create and communicate a vision for followers; they describe a desired state of affairs to which followers commit themselves. Symbolic leaders create and communicate purpose; they help participants to understand that their mundane work is important and highly relevant to the success of the overall mission. Symbolic leaders do not assume that everyone sees the whole picture; they use words (spoken and written) and other symbols (such as time, attention, and their personal presence) to continually reemphasize what is important, what is good, what is wanted. Symbolic leaders seek to make clear to subordinates the connections between what they do, on the one hand, and *what they can do*, on the other, toward the achievement of excellence.

Obviously, symbolic leadership goes beyond the "nuts and bolts" of managing a good school. Perhaps not so obvious is the fact that symbolic leadership does not "just happen" any more than the technical, human, and educational forms of leadership do. It has to be valued, thought about, and planned. The symbolic school leader must, for example, devote time to signaling to others what is important and what is valuable. Such a leader tours the school, visits classrooms, seeks out students, and is seen spending time with them. Such a leader actively seeks opportunities to preside at ceremonies and rituals that symbolize and support the goals and values that he or she seeks to emphasize. The symbolic leader works at downplaying management activities in favor of underscoring the importance of educational activities. In other words, the symbolic leader organizes his or her personal time and energies so as to provide a unified vision of the school to students and teachers alike. Such a vision provides them with a clear sense of order and direction around which consensus can be formed as to what school is really all about; it is a vision to which they can commit themselves wholeheartedly.

There is a precondition for symbolic leadership: the leader has had to think clearly about what is important, has had to develop a vision about a desired state of affairs that is clear and that can be articulated to others in ways that they can readily understand. Indeed, symbolic leadership is not possible unless the leader has developed a vision of what ought to be that has some substance, some quality that can stir the awareness and enthusiasm of others and induce their commitment to sharing it as their own purpose. The symbolic leader, after all, stands for something that is important and that gives meaning and purpose to the seemingly mundane and routine work of others in the school. It is crucial that careful thought be given to this something, this vision, this desired better state of affairs. If ever thoughtful planning was called for, symbolic leadership calls for it.

However, a substantial body of research carried forward over a period of many years—and still developing—strongly suggests that even symbolic leadership is insufficient if we are to achieve excellence in schooling. The research of such pioneers as George Stern[46] and Andrew Halpin[47] made clear that excellent schools are characterized by a distinctive organizational climate that seems to set such schools apart from others. Later studies, such as the work of Seymour Sarason[48], Wilbur Brookover[49], and Joyce Epstein[50] have extended this concept and taught us that each school has a particular *culture* that is describable and highly specific. This means that a school has a uniqueness, a history, traditions, and customs that leaders emphasize and make coherent and important.

Recent research in schools—such as reported in Ernest Boyer's *High School*[51], Theodore Sizer's *Horace's Compromise,*[52] and John Goodlad's *A Place Called School*[53] as well as more popular portrayals of good schools, such as Sarah Lawrence Lightfoot's *The Good High School*[54]—have strongly underscored the importance of managing schools so that teachers in them feel that they belong to effective work groups, feel good about the work that they do, and feel that they achieve something on the job that is worthwhile. From such research, it is becoming increasingly clear that the leaders of excellent schools take care not only to preserve the traditions that may happen to have been inherited from the past, but they set about the building of new higher-order traditions. In this regard, findings from research in schools seem to parallel findings being reported from studies in the corporate world such as in John Naisbett's *Megatrends*,[55] Thomas Peters' and Robert Waterman's *In Search of Excellence*,[56] and Terrence Deal's and Allan Kennedy's *Corporate Cultures*.[57]

Leadership through the development of an organization's culture means building behavioral norms that exemplify the best that a school stands for. It means building an institution in which people believe strongly, with which they identify personally, and to which they gladly render their loyalty. All of this gives meaning to the work that they do, gives it significance, and this—as we know—is highly motivating.

Leaders who would build strong organizational cultures in schools spend time articulating the purposes and the mission of the school; they socialize others to these values; they define and redefine the uniqueness of the school; they develop systems of symbols that reinforce this uniqueness and make sure that the symbols are highly visible; they reward those who accept and reflect the norms and values of the school. Schools in which this happens are characterized by the bonding that occurs between people, and between people and organizations in which they have faith and toward which they have commitment. Under such leadership, students and teachers alike come to understand that they are part of an important and worthwhile larger mission. This, in itself, gives meaning to their daily efforts and includes them as part of something special and important. Under cultural leadership, therefore, students and teachers find satisfaction in being part of a special group at a special moment of achievement.

The culture of the school shapes and molds how people think, feel, and behave. It is communicated through customs, traditions, expectations, common meanings, norms, and habits. It is visible in words and behavior of all kinds as people go about their daily activities for it is ordinary daily behavior that reveals values, beliefs, and commitment. The culture of a school is a constructed reality, after all, and it takes strong, skilled, dedicated leadership to construct a vision of reality that will coalesce students and teachers in a move together toward higher levels of excellence.

SUMMARY

Classical organization (mechanistic, bureaucratic) tends to view leadership as (1) largely a matter of hierarchical power over subordinates and (2) almost wholly concerned with getting the task accomplished. *Human relations* adherents see leadership as interaction between the leader and others in the group, which (1) helps the social system to maintain itself (cohesiveness, productive group norms) and (2) achieves the group's goals. *Behavioral* views generally accept that effective leaders exhibit high task-oriented (that is, structuring the work) and relationships-oriented (that is, showing concern for others) behaviors. *Contingency* views of leadership posit that (1) there is no single, "best" leadership style suitable to all situations, and (2) the criterion for leader effectiveness is the success of the organization or group in achieving its goals.

For the administrator in a complex formal organization, such as a school system, perhaps nothing about leadership is more confusing than the difference between position power and leadership. Position power (for example, superintendent of schools or principal of a school) provides the incumbent with at least the potential of forcible domination and coercion. This is not leadership. In organizations, particularly, we must distinguish between superordination and leadership. Jacob Getzels instructs us:

> The source of superordination is *vested authority* [while] the source of leadership is *entrusted authority.* Authority is vested in a superordinate when power resides in the institution, and obedience is owed the superordinate by the subordinate in virtue of the role each occupies, roles the subordinate cannot alter. Authority is entrusted in a leader when power resides in the individuals themselves, and cooperation is *granted* the leader by the follower...a judgment...the follower can alter. The superordinate may legitimately *compel* subordination; the leader can legitimately only *elicit* followership. The relationship between subordinate and superordinate is *compulsory,* between follower and leader *voluntary.*[58]

James MacGregor Burns, emphasizing the symbiotic relationship between leadership and *followership,* points out that, although they do exercise various kinds of power, leaders *engage with followers* in seeking to achieve not only their own goals but also significant goals of the followers. "Leadership over human beings," he tells us, "is exercised when persons with certain purposes mobilize, in competition or conflict with others, institutional, political, psychological and other resources so as to arouse, engage, and satisfy the motives of followers."[59] Thus, leadership is distinguished from the exercise of naked power over others, wherein there is no *mutual* engagement. "To control *things*—tools, mineral resources, money, energy—is an act of power," Burns emphasizes, "not leadership, for things have no motives. Power wielders may treat people as things. Leaders may not."[60]

Research in the first three-quarters of this century emphasized two-dimensional leadership in education (that is, the task dimension and the human dimension). Newer perspectives on educational leadership make clear that such emphasis tends to produce what may be called competent schools (well-organized, well-run, but not highly educationally effective).

Recent research emphasizes the need for three additional forms of leadership in the educational organization if it is to move from competence to excellence. One of these is educational leadership: this includes diagnosing and solving pedagogical and curricular problems and helping teachers to solve instructional problems. The second is symbolic leadership wherein the leader communicates purpose, values, and significance to followers. The symbolic leader seeks to develop a consensus as to a vision of the total enterprise and the followers' role in it, a vision to which they can personally commit themselves because they share and support the mission and the values of the organization. Symbolic leaders make use of words, time, and their personal presence and participation in the organization's rituals, ceremonies, and other symbolic behaviors. They attend to these as primary activities rather than as peripheral activities to be squeezed in after managerial work is attended to.

The third form of leadership emerging in the newer perspectives—cultural leadership—is focused on developing a strong organizational culture in which people believe strongly, with which they identify personally, and to which they gladly render their loyalty. Thus powerful norms are created which unite the participants in a common cause, give significance to their daily work, and influence how they think, feel, and behave. Cultural leaders devote considerable time and energy to attending to customs, traditions, group norms, and daily habits which exemplify the best that the school stands for.

SUGGESTED READING

ARGYRIS, CHRIS, *Increasing Leadership Effectiveness*. New York: John Wiley & Sons, Inc., 1976.
In an experiment involving six corporation executives, Argyris applied his "theory of action" concept to the problem of improving their leader behavior. This involved (1) helping the executives to assess the assumptions and beliefs that prompted their leader behavior, (2) evaluating the consequences, and (3) developing and practicing a broader range of behavior style. This book makes important contributions not only to a theory of leadership but also to thinking about programs to train leaders.

BENNIS, WARREN, "The Artform of Leadership," in *The Executive Mind*, ed. Suresh Srivastva and associates. San Francisco: Jossey-Bass, 1983.
A noted scholar and experienced educational leader challenges some cherished orthodoxy about leadership in a brief discussion of newer perspectives.

BURNS, JAMES MACGREGOR, *Leadership*. New York: Harper & Row, Publishers, Inc., 1978.
In this Pulitzer Prize-winning volume, political historian Burns lucidly weaves social-psychological concepts into a tapestry that vividly interprets modern understanding of the essence of leadership. Though the aim of the book is to illuminate the dilemmas of contemporary political leadership (hence it draws many of its illustrations from great political leaders), the lessons for educators are clear and readily understandable. A work of impeccable scholarship distinguished by being highly readable; it is strongly recommended.

SCHEIN, EDGAR H., *Organizational Culture and Leadership*. San Francisco: Jossey-Bass, 1985.
Defines organizational culture and goes on to describe how organizational cultures begin, develop, and change. This is an authoritative, well-written book and—though its focus is not primarily on schools—one that is useful to the practitioner.

SERGIOVANNI, THOMAS J., "Leadership and Excellence in Schooling," *Educational Leadership*, 41, no. 5 (February 1984), 4–13.
Describes the five kinds of leadership necessary for excellence in education—technical, human, educational, symbolic, and cultural—as a hierarchy of leader behavior (somewhat reminiscent of Maslow's hierarchy of motivational needs). While the notion of such a hierarchy is problematic, this discussion is lucid, well-informed, and strongly recommended.

VIDICH, ARTHUR J., AND CHARLES MCREYNOLDS, "Rhetoric versus Reality: A Study of New York City High School Principals," in *Anthropological Perspectives in Education*, eds. Murray L. Wax, Stanley Diamond, and Fred O. Gearing. New York: Basic Books, Inc., Publishers, 1971.
Sensitively describes many of the "real-world" forces that cause school administrators to shun leadership by immersing themselves in the day-to-day demands of the job, resulting in what the authors call "bureaucratization of the imagination." Makes an excellent case study for group discussion.

YUKL, GARY A., *Leadership in Organizations*, 2nd ed. Englewood Cliffs: Prentice Hall, 1989.
This textbook surveys the literature on leadership, both of the present and the recent past, explaining the many competing views and understandings that have attracted significant attention. While the focus is on corporate management, nearly all of the theories and concepts have been used in educational thinking, as well. This otherwise helpful source is badly marred by the author's utter confusion as to the differences between charismatic leadership and transformational leadership, which the second edition seeks to deal with.

NOTES

[1]Thomas J. Sergiovanni, "Leadership Behavior and Organizational Behavior," *Notre Dame Journal of Education*, 4, no. 1 (Spring 1973), 16.
[2]Warren Bennis and Burt Nanus, *Leaders: The Strategies for Taking Charge* (New York: Harper & Row, Publishers, Inc., 1985), p. 21.

[3]Ralph M. Stogdill, "Personal Factors Associated with Leadership: A Survey of the Literature," *Journal of Psychology*, 25 (1948), 35–71.

[4]Richard D. Mann, "A Review of the Relationships between Personality and Performance in Small Groups," *Psychological Bulletin*, 56 (1959), 241–70.

[5]Bernard M. Bass, *Leadership, Psychology and Organizational Behavior* (New York: Harper & Row, Publishers, Inc., 1960).

[6]Bennis and Nanus, *Leaders*.

[7]John K. Hemphill, *Situational Factors in Leadership* (Columbus: Bureau of Business Research, College of Commerce and Administration, The Ohio State University, 1949).

[8]Robert J. Starratt, "Contemporary Talk on Leadership: Too Many Kings in the Parade?" *Notre Dame Journal of Education*, 4, no. 1 (Spring 1973), 14.

[9]Edwin A. Fleishman and Edwin F. Harris, "Patterns of Leadership Behavior Related to Employee Grievances and Turnover," *Personnel Psychology*, 15, no. 1 (Spring 1962), 43–44.

[10]James MacGregor Burns, *Leadership* (New York: Harper & Row, Publishers, Inc., 1978), p. 19.

[11]Dorwin Cartwright and Alvin Zander, eds., *Group Dynamics: Research and Theory*, 2nd ed. (Evanston, IL: Row, Peterson and Company, 1960).

[12]Daniel Katz, N. Maccoby, and Nancy C. Morse, *Productivity, Supervision and Morale in an Office Situation* (Ann Arbor: Survey Research Center, University of Michigan, 1950).

[13]Rensis Likert, *New Patterns of Management* (New York: McGraw-Hill Book Company, 1961), p. 7.

[14]*Leader Behavior Description Questionnaire—Form XII*. Copyright © 1962 by the Bureau of Business Research, College of Commerce and Administration, The Ohio State University, Columbus, OH.

[15]Andrew W. Halpin, *Theory and Research in Administration* (New York: Macmillan Inc., 1966), p. 86.

[16]Robert R. Blake and Jane Srygley Mouton, *The Managerial Grid* (Houston, TX: Gulf Publishing Company Inc., 1985).

[17]Robert R. Blake and others, "Breakthrough in Organizational Development," *Harvard Business Review*, 42 (November–December 1964), 136.

[18]Ibid.

[19]Ibid.

[20]Ibid.

[21]Albert F. Siepert and Rensis Likert, "The Likert School Profile Measurements of the Human Organization" (paper presented at the National Convention of the American Educational Research Association New Orleans, February 27, 1973), p. 1.

[22]Bernard M. Bass is generally credited with first describing the difference between successful and effective leadership. See his *Leadership, Psychology and Organizational Behavior* (New York: Harper & Brothers, Publishers, 1960).

[23]Fred E. Fiedler and Martin M. Chemers, *Leadership and Effective Management* (Glenview, IL: Scott, Foresman & Company, 1974), pp. 94–95.

[24]Ibid.

[25]Ibid., pp. 96–97.

[26]Fred E. Fiedler, "The Leadership Game: Matching the Man to the Situation," *Organizational Dynamics* (New York: AMACOM, 1977), p. 12.

[27]Fred E. Fiedler, *A Theory of Leadership Effectiveness* (New York: McGraw-Hill Book Company, 1967), p. 51.

[28]Terence R. Mitchell, "Leader Complexity and Leadership Style," *Personality and Social Psychology*, 16 (September 1970), 166–74.

[29]Fred E. Fiedler, "How Do You Make Leaders More Effective? New Answers to an Old Puzzle," in *Making Leaders More Effective*, rev. ed., ed. William F. Dowling (New York: AMACOM, 1975), p. 9.

[30]Fiedler, *A Theory of Leadership Effectiveness*, p. 261.

[31]Fred E. Fiedler, "The Leadership Game: Matching the Man to the Situation," in Fred E. Fiedler, Victor H. Vroom, and Chris Argyris, *Leadership: Fiedler, Vroom, and Argyris* (New York: AMACOM, 1977).

[32]Vincent McNamara and Frederick Enns, "Directive Leadership and Staff Acceptance of the Principal," *Canadian Administrator*, 6 (1966), 5–8.

[33]Vincent D. McNamara, "The Principal's Personal Leadership Style, the School Staff Situation, and School Effectiveness" (unpublished doctoral dissertation, University of Alberta, 1968).

[34]Parnell Garland and Robert R. O'Reilly, "The Effect of Leader-Member Interaction on Organizational Effectiveness," *Educational Administration Quarterly*, 12, no. 3 (Fall 1976), 9–30.

[35]McNamara, "The Principal's Personal Leadership Style."

[36]Peter F. Drucker, *Management: Tasks, Responsibilities, Practices* (New York: Harper & Row, Publishers, Inc., 1974), pp. 264–65.

[37]Victor H. Vroom and Philip W. Yetton, *Leadership and Decisionmaking* (Pittsburgh: University of Pittsburgh Press, 1973).

[38]William J. Reddin, "The 3-D Management Style Theory: A Typology Based on Task and Relationships-Orientation," *Training and Development Journal*, 21 (April 1967), 11.

[39]William J. Reddin, *Managerial Effectiveness* (New York: McGraw-Hill Book Company, 1970), Chapter 24.

[40]Fred Luthans, *Organizational Behavior* (New York: McGraw-Hill Book Company, 1977), p. 452.

[41]Paul Hersey and Kenneth H. Blanchard, *Management of Organizational Behavior: Utilizing Human Resources*, 3rd ed. (Englewood Cliffs, NJ: Prentice-Hall, 1977), p. 161.

[42]Ibid., p. 162.

[43]This illustration is adapted from Philip E. Gates, Kenneth H. Blanchard, and Paul Hersey, "Diagnosing Educational Leadership Problems: A Situational Approach," *Educational Leadership*, 33, no. 5 (February 1976), 348–54.

[44]Thomas J. Sergiovanni, "Leadership and Excellence in Schooling," *Educational Leadership*, 41, no. 5 (February 1984), 4–13.

[45]The following discussion is based on Sergiovanni, "Leadership and Excellence in Schooling."

[46]George G. Stern, *People in Context: Measuring Person-Environment Congruence in Education and Industry* (New York: John Wiley & Sons, Inc., 1970).

[47]Andrew Halpin and Don B. Croft, *The Organizational Climate of Schools* (Washington, DC: United States Office of Education Research Project, Contract #SAE 543-8639).

[48]Seymour Sarason, *The Culture of the School and the Problem of Change* (Boston: Allyn & Bacon, 1970).

[49]Wilbur Brookover and others, "Elementary School Social Climate and School Achievement," *American Educational Research Association Journal*, 15 (1978), 301–318.

[50]Joyce L. Epstein, ed., *The Quality of School Life* (New York: D.C. Heath/Lexington Books, 1981).

[51]Ernest L. Boyer, *High School: A Report on Secondary Education in America* (New York: Harper & Row, Publishers, Inc., 1983).

[52]Theodore R. Sizer, *Horace's Compromise: The Dilemma of the American High School* (Boston: Houghton Mifflin Company, 1984).

[53]John I. Goodlad, *A Place Called School: Prospects for the Future* (St. Louis: McGraw-Hill Book Company, 1983).

[54]Sara Lawrence Lightfoot, *The Good High School: Portraits of Character and Culture* (New York: Basic Books, Inc., Publishers, 1983).

[55]John Naisbitt, *Megatrends: Ten New Directions for Transforming Our Lives* (New York: Warner Books, 1982).

[56]Thomas J. Peters and Robert H. Waterman, Jr., *In Search of Excellence: Lessons from America's Best-Run Companies* (New York: Harper & Row, Publishers, Inc., 1982).

[57]Terrence E. Deal and Allan A. Kennedy, *Corporate Cultures: The Rites and Rituals of Corporate Life* (Reading, MA: Addison-Wesley, 1982).

[58]Jacob W. Getzels, "Theory and Research on Leadership: Some Comments and Some Alternatives," in *Leadership: The Science and the Art Today*, eds. Luvern L. Cunningham and William J. Gephart (Itasca, IL: F. E. Peacock, Publishers, Inc., 1973), pp. 40–41.

[59]Burns, *Leadership*, p. 18.

[60]Ibid.

7

ORGANIZATIONAL CULTURE AND ORGANIZATIONAL CLIMATE

"An institution is like a tune; it is not constituted by individual sounds but by the relations between them."

—*Peter F. Drucker*[1]

The goal of human resources development (HRD) as a field of research and practice is to discover the technology through which organizations will become more effective while employees become more productive and satisfied in their work. As we have seen in the chapter on motivation, the mainstream approach to human resource development holds that the inner state of organizational participants is an important key to understanding and managing their behavior. Thus, while immediate antecedent conditions may well evoke behavioral responses, so, too, do the perceptions, values, beliefs, and motivations of the participants. In other words, participants commonly respond to organizational events very much in terms of learnings that have developed through their experience over time and not merely to antecedent events immediately preceding or following their behavior. Therefore, modern HRD is much concerned with the forces and processes through which organizational participants are socialized into the organization: how they develop perceptions, values, and beliefs concerning the organization and what influence these inner states have on behavior. In contemporary organizational behavior literature, this is the realm of organizational climate and organizational culture.

Neither organizational climate nor organizational culture is a new concept. They have a long tradition in the literature of organization studies, going back at least as far as the Western Electric research of the 1930s, which noted—as described earlier—that some management styles elicited feelings of affiliation, competence, and achievement from workers, leading to more productive work than had been done previously as well as eliciting greater satisfaction from workers than under different styles of management. Beginning in the 1940s, Kurt Lewin and his colleagues and students conducted numerous studies to explore the proposition that organizations could be made more effective by using planned interventions designed to shift the social norms of managers and workers alike.

Perhaps the most notable of these early efforts occurred in the Weldon Manufacturing Company—which made men's pajamas—after its merger with the Harwood Manufacturing Corporation.[2]

Many different names have been used over the years to allude to the subtle, elusive, intangible, largely unconscious forces that comprise the symbolic side of organizations and shape human thought and behavior in them.[3] In the late 1930s, Chester Barnard described culture as a social fiction created by people to give meaning to work and life.[4] In the 1940s, Philip Selznick used the term "institution" to describe what it is that creates solidarity, meaning, commitment, and productivity in organizations,[5] Marshall Meyer and his associates used the term somewhat similarly in the 1970s.[6] In the 1960s, the term "organizational climate" became very popular with students of organization, in no small measure due to the research on elementary schools by Andrew Halpin and Don Croft.[7] In his studies of universities in the 1970s, Bernard Clark used the term "organizational saga."[8] Michael Rutter and his colleagues noted the importance of "ethos" in determining the effectiveness of the high schools that they studied.[9] These studies are illustrative of a substantial body of research literature that seeks to describe and explain the learned pattern of thinking, reflected and reinforced in behavior, that is so seldom seen yet is so powerful in shaping people's experiences. This pattern of thinking and the behavior associated with it provide stability, foster certainty, solidify order and predictability, and create meaning.[10]

DEFINING AND DESCRIBING ORGANIZATIONAL CLIMATE AND CULTURE

An observer who moves from school to school ineluctably develops an intuitive sense that each school is distinctive, unique in some almost indefinable yet powerful way. This sense, seemingly palpable when we are in a school, more than describes that school: it *is* that school. As I have described, many different terms have been used to identify that sense of the unique characteristics that organizations have. People sometimes use such terms as atmosphere, personality, tone, or ethos when speaking of this unique characteristic of a school. But the term *organizational climate* has come into rather general use as a metaphor for this distinctive characteristic of organizations. But just what is organizational climate? And how is it created?

Climate is generally defined, as Renato Tagiuri suggested, as *the characteristics of the total environment* in a school building.[11] But we need to understand what those characteristics are, and to lay the groundwork for that we turn to the work of Tagiuri.

Tagiuri described the total environment in an organization, that is, the organizational climate, as comprised of four dimensions:

1. The ecology,
2. The milieu,
3. The social system,
4. The culture.

Ecology refers to physical and material factors in the organization: for example, the size, age, design, facilities, and condition of the building or buildings. It also refers to the technology used by people in the organization: desks and chairs, chalkboards, elevators, everything used to carry out organizational activities.

Milieu is the social dimension in the organization. This includes virtually everything relating to the people in the organization. For example, how many there are and what they are like. This would include race and ethnicity, salary level of teachers, socioeconomic level of students, education levels attained by the teachers, the morale and motivation of adults and students who inhabit the school, level of job satisfaction, and a host of other characteristics of the people in the organization.

Social system refers to the organizational and administrative structure of the organization. It includes how the school is organized, the ways in which decisions are made and who is involved in making them, the communication patterns among people (who talks to whom about what), what work groups there are, etc.

Culture refers to the values, belief systems, norms, and ways of thinking that are characteristic of the people in the organization. It is "the way we do things around here." This aspect of the organization's total environment is described more fully a little later in this chapter.

As Figure 7–1 shows, these four dimensions are dynamically interrelated and, together, give rise to organizational climate. In creating Figure 7–1, I have substituted the term *organization* for Tagiuri's original term *social system,* because it seems to me to be more descriptive of what that dimension actually encompasses. Much of the organization dimension of climate arises from factors that administrators control directly or strongly influence. It is important, I think, that administrators understand the close connections between the choices they make about the way they organize and the climate manifested in the organization. To some, *social system* conveys a sense of a somewhat uncontrollable natural order of things whereas *organization* makes the influence of the administrator's responsibility for establishing that order a little clearer.

However, contemporary thought does not view each of the four dimensions cited above as being equally potent in producing the character and quality of the climate in a given organization. Recent research has concentrated attention on the primacy of the culture of the organization in defining the character and quality of the climate of an organization.

RECENT RESEARCH ON ORGANIZATIONAL CULTURE

Research on organizational culture, which had stood for some time in the wings of organization studies, shifted to center stage in the two-year span of 1981–1982. It was a dramatic shift and was due to the publication of two books. The first of these—William Ouchi's *Theory Z*—appeared in 1981 and became the first book by a researcher of organizational behavior to enjoy a lengthy stay on the nonfiction best-seller lists.[12] Published at a moment when American corporate managers were groping for some solution to their difficulties in meeting Japanese competition, Ouchi—a Japanese-American—compared and contrasted the management styles used in the two nations. He found that Japanese management practices tended to be quite different from American and that some of them (not all, due to societal

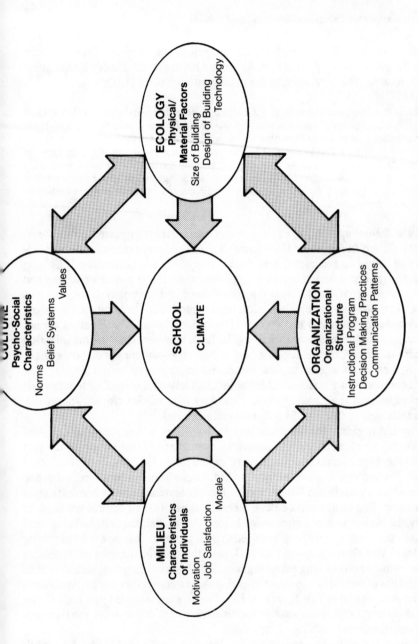

FIGURE 7–1. Interactive model showing relationships between and among key environmental factors that shape and mold school climate. Figure 2. in Carolyn S. Anderson, "The Search for School Climate: A Review of the Research," *Review of Educational Research*, 52 (Fall 1982). © 1982 by the American Educational Research Association. Adapted by Robert G. Owens with permission of the publisher.

Text within the figure:

ECOLOGY
Physical/
Material Factors
Size of Building
Design of Building
Technology

CULTURE
Psycho-Social
Characteristics
Norms   Belief Systems   Values

SCHOOL
CLIMATE

ORGANIZATION
Organizational
Structure
Instructional Program
Decision Making Practices
Communication Patterns

MILIEU
Characteristics
of Individuals
Motivation   Job Satisfaction   Morale

differences) could profitably be adopted by American corporations. Taking his cue from McGregor's Theory X-Theory Y, he named his approach Theory Z to suggest a new alternative. Theory Z accepts the main assumptions of HRD:

> Of all its values, commitment of a Z culture to its people—its workers—is the most important....Theory Z assumes that any worker's life is a whole, not a Jekyll-Hyde personality, half machine from nine to five and half human in the hours preceding and following. Theory Z suggests that humanized working conditions not only increase productivity and profits to the company but also the self-esteem for employees....Up to now American managers have assumed that technology makes for increased productivity. What Theory Z calls for instead is a redirection of attention to *human* relations in the corporate world.[13]

In the following year, 1982, another research report appeared on the best-seller lists. Called *In Search of Excellence,* it described eight management characteristics that sixty-two successful American corporations had in common.[14] Cutting across the eight characteristics was a consistent theme: the power of values and culture in these corporations, rather than procedures and control systems, provides the "glue" that holds them together, stimulates commitment to a common mission, and galvanizes the creativity and energy of their participants. These values are not usually transmitted formally or in writing. Instead, they permeate the organization in the form of stories, myths, legends, and metaphors—and these companies have people in them who attend to this awareness of organizational culture: "The excellent companies are unashamed collectors and tellers of stories, of legends and myths in support of their basic beliefs. Frito-Lay tells service stories. Johnson & Johnson tells quality stories. 3M tells innovation stories."[15]

Why did organizational culture stay in the wings in America so long? And why is it today a central concern in American management? One answer to the first question is that the human underpinning of organization has long been considered to be *soft.* Technology is *hard.* Money is hard. Organizational structure, rules and regulations, policy decisions—these are hard, in the lexicon of many administrators and managers. The things that one can measure, quantify, and control are hard. In this view, the human side of organization is soft. Values, beliefs, culture, behavioral norms have therefore widely been believed to be less potent, less powerful in getting things done. But Ouchi showed that in Japan, the current nemesis of American business, managers have long taken organizational culture far more seriously than Americans have—and it is important in giving them a competitive edge. And Peters and Waterman, authors of *In Search of Excellence,* demonstrated that high-flying American corporations show similar sophistication and concern for the development of organizational culture.

Further, these books—together with Terrence Deal's and Allan Kennedy's *Corporate Cultures: The Rites and Rituals of Corporate Life,* which also appeared in 1982[16]—helped to clarify what culture is: a system of shared values and beliefs that interact with an organization's people, organizational structures, and control systems to produce behavioral norms. They helped make clear that, in practical terms, *shared values* means "what is important"; *beliefs* means "what we think is true"; and *behavioral norms* means "how we do things around here." With the obvious success of companies using these ideas, and with the ideas themselves clarified, the concept of organizational culture suddenly became of practical importance to managers and administrators. As Peters and Waterman put it, "Now, culture is the 'softest' stuff around. Who trusts its leading analysts—anthropologists and sociologists—after all? Businessmen surely don't. Yet culture is the hardest stuff around, as well."[17]

It became clear to American businessmen—confronted by recession, deregulation, technological upheavals, foreign competition, and transforming economic and social change—that an organizational culture that stifles innovation and hard work may be the biggest stumbling block to adapting to uncertain times. The lesson was not lost on educational administrators: confronted by shrinking finances, faltering public support, divided constituencies with conflicting interests, and rampant charges of organizational ineffectiveness, they became riveted by the implications of organizational culture for educational organizations.

ORGANIZATIONAL CULTURE AND ORGANIZATIONAL CLIMATE COMPARED AND CONTRASTED

The terms *culture* and *climate* are both abstractions that deal with the fact that the behavior of persons in organizations is not elicited by interaction with proximate events alone but is also influenced by interaction with intangible forces in the organization's environment. As I shall explain more fully, culture refers to the behavioral norms, assumptions, and beliefs of an organization, whereas climate refers to perceptions of persons in the organization that reflect those norms, assumptions, and beliefs.

Organizational culture. Though many definitions of organizational culture are found in the literature, the high degree of agreement between and among them makes it relatively easy to understand what culture is and how it relates to and differs from organizational climate. Organizational culture is the body of solutions to external and internal problems that has worked consistently for a group and that is therefore taught to new members as the correct way to perceive, think about, and feel in relation to those problems.[18]

Culture develops over a period of time and, in the process of developing, acquires significantly deeper meaning. Thus, "such solutions eventually come to be assumptions about the nature of reality, truth, time, space, human nature, human activity, and human relationships—then they come to be taken for granted and, finally, drop out of awareness."[19] Therefore, "culture can be defined as the shared philosophies, ideologies, values, assumptions, beliefs, expectations, attitudes, and norms that knit a community together."[20] In this case, the community is an organization—a school, for example—and all of these interrelated qualities reveal agreement, implicit or explicit, among teachers, administrators, and other participants on how to approach decisions and problems: "the way things are done around here."[21]

As Terrence Deal points out, "At the heart of most...definitions of culture is the concept of a learned pattern of unconscious (or semiconscious) thought, reflected and reinforced by behavior, that silently and powerfully shapes the experience of a people."[22] This pattern of thought, which is organizational culture, "...provides stability, fosters certainty, solidifies order and predictability, and creates meaning."[23]

It also gives rise to simpler, though highly compatible, common-sense definitions, such as "[Organizational culture] is the rules of the game; the unseen meaning between the lines in the rulebook that insures unity"[24] or "Culture consists of the conclusions a group of people draws from its experience. An organization's culture consists largely of what people believe about what works and what does not."[25]

While anthropologists and sociologists understand that culture—whether of a larger society or of an organization—can be inferred by observing the behavior of people, it is not really a study of that behavior. Through the observation of behavior one can develop an understanding of the systems of knowledge, beliefs, customs, and habits of people—whether it be in a larger society or an organization. In studying organizational culture, therefore, one looks at the artifacts and technology that people use, and one listens to what they say and observes what they do in an effort to discover the patterns of thoughts, beliefs, and values that they use in making sense of the everyday events that they experience. Thus, organizational culture is the study of the wellsprings from which the values and characteristics of an organization arise.

Two major themes in a definition of organizational culture.   Two themes consistently pervade the literature describing and defining organizational culture: one theme is *norms* and the other theme is *assumptions*. Norms and assumptions are widely regarded as key components of organizational culture.

Norms.   An important way in which organizational culture influences behavior is through the norms or standards that the social system institutionalizes and enforces. These are encountered by the individual as group norms, which are ideas "that can be put into the form of a statement specifying what members...should do."[26] They are, in other words, "rules of behavior which have been accepted as legitimate by members of a group."[27] They are, of course, unwritten rules, that nonetheless express the shared beliefs of most group members about what behavior is appropriate in order to be a member in good standing.[28]

Assumptions.   Underneath these behavioral norms lie the assumptions that comprise the bedrock upon which norms and all other aspects of culture are built. These assumptions deal with what the people in the organization accept as true in the world and what is false, what is sensible and what is absurd, what is possible and what is impossible. I agree with Edgar Schein: these are not values, which can be debated and discussed. Assumptions are tacit instead, unconsciously taken for granted, rarely considered or talked about, and accepted as true and nonnegotiable.[29] The cultural norms in the organization—informal, unwritten, but highly explicit and powerful in influencing behavior—arise directly from the underlying assumptions.

Specifying what organizational culture is.   Edgar Schein describes organizational culture as being comprised of three different but closely linked concepts. Thus, organizational culture may be defined as:

1. a body of solutions to external and internal problems that has worked consistently for a group and that is therefore taught to new members as the correct way to perceive, think about, and feel in relation to those problems;

2. these eventually come to be assumptions about the nature of reality, truth, time, space, human nature, human activity, and human relationships;

3. over time, these assumptions come to be taken for granted and finally drop out of awareness. Indeed, the power of culture lies in the fact that it operates as a set of unconscious, unexamined assumptions that are taken for granted.[30]

Thus, culture develops over a period of time and, in the process of developing, acquires significantly deep meaning. Therefore, culture can be defined as the shared philosophies, ideologies, values, assumptions, beliefs, expectations, attitudes, and norms that knit a community together.[31] The school is viewed as having all of these interrelated qualities that reveal agreement, implicit or explicit, among teachers, administrators, and other participants on how to approach decisions and problems: "the way things are done around here."[32] As with most definitions of organizational culture, this pivots on the concept of a learned pattern of unconscious thought, reflected and reinforced by behavior, that silently and powerfully shapes the experience of a people.[33]

In Schein's model (Figure 7–2), the most obvious manifestations of organizational culture are visible and audible: these are artifacts such as tools, buildings, art, and technology as well as patterns of human behavior, including speech. Because these are visible, they have been frequently studied usually using naturalistic field methods such as observation, interviews, and document analysis. Though these manifestations are readily visible, they are merely symbolic of the culture

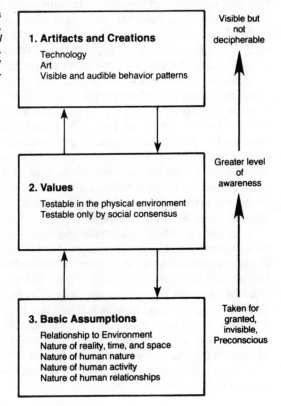

FIGURE 7–2. Schein's Model of Levels of Culture. Schein, Edgar H. *Organizational Culture and Leadership.* San Francisco: Jossey Bass, 1985, p. 14. (Figure 1).

1. Artifacts and Creations
Technology
Art
Visible and audible behavior patterns

Visible but not decipherable

2. Values
Testable in the physical environment
Testable only by social consensus

Greater level of awareness

3. Basic Assumptions
Relationship to Environment
Nature of reality, time, and space
Nature of human nature
Nature of human activity
Nature of human relationships

Taken for granted, invisible, Preconscious

itself, which is not visible and which is not even in the awareness of the people we observe. Therefore, to make sense of the artifacts and the behaviors that we observe requires us to decipher their meaning, and this is difficult to do.

Below this publicly visible level of the manifestations of culture lie the values of the organization, sometimes encoded in written language such as in a "mission statement," a statement of philosophy, or a "credo." Documents such as these move us closer to understanding the basic assumptions of the organization but they, too, merely reflect the basic assumptions that are the essence of the culture.

Finally, at the third and lowest level, we find the essence of the culture: those assumptions that are taken for granted, invisible, and out of consciousness. These have to do with the relationships of individuals to the environment; the nature of reality, time, and space; the nature of human activity; the nature of human nature, and the nature of human relationships. These unseen assumptions, of which the organization's members are unaware, form patterns but they remain implicit, unconscious, and taken-for-granted unless they are called to the surface by some process of inquiry.

Symbolism and culture.   Though organizational culture is usually studied through inferences derived from the observation of organizational behavior, the focus is not limited to the impact of the environment on the behavior of individual persons. It extends to understanding what the elements of such environments are, how they develop, and how these elements relate to one another so as to form (in effect) the lexicon, grammar, and syntax of organization. Thus, for example, the study of symbolism is central to the study of organizational culture: the rituals, myths, traditions, rites, and language through which human meanings and values are transmitted literally from one generation of the organization to another.

A school climate may be characterized by certain perceptions held by participants as to the nature of the organization ("What things are really like here"), but how are those perceptions developed, communicated, and transmitted? A school may be viewed by members as holding certain values, extolling particular virtues, standing for describable standards and practices that have a deep effect on the behaviors of the members. But how are these made explicit and communicated to the members? What are the mechanisms used by the organization to influence and control behavior in predictable, desired ways? In schools, as well as in societies, the answer is through institutionalized rituals and symbols. Understanding these is essential to understanding culture.

In many societies, for example, marriage rites constitute powerful symbols that evoke a great deal of behavior considered "right" and "proper," if not inevitable. This might include deciding where the married couple live, how the members of the family take on new roles (such as mother-in-law), and division of labor between the sexes. Thus the institution of marriage, symbolized by ceremonies and rituals handed down through the generations, communicates values to people that the society holds to be important. Much more than that, the communication results in behaviors that may seem ordinary and even mundane to the participants but which are powerful in developing their perceptions as to what is right or wrong, or even possible.

Similarly, to join the faculty of a typical American high school brings with it many obligations and expectations. Some of these are inexorably demanded by the daily schedule of classes (the bell schedule), which signals powerfully to participants who should be where—and doing what—virtually every minute of the day. To many educators the schedule is such an inherent part of the culture of the school as to be taken for granted, accepted without question, an overriding symbol of what defines the school itself. That is a powerful cultural feature of the high school, and it has great impact on what participants do, see as possible, and value as important in the life of the school. The bell schedule is one of many powerful cultural symbols that help to create the organizational climate found in an American high school.

Organizational climate.   Organizational climate is the study of *perceptions* that individuals have of various aspects of the environment in the organization. For example, in their pioneer study of organizational climate in schools Andrew Halpin and Don Croft examined "the attributes of leadership and group behavior" found to exist in elementary schools.[34] To do this, they asked teachers to describe their perceptions of certain human interactions in a sample of elementary schools that seemed to result from such causes as the principal's behavior in his or her official role in the hierarchy, the personality characteristics of individual teachers, the social needs of individual teachers as members of a work group, and such group characteristics of the teachers in the school as morale. A major outcome of the Halpin and Croft research was the demonstration that, by using the set of perceptions that the Halpin and Croft questionnaire probed, the organizational climate of elementary schools may be systematically assessed.

The notion of satisfaction is usually closely associated with the concept of organizational climate. That is, to what extent are the perceptions that participants have of the environment of the organization satisfying to them? This association of satisfaction with the perceptions of participants is implicit in some techniques for studying climate whereas many studies have inquired directly into possible discrepancies between the participants' perceptions of the existing state of affairs in contrast to whatever desired state the respondents think ought to prevail.

Studies of organizational climate depend heavily on eliciting the perceptions of participants. This has led to the use of questionnaires in which respondents are asked directly about their perceptions. Although interviews could also be an effective means of gathering such information, this has not been done very often whereas the development of questionnaires has proliferated.

Earlier studies of organizational climate in schools tended to gather data from adults, almost always teachers, with occasional inquiries of principals. In more recent years, the trend in school climate studies has been in the direction of examining the perceptions of pupils and students, rather than adults in the school.

The affective aspects of culture and climate.   The culture of an organization exerts powerful influence on the development of climate. Inasmuch as culture of the organization, even though it is intangible, influences the way that participants perceive events and make sense of those events, it is clear that culture has influence on the attitudes and feelings of participants. Rosabeth Moss Kanter captures much of the impact of organizational culture and climate in reporting her studies comparing highly successful and less successful American corporations.

She speaks of high-performing companies as having a culture of pride and a climate of success. By a culture of pride she means "...there is emotional and value commitment between person and organization; people feel that they 'belong' to a meaningful entity and can realize cherished values by their contributions."[35] With this feeling of pride in belonging to a worthwhile organization with a record of achievement, of being a member rather than merely an employee, the confidence of the individual is bolstered: confidence that the organization will be supportive of creative new practices and will continue to perform well and confidence also that the individual will be effective and successful in his or her own realm of work in the organization.

Kanter's research leads her to believe that the culture of pride is widely found in organizations that are integrative, which means organizations that emphasize the wholeness of the enterprise, that actively consider the wider implications of things that they do, and that thrive on diversity and stimulate challenges to traditional practices. These organizations tend to a large extent to be successful because their cultures foster a climate of success.

In contrast, Kanter describes less successful organizations as being segmented. In segmented organizations members find it difficult even to discover what is going on beyond their own little sphere of operations much less to deal with problems that affect the whole organization. People are kept isolated, stratified away from the larger decisions in the organization, focused on the narrow piece of action in which they are directly involved. In these organizations people find it difficult to take pride in the organization because they really know little about it and what it is doing. Thus, such organizations are characterized by climates of something other than success.

Multiple cultures.   Although a given organization will have an overall organizational culture, many organizations also have other additional workplace cultures. In other words, in describing organizational culture we must be aware that subunits of the organization have cultures of their own which possess distinctive attributes. As an example, consider the school district that has central administrative offices, a senior high school, a junior high school, and several elementary schools.

Whereas the school board and top-level administrators in such a district may understand that the district as an organization has a shared set of understandings, assumptions, and beliefs reflected in and reinforced by the behaviors of people—in short, an organizational culture—they should also understand that each individual school will be characterized by its own culture. The culture of a given school is likely to reflect certain of the principal characteristics of the school district's organizational culture and, yet, be different in some ways. Moreover, the cultures of the various schools are likely to differ. Further, it is more than likely that the central office will exhibit an organizational culture of its own which is distinctive from that of any of the schools.

To carry the illustration further, consider the organizational culture of the senior high school in that district. The school itself will have an organizational culture as I have described and it will also have workplace cultures within it. For example, the counselors in the Guidance and Counselling department of the school may interpret their role—and that of the department—as being supportive and helping in their relationship to students, encouraging students to grow and mature in the ability to make informed decisions regarding their lives, and to increasingly take charge of their lives. In their work, such counselors would tend to value developing high trust relationships with students in order to engender openness in dealing with problems. Across the hall, however, one might find the unit responsible for managing attendance and discipline. Quite possibly the faculty in this unit could adopt—for whatever reasons—a shared understanding that toughness counts along with fairness, that it is the responsibility of the school to be sure that students toe the mark and to mete out punishment when they fail to do so, and to leave no mistake as to who is in charge. One could go on, demonstrating that other departments in the school are likely to exhibit cultures of their own—in some ways distinctive and in other ways mirroring the culture of the school as a whole.

The fact that multiple cultures are likely to be found in school districts and schools is not surprising inasmuch as the subunits of the organization do many of the same culture-building things as the larger organization itself does. It is the subunits—such as schools and departments—that regularly bring together people who share some constellation of interests, purposes, and values; they are the settings in which people seek social affiliation in face-to-face groups; they facilitate the sharing and cooperative effort required to get the work done. These functions of the subunits provide the impetus for developing multiple cultures in the organization, rather than a single organizational culture from top to bottom.

Indeed, it appears likely that Theory X administrators tend to think of organizational culture as being conceptualized at top levels in the organization and managed in such a way as to be implemented down the line of authority. This approach to the development of organizational culture, which is in harmony with classical concepts of organization, is problematic inasmuch as it is difficult to change the assumptions of people and compel their sharing of assumptions with others by issuing directives. On the other hand, Theory Y administrators are likely to more readily accept the concept of multiple cultures existing within the organization. The development of multiple cultures within the organization is facilitated by the use of participative methods associated with HRD.

No concept in the realm of organizational behavior relies more heavily on social systems concepts than does organizational culture (recall the discussions of general systems theory, social systems theory, and sociotechnical systems theory in Chapter 3). Clearly, however, the culture of an organization is readily seen as important to eliciting and shaping the behavior of participants, which gives rise to the notion of *person-environment interaction*.

Group norms. An important way in which organizational culture influences behavior is through the norms or standards that the social system institutionalizes and enforces. These are encountered by the individual as group norms, which are "an idea that can be put in the form of a statement specifying what members...should do."[36] They are, in other words, "rules of behavior which have been accepted as legitimate by members of a group."[37] Groups typically exert pressures on an individual to conform to group norms that are more pervasive than the individual is likely to comprehend. These pressures are often felt as an obligation to behave in certain ways; this is often manifested in positive forms, such as support from the group for opinions and behavior that the group approves and wishes to reinforce.

Especially if the individual highly values the esteem and acceptance of members of the group and, more especially, if the group is highly cohesive, the pressure to conform to group standards and expectations can even influence one's perceptions of "reality." He or she tends to "see" things in terms of the expectations that the group has. Thus, the interaction of the individual with groups reaches far deeper than merely observable behavior: it strongly influences the development of perceptions, values, and attitudes.

Person-environment Interaction. Any discussion of organizational culture has its roots in the work of Kurt Lewin, who demonstrated that understanding human behavior requires us to consider the whole situation in which behavior occurs.[38] The term "whole situation" is defined as meaning both the person and the environment. Essentially, then, behavior is a function of the interaction of person and environment. Thus,

$$B = f(P, E)$$

in which B = behavior
    f = function
    P = person
    E = environment

Consequently, in conceptualizing organizational culture, it is necessary to think of the person and the organizational environment as complementary parts of one situation. They are inseparable.

The group (human social system), as it is being discussed here, is an important part of the environment that the individual encounters as a member of an organization. "The postulate that behavior is a function of the interaction of organism and environment is widely accepted,..." Garlie Forehand and B. Von Haller Gilmer point out, but "the concept of environment has been a difficult one for psychologists to deal with empirically."[39] This is, in part, because formal models of the organization (such as organizational charts) provide tidy, rational diagrams, but people often do not behave in the ways that the model depicts.[40] On the other hand, the behavior of individuals in organizational settings does not arise *only* from the personal characteristics of the individuals, but is also influenced by the total situation in which they find themselves.[41]

The perspective of organizational culture helps us to understand that the environment with which people interact is constituted of more than the immediate circumstances in which they find themselves. A crucial aspect of understanding the culture of an organization is to understand the organization's history and its traditions because individuals in an organization are socialized to accept them. Thus, unseen but present in every human encounter with the organization, is the understanding and acceptance by participants of values and expectations that are inherent in the tradition of the organization. Organizations normally expend considerable effort, both formally and informally, to transmit and reinforce these values and expectations through socialization processes.

In many an American high school, to return to an earlier example, it is difficult for teachers and administrators alike to conceptualize organizing their work in any other way than by using a bell schedule built upon Carnegie Units of Instruction. This is a strong tradition in American secondary education, often associated with quality and sound professional practice, that has continually been reinforced by the teachers' own experience as students in high schools, by their university training, and by their experience as professionals. It is an illustration of the forces that are always present in organizational culture as part of the unseen, intangible environment which shapes and molds the behavior of participants.

The term "tradition" used in this sense does not necessarily mean repeating old solutions to newly emerging problems. Some organizations try to create what might be called new cultural traditions in an effort to break the habits of the past and emphasize the value of originality and creativity in finding fresh solutions to problems encountered in the life of the organization. Contemporary examples are readily found in the relatively young entrepreneurial computer firms in the Silicon Valley and other locations that place high value on bold thinking and inventiveness. Apple Computer is frequently cited as an illustration of an organization that was built on this concept. At this writing, with that company having developed into a large corporation whose culture was taking on values and assumptions that the original founders no longer found congenial, there was doubt whether or not the "old" corporate culture could be maintained into the future or whether it had outlived its usefulness and needed to be replaced by different cultural traditions.

Concept of behavior settings.   Roger Barker theorized that environments have great influence in evoking and shaping the patterns of behavior of the people in them.[42] Indeed, according to his view of what is now known as "ecological psychology," the influence of environment is so great that it tends to overcome many individual differences among people who populate organizations. The result is that, in specific organizations, people tend to exhibit patterns of behavior that are so regular and distinct that we tend to view their behavior as "belonging to" those particular organizations. Barker posited, therefore, that organizational behavior is best understood in terms of *behavior settings,* referring to the whole complex physical and psychological environment with which people are in constant interaction.

In a remarkable pioneer study of the relationship between the size of high schools and the behavior of students in them, Roger Barker and Paul Gump discovered, for example, that the extent to which students participate in extraclass and extracurricular activities is directly related to the size of the school.[43] In similar research, Leonard Baird showed that the achievement of students, as well as the degree of their participation in extraclass activities, is related not only to the size of the school but also to the type of community in which the school is located (for example, small city, suburb, or large city).[44] In another study, Baird found that success at college was related not so much to the size of the high school from which students came as it was to the size of the college itself.[45]

Barker's work has had considerable influence on Seymour Sarason, whose book, *The Culture of the School and the Problem of Change,* speaks so lucidly and persuasively of the necessity of finding ways of altering the patterns of activities, group norms, and the temporal qualities that are characteristic of American public schools, before we can hope to change the impact that they have on the people in them.[46] This milieu, which Sarason called the "culture of the school," is not necessarily planned or deliberately created; it tends, instead, to be a phenomenon that is generated from (1) the activities of people in the school (for example, lecturing, listening, moving about according to schedule), (2) the physical objects in the environment (for example, walls, furniture, chalkboard, playground), and (3) the temporal regularities observed (for example, the length of classes, the pattern of the daily schedule, the pattern of the school calendar).

The influence of this interaction among activities, physical environment, and temporal regularities is seen as not only pervasive and relatively stable, but also as having very great power to mold the behavior of the people in the organization. Sarason has extended this insight to attempts to plan and create settings in newly created organizations that presumably would elicit kinds of behaviors thought to be functional and productive in terms of the organization's mission.[47]

The interaction-influence system. A central concept in organizational behavior is that of the interaction-influence system of an organization. We should keep in mind that the basic function of organizational structure is to establish patterns of human interaction to get the tasks accomplished (who deals with whom, in what ways, and about what). Thus, departments, teams, schools, and divisions are typical formal structures, while friendship groups, people who work in close proximity to one another, and coffee-klatch groups are typical informal structures. The interactions between and among people thus put into contact with each other in conducting the day-to-day business of the organization establish the norms that are so powerful in shaping organizational behavior.

The interaction-influence system of the organization deals simultaneously with both structure and the processes of interaction. The two are mutually interdependent in such a dynamic way that they cannot be considered independently. In this sense, the interaction-influence patterns in shaping the organizational behavior of work groups are roughly the counterparts of person and environment in eliciting and shaping the behavior of individuals.

The interaction processes in the interaction-influence system include communication, motivation, leadership, goal setting, decision making, coordination, control, and evaluation. The ways in which these interactions are effected in the organization (their characteristics and quality) exercise an important influence on eliciting and shaping human behavior. Efforts to describe the organizational culture of educative organizations are, therefore, efforts to describe the characteristics of the organization's interaction-influence system.

DESCRIBING AND ASSESSING ORGANIZATIONAL CULTURE IN SCHOOLS

The study of organizational culture presents nettlesome problems to the traditional researcher primarily because important elements of culture are subtle, unseen, and so familiar to persons inside the organization as to be considered self-evident and unworthy of discussion. Collecting, sorting, and summarizing data such as the significant historical events in the organization and their implications for present-day behavior, the impact of organizational heroes on contemporary thinking, and the influence of traditions and organizational myths, is a task that does not lend itself to the tidiness of a printed questionnaire and statistical analysis of the responses to it. As the work of Ouchi, Peters and Waterman, Kanter, and Deal and Kennedy demonstrated, it is necessary to get inside the organization: to talk at length with people; to find out what they think is important to talk about; to hear the language they use; and to discover the symbols that reveal their assumptions, their beliefs, and the values to which they subscribe. For that reason, students of organizational culture tend to use qualitative research methods rather than traditional questionnaire-type studies. This has raised vigorous debate in many schools of education as to the epistemological value of qualitative research methods as contrasted with the more traditional statistical studies (of the experimental or quasi-experimental type) that have long been the stock-in-trade of educational researchers.

RELATIONSHIP BETWEEN ORGANIZATIONAL CULTURE
AND ORGANIZATIONAL EFFECTIVENESS

Do various organizational cultures produce different outcomes, in terms of effectiveness, in the organization achieving its goals? The issue is far from simple: measuring organizational effectiveness is, in itself, a complex undertaking, and the traditional need felt by many people in management to control and direct subordinates in the *command* sense of the term tends to tinge with emotion discussion of the issue.

To a large extent, accepted conventions of research and rules of evidence, discussed above, form the heart of this controversy. It has long been accepted in the logic of science that cause-and-effect relationships are best established by such rationalistic research designs as the controlled experiment. Experimental research, of course, requires that one can control the relevant variables under study.

There is a substantial body of carefully controlled experimental research conducted in laboratory settings that strongly undergirds the psychological concepts from which students of organizations draw in conceptualizing organizational behavior.[48] However, studies of actual organizations in the real world often must be conducted under conditions wherein such control is not possible. There is an analogous situation here with the extensive research literature on the possibility that "cigarette smoking causes cancer in humans," which is not a body of controlled experimental research that *proves* that cigarette smoking is the single causative factor. Research evidence *suggesting* (however strongly) a causal link between cigarette smoking and the incidence of cancer in humans is generally derived from such nonexperimental research as survey studies (many of which are longitudinal in design) or controlled research conducted on animals. Generally, there is such a strong *association* between the incidence of smoking and the incidence of cancer that many people accept that a cause-and-effect relationship exists. In terms of scientific rules of evidence, however, this is not *proof* and one can argue that, until evidence from fully controlled experiments is produced, the cause-and-effect relationship cannot be accepted as conclusive.

So it is with the link between organizational culture and organizational effectiveness: no significant body of *experimental* research in which the variables are fully controlled exists, and, therefore, discussion of the issue must be in the realm of *association* of significant variables. There is little question that many students of organizational behavior have ducked this issue by contenting themselves with refining techniques for defining and describing the variables of organizational culture or—in some cases—cautiously suggesting a possible relationship.

Cause and effect. Rensis Likert was distinctive in that—unlike many students of organizational culture who are content merely to describe and assess relevant variables—he sought to link organizational performance to the internal characteristics of the organization. His analysis is that the performance of an organization is determined by a three-link chain of causes and effects.

The first link in the chain is composed of the *causal variables,* which are under the control of the administration. Thus, administration (management) can *choose* the design of the organization's structure (mechanistic or organic, bureaucratic or flexible). Similarly, administration can *choose* the leadership style (for example, authoritarian or participative); it can *choose* a philosophy of operation (for example, teamwork or directive, problem-solving or rule-following). The choices that administration makes in selecting the options available are critical to and powerful in determining the nature of the management system in the organization (namely, Systems 1, 2, 3, or 4). These are seen as causing the interaction-influence system of the organization—in other words, its culture—to have the characteristics that it does have.

Intervening variables flow directly from (are caused largely by) these causal variables (that is, the choices that administration makes). Thus, the nature of motivation, communication, and other critical aspects of organizational functioning is determined.

End-result variables, the measures of an organization's success, depend heavily, of course, on the nature and quality of the internal functioning of the organization.

This analysis fits nicely with recent reports of qualitative research in American public schools—such as Theodore Sizer's *Horace's Compromise,*[49] Ernest Boyer's *High School,*[50] and John Goodlad's[51]—and their counterparts from the corporate world—such as *In Search of Excellence, Theory Z, Corporate Cultures,* and *The Change Masters.* For, as Rosabeth Moss Kanter pointed out in the latter work and I discussed earlier, innovative companies are marked by a culture of pride and a climate of success in which the organizational norms support success-oriented effort—and that depends upon the values which the leaders enact in the daily life of the organization.

The problem of measuring school effectiveness. Any effort to relate organizational culture (however described and measured) to the effectiveness of educative organizations squarely confronts the difficulties of assessing the effectiveness dimension. This problem requires that we identify indicators of organizational effectiveness for schools and ways of measuring them. Needless to say, this problem has been receiving markedly increased attention over the years.

In research parlance, we are dealing with sets of variables. Organizational climate and other internal characteristics of the school (for example, style of leadership, communication processes, motivational forces) are examples of *independent* variables. Other independent variables are characteristics of the situation in which the school, as an organization, is embedded. This, of course, would include such characteristics of the community as its wealth, its social-cultural traditions, its political power structure, and demography. Very often it seems clear that these two independent variables are highly interactive, but little has been done to explore this possibility. For example, we have scant firm evidence of what impact the situational variables with which a school contends have on shaping the characteristics of the interaction-influence system of the school. We must remember that the school is an open system, interactive with and responsive to its external environment. Though organizational culture focuses on the internal arrangements of schools, those always reflect, to some degree, the larger environment of the school's situation.

Dependent variables are indicators of organizational effectiveness. These can be grouped roughly as objective indicators and subjective indicators. Measures of achievement (such as test scores) and measures of some behaviors (for example, dropouts, absences) often can be quantified objectively. Very often we use subjective measures of school effectiveness, too. These could include performance ratings by various of the school's publics, as well as surveys of attitudes toward the school's performance.

One recent, sophisticated attempt to "get at" the complexities of this problem was a study by Wilbur Brookover and his associates of a random sample of 2,226 Michigan elementary schools. The dependent variable, by which effectiveness was measured, was the mean achievement scores of fourth-grade pupils in the standardized Michigan Assessment Program.

The key independent variable was a measure of school climate that was developed from the following definition:

> The school climate encompasses a composite of variables as defined and perceived by members of this group. These factors may be broadly conceived as the norms of the social system and expectations held for various members as perceived by the members of the group and communicated to members of the group.[52]

The investigators noted that a good deal of the previous research of this kind had used the socioeconomic status (SES) of the children or the racial composition of the school as a proxy for organizational climate. Among such studies that are well known to educators are the famous "Coleman report"[53] and the work of Christopher Jencks on inequality of schooling.[54] In this case, however, the researchers chose to devise an instrument to measure climate directly in the schools under study. The climate variable was essentially a measure of the norms and expectations in the school. Appropriately enough, the researchers called this the Student Sense of Academic Futility. Thus, the principal independent variables in the study were (1) mean school-level SES, (2) racial composition of the school (that is, percent of students who were white), and (3) climate of the school.

In commenting on their findings, the investigators said, "The first and foremost conclusion derived from this research is that some aspects of school social environment clearly make a difference in the academic achievement of schools."[55] Although there were large differences between the achievement levels in various schools, the socioeconomic and racial composition of the student bodies in those schools accounted for only a small percentage of the variance. The crucial variable, strongly associated with objective measures of student achievement, was the social climate of the school (measured, in this case, by the student's sense of academic futility).

The researchers concluded that this concept of climate, at least, is clearly related to school achievement and observe that:

> If we apply these findings to the school desegregation issue, it seems safe to conclude that neither racial nor socioeconomic desegregation of schools automatically produces higher school achievement. If the unfavorable social-psychological climate which typically characterizes segregated black and lower SES schools continues to prevail for the poor or minority students in the desegregated schools, desegregation is not likely to materially affect achievement of the students. If the social-psychological climate relevant to the poor and minority [students] is improved in conjunction with desegregation, higher achievement is likely to result.[56]

Strong research support for a close relationship between the culture of the school and outcomes also comes from a study of twelve inner-city London schools.[57] The research questions were:

1. Do a child's experiences at school have any effect?
2. Does it matter which school a child attends?
3. If so, which are the features of the school that matter?

The first question was prompted, of course, by a number of American studies that raise serious questions as to what effect attendance at school actually has (for example, Coleman's and Jencks's work). The second and third questions deal specifically with the cause-and-effect problem under discussion here.

To measure school outcomes the researchers used the following dependent variables: (1) pupil behavior, (2) pupil attendance, and (3) regularly scheduled public school examinations. The study showed, first, that there was a marked difference in the behavior, attendance, and achievement of the students in various secondary schools. Second, these differences between schools was not accounted for by the socioeconomic or ethnic differences of their students: clearly, students were likely to behave better and achieve more in some schools than in others. Third, these differences in student behavior and performance

> ...were *not* due to such physical factors as the size of the school, the age of the buildings or the space available; nor were they due to broad differences in administrative status or organization [for example, structure]. It was entirely possible for schools to obtain good outcomes in spite of initially rather unpromising and unprepossessing school premises, and within the context of somewhat differing administrative arrangements...the differences between schools in outcome *were* systematically related to their characteristics as social institutions.[58]

Key among these latter characteristics (that is, the independent variables) were (1) the behavior of teachers at work, (2) the emphasis placed on academic performance, (3) the provision for students to be rewarded for succeeding, and (4) the extent to which students were able to take responsibility. All these factors, the researchers pointed out, were open to modification by the staff, rather than fixed by external constraints. In short, this research strongly suggests that organizational culture (which they call "ethos") is a critical factor in student behavior and achievement. And, much as Likert did, they point out that organizational culture is in the control of the people who manage the organization.

Joyce Epstein has reported studies in schools which describe the perceptions of students' satisfaction with school in general, their commitment to school work, and their attitudes toward teachers.[59] Taken together, these are thought by Epstein to describe the quality of school life as the students perceive it. Further, this perception is described as, of course, being related to the behaviors of the students as participants in the organization. To conduct such studies, Epstein has developed and validated a 27-item questionnaire designed to be used across school levels (that is, elementary, middle, and high school).

Rudolf Moos has reported large-scale research in the United States, in both secondary school and college settings, that supports the mounting evidence in the literature that the learning and development of students are significantly influenced by characteristics of organizational culture.[60] After studying some 10,000 secondary school students in over 500 classrooms, he was able to identify characteristics of classroom organizational culture that facilitate academic achievement, on the one hand, and those that induce stress, alienate students, and thereby inhibit learning, on the other hand. He measured the variances from classroom to classroom in such contextual influences as (1) stress on competition, (2) emphasis on rules, (3) supportive behavior by the teacher, and (4) extent of innovative activities. They were the independent variables. These measures were then correlated with measures of dependent variables, such as (1) student rate of absence, (2) grades earned, (3) student satisfaction with learning, and (4) student satisfaction with the teacher.

In college settings Moos studied 225 living groups (for example, coed and single-sex residence halls, fraternities and sororities), involving about 10,000 students. Using questionnaires, he measured distinctive characteristics of these various groups such as (1) emphasis on intellectuality, (2) social activities, and (3) group unity. He then sought to assess the effects of these variables on such dependent variables as (1) students' concepts of themselves, (2) personal interests and values, (3) aspirations, and (4) achievement.

Essentially, Moos found that students' learning and development are strongly influenced by the nature and qualities of the person-environment interaction in such educational settings as secondary school classrooms and college residence arrangements. An interesting aspect of his research is his attempt to demonstrate how organizational culture and human behavior are influenced, not only by the interaction-influence system of the group but also by other factors in the environment such as room design, schedule of activities, and layout of building. In his view, our knowledge of the causes and effects of organizational culture enables us to create and manage specified learning environments by controlling critical variables (such as competition, intellectuality, and formal structure). This, in turn, improves our ability to place students in the settings best suited to their needs—settings in which they will feel most comfortable and be most successful. This, he contends, is highly practical knowledge that can be used to develop administrative policies and peda-gogical practices that are effective in dealing with student apathy, alienation, absenteeism, and dropouts.

DESCRIBING AND ASSESSING ORGANIZATIONAL CLIMATE IN SCHOOLS

To describe and assess the climate of a school requires (1) the development of a clear concept of what the key factors are in the interaction-influence system that determines climate, (2) the creation of some method of collecting data that describes these factors (usually a paper-and-pencil questionnaire), and (3) a procedure by which the data may be analyzed and, ultimately, displayed in a way that informs us.

Literally scores of ways of describing and assessing organizational climates of various kinds of organizations have been proffered in the literature. The great bulk of these can be dismissed because they are largely intuitive in nature, giving little attention to a clear, systematic concept of the nature of climate itself on which to develop data-gathering and data-analysis procedures. This leaves at least a dozen well-developed scientific approaches that have been used in many kinds of organiza-tional settings, ranging from the crews of space capsules to universities, from pris-oner-of-war camps to the employees of large offices. Since our concern here is focused on education, only climate-assessment techniques that deal specifically with educa-tional organizations are discussed. Criteria for selecting the three climate-assessment techniques included in the discussion were:

1. The contribution that the theoretic construct on which the technique is based can make to our understanding of the organizational climate itself;
2. The relative frequency with which the technique actually has been used in studies of *education.*
3. The scientific quality of the technique.

ORGANIZATIONAL CLIMATE DESCRIPTION QUESTIONNAIRE (OCDQ)

With the publication in 1962 of a research report, entitled *The Organizational Climate of Schools,*[61] Andrew W. Halpin and Don B. Croft introduced the notion of organizational climate to educators. Because, by definition, organizational climate is experienced by people in the organization, they assumed that the *perceptions* of these people are a valid source of data. Though one may argue that perceptions themselves are not objective reflections of "reality" (but may be influenced by subjective factors), the point is that whatever people in the organization *perceive* as their experience is the reality to be described. The purpose of an assessment of organizational climate is to obtain an objective description of those perceptions. Therefore, Halpin and Croft sought to elicit from teachers the critical factors that they generally agreed were central to describing the climate of a school. It should be remembered that, at the time of the Halpin and Croft research the concept of organizational cultures was unknown. It is now understood that climate is the study of the perceptions of participants of factors in the organizational environment that are likely to reflect the culture of the organization.

Eventually they identified two clusters of factors. One cluster consisted of four factors that describe the teachers' perceptions of the teachers as a human group:

> *Intimacy*—the degree of social cohesiveness among teachers in the school;
>
> *Disengagement*—the degree to which teachers are involved and committed to achieving the goals of the school;
>
> *Espirit*—the apparent morale of the group;
>
> *Hindrance*—the extent to which teachers see rules, paper work, and "administrivia" as impeding their work.

The other cluster of climate factors was the collective perception of teachers concerning the principal:

> *Thrust*—the dynamic behavior with which the principal sets a hard-working example;
>
> *Consideration*—the extent to which the principal is seen as treating teachers with dignity and human concern;
>
> *Aloofness*—the extent to which the principal is described as maintaining social distance (for example, cold and distant or warm and friendly);
>
> *Production emphasis*—the extent to which the principal tries to get teachers to work harder (for example, supervising closely, being directive, demanding results).

To obtain data from teachers on these eight factors, Halpin and Croft devised a simple questionnaire. Each of the sixty-four items on the questionnaire elicited a perception on one of the eight factors. A sample from the OCDQ is shown in Figure 7–3. A scoring procedure yielded group scores for a given school faculty.

FIGURE 7–3. Sample items from the Organizational Climate Description Questionnaire. From Andrew W. Halpin and Don B. Croft, *The Organizational Climate of Schools* (Chicago: Midwest Administration Center, University of Chicago, 1963), pp. 122–24.

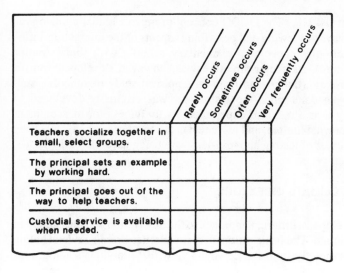

Halpin's and Croft's central finding (based on initial data obtained in seventy-one suburban elementary schools) was that descriptions of the teachers as a human social group tend to be associated with the teachers' perceptions of the principal in relatively consistent patterns. For example, some schools—said to have a *closed climate*—appear thus in the perceptions of teachers: teachers tend not to be highly engaged in their work, they do not work well together, and their achievement as a group is minimal. The principal in such a school is seen by the teachers as ineffective in leading them, as creating a great deal of hindrance to their work, and as not inclined to be concerned about their personal welfare. Teachers get little satisfaction from their work, morale is low, and there is likely to be a high turnover of teachers. The principal is seen as aloof and impersonal, and tends to urge teachers to work harder. Such a principal tends to emphasize rules, is often arbitrary, and generally "goes by the book"—keeping good records and getting reports out punctiliously. Such a principal is viewed by teachers as working with little personal drive, as being not terribly inventive or creative in reducing the obstacles and annoyances that teachers encounter, and as often philosophically ascribing problems in the school to outside forces over which he or she has no control.

Using the OCDQ, Halpin and Croft identified a range of types of climates that ran from the "closed" (as just described) to the *open climate* school which is, of course, quite different. The teachers of a school with an open climate tend to see the principal's behavior as an easy, authentic integration of the official role and his or her own personality. Such a principal works energetically, shows concern and even compassion for teachers, and yet is well able to lead, control, and direct them; he or she is not especially aloof or distant, seems to know how to follow rules and regulations with minimum hindrance to teachers, and does not feel the need to monitor teachers and supervise them closely, yet is in full control. Under such leadership, teachers obtain considerable satisfaction from their work and are sufficiently motivated to overcome most difficulties and frustrations. The teachers are proud to be part of the school, do not feel burdened by busywork, regulations, and "administrivia," and have enough incentive to solve their own problems and keep the organization moving.

Comments on OCDQ.   The OCDQ concept of organizational climate produced some useful ways of viewing and describing aspects of the interaction-influence systems of schools (especially elementary schools with their simpler organizational structure). Its factor structure was, however, developed from a strictly deductive process (rather than from an empirical study of schools), and, indeed, little has been done since the instrument was originally developed to validate it or modify it as a result of experience. Its usefulness for measurement purposes is now somewhat limited, and more recent approaches—which have been under constant processes of testing and revision—are being used increasingly.

ORGANIZATIONAL CLIMATE INDEX (OCI)

George C. Stern developed a different approach to the description and measurement of organizational climate. The basic rationale that underlies Stern's understanding of climate emanates directly from the Lewinian view that individuals and groups in organizations must be understood in the context of their interaction with the environment (B = fP, E). In this view, behavior is related to *both* person and environment. Efforts to assess the climate of a given organization must, therefore, measure *both* characteristics of individuals and characteristics of the environment.

Stern, a psychologist, saw an analogy between human personality and the personality of the institution, and he drew on the much earlier work of Henry A. Murray, who had developed the concept of *need-press* as it shaped human personality.[62] Murray postulated that personality is the product of dynamic interplay between need, both internal and external, and press, which is roughly equivalent to the environmental pressures that lead to adaptive behavior.[63] Two questionnaire instruments were devised to determine the need-press factors Stern felt influenced the development of climate in institutions of higher education: the Activities Index (AI), which assessed the need structure of individuals, and the College Characteristics Index (CCI), which probed the organizational press as experienced by persons in the organization.[64]

Over the years, these two questionnaires have been used on a number of campuses, where they have helped researchers assess organizational climate in higher education settings. Differences among various institutions of higher learning—denominational colleges, state universities, liberal arts colleges, and teachers colleges, among others—are observable for measurable factors such as staff and facilities, achievement standards, aspirations of students, extent of student freedom and responsibility, academic climate, and social life on the campus. The level of intellectual press seems to be particularly valuable in explaining important differences among collegiate institutions.

George Stern and Carl Steinhoff developed an adaptation of the CCI, applicable to schools and other organizations, called the Organizational Climate Index (OCI), which was first used in 1965 in a study of the public schools in Syracuse, New York.[65] The OCI presents teachers with statements that could apply to their schools; the teachers then are asked to mark these statements true or false, as applicable to their schools. Typical statements presented in the OCI are shown in Figure 7–4. Analysis of the data from studies of a number of schools has led to the formulation of the six OCI Climate Index Factors, shown in Figure 7–5.

A school's Development Press score is computed from the sum of the scores for Factors 1, 2, and 3 minus the score for Factor 6. Schools with high scores on Development Press are characterized by organizational environments that emphasize intellectual and interpersonal activities. In general, these environments are intellectually stimulating, maintain high standards for achievement, and are supportive of personal expression. Such schools characteristically tend to motivate

FIGURE 7–4. Sample of the forty true-false items that comprise the Organizational Climate index. Short Form (OCI-375 SF). Copyright © 1975 by George G. Stern and Joel Richman.

Social events get a lot of enthusiasm and support.
People find others eager to help them get started.
People are expected to have a great deal of social grace and polish.
People here speak up openly and freely.
Good work is really recognized around here.
Everyone here has a strong sense of being a member of the team.
Personality and pull are more important than competence in getting ahead around here.

Factor 1: Intellectual Climate. Schools with high scores on this factor have environments that are perceived as being conducive to scholarly interests in the humanities, arts, and sciences. Staff and physical plant are seen to be facilitative of these interests and the general work atmosphere is characterized by intellectual activities and pursuits.

Factor 2: Achievement Standards. Environments with high scores on this factor are perceived to stress high standards of personal achievement. Tasks are successfully completed and high levels of motivation and energy are maintained. Recognition is given for work of good quality and quantity and the staff is expected to achieve at the highest levels.

Factor 3: Personal Dignity (Supportiveness). Organizational climates scoring high on this factor respect the integrity of the individual and provide a supportive environment that would closely approximate the needs of more dependent teachers. There is a sense of fair play and openness in the working environment.

Factor 4: Organizational Effectiveness. Schools with high scores on this factor have work environments that encourage and facilitate the effective performance of tasks. Work programs are planned and well organized, and people work together effectively to meet organizational objectives.

Factor 5: Orderliness. High scores on this factor are indicative of a press for organizational structure and procedural orderliness. Neatness counts and there are pressures to conform to a defined norm of personal appearance and institutional image. There are set procedures and teachers are expected to follow them.

Factor 6: Impulse Control. High scores on this factor imply a great deal of constraint and organizational restrictiveness in the work environment. There is little opportunity for personal expression or for any form of impulsive behavior.

FIGURE 7–5. Organizational Climate Index factors and their definitions. © 1975 by Joel Richman.

FIGURE 7–6. Development Press and Control Press are scalar dimensions of organizational climate measured by the OCI.

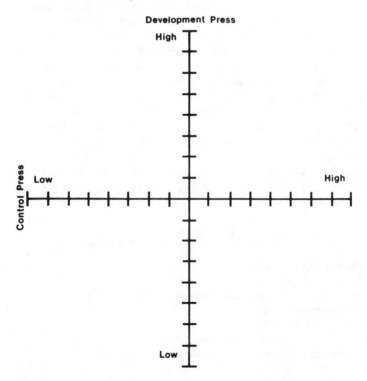

people, are concerned about their personal needs, and accept (indeed, encourage) a wide range of behavior styles among participants.

A school's score on Control Press (Task Effectiveness) is computed by adding together the scores for Factors 4 and 5. Schools high in Control Press are characterized by internal environments that emphasize orderliness and structure. Rules and going through channels are important in such schools, and concepts of what constitutes appropriate behavior tend to be clear-cut, narrow, and emphasized. In short, schools with such environments tend to be task-oriented rather than people-oriented.

In sum, the two key dimensions that describe the organizational climate of a school, using the Stern-Steinhoff Organizational Climate Index, are development press and control press. By representing these dimensions, as shown in Figure 7–6, we can plot the OCI score of a school and describe its organizational climate, either in terms of the dimensions or in relationship to the data from other schools. As the OCI has been applied to a number of schools, normative data have been developed which are useful for interpreting the score of an individual school. In 1968, Steinhoff administered the OCI to a number of New York City schools in an effort to obtain such normative data for that big-city situation, in order to supplement the normative data that he had already obtained from medium-sized Syracuse.

There is a general tendency for the climate of schools to fall within a rough elongated oval when plotted on a scattergram, as shown in Figure 7–7. Obviously,

FIGURE 7–7. When assessed with the OCI, the organizational climates of schools generally tend to fall within a rough, oval pattern in either of two combinations: (a) emphasizing High Development Press and Low Control Press or (b) Low Development Press and High Control Press.

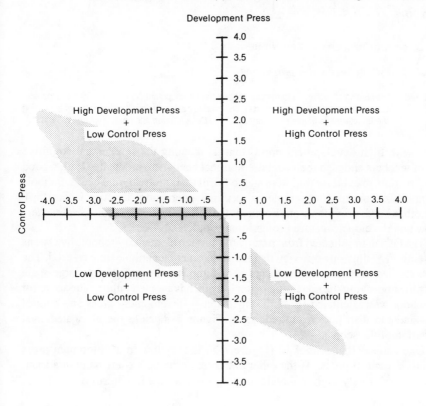

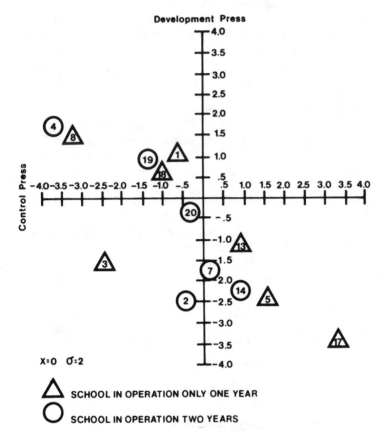

Development Press

X=0 σ=2

△ SCHOOL IN OPERATION ONLY ONE YEAR

○ SCHOOL IN OPERATION TWO YEARS

FIGURE 7–8.   Distribution of fourteen elementary schools on Development-Control axes of the Organizational Climate Index. From Robert G. Owens and Carl R. Steinhoff, "Strategies for Improving the Effectiveness of Inner-City Schools," *Phi Delta Kappan,* 50, no. 5 (January 1969),261.

schools with high development press (that is, meeting the intellectual-cognitive needs of teachers and also their social-emotional needs) are associated with a good deal of freedom to exercise initiative and to fulfill their motivational needs. Schools that emphasize control (for example, rules, close supervision, directive leadership), on the other hand, provide an environment that offers less opportunity for teachers to grow and develop as mature professional people.

The OCI data collected from a study of fourteen elementary schools by Owens and Steinhoff [66] illustrate one way that this assessment technique may be used. The schools studied were selected from a group of demonstration schools in a large-scale project for improving the education of socially disadvantaged pupils. The score for each school was calculated for both dimensions—development press and control press—and the distribution plotted, as in Figure 7–8. Note the elongated oval distribution of the scores.

One can see that school 17 (Figure 7–8) is very low in development press and high in control press. At the other extreme, in the upper-left-hand quadrant, school 4 is relatively high in development press and low in control press. These data—which represent the perceptions of teachers in the schools—include those for one school in which there is obviously little chance to be self-actualizing or to exercise initiative, a situation in which freedom is quite inhibited (that is, school 17). In contrast, another school offers participants a great deal of freedom to "be themselves," and there is little in the environment that is inhibiting (school 4). The sample of schools represented here is an especially interesting distribution, because before the project it was generally felt by professionals in the educational community that the schools in the project were "all alike." Yet, as we can see, there is a relatively broad, even range along the two axes, which indicates not only that the schools were not alike—in terms of their organizational climates—but also that they exhibited a variety of climate types that are not clustered or likely to have occurred merely by chance.

Comments on the OCI.　Though the Stern need-press theory of the psychological environments in educative organizations has not enjoyed popularity among those concerned with public schools that the OCDQ has, it has been used in a number of studies. A deterrent to early popularity was the length and complexity of the questionnaires (the full OCI once having 300 items). Another deterrent was the relative complexity of the data analysis and interpretation procedures. A short form of the OCI that is simple to use has been available since 1975, however. This can be hand-scored, and school norms for elementary, junior high, senior high, rural, suburban, and urban, which also are simple to use, have been published.

Among the many strengths of the need-press approach are that (1) it is based upon a strong (if not simple) theoretic concept of organizational climate that has held up well, and (2) it has a long history of meticulous research that has yielded assessment instruments that have been carefully scrutinized for validity and reliability. Consequently, the OCI is a powerful assessment tool that yields relatively rich and fine-grained data suited to the analysis of climates of individual schools. It is, at the same time, capable of producing the kinds of normative data needed to study groups of schools (for example, the schools in a given district or the schools involved in an experimental project).

In addition, the OCI appears to be applicable to a wide variety of educative organizations—elementary, secondary, and college,[67] urban or suburban. Various forms of the questionnaire instruments make it possible, also, to obtain data from pupils and students, as well as from adults such as teachers.

PROFILE OF A SCHOOL (POS)

For more than thirty years, beginning in 1947, Rensis Likert directed an extensive, large-scale program of research that was basically intended to identify the human factors that influence the ultimate effectiveness of organizations to achieve their goals. Most of the research was carried out in industrial firms, although in later years it included schools and universities, health-care organizations, public agencies, and military organizations. By 1961, Likert was able to describe significant relationships among (1) the management styles, (2) the characteristics of the organization's interaction-influence system, and (3) the effectiveness of the organization.[68] In 1967, Likert published a comprehensive theory of management that is derived from the extensive data that had been gathered up to that time.[69]

Essentially, Likert's approach is to measure characteristics of the internal functioning of the organization and to relate those to measures of organizational performance. Performance of the organization is determined by such measures as:

1. Productivity (for example, profitability, return on investment, share of the market).
2. Rate of absence and turnover.
3. Loss through scrap and waste.
4. Quality control.

These measures are objective and may be obtained from the records usually maintained by industrial and business firms.

Measuring the internal functioning of the organization, however, required the development of a data-gathering procedure based on some notion as to what was significant. Likert devised a paper-and-pencil questionnaire that employees fill out and that describes six characteristics of the organization:

1. Leadership processes.
2. Motivational forces.
3. Communication processes.
4. Decision-making processes.
5. Goal-setting processes.
6. Control processes.

Four management systems.   One basic concept that Likert derived from his data was that there are four identifiable management systems. Each is describable in terms of organizational climate and leadership behavior, as measured in terms of the organization's characteristics. System 1 is called *exploitive-authoritative* (or punitive-authoritarian) and, as is shown in Figure 7–9, is based upon classical management concepts, a Theory X view of motivation, and a directive leadership style. System 2 is *benevolent-authoritative,* (or paternalistic-authoritarian). It emphasizes a one-to-one relationship between subordinate and leader in an environment in which the subordinate is relatively isolated from others in work-related matters. System 3, called *consultative,* employs more of a participative leadership style in which the leader tends to consult with people *individually* in the process of making decisions (for example, Hersey's-Blanchard's S2, Vroom's CI). System 4, the *participative* (or group interactive) model of an organizational system, uses Theory Y concepts of human functioning and emphasizes team interaction in all of the critical organizational processes (for example, Hersey's-Blanchard's S3, Vroom's GII).

FIGURE 7–9.   Likert's four management systems. From David G. Bowers, *Systems of Organization: Management of the Human Resource* (Ann Arbor: University of Michigan Press, 1976), pp. 104–5.

SYSTEM 1: EXPLOITIVE AUTHORITATIVE

Motivational Forces

Taps fear, need for money and status. Ignores other motives, which cancel out those tapped. Attitudes are hostile, subservient upward, contemptuous downward. Mistrust prevalent. Little feeling of responsibility except at high levels. Dissatisfaction with job, peers, supervisor and organization.

Communication Pattern

Little upward communication. Little lateral communication. Some downward communication, viewed with suspicion by subordinates. Much distortion and deception.

Interaction-Influence Process

No cooperative teamwork, little mutual influence. Only moderate downward influence, usually overestimated.

Decision-Making Process

Decisions made at top, based upon partial and inaccurate information. Contributes little motivational value. Made on man-to-man basis, discouraging teamwork.

Goal-Setting Process

Orders issued. Overt acceptance. Covert resistance.

Control Process

Control at top only. Control data often distorted and falsified. Informal organization exists, which works counter to the formal, reducing real control.

SYSTEM 2: BENEVOLENT AUTHORITATIVE

Motivational Forces

Taps need for money, ego motives such as desire for status and for power, sometimes fear. Untapped motives often cancel out those tapped, sometimes reinforce them. Attitudes are sometimes hostile, sometimes favorable toward organization, subservient upward, condescending downward, competitively hostile toward peers. Managers usually feel responsible for attaining goals, but rank and file do not. Dissatisfaction to moderate satisfaction with job, peers, supervisor and organization.

Communication Pattern

Little upward communication. Little lateral communication. Great deal of downward communication, viewed with mixed feelings by subordinates. Some distortion and filtering.

Interaction-Influence Process

Very little cooperative teamwork, little upward influence except by informal means. Moderate downward influence.

Decision-Making Process

Policy decided at top, some implementation decisions made at lower levels, based on moderately accurate and adequate information. Contributes little motivational value. Made largely on man-to-man basis, discouraging teamwork.

Goal-Setting Process

Orders issued, perhaps with some chance to comment. Overt acceptance, but often covert resistance.

Control Process

Control largely at top. Control data often incomplete and inaccurate. Informal organization usually exists, working counter to the formal, partially reducing real control.

SYSTEM 3: CONSULTATIVE

Motivational Forces

Taps need for money, ego motives, and other major motives within the individual. Motivational forces usually reinforce each other. Attitudes usually favorable. Most persons feel responsible. Moderately high satisfaction with job, peers, supervisor and organization.

Communication Pattern

Upward and downward communication is usually good. Lateral communication is fair to good Slight tendency to filter or distort.

Interaction-Influence Process

Moderate amount of cooperative teamwork. Moderate upward influence. Moderate to substantial downward influence.

Decision-Making Process

Broad policy decided at top, more specific decisions made at lower levels, based upon reasonably accurate and adequate information. Some contribution to motivation. Some group-based decision making.

Goal-Setting Process

Goals are set or orders issued after discussion with subordinates. Usually acceptance both overtly and covertly, but some occasional covert resistance.

Control Process

Control primarily at top, but some delegation to lower levels. Informal organization may exist and partially resist formal organization, partially reducing real control.

SYSTEM 4: PARTICIPATIVE GROUP

Motivational Forces

Taps all major motives except fear, including motivational forces coming from group processes. Motivational forces reinforce one another. Attitudes quite favorable. Trust prevalent. Persons at all levels feel quite responsible. Relatively high satisfaction throughout.

Communication Pattern

Information flows freely and accurately in all directions. Practically no forces to distort or filter.

Interaction-Influence Process

A great deal of cooperative teamwork. Substantial real influence upward, downward and laterally.

Decision-Making Process

Decision making done throughout the organization, linked by overlapping groups and based upon full and accurate information. Made largely on group basis encouraging teamwork.

Goal-Setting Process

Goals established by group participation, except in emergencies. Full goal acceptance, both overtly and covertly.

Control Process

Widespread real and felt responsibility for control function. Informal and formal organization are identical, with no reduction in real control.

FIGURE 7–9. *(cont'd.)* Likert's four management systems. From David G. Bowers, *Systems of Organization: Management of the Human Resource* (Ann Arbor: University of Michigan Press, 1976), pp. 104–5.

Application to school systems. In 1968, Rensis Likert and Jane Gibson Likert developed questionnaires for use in schools, called *Profile of a School* (POS) questionnaires, which are based upon the survey questionnaires that had been used in business and industry. Interrelated POS questionnaires are available for use with school board members, superintendents, central office people, principals, department heads and chairpersons, teachers, students in grades four through six, students in grades seven through twelve, and parents—thus making possible broad-scale studies in school districts.

A sample of items from the POS for teachers is shown in Figure 7–10. Sample items from the Student's Questionnaire, Form 3, are shown in Figure 7–11. Likert and Likert also have produced *Profile of a College or University* questionnaires, which have been used in various kinds of institutions of higher education, including large universities, liberal arts colleges, and community colleges.

By plotting the data obtained from a questionnaire survey, one can represent graphically the characteristics of an organization's interaction-influence system. Since, by definition, a graphic display of the measurements of the dimensions of a variable is a profile, the Likerts refer to this as the Profile of a School (POS). One can readily ascertain from a graphic display such as this which management system

FIGURE 7–10. Sample items from *Profile of a School, Teacher's Questionnaire, Form 3.* © 1977 by Jane Gibson Likert and Rensis Likert. Distributed by Rensis Likert Associates, Inc., Ann Arbor, Michigan 48108.

	SYSTEM 1		SYSTEM 2		SYSTEM 3		SYSTEM 4	
50. How accurate is upward communication to the principal?	USUALLY INACCURATE		OFTEN INACCURATE		FAIRLY ACCURATE		ALMOST ALWAYS ACCURATE	
	①	②	③	④	⑤	⑥	⑦	⑧
60. To what extent are you involved in major decisions related to your work?	VERY LITTLE		SOME		CONSIDER-ABLE		VERY GREAT	
	①	②	③	④	⑤	⑥	⑦	⑧
61. How much does the principal try to help you with your problems?	VERY LITTLE		SOME		QUITE A BIT		A VERY GREAT DEAL	
	①	②	③	④	⑤	⑥	⑦	⑧
62. How much help do you get from the central staff of your school system?	①	②	③	④	⑤	⑥	⑦	⑧
63. To what extent are decision makers aware of problems, particularly at lower levels?	VERY LITTLE		SOME		CONSIDER-ABLE		VERY GREAT	
	①	②	③	④	⑤	⑥	⑦	⑧
What is the administrative style of:	HIGHLY AUTHORI-TARIAN		SOMEWHAT AUTHORI-TARIAN		CONSULT-ATIVE		PARTICI-PATIVE GROUP	
64. the principal	①	②	③	④	⑤	⑥	⑦	⑧
65. the superintendant of schools	①	②	③	④	⑤	⑥	⑦	⑧
68. How high are the principal's goals for educational performance?	LOW		ABOUT AVERAGE		QUITE HIGH		VERY HIGH	
	①	②	③	④	⑤	⑥	⑦	⑧

	SYSTEM 1 RARELY		SYSTEM 2 SOMETIMES		SYSTEM 3 OFTEN		SYSTEM 4 VERY OFTEN	
1. How often is the behavior of your teachers friendly and supportive?	①	②	③	④	⑤	⑥	⑦	⑧

	VERY LITTLE		SOME		QUITE A BIT		A VERY GREAT DEAL	
8. How much confidence and trust to your teachers have in you?	①	②	③	④	⑤	⑥	⑦	⑧
11. How much do you feel that your principal is interested in your success as a student?	①	②	③	④	⑤	⑥	⑦	⑧

	RARELY		SOMETIMES		OFTEN		VERY OFTEN	
17. How often do your teachers ask for and use your ideas about academic matters, such as course content, subjects to be studied, books?	①	②	③	④	⑤	⑥	⑦	⑧

	NOT WELL		SOMEWHAT WELL		QUITE WELL		VERY WELL	
30. How well do your teachers know the problems you face in your school work?	①	②	③	④	⑤	⑥	⑦	⑧
31. How well does your principal know the problems you face in your school work?	①	②	③	④	⑤	⑥	⑦	⑧

FIGURE 7–11. Sample items from the *Profile of a School, Student's Questionnaire, Form 2.* © 1972 and 1978 by Jane Gibson Likert and Rensis Likert. Distributed by Rensis Likert Associates, Inc., Ann Arbor, Michigan 48108.

more nearly fits the description of the organization under study. A number of studies of schools and school systems has used the POS questionnaires. A description of a few of these will give some of the flavor of the kinds of research that the POS measurement technique makes possible.

Likert and Likert report studies of high schools, for example, in which teachers were asked to indicate the extent to which they thought that their department heads

Were friendly and supportive;
Showed confidence and trust in teachers;
Sought and used teachers' ideas;
Were interested in teachers' success;
Helped teachers with their problems.

Teachers were absent less often in those departments whose leaders were rated high in these items (System 4) than those in departments whose leaders were rated low (System 1). In addition, the teachers in departments with System 4 leadership tended to view the school principal more favorably than those in departments with System 1 leadership.[70] Use of the POS with teachers and with principals also reveals that there is often a discrepancy between the perception that principals have of their own leadership style and the perceptions that teachers have of their principals, with a tendency for principals to rate themselves as having styles much closer to System 4 behavior than teachers do (recall the discussion in Chapter 6 in which Fiedler reported a similar phenomenon in an experimental study of the behavior of school superintendents).[71]

A comparative study of thirty-four Individually Guided Education (IGE) elementary schools with twenty-five non-IGE schools reports that descriptions of principals' leader behavior were no different in one group of schools than in another: they generally clustered somewhere between System 2 and System 3 in style.[72] It would appear that the adoption of IGE does not necessarily assure the development of a more open, considerate, or otherwise effective leadership style on the part of a school principal.

A typical Profile of a School (POS) is shown in Figure 7–12. This particular profile is of a high school in which data were collected from 308 students and 94

FIGURE 7–12. Example of a high school profile derived from student and teacher questionnaires. From Albert F. Siepert and Rensis Likert, "The Likert School Profile Measurements of the Human Organization" (paper presented at the American Educational Research Association, New Orleans, 1973).

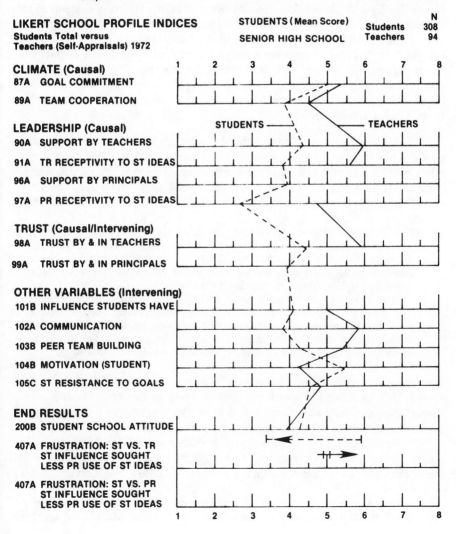

teachers. Through a data-analysis process, responses to various items on the questionnaires have been clustered into indices, and it is the mean scores of these indices that are plotted on the graph.

At the top are the significant causal variables (climate and leadership). The intervening variables (for example, mutual trust, communication process, and personal motivation) are arrayed next on the profile. Finally, end results are graphed in terms of student attitude and a measure of frustration.

This particular example is interesting because the researchers asked the respondents to answer the questionnaires in two ways: (1) as a self-appraisal of their own behavior and (2) as a perception of the behavior of others. The discrepancy between these was used as a measure of frustration (that is, the extent to which a person *expects* to be involved in decisions affecting him or her and the extent to which the person *experiences* this involvement). This is illustrated in item 407A in Figure 7–12, which shows a discrepancy between (a) the efforts of students to gain influence over events and (b) the extent to which teachers used student input.

Figure 7–13 further illustrates the kind of information a Profile of a School can yield. In this case, though the arrangement of data items differs slightly from that in Figure 7–12, the profile clearly reveals the tendency of principals to rate the school close to System 4, the teachers somewhat lower, and students significantly lower. This profile was generated from data from a group of California junior high schools in six school districts.

The linking-pin model for schools. Perhaps one of the most potentially powerful outcomes of the body of research utilizing the POS as a measure of climate arises from Likert's own analysis of the shortcomings of the organizational structure of American schools and its impact on the interaction-influence system (recall the discussion of the school as a loosely coupled system in Chapter 1). Likert observed that:

> The interaction-influence networks of our schools all too often are proving to be incapable of dealing constructively even with the internal school problems and conflicts, not to mention the conflicts impinging from the outside. Moreover, the present decision-making structure of the schools requires patterns of interaction that often aggravate conflict rather than resolving it constructively.
>
> Faculty meetings, for example, almost always employ parliamentary procedures that force a System 2 win-lose confrontation. The systematic, orderly problem solving that small groups can use does not and cannot occur in large meetings....[I]t is distressing to observe the extraordinary capacity of *Robert's Rules of Order* to turn the interaction of sincere, intelligent persons into bitter, emotional, win-lose confrontation.[73]

He goes on to point out that in meetings of fifty to one hundred faculty members there is little likelihood of creative problem solving, as factions of members joust through parliamentary maneuvering, and, in the end, few emerge with anything like genuine commitment to the actions that are finally taken.

In discussing Likert's approach to this problem, David Bowers points out that a place to begin is to understand what an organization is and what it is not (recall the discussions of organizational theory in Chapter 2). Bowers observes:

> An organization is not simply a physical plant or its equipment. It is not an array of positions, nor a collection of persons who fill these positions. [Recall the discussion of

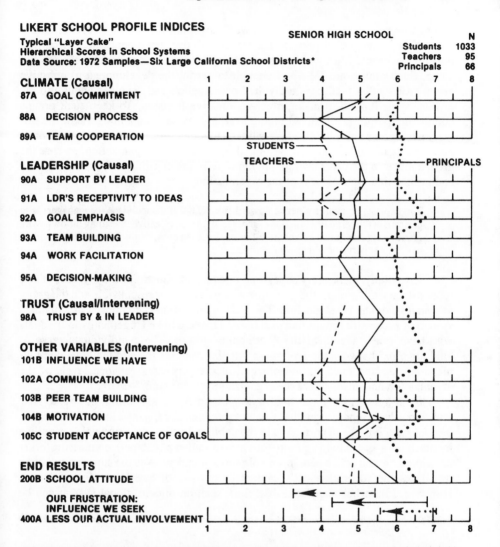

LIKERT SCHOOL PROFILE INDICES
Typical "Layer Cake"
Hierarchical Scores in School Systems
Data Source: 1972 Samples—Six Large California School Districts*

SENIOR HIGH SCHOOL
Students   1033
Teachers   95
Principals   66
N

CLIMATE (Causal)
87A   GOAL COMMITMENT
88A   DECISION PROCESS
89A   TEAM COOPERATION

STUDENTS
TEACHERS
PRINCIPALS

LEADERSHIP (Causal)
90A   SUPPORT BY LEADER
91A   LDR'S RECEPTIVITY TO IDEAS
92A   GOAL EMPHASIS
93A   TEAM BUILDING
94A   WORK FACILITATION
95A   DECISION-MAKING

TRUST (Causal/Intervening)
98A   TRUST BY & IN LEADER

OTHER VARIABLES (Intervening)
101B   INFLUENCE WE HAVE
102A   COMMUNICATION
103B   PEER TEAM BUILDING
104B   MOTIVATION
105C   STUDENT ACCEPTANCE OF GOALS

END RESULTS
200B   SCHOOL ATTITUDE

OUR FRUSTRATION:
INFLUENCE WE SEEK
400A   LESS OUR ACTUAL INVOLVEMENT

FIGURE 7–13.   Example of a "layer cake" profile of a school in which students, teachers, and principals hold different perceptions of school profiles. From Albert F. Siepert and Rensis Likert, "The Likert School Profile Measurements of the Human Organization" (paper presented at the American Educational Research Association, New Orleans, 1973).

role theory and the Getzels-Guba model in Chapter 3.] It is not a sequence of work tasks or technical operations. It is all of these things, to be sure, but it is fundamentally something more. The basic building block of the organization is the face-to-face group, consisting of the supervisor and those subordinates immediately responsible to him. *The organization consists most basically of a structure of groups, linked together by overlapping memberships into a pyramid through which the work flows.*[74] [Emphasis added.]

Thus, the organization is conceptualized as a roughly pyramidal structure whose basic unit is the face-to-face work group: people who regularly interact (communicate, influence, motivate) at work, together with their supervisor. Examples are department chairpersons and teachers in the departments, head librarians plus librarians and library aides, grade chairpersons and homeroom teachers, and so on. Such groups are (1) small enough to permit the development of effective group process that facilitates individual participation and (2) close enough to the task to be performed to make effective, creative decision. To keep such groups coordinated requires effective communication between and among them: the primary work groups must be effectively linked together. And, especially, Likert points out, it is essential that groups be linked *upward* in the organization, so that the groups lower in the organizational pyramid have the capability of interacting with and influencing higher levels of the organization.

> The capacity to exert influence upward is essential if a supervisor (or manager) is to perform his supervisory functions successfully. To be effective in leading his own work group, a superior must be able to influence his own boss, that is he needs to be skilled both as a supervisor and as a subordinate.[75]

Essentially, then, every supervisor or every administrator is a member of two face-to-face work groups: the group *for which* he or she is responsible and the group *to which* he or she is responsible. The total organization is composed of a planned system of such work groups that *overlap* and that are linked together by individuals who have roles in both of the overlapping groups. These individuals serve as "linking pins" between the groups—a role that requires them to facilitate communication, decision making, and other influence processes between levels of the organization and, also, across the organization (see Figure 7–14).

Such a structure is not totally new in American schooling, of course. The traditional high school principal's cabinet, for instance, generally includes chairpersons who link the departments to the cabinet. In turn, the principal is usually a member of a districtwide group (often also called a cabinet) comprising other principals, central office people, and the superintendent. And the superintendent, in turn links the superintendent's cabinet to the school board (see Figure 7–15). However, Likert has suggested that, *first*, such an organizational system can be

FIGURE 7–14.   The linking pin. From Rensis Likert, *New Patterns of Management* (New York: McGraw-Hill Book Company, 1961), p. 113.

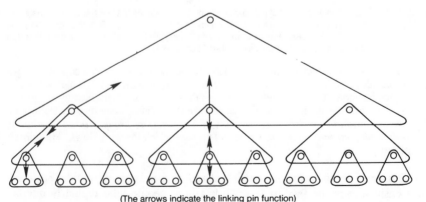

(The arrows indicate the linking pin function)

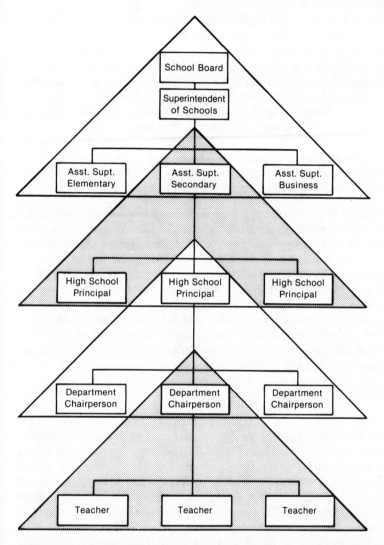

FIGURE 7–15. The linking-pin concept as applied to the decision-making structure of a medium-sized school district.

extended and elaborated to include all facets of the school district organization (including elementary schools).[76] *Second*—and more important—Likert has described how such an arrangement can facilitate the development of a more functional interaction-influence system: one that is not characterized by the traditional, directive, downward-oriented concepts of line-and-staff organization but, instead, is characterized by free communication and influence, up, down, and across the organization, featuring a teamwork approach to problems at all levels.

In sum, "the effectiveness of the interaction-influence system of an organization and the capacity of this system to deal with difficult problems depend upon the effectiveness of the work groups of which the structure consists and upon the extent to which multiple linkage is provided."[77] Considering, therefore, the dynamic interdependence between structure (for example, linked, overlapping groups) and the influence system (for example, directive or collaborative) brings us back to the central issue of leadership that was discussed in Chapter 6: participation in making decisions. One seeking to develop a collaborative interaction-influence system must attend to developing a leadership or administrative style that will develop the skills and motivation of subordinates that support such an approach. In other words, one would seek to move from System 1 to System 4. The ideas of Tannenbaum and Schmidt, Vroom, Reddin, and Hersey and Blanchard concerning leadership (all discussed in Chapter 6) suggest approaches to making such a shift possible. All of this conforms to the major approaches to motivation (that is, the ideas of Maslow, Porter and Lawler, Herzberg, and others) discussed in Chapter 5.

Comments on POS. The POS survey questionnaire approach can be understood only in the context of the extensive research upon which the concepts underlying Likert's theory of management systems rest. The theory itself is empirically derived— that is, Likert and his colleagues went into the real world and, using systematic quantitative measurements, looked at what members of organizations and organizations themselves do.[78] It is not armchair speculation. Through the analysis of numerous studies a critical mass of data has been assembled that gives strong support to the concepts, as well as to the validity and reliability of the survey questionnaire instruments themselves. Clearly, we are dealing with a major formal theory of organizational behavior that is matched only by the work of McGregor and Herzberg in impact and significance for both researchers and practitioners in this country.

SUMMARY

In the 1980s, the concept of organizational culture emerged as central in the analysis of organizational behavior and organizational effectiveness. Organizational culture is the body of solutions to problems that has worked consistently for a group and that is therefore taught to new members as the correct way to perceive, think about, and feel in relation to those problems. Over time, organizational culture takes on meaning so deep that it defines the assumptions, values, beliefs, norms, and even the perceptions of participants in the organization. Though culture tends to drop from the conscious thoughts of participants over time, it continues to powerfully create meaning for them in their work and becomes "the rules of the game."

By the mid-1980s studies of schools, such as the work of Meyer and Rowan, Deal, Weick, Lightfoot, Goodlad, and Sizer had lent strong support to earlier work of Sarason and Barker demonstrating that organizational culture is a fundamental factor in determining the quality of educational organizations. Culture cannot be studied directly but is inferred from observed behavior such as language, use of artifacts, rituals, and symbolism commonly encountered in the workplace.

Organizational climate, which is the study of the perceptions of participants of certain intangible aspects of the environment, reflects the culture. Studies of organizational climate ordinarily use questionnaires to elicit perceptions from participants. The trend in the study of organizational climate in schools has been away from the study of the perceptions of adults toward the study of those of pupils and students.

As the study of organizational culture moved to a central position in organizational behavior in education, it was accompanied by increasing use of such qualitative research methods as participant observation and open-ended unstructured interviews to replace traditional statistical research methods. The use of qualitative research methods makes it possible to produce richly detailed "thick" descriptions of the organizational culture of schools which are necessary in order to explain what is happening in them. While the use of such methods is relatively recent in the study of organizational behavior in comparison with traditional statistical methods, they are derived from a long and respected research tradition in anthropology and sociology as well as educational administration. Qualitative research methods, such as ethnography, are based on very clear concepts of the nature of inquiry that are quite different from conventional rationalistic concepts and observe rules of procedure and rigor that are equally clear and different from those of conventional quantitative methods.

Much of the research on organizational culture, in both corporate and educational organizations, is related to the effectiveness of the organizations. The studies of Peters and Waterman, Deal and Kennedy, and Kanter, for example, all describe relationships between performance of the company (in such terms as market share, sales, and profitability) and the organizational culture within the company. There is comparable support for a similar thesis in education. In large measure, clearly establishing such causal connections in schooling is hampered by the extraordinary complexity of the organization and the confusion and ambiguity among and between various constituencies of schooling as to the criteria for determining what high performance is in a school.

A substantial and growing body of empirical evidence, derived from vigorous research in schools and other educative organizations, indicates that the effectiveness of these organizations, in terms of student learning and development, is significantly influenced by the quality and characteristics of the organizational culture. Not surprisingly, the research clearly suggests that schools that emphasize supportiveness, open communication, collaboration, intellectuality, and that reward achievement and success outperform (in terms of achievement, attendance, dropout rate, frustration, and alienation) those that emphasize competition, constraint and restrictiveness, rules and standard operating procedures and that reward conformity. Further, by delineating the critical factors involved, the concepts arising from this body of research make it possible and practicable to plan and manage organizational culture purposefully. It would be difficult to overemphasize the implications arising from this research for administrative practice in the era marked by declining confidence in schools and school systems and by increasing demands for accountability for performance.

SUGGESTED READING

COHEN, ALLAN R., AND HERMAN GADON, "Changing the Management Culture in a Public School System," *The Journal of Applied Behavioral Science*, 14, no. 1 (1978), 61–78.
A case study of an effort to shift the management style (of school board members, superintendent and assistants, central office specialists, and principals) in a New England school district toward, in effect, System 4 style. Specific and practical insights for the practitioner who wants to know how to plan and manage such a change.

LEVINE, SARAH, L., *Promoting Adult Growth in Schools: The Promise of Professional Development.* Boston: Allyn and Bacon, 1989.

This book starts with an examination of the professional lives of school teachers and finds what many have found before: that teaching is isolating, inhibiting of personal growth and development, and for these reasons is unsatisfying and rewarding. Moreover, this is inevitably reflected in the effectiveness of the schools. Levine goes on, however, to discuss what can be done by school principals and others to change all this so as to develop schools as growth-enhancing environments for the adults who work in them. Contains a great deal of useful, practical advice.

LIEBERMAN, ANN, ed., *Building a Professional Culture in Schools*. New York: Teachers College Press, 1988.

Note that the title of this book uses the term "professional culture" rather than "organizational culture." This is not by chance: it reflects the belief that schools should be developing a very definite kind of culture. It is an interesting book of readings in which a number of currently popular writers, including activists, researchers, academics, and unionists, advocate various aspects of developing schools which are more collegial and in which teachers enact greater leadership than in the past.

LUTZ, FRANK W., AND LAURENCE IANNACCONNE, *Understanding Educational Organizations: A Field Study Approach*. Columbus, OH: Charles E. Merrill Publishing Company, 1969.

Two pioneers in the long history of qualitative research in educational administration—known particularly for their study of the exercise of power in schools—describe their theory, their research methods, and procedures to use in the field. A sound introduction for the reader inexperienced in using field methods in the study of school culture.

MEYER, JOHN W., W. RICHARD SCOTT, AND TERRENCE E. DEAL, "Institutional and Technical Sources of Organizational Structure: Explaining the Structure of Educational Organizations," in *Organizations and Environments: Ritual and Rationality*, John W. Meyer and W. Richard Scott, eds. Beverly Hills, CA: Sage Publications, Inc., 1983.

A provocative discussion of the contrast between the conventional structuralist explanation of organizational characteristics of schools with the emerging cultural (or, as the authors put it, "institutional") explanation. Other chapters in this book elaborate important new perspectives on organizational characteristics of schools which generally begin with the understanding that much of what we have come to accept as organizational structure is, in reality, myth and ceremony.

OTT, J. STEVEN, *The Organizational Culture Perspective*. Pacific Grove, CA: Brooks/Cole Publishing Company, 1989.

A comprehensive textbook that provides a readable survey of contemporary organizational culture theory and research. Although it primarily deals with corporate culture, and includes numerous examples from business and industry, educators will find it a useful source for illuminating concepts of organizational culture that are readily applicable to educational settings.

SARASON, SEYMOUR B., *The Culture of the School and the Problem of Change*. Boston: Allyn & Bacon, Inc., 1971.

Based on his own extensive experiences in schools, this now classic small volume presents a sensitive, insightful description of schools, how they are "really" organized, and what this means for developing effective ways of facilitating change in them. An easy-to-read book that endures as an exceptional example of the use of the concept of culture as an organizer for the analysis of the school as an organization.

STINCHCOMBE, JEAN, *Response to Declining Enrollment: School Closing in Suburbia*. Lanham, MD.: University Press of America, 1984.

Using qualitative research methods, this investigation chronicles five years of the history of a school district wrestling with the prospect of closing a school. While it analyzes the situation as an example of community politics, and does not use organizational culture itself as an organizer, the study will raise many relevant questions for those interested in understanding the culture of schools. A particular contribution of this study is that the author relates the observations and findings to the considerable body of previous qualitative research literature in educational administration to demonstrate that the events described in this research are part of a pattern that is well-established in American school districts.

NOTES

[1]Peter F. Drucker, *Concept of the Corporation* (New York: The John Day Co., 1946), p. 26.
[2]Alfred J. Marrow, David G. Bowers, and Stanley E. Seashore, *Management by Participation* (New York: Harper & Row, Publishers, Inc., 1967).

[3]Terrence E. Deal, "Cultural Change: Opportunity, Silent Killer or Metamorphosis?" (unpublished paper, no date).

[4]Chester A. Barnard, *Functions of the Executive* (Boston: Harvard University Press, 1938).

[5]Philip Selznick, *TVA and the Grass Roots* (Berkeley: University of California Press, 1949).

[6]Marshall W. Meyer and associates, eds., *Environments and Organizations* (San Francisco: Jossey-Bass, 1978).

[7]Andrew W. Halpin and Don B. Croft, *The Organizational Climate of Schools* (Chicago: Midwest Administration Center, The University of Chicago, 1962).

[8]Bernard Clark, "The Organizational Saga in Higher Education," in *Managing Change in Educational Organizations*, J. Victor Baldridge and Terrence E. Deal, eds. (Berkeley, CA: McCutchan, 1975).

[9]Michael Rutter, Barbara Maughan, Peter Mortimore, and Jane Ouston, with Alan Smith, *Fifteen Thousand Hours: Secondary Schools and Their Effects on Children* (Cambridge, MA: Harvard University Press, 1979).

[10]Deal, "Cultural Change," p. 6.

[11]Renato Tagiuri, "The Concept of Organizational Climate," in Renato Tagiuri and George H. Litwin, eds., *Organizational Climate: Exploration of a Concept* (Boston: Harvard University, Division of Research, Graduate School of Business Administration, 1968). See also, Carolyn S. Anderson, "The Search for School Climate: A Review of the Research." *Review of Educational Research*, 52 (Fall 1982), 368–420, and Cecil Miskel and Rodney Ogawa, "Work Motivation, Job Satisfaction, and Climate," in Norman J. Boyan, ed., *Handbook of Research on Educational Administration* (New York: Longman, Inc., 1988).

[12]William Ouchi, *Theory Z: How American Business Can Meet the Japanese Challenge* (Reading, MA: Addison-Wesley, 1981).

[13]Ibid., p. 165.

[14]Thomas J. Peters and Robert H. Waterman, Jr., *In Search of Excellence: Lessons from America's Best-Run Companies* (New York: Harper & Row, Publishers, Inc., 1982).

[15]Ibid., p. 282.

[16]Terrence E. Deal and Allan A. Kennedy, *Corporate Cultures: The Rites and Rituals of Corporate Life* (Reading, MA: Addison-Wesley, 1982).

[17]Peters and Waterman, *In Search of Excellence*, p. 319.

[18]Edgar H. Schein, "How Culture Forms, Develops, and Changes," in *Gaining Control of the Corporate Culture*, Ralph H. Kilmann, Mary J. Saxton, Roy Serpa, and associates (San Francisco: Jossey-Bass, 1985), p. 19–20.

[19]Ibid., p. 20.

[20]Ralph H. Kilmann, Mary J. Saxton, and Roy Serpa, "Five Key Issues in Understanding and Changing Culture," in Kilmann and others, *Gaining Control of the Corporate Culture*, p. 5.

[21]Ibid.

[22]Terrence E. Deal, "Cultural Change: Opportunity, Silent Killer, or Metamorphosis?", in *Gaining Control of the Corporate Culture* (revision of previously unpublished paper), p. 301.

[23]Ibid.

[24]Ralph H. Kilmann, "Five Steps for Closing Culture-Gaps," in Kilmann and others, *Gaining Control of the Corporate Culture*, p. 352.

[25]Alan L. Wilkins and Kerry J. Patterson, "You Can't Get There from Here: What Will Make Culture Projects Fail," in Kilmann and others, *Gaining Control of the Corporate Culture*, p. 267.

[26]George C. Homans, *The Human Group* (New York: Harcourt, Brace, & World, 1950), p. 123.

[27]A. Paul Haire, *Handbook of Small Group Research*, (New York: The Free Press, 1962), p. 24.

[28]A. R. Cohen and others, *Effective Behavior in Organizations*, 3rd ed. (Homewood, IL: Richard D. Irwin, 1984), p. 62.

[29]Schein, "How Culture Forms, Develops, and Changes," in Kilmann and others, *Gaining Control of the Corporate Culture*, p. 21.

[30]Ibid., pp. 19–20.

[31]Ralph H. Kilmann, Mary J. Saxton, and Roy Serpa, "Five Key Issues in Understanding and Changing Culture," in Kilmann and others, *Gaining Control of the Corporate Culture*, p. 5.

[32]Ibid.

[33]Terrence E. Deal, "Cultural Change: Opportunity, Silent Killer, or Metamorphosis?" in Kilmann and others, *Gaining Control of the Corporate Culture*, p. 301.

[34]Halpin and Croft, *The Organizational Climate of Schools*.

[35]Rosabeth Moss Kanter, *The Change Masters: Innovation and Entrepreneurship in the American Corporation* (New York: Simon & Schuster, Inc., 1983), p. 149.

[36]George C. Homans, *The Human Group* (New York: Harcourt, Brace, & World, 1950), p. 123.

[37]A. Paul Haire, *Handbook of Small Group Research* (New York: The Free Press, 1962), p. 24.

[38]Kurt Lewin, *Principles of Topological Psychology* (New York: McGraw-Hill Book Company, 1936).

[39]Garlie A. Forehand and B. Von Haller Gilmer, "Environmental Variations in Studies of Organizational Behavior," Psychological Bulletin, 62, no. 6 (December 1964), 361–82.

[40]James G. March and Herbert A. Simon, *Organizations* (New York: John Wiley & Sons, Inc., 1959).

[41]Renato Tagiuri, ed., *Research Needs in Executive Selection* (Boston: Harvard University, Graduate School of Business Administration, 1961).

[42]Roger G. Barker describes the theory of behavior settings and ways of studying them in *Ecological Psychology: Concepts and Methods for Studying the Environment of Human Behavior* (Stanford, CA: Stanford University Press, 1968).

[43]Roger G. Barker and Paul V. Gump, eds., *Big School, Small School* (Stanford, CA: Stanford University Press, 1964).

[44]Leonard L. Baird, "Big School, Small School: A Critical Examination of the Hypothesis," *Journal of Educational Psychology,* 60 (1969), 253–60.

[45]Leonard L. Baird, "The Relation of Vocational Interests to Life Goals, Self-Ratings of Ability and Personality Traits, and Potential for Achievement," *Journal of Educational Measurement,* 7 (1970), 233–39.

[46]Seymour B. Sarason, *The Culture of the School and the Problem of Change* (Boston: Allyn & Bacon, Inc., 1971).

[47]Seymour B. Sarason, *The Creation of Settings and Future Societies* (San Francisco: Jossey-Bass, 1972).

[48]This field is well surveyed in Marvin D. Dunnette, ed., *Handbook of Industrial and Organizational Psychology* (Chicago: Rand McNally & Company, 1976).

[49]Theodore R. Sizer, *Horace's Compromise: The Dilemma of the American High School* (Boston: Houghton Mifflin, 1984).

[50]Ernest L. Boyer, *High School: A Report on Secondary Education in America* (New York: Harper & Row, Publishers, Inc., 1983).

[51]John I. Goodlad, *A Place Called School: Prospects for the Future* (St. Louis: McGraw-Hill, 1983).

[52]Wilbur B. Brookover and others, "Elementary School Social Climate and School Achievement," *American Educational Research Journal,* 15, no. 2 (Spring 1978), 302.

[53]James S. Coleman and others, *Equality of Educational Opportunity* (Washington, DC: Government Printing Office, 1966).

[54]Christopher Jencks and others, *Inequality* (New York: Basic Books, Inc., Publishers, 1972).

[55]Brookover and others, "Elementary School Social Climate and School Achievement," p. 316.

[56]Ibid., p. 317.

[57]Rutter and others, *Fifteen Thousand Hours.*

[58]Ibid., p. 178.

[59]Joyce L. Epstein, ed., *The Quality of School Life* (Lexington, MA: D. C. Heath & Co., 1984).

[60]Rudolf H. Moos, *Evaluating Educational Environments* (Palo Alto, CA: Consulting Psychologists Press, 1979).

[61]Andrew W. Halpin and Don B. Croft, *The Organizational Climate of Schools* (U.S.O.E. Research Project, Contract no. SAE 543-8639, August 1962).

[62]Henry A. Murray and others, *Explorations in Personality* (New York: Oxford University Press, 1938), p. 124.

[63]For a full description of Stern's extensive research in this field, see George G. Stern, *People in Context: Measuring Person-Environment Congruence in Education and Industry* (New York: John Wiley & Sons, Inc., 1970).

[64]George G. Stern, "Characteristics of Intellectual Climate in College Environments," *Harvard Educational Review,* 31 (Winter 1963), 5–41.

[65]Carl R. Steinhoff, *Organizational Climate in a Public School System* (U.S.O.E. Cooperative Research Program, Contract no. OE-4-255, Project no. S-083, Syracuse University, New York, 1965).

[66]Robert G. Owens and Carl R. Steinhoff, "Strategies for Improving Inner-City Schools," *Phi Delta Kappa,* 50, no. 5 (January 1969), 259–63.

[67]See, for example, Carl R. Steinhoff and Lloyd Bishop, "Factors Differentiating Preparation Programs in Educational Administration: U.C.E.A. Study of Student Organizational Environment," *Educational Administration Quarterly,* 10 (1974), 35–50; and Lloyd Bishop and Carl R. Steinhoff, "Organizational Characteristics of Administrative Training Programs: Professors and Their Work Environments," *Journal of Educational Administration,* 13 (1975), 54–61.

[68]Rensis Likert, *New Patterns of Management* (New York, McGraw-Hill Book Company, 1961).

[69]Rensis Likert, *The Human Organization: Its Management and Value* (New York: McGraw-Hill Book Company, 1967).

[70]Rensis Likert and Jane Gibson Likert, *New Ways of Managing Conflict* (New York: McGraw Hill Book Company, 1976).

[71]See, for example, Benjamin Cullers, Clarence Hughes, and Thomas McGreal, "Administrative Behavior and Student Dissatisfaction: A Possible Relationship," *Peabody Journal of Education*, 50 (January 1973), 155–63.

[72]William Joseph Gauthier, Jr., "The Relationship of Organizational Structure, Leader Behavior of the Principal and Personality Orientation of the Principal to School Management Climate" (unpublished doctoral dissertation, University of Connecticut, 1975).

[73]Likert and Likert, *New Ways of Managing Conflict*, pp. 218–19.

[74]David G. Bowers, *Systems of Organization: Management of the Human Resource* (Ann Arbor: University of Michigan Press, 1976), pp. 2–3.

[75]Likert, *New Patterns of Management*, p. 144.

[76]Likert and Likert, *New Ways of Managing Conflict*, Chapter 12.

[77]Likert, *New Patterns of Management*, p. 181.

[78]Bowers, *Systems of Organization*, p. 2.

8

ORGANIZATIONAL CHANGE

"We trained hard...but it seemed every time we were beginning to form up into teams we were reorganized. I was to learn later in life that we tend to meet any situation by reorganizing, and a wonderful method it can be for creating the illusion of progress while producing confusion, inefficiency, and demoralization."

—*Gaius Petronius*

One of the dominant concepts that has emerged in the twentieth century is that of planned, controlled, and directed social change. It is a worldwide belief today that societies need not be confined to adaptive reaction to changing values and events as they unfold but that they can consciously direct the forces of change to suit predetermined goals and social values. A related and equally important trend, which has given impetus to the notion that social change can be successfully planned and managed, is the emphasis upon the growing belief that planned and controlled change in *individual* lives is not only possible, but necessary if the long-range goals of each one of us are to be realized.

This dynamic concept of social change has been fueled and shaped by the theories and values from two principal sources: one is Marxist political and social theory, and the other is the empirically based social sciences largely as developed in the United States. The impact of this emerging concept upon educational institutions and organizations has been extraordinary, for it implies that the processes of creating a desirable society require creating a compatible educational system. Although there is some debate about the power of educational systems to create societies, there is little argument that planned social change is supported by compatible educational systems.

Early in the century, prevailing views emphasized social change as flowing from economic and technological transformations in the world. Since mid-century, however, ever-increasing attention has been given to the centrality of social and cultural values as a dynamic in change processes. Clearly, in the second half of the twentieth century, for example, education has come to be viewed as a key to equality and equity in all societies. In this sense, education has been thrust into a central position in the political world, for deciding what equity is and what social values are crucial is clearly a political issue and not merely a technical educational issue.

In order for an educational system to reflect the will of the political community, change in educational organizations cannot be planned and managed by educational policy makers alone: provision must be made for orchestrating the participation of all the social groups involved.

But educational organizations are expected not only to be vehicles for social change, they are expected also to preserve and transmit traditional values to younger members of society at the same time as they are expected to prepare them to deal with an ever-changing world. As Seymour Sarason has pointed out:

> There are few, if any, social problems for which explanations and solutions do not in some way involve the school—involvement that may be direct or indirect, relevant or irrelevant, small or large. After all, the argument usually runs, the school is a reflection of our society as well as the principal vehicle by which its young are socialized or prepared for life in adult society.[1]

Thus, schools and other educational organizations must confront not merely change but, rather, the integration of stability *and* change. And, many observers, impatient to bring about change in schools, have pointed out again and again that the more things change in schools, the more they remain the same. Yet, as Matthew Miles reminds us:

> ...many aspects of schools as organizations, and the value orientations of their inhabitants, are founded on history and constitute...genotypical properties. These are important to the schools; they help maintain continuity and balance in the face of the school's ambiguous mission and its vulnerability to external pressures from parents and others. Therefore, it is likely that, while rapid shifts in specific school practices are relatively more possible, changes touching on the central core of assumptions and structures will be far more difficult to achieve.[2]

THE TRADITION OF CHANGE IN AMERICAN EDUCATION

Historically, change in American education was viewed largely as a process of "natural diffusion." That is, new ideas and practices arose in some fashion and spread in some unplanned way from school to school and from district to district. The result was that schools generally changed very slowly: in the late 1950s Paul Mort observed that it then took about fifty years for a newly invented educational practice to be generally diffused and accepted in schools throughout the country and that the average school lagged some twenty-five years behind the best practice of the time.[3]

Natural diffusion processes. Mort observed in the late 1950s that there was a pattern to this unplanned process of diffusion:

> Educational change proceeds very slowly. After an invention which is destined to spread throughout the school appears, fifteen years typically elapse before it is found in three percent of the school systems....After practices reach the three percent point of diffusion, their rate of spread accelerates. An additional 20 years usually suffices for an almost complete diffusion in an area the size of an average state. There are indications that the rate of spread throughout the nation is not much slower.[4]

This is well illustrated by the introduction and spread of kindergartens. In 1873—nearly twenty years after the introduction of private kindergartens to America from Germany—the city of St. Louis established the first public school kindergartens. By the mid-1950s, there was little doubt that kindergarten education had been firmly established in the profession as a desirable educational practice, and, indeed, such federally funded projects as Head Start provided strong stimuli for spurring its development. However, as late as the 1967–1968 school year (ninety-four years after the introduction of kindergartens in St. Louis), only 46 percent of the nation's school districts provided kindergarten education for their children.[5]

For many years, Mort was considered the leading student of educational change in this country. The main thesis of his work was that adequacy of financial support is the key factor in determining how much lag a school system exhibits in adopting innovative practices. Vigorously active in his many years as a teacher and researcher at Teachers College, Columbia University, Mort left a storehouse of knowledge and a large number of devoted students who have heavily influenced the thinking of school administrators with regard to the factors that enhance change and innovation in schools. Largely because of this influence, per pupil expenditure has long been considered the most reliable predictor of a school's chances of adopting educational innovations.

The systematic underpinnings of the cost-quality relationship in education are generally felt to have been established in 1936 by Paul Mort's and Francis Cornell's study of Pennsylvania schools.[6] Numerous studies dealing with the relationship between expenditure and measures of school output have followed, which generally support the not-too-surprising notion that high expenditure is generally associated with various indicators of superior school output. A troublesome fact was noted rather early in this research, however: it is possible for school districts to have high per pupil costs and still have inferior schools.[7] Considerable research has been undertaken since 1938 to explain this fact, much of it exploring the nature of the cost-quality relationship itself. Mort tended to think of this relationship as linear: more money would tend to assure higher educational quality, and there was no point of diminishing returns. Since 1965, however, increasing attention has been paid to the possibility that cost-quality relationships in education are actually curvilinear and have an optimum point beyond which additional expenditure fails to yield increased school output.[8]

Sociological views of diffusion.   Although it would be absurd to say that the schools' efforts to reduce the lag in change would be enhanced by penurious circumstances, more recent research tends to emphasize the influences of social structure on the amount and rate of change. For example, Richard O. Carlson studied the rate and pattern of the adoption of "new math" in a West Virginia county.[9] Carlson reported that the position that a superintendent of schools held in the social structure of the school superintendents of the county made it possible to make reasonable predictions about the amount and rate of innovation in that superintendent's school district. When the superintendent was looked upon as a leader by his or her peers, as influential among other superintendents, and as in communication with many of them, his or her district tended to adopt innovations early and thoroughly. Contrary to the bulk of existing research on cost-quality relationships, Carlson did not find a parallel between innovation and the financial support level of the school district. If nothing else, such studies—and Carlson's study represents only one of many sociological studies of organizational change and innovation—indicate that money spent is only one factor in the adaptability of schools, to use Mort's term. Within limits that are not yet clear, it is probably not even the major factor.

Planned, managed diffusion. The strategy by which money is spent may have a greater impact on change in schools than conventional indices such as per pupil expenditure may indicate. One of the more spectacular and better-known attempts to alter significantly the pattern of change in the public schools in the post-Sputnik era was undertaken by the Physical Science Study Committee (PSSC) in 1956, under the leadership of Professor J. R. Zacharias of the Massachusetts Institute of Technology.[10] Briefly, the PSSC group wanted to improve the teaching of physical science in American high schools. Retraining thousands of teachers, developing new curricula for all sizes of school districts, and persuading the local school boards to buy the needed materials and equipment all, by traditional methods, might well have taken half a century to accomplish. Instead, within ten years after the project was inaugurated, high schools were considered to be behind the times if they did not offer a PSSC course.

This incredibly swift mass adoption was achieved by a strategy that involved three phases: (1) inventing the new curriculum, (2) diffusing knowledge of the new curriculum widely and rapidly among high school science teachers, (3) and getting the new curriculum adopted in local schools. This was a strategy that involved the use of a number of new ideas. In addition to bypassing local school districts wherever possible, the PSSC group invested its money in novel and powerful ways. First, by spending $4.5 million in two and one-half years to hire a full-time professional "team," a portable, self-contained curriculum "package" was developed and tested in practice. This "package" included filmed lessons, textbooks, teachers' guides, tests, and laboratory guides and apparatus—a completely unified, integrated unit that could be moved *in toto* into almost any high school. Second, physics teachers were introduced to the new techniques by attending institutes, for which they received financial grants and stipends. Some forty institutes were made available each year throughout the country for this purpose. Third, by providing funds to be matched by the federal government (largely through the National Defense Education Act), the PSSC group persuaded local school boards to buy the package for their schools.

Three strategies of planned change. Contemporary approaches to change are dominated by efforts to develop strategies and tactics that may enable us to plan, manage, and control change. In this book, the taxonomy suggested by Robert Chin is used as the basis for discussion.[11] As I shall explain, Chin posits that there are three major "strategic orientations" that are useful in planning and managing change:

1. empirical-rational strategies,
2. power-coercive strategies,
3. normative-reeducative strategies.

EMPIRICAL-RATIONAL STRATEGIES OF CHANGE

The traditional processes of unplanned dissemination of new ideas to schools have given way to strategies of planned, managed dissemination intended to spread new ideas and practices swiftly. Much research and study have been devoted to these strategies, which are primarily focused upon more closely linking the findings of research to the practices of education. This linkage requires improving communication between researchers and practitioners (users, consumers of research) so that the traditional, scornful distance between them will be replaced by a more productive, cooperative (if not collaborative) relationship.

This approach sees the scientific production of new knowledge and its use in daily activities as the key to planned change in education. It is referred to broadly as Knowledge Production and Utilization (KPU). Numerous models for implementing the strategy have been proposed and tried; all of these attempt to develop an orderly process, with a clear sequence of related steps leading from the origination of new knowledge to its ultimate application in practice. The aim is to bridge the gap between theory and practice. To do this requires not only that the functions or activities of the process be described but also that someone (or some agency) be designated to carry them out.

Research, development, and diffusion (R, D, and D).   Various models for implementing KPU concepts of change appear under different appellations, depending upon the number of steps that are seen as important. An R and D model, for example, suggests that someone ought to be conducting research and that someone ought to be developing some useful products from that research. As in all KPU models, research is meant here to be the invention or discovery of new knowledge, regardless of its applicability to immediate problems. In R and D work, the quality and validity of the research are of paramount importance. The model recognizes, however, that the research scientist is not always the person best equipped to translate research findings into useful products.

The *development* phase of R and D includes such things as solving design problems, considering feasibility in "real-world" conditions, and cost. Development essentially means translating research into products that are practical for use; these can range from school buildings to pupil seating, from textbooks to comprehensive packaged curricula, or from instructional techniques to new types of football helmets. In free enterprise societies this stage has been largely the province of profit-seeking firms that have the necessary financial resources and entrepreneurial skills.

The *diffusion* phase of R, D, and D is seen as a third and distinctive phase; it is, more or less, the "marketing" activities of R, D, and D. The aim is to make the new products readily available in attractive, easy-to-use form at reasonable cost to the adopter.

Of course, the ultimate goal of all of this is to get the new ideas into use. Some, therefore, treat *adoption* as a separate aspect of the process and may even call it Research, Development, Dissemination, and Adoption (R, D, D, A) to emphasize this point. As David Clark and Egon Guba have made clear,[12] the processes of adoption are not simple. They describe a three-stage process: (1) *a trial,* during which the new product is tested in some limited way, (2) *installation,* a process of refinement and adaptation to local conditions if the trial appears promising, and finally—if all goes well—(3) *institutionalization,* which means that the innovation becomes an integral part of the system. A test of institutionalization is whether or not the invention continues in use if external support and encouragement are withdrawn. (See Figure 8–1.)

FIGURE 8–1. Concept of the Research, Development, Diffusion, and Adoption (R, D, D, A) model of change.

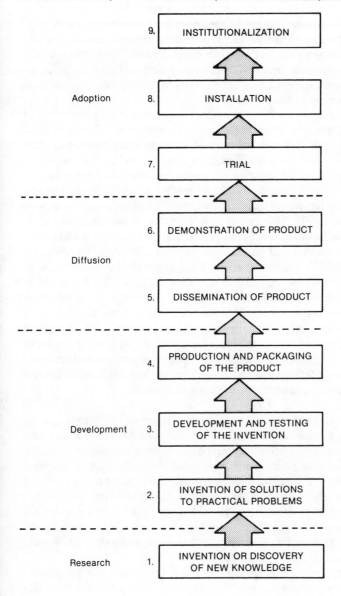

The "agricultural model."   It would be difficult to overemphasize the impact that the American experience with planned, controlled change in agriculture has had upon the thinking of those who advocate KPU strategies for education. Rural sociologists early discovered the processes and linkages that facilitated the rapid spread of new and better farming practices through the social system. The development of a network of land grant universities, agricultural experimentation stations, and the ubiquitous county agent are a few of the readily visible key parts of the extensive system that helps farmers to use new, yet proven, knowledge in the practical business of boosting production and lowering costs. When agriculture is compared to the public schools in terms of the speed with which new knowledge and techniques are put into widespread use, it is quickly apparent that agriculture has adopted innovations with far less lag than schools have. Thus, much of the model building and formalistic process development usually found in KPU approaches to change in education is based upon efforts to replicate the "agricultural model" in terms appropriate to education.

Beginning in the late 1950s, federal activity was considerably increased in this direction. For example, the National Defense Education Act (NDEA) of 1958 triggered the production of the spate of innovative curriculum "packages" that appeared in the 1960s.[13] Title IV of the Elementary and Secondary Education Act (ESEA) of 1965 provided for the creation of twenty regional educational laboratories and ten Educational Research and Development Centers throughout the country. The Educational Resources Information Center (ERIC) also appeared, with federal support, in the 1960s. This nationwide network of twenty information clearinghouses seeks to facilitate the rapid communication of research and development activities in forms that will be useful to those in education. The National Institute of Education (NIE) was organized in 1972 expressly for the purpose of fostering research, experimentation, and dissemination of knowledge that could be applied to the improvement of public schooling. The creation of a cabinet-level Department of Education in the executive branch of the federal government in 1979 was strongly supported by many who believed that such an agency was needed to exercise greater order, system, and control in educational KPU. Thus, in a span of a quarter-century, the nation moved vigorously to systematize and stimulate planned KPU in education through federal leadership, in place of the traditional, relatively unplanned, scattered, local, and small-scale efforts of the past.

Assumptions and implications of KPU approaches to change.   KPU approaches to change are based on two critical assumptions: (1) that the new knowledge (product, technique) will be perceived by potential adopters as desirable and (2) that adopters—being rational and reasonable—will do what is desirable because it is in their own self-interest. In other words, "the belief is that good ideas will be used to improve education."[14] It typifies what Robert Chin has described as an *empirical-rational strategy of change:* that is, the new knowledge or practice is empirically demonstrated to be good, and, therefore, one rationally expects it to be adopted.[15] It is a strategy that fits neatly into the traditions and values of Western scientific-technological culture.

To facilitate adoption, new ideas have to reach the adopters in practicable form. Thus, the local physician uses a new "wonder drug" with patients in the office when it is available in convenient containers and when the directions permit easy application with familiar implements. Increasingly, schools are being offered relatively complete instructional "delivery systems" that seek to provide comprehensive "packages" for instruction that, in turn, are based on demonstrably effective concepts and are complete enough to meet a significant need of the school. These are often referred to as *innovations*, and much attention is given to the difficulties of "installing" innovations in schools.

The term, "innovation," has been severely debased through misuse in the literature on organizational change and stability. Some people simply use it more or less as a synonym for "change." For example, H. G. Barnett posits that "innovation is any thought, behavior or thing that is new because it is qualitatively different from existing forms."[16] But such a broad generalization fails to convey the essence of innovation as it is used in organizational change. In fact, it fails to differentiate innovation from *organizational drift:* the inevitable, unplanned, incremental changes that pervade all organizations that exist in a culture whose dominant characteristic is change. Innovation has acquired a pejorative sense in educational circles owing to the frequency with which innovations have been introduced, tried, used, and abandoned.

In this book, the term *innovation* is used in referring to planned, novel, deliberate, specific change that is intended to help the organization (1) achieve existing goals more effectively or (2) achieve new goals. The concept of specificity is crucial: "...innovations in education...ordinarily have a defined, particular, specified character...."[17] Thus, one usually speaks of *an* innovation: something that can be specified in terms of (a) concepts, (b) a set of operating procedures, and (c) a relevant technology to which we attach a name (for example, magnet schools, alternative education, DISTAR reading program, individually prescribed instruction, and minimal competency testing). Thus, not all organizational change can be described as innovation: indeed, as I shall describe shortly, much desirable organizational change is not necessarily innovative in the sense that the term is used here.

The point to be emphasized, however, is that such empirical-rational strategies of change as KPU and R, D, and D tend to focus upon innovation. The concept is that good ideas are developed outside the school and are, ultimately, *installed* in the school. Thus, there is much concern about problems of disseminating the innovation and of installing the innovation in adopting schools. At the installation level, those who favor the innovation see it as empirically proven and view adoption as rational; conversely, they tend to view barriers to installation at the school level as nonrational (if not irrational). It is at this point that the empirical rationalist becomes concerned, not with *educational* change in a broad sense, but with *organizational* change to facilitate the adoption process.

Other empirical-rational strategies. In order to simplify this discussion, I have focused on one empirical-rational strategy, namely, linking basic research to practice by building diffusion networks and stimulating applied research. This typically involves creating research and development centers, linking state education departments to regional educational laboratories, and developing consortia of universities and school districts. Other empirical-rational strategies for change include:

Personnel selection and replacement. This includes "clearing out the deadwood" (through dismissal, early retirement, reorganization, transfers), as well as changing the criteria for the certification and employment of new people. Though many proponents of school reform advocated use of this strategy in the 1980s, many administrators confronted with a chronic shortage of teachers considered it of problematic value.

Utopian thinking. Futurists seek to develop scientific techniques for improving forecasting of the future. Their efforts are, of course, based upon the highly rational premise that skill in predicting the future can be helpful in making decisions at the present time. Their empirical rational attempts to project what *might* exist in the future, what the alternatives may be, and what *ought* to be can lead to planned efforts to direct the course of events toward some desired goal, rather than to accept whatever may occur.

POWER-COERCIVE STRATEGIES OF CHANGE

A power-coercive approach to change differs significantly from an empirical-rational one in its willingness to use (or threaten to use) *sanctions* in order to obtain compliance from adopters. Sanctions are usually political, financial, or moral. In the power-coercive point of view, rationality, reason, and human relations all are secondary to the ability to effect changes directly through the exercise of power.

One way of exercising political power is to gain control over the political institutions that pass legislation, issue executive orders, and hand down court decisions. These are commonly accompanied by financial sanctions to heighten their coercive effect. The popularity of this strategy in America is visible in the welter of legislation, judicial decisions, and governmental regulations—each with sanctions for noncompliance—that draw so much time and attention from educational policymakers and administrators.

Robert Chin and Kenneth Benne describe the restructuring of power elites as another power-coercive strategy to bring about change.[18] It is well recognized that our society has a power structure in which relatively limited groups have extraordinary power to affect change: either to make things happen or to keep them from happening. Instead of accepting the existing power structure as fixed and inevitable, it is possible to change the power structure. If this is done—either by shifting power to new hands or by spreading power more equitably among more people—it is possible to achieve new goals.

This has, of course, been well illustrated by the efforts of minority groups and women to gain representation in the key decision-making groups concerning schools, such as school boards, administrative positions, and boards that control finances. It is illustrated, too, by teachers—long maintained in a powerless and dependent state—who have unionized in an effort to shift their power relationships with administrators and school boards so as to bring about change. A third illustration is the coalition of groups concerned about the education of the handicapped, which has resulted in a series of laws and judicial decisions sharply rearranging the power structure in some key areas of educational decision making.

A THIRD STRATEGY: ORGANIZATIONAL SELF-RENEWAL

Both empirical-rational and power-coercive strategies of change share two assumptions: (1) that good ideas are best developed outside of the organization and (2) that the organization is the target of external forces for change. Implicit in these strategies is the notion that organizations—when left to their own devices—generally emphasize stability over change and generally are resistant to change; they therefore must be *made* to change. There is little question that both of these strategic orientations are effective under certain conditions. But there also is little question that educational organizations have demonstrated remarkable resilience in dealing with these external forces for change—maintaining considerable stability over time and often frustrating even vigorous empirical-rational and power-coercive efforts. The nature and extent of this frustration are illustrated by research conducted by the Rand Corporation for the United States Office of Education between 1973 and 1977.

The Rand study of federal programs supporting educational change. The concerns that led to this research were well expressed in 1975, in a publication of the National Institute of Education, which reflected the then-prevailing mood of the Congress:

> Over the past decade and a half, the federal government has spent over a billion dollars on research and development on the country's educational problems, and billions more on categorical aid to schools and districts. Yet, the problems remain intractable, and the repeated research finding that innovations produce "no significant differences" has engendered such frustration that some have begun to despair of the schools' potential for improvement. A disturbingly familiar national behavior pattern is beginning to manifest itself in education. We are a "can-do," "quick-fix" society. The answer to a problem is a program. If the program fails, we try another one, and if a whole series of programs fails, we tire of that problem and go on to fresher ones.[19]

In an effort to understand this situation, Rand undertook a study of federally funded programs that had been designed to introduce and spread innovative practices in public schools. "These change agent programs," it was noted, "normally offer temporary federal funding to school districts as 'seed money.' If an innovation is successful, it is assumed that the district will incorporate and spread part or all of the project using other sources of funds."[20] (Recall the discussion earlier in this chapter concerning the adoption and institutionalization of innovations, and see again Figure 8–1.)

The study consisted of a series of related investigations of 293 projects in eighteen states sponsored under the following federal programs:

a. Elementary and Secondary Education Act (ESEA), Title III—Innovative Projects.

b. ESEA, Title VII—Bilingual Projects.

c. Vocational Education Act, 1968 amendments, Part D—Exemplary Programs.

d. Right to Read Program.

The research focused on two main issues: (1) the kinds of strategies and conditions that tend to promote change in the school and the kinds that do not and (2) the factors that promote or deter the institutionalization of innovation (which has been tried and adopted) after the federal "seed money" runs out.[21]

Although there is no pretense of summarizing this large and complex research here, the salient finding is clear: the differences among school districts in the extent to which they successfully adopted and implemented innovations are explained not so much by either (1) the nature of the innovation itself or (2) the amount of federal funding but, rather, are explained more by the *character- istics of the organization and the management of the local school districts and schools themselves*. For example:

> In cases of successful implementation, the districts were generally characterized by...a "problem-solving" orientation. That is, they had identified and frequently had already begun to attack the problem before federal money became available. By contrast, failures in implementation were associated with an "opportunistic" orientation. These districts simply supplemented their budgets with money that happened to be available.[22]

School districts that were successful in implementing innovative programs tended, also, to exhibit other characteristics:

- They tended to reject rigidly packaged innovations that did not permit adaptation to local conditions.
- They were strongly involved in developing their own local materials, rather than simply adopting materials that had been developed elsewhere.
- They engaged in continuous planning and replanning rather than in "one-shot" planning at the beginning of a project.
- They engaged in ongoing training of people as needs arose in the projects and as defined by the participants (rather than in "one-shot" training at the outset or in having training needs identified by outside "experts").
- Consistent technical assistance was available locally for projects, rather than one or two-day visits from outside "experts."
- Innovative projects received strong support from key administrators at both the district and the school levels (for example, superintendent of schools and principal).

In sum, this research gives strong support to the view, long held by applied behavioral scientists, that organizational characteristics of the target school systems and schools at which empirical-rational and power-coercive strategies of change are aimed are crucial to determining the effectiveness of those schools *and* their capacity to change. In the words of the NIE report, increasing of productivity is not primarily

> ...a problem which can be solved by installing new accountability systems, teaching administrators improved purchasing techniques, or utilizing superior technology, but is a problem of improving the organizational culture (problem-solving and decisionmak- ing structures, incentives to change, skills in managing collaborative planning and implementation, mutual support and communication, opportunities for relevant train- ing, etc.) in which people work.[23]

This development at the local school district and school level is viewed as a necessary precondition to effective utilization of knowledge, no matter how it is produced, packaged, and disseminated:

No matter how good the channels which transmit knowledge and products to practitioners, it appears that such products will spread slowly and see little effective use until schools and districts develop the capacity to engage in an active search for solutions to their own problems, to adapt solutions to the particulars of their own situation, and equally important, to adapt themselves as organizations to the requirements of the selected solutions.[24]

A normative-reeducative strategy. These views express the essence of the third major strategy orientation to change identified by Chin: the normative-reeducative strategies. This orientation is based upon an understanding of organizations and people in them that is quite different from the orientation usually held by the empirical-rational or power-coercive views, which are essentially classical or bureaucratic and tend to see the organization as a creation apart from people. Organization theory, in this view, "deals with human *response* to organization rather than with human activity in *creating* organizations."[25]

Normative-reeducative strategies of change, on the other hand, posit that the norms of the organization's interaction-influence system (attitudes, beliefs, and values—in other words, culture) can be deliberately shifted to more productive norms by collaborative action of the people who populate the organization. Andrew Halpin would describe this as shifting from a closed climate to a more open climate. In George Stern's terminology it would be enhancing development press of the organizational climate. Rensis Likert would speak of moving away from System 1 management style toward System 4 (see Chapter 7).

Organizational health. In order to be effective, an organization must accomplish three essential core activities *over time:*

1. Achieve its goals
2. Maintain itself internally
3. Adapt to its environment.[26]

Thus, the organization must be effective, stable, yet capable of changing appropriately. Organizations differ in their abilities to accomplish these things; in other words, they exhibit different degrees of *organizational health*. A healthy organization "not only survives in its environment, but continues to cope adequately over the long haul, and continuously develops and extends its surviving and coping activities. Short-run operations on any particular day may be effective or ineffective, but continued survival, adequate coping, and growth are taking place."[27]

The unhealthy organization, on the other hand, is steadily ineffective. It may cope with its environment effectively on a short-term basis with a "crash program," a concentrated drive to meet a particularly threatening situation, or other "administration-by-crises" techniques, but in the long run the unhealthy organization becomes less and less able to cope with its environment. Rather than gaining in its ability to cope with a situation, it declines in this capacity over time and tends to become dysfunctional.

No single output measure or time slice of organizational performance can provide a reliable, accurate measure of organizational health: a central concern is the organization's continuing ability to cope with change and to adapt to the future.

This ability is best viewed in the perspective of time. There are, however, some relatively specific indicators of organizational health:

1. *Goal focus.* This is the extent to which people in the organization understand and accept the achievable and appropriate goals of the organization.
2. *Communication adequacy.* This is vertical and horizontal internal communication and external communication with the environment, and the ease and facility of communication (as against the amount of 'noise' and 'distortion' that can inhibit and confuse communication).
3. *Optimal power equalization.* An important element of this dimension is the issue of collaboration versus coercion.
4. *Human resources utilization.* This is the effective use of personnel, so that they—as persons—feel that they are growing and developing in their jobs.
5. *Cohesiveness.* This is the extent to which participants like the organization and want to remain in it in order to influence the collaborative style.
6. *Morale.* This is exhibited as feelings of well-being and satisfaction.
7. *Innovativeness.* This is the tendency to devise new procedures and goals, to grow, to develop, and to become more differentiated over a period of time.
8. *Autonomy.* Rather than being merely a "tool of the environment" that responds passively to outside stimuli, the autonomous organization tends to determine its own behavior in harmony with external demands.
9. *Adaptation.* Healthy organizations should be able to change, correct, and adapt faster than the environment.
10. *Problem-solving adequacy.* This includes mechanisms for sensing and perceiving problems, as well as those for solving problems permanently and with minimum strain.[28]

Organization self-renewal. It is a commonplace observation, of course, that organizations have a tendency to atrophy over time, becoming obsessed with maintaining themselves, increasing bureaucratic rigidity, and seeking to shore up traditional practices. In a world characterized by rapid change, such organizations tend to be viewed as *un*healthy, emphasizing maintenance of the organization at the expense of the need for constant adaptability so as to keep pace with the change in the demands and expectations of its external environment.

The concept of organization self-renewal was first comprehensively described by Rensis Likert in 1961.[29] He, of course, described ways of managing the interaction-influence system of the organization in ways that would stimulate creativity, promote growth of people in the organization, and facilitate solution of the organization's problems (see the discussion of System 1-System 4 in Chapter 7). In 1969 Gordon Lippitt elaborated a well-developed approach to the processes of renewal based on the view that every organization has a life cycle (birth-youth-maturity) with different renewal needs at each stage of its existence.[30] As early as 1967, Matthew Miles and Dale Lake described an application of the concept to school systems in the Cooperative Project for Educational Development.[31]

Organization self-renewal postulates that effective change cannot be imposed on a school; rather, it seeks to develop an internal capacity for continuous problem solving. The processes of renewal include the increased capacity to (1) sense and identify emerging problems, (2) establish goals, objectives, and priorities, (3) generate valid alternative solutions, and (4) implement a selected alternative. An outcome of renewal processes is to shift the culture of the school from emphasis on traditional routines and bureaucratic rigidity toward a culture that actively supports the view that much of the knowledge needed to plan and carry out change in schools is possessed by people in the schools themselves.[32] Further, it recognizes that "the optimal unit for educational change is the single school with its pupils, teachers, principal—those who live there every day—as primary participants."[33]

The self-renewing school possesses three essential characteristics: *First,* a culture that supports adaptability and responsiveness to change. Such a culture is supportive of open communication, especially from the bottom upward, and values problem solving as a high priority. *Second,* a set of clear-cut, explicit, and well-known procedures through which participants can engage in the orderly processes of systematic, collaborative problem solving. *Third,* such a school is not a parochial institution relying solely on internal energy, ideas, and resources for solving problems. Rather, it is a school that knows when and how to reach out to seek appropriate ideas and resources for use in solving its problems.[34]

Organization development (OD). Organization development (OD) is the principal process for increasing the self-renewal capability of school districts and schools. OD has been defined in many ways because it is difficult to capture the full essence of such a complex approach to improving organizational performance. However, after a comprehensive study of OD in American and Canadian schools, Michael Fullan, Matthew Miles, and Gib Taylor offered this definition in 1978:

> Organization development in school districts is a coherent, systematically-planned, sustained effort at system self-study and improvement, focusing explicitly on change in formal and informal procedures, processes, norms or structures, using behavioral science concepts. The goals of OD include *both* the quality of life of individuals as well as improving organizational functioning and performance.[35]

In practice, OD involves a cluster of at least ten concepts that characterize the process:

1. The goal of OD
2. System renewal
3. A systems approach
4. Focus on people
5. An educational strategy
6. Learning through experienced behavior
7. Dealing with real problems
8. A planned strategy
9. Change agent
10. Involvement of top-level administration.

Each of these ten OD concepts is briefly described as follows.[36]

1. The goal of OD.   The primary goal of OD is to improve the functioning of the organization itself. Improving the productivity and effectiveness of the organization is seen as largely dependent upon developing the organization's capability to make better-quality decisions about its affairs—decisions affecting its structure, its tasks, its use of technology, its use of human resources, and its goals. The primary approach to this is to develop a work-oriented culture in the organization that will maximize the involvement of the organization's people in more effective decision making regarding matters of importance to them and to the goals of the organization.

Although OD may very well lead to the adoption of a new program or curriculum, to a restructuring of the organization, or to a commitment to new goals, these are not considered to be first steps to improved effectiveness of schools and school systems. Neither does OD assume—as some have speculated—that significant organizational change will result from programs limited to improving the personal and interpersonal skills of individuals or groups, whether through counseling, sensitivity training, conventional education, or any other means. This is not likely to be enough to alter significantly established norms that shape the work-related behavior of the organization: rules, expectations, traditions, and habits.

2. System renewal.   Organization development rejects the notion that atrophy is inevitable in organizations. Stated positively, the view is that an organization can develop self-renewing characteristics, enabling it to increase its capability, to adapt to change, and to improve its record of goal achievement.

This concept of system self-renewal sees the organization not as being helplessly buffeted about by exigencies and changes thrust upon it, but as growing in its ability to initiate change, to have an increasing impact upon its environment, and to develop an increasing capability to adapt to new conditions and solve new problems over time. Perhaps more important is its ability to develop a growing sense of purpose and direction over time. The view is of an energized system marked by increasing vitality and imaginative creativity.

The self-renewal concept is at the center of the difference between organization development and organization improvement. The goal is not merely to overcome an immediate problem and arrive at a new "frozen" state of organizational functioning. The concept is one of building into the organizational system the conditions, the skills, the processes, and the culture that foster continual development of the organization over a sustained period of time. Although OD may be triggered by a specific event—such as initiating a new school or facing up to community criticism—the event itself merely provides an entry point for action.

If OD techniques are used to develop responses to the event and then are dropped, rather than continued and extended, then the project is not OD at all, but another piecemeal change effort so characteristic of public schools. The concept of management by crisis is so firmly embedded in American educational administration that developing planned, systematic, and sustained approaches has quite possibly become the central problem of administering change in schools.

3. A systems approach.   Organization development is based upon the concept of the organization as a complex sociotechnical system. Such a view of the organization, of course, emphasizes the wholeness of the organizational system and the dynamic interrelatedness of its component subsystems: human, structural, technological, and task.

The school, for example, is a sociotechnical system. It comprises subsystems, of course—departments, grade levels, informal groups, teams, and work groups— that are in a constant state of dynamic interrelationship. The school is also a subsystem of larger systems: the school district, for example, and the community in which it functions.

As we have described, such a view has fundamental implications for those concerned with administering organizational change; these are translated into certain fundamental assumptions:

a. To effect change that has long-range staying power one must change the whole system and not merely certain of its parts or subsystems.

b. Moreover, because of the dynamic interrelatedness and interdependency of the component subsystems, any significant change in a subsystem will produce compensatory or retaliatory changes in other subsystems.

c. Events very rarely occur in isolation or from single causes. Systems concepts of the organization emphasize the importance of dealing with events as manifestations of interrelated forces, issues, problems, causes, phenomena, and needs. The world of the organization is recognized as the complex system that it is, and ascribing single causation to phenomena or treating events as isolated incidents can mask our full understanding of them.

d. The organizational system is defined, not by walls or membranes, but by existing patterns of human behavior. These patterns are not static, but are in constant dynamic equilibrium—as Kurt Lewin's concept of force-field analysis illustrates. Therefore, the crucial information that the administrator requires comes from analyzing the specific field of forces at a particular time, rather than from analyzing generalized historical data from the past or from other organizations.

4. Focus on people. The main concern for OD is the human social system of the organization, rather than task, technology, or structure dimensions. Specifically, the focus is upon the organizational culture that characterizes the climate of beliefs influencing behavior—such as the ways in which superordinates and subordinates deal with one another, the ways in which work groups relate to each other, and the extent to which people in the organization are involved in identifying organizational problems and seeking solutions to them. Attitudes, values, feelings, and openness of communication are typical concerns for OD. It matters what people think, how open their communication is, how they deal with conflict, and to what extent they feel involved in their jobs, because these kinds of human concerns help determine how much work gets done and how well. People who have learned to keep their thoughts to themselves, to be discreet in proffering a new idea or in voicing doubt or criticism, contribute little to the organization's ability to diagnose its problems and find solutions. The culture of many schools encourages this kind of behavior—leaving decisions to the upper echelons and frowning upon lower participants who "cause trouble" by raising questions.

Commonly, the school's culture carefully structures organizational behavior so as to minimize open, free, and vigorous participation in central decisions—witness the typical faculty meeting with its crowded agenda of minutiae or the superintendent's *pro forma* appearances before the staff, which are filled with routine platitudes. Organizations with such characteristics tend to be relatively inflexible, slow to change, and defensive in a fast-changing environment.

In the OD view, one of the great resources available to an organization trying to improve its effectiveness is its own people. By encouraging people to become involved, concerned participants, rather than making them feel powerless and manipulated by unseen and inscrutable forces, the organization can draw ever-increasing strength, vitality, and creativity from its people.

5. An educational strategy. Organization development seeks to stimulate organization self-renewal by changing the behavior of people in the organization in significant ways through education. In this sense, however, education has little relationship to conventional, in-service education concepts that usually (a) are chiefly concerned with the acquisition of cognitive knowledge, and (b) take place in a typical classroom setting that emphasizes the learner as a dependent recipient of knowledge.

The educational strategy and processes of OD focus primarily upon the elements important to shaping the organizational climate and culture of the organization: the complex web of dynamic organizational variables that so deeply influences the way that people feel about their role in the organization, the attitudes and expectations they develop toward their co-workers, and the quality of the relationships between individuals and groups within the organization. Conventionally, these kinds of problems—involving conflict, communication barriers, suspicion and fear, and questions of organizational effectiveness—have been skirted carefully in organizations: they are too "touchy," too sensitive to treat adequately. OD seeks to find ways not only to face such problems, which are central to the organization's functioning, but also to increase the participants' abilities to solve them in productive ways. Because it changes the norms of the organization through a strategy of study and learning the process is a normative-reeducative strategy.

6. Learning through experience. The concept of learning by doing applied to organizational life is the basis for learning in OD. Educative techniques strongly stress the building of knowledge and skill in organizational behavior through a two-step, experience-based process in which a work-related group of people (1) shares a common experience and then (2) examines that experience to see what it can learn from it.

This can be done in relatively controlled conditions of laboratory training, such as in a T-group. It also can be a study of real-life experiences that group members actually have shared in the organization. But the basis for learning is the group's actual experience, not hypothetical situations. The group members are encouraged to question and to raise issues concerning group functioning, drawing insights and learning directly from this experience.

One purpose of this insistence upon examining experience in this way is to develop within the participants a long-lasting set of techniques and understandings that will enable them to learn and profit repeatedly from their own experiences over a sustained period of time. If this can be developed as a significant part of the group life of an organization, it can be a strong element of the desired self-renewal process.

7. Dealing with real problems. Organization development is applied to an organization in order to deal with existing, pressing problems. In some cases these problems may be serious enough to threaten the very survival of the organization, although they usually are not so dramatic. The educational processes do not involve learning about someone else's problem or discussing general cases but are directed to the specific organization under consideration—with its special conditions that make it unique.

What kind of problems might call for OD in a school? An attempt to catalogue such a wide range of possibilities would not be helpful, but it might be useful to mention a few typical situations:

1. Conditions of rapid change—such as a major school-district reorganization or the result of a sweeping court order—that might promote an "identity crisis" and organizational confusion of considerable magnitude.

2. A leadership crisis, such as the situation in which the new superintendent finds that there is little response to his or her initiatives.

3. Poor organizational effectiveness (however it is measured) that must be resolved in ways other than defensiveness or seeking excuses.

4. A high level of conflict, whether evidenced by excessive bickering and infighting or by the apathy characteristic of withdrawal from too painful a situation.

Often, of course, these kinds of problems are interrelated; opening up one for examination and solution may well lead to other problems that were not considered to be of great concern at the outset. This heuristic characteristic of OD concepts and processes has great power to penetrate to the central problems of the organization. Therefore, the major criterion in identifying the problem to be worked on in the initial stages is that it be of genuine concern to the organization's participants—something they feel is important to them, rather than something about which only someone else is concerned.

Organization development efforts should be viewed in the long-term sense suggested by the self-renewal concept, enabling the process to start from seemingly superficial problems and eventually reach the core. Thus, OD is not a one-shot approach to the alleviation of some limited, narrowly defined crisis, after which it will be abandoned. Indeed, as OD techniques become more popular and respectable in the eyes of administrators and managers, there is rising concern that the demand for such a "Band-Aid" approach (identifying OD with management by crisis rather than with the development of self-renewal) could discredit more ethical OD approaches.

8. A planned strategy. Another characteristic of OD—again in harmony with its overall systems approach—is that the effort must be planned systematically. The technology of OD embraces a wide range of possible activities and techniques. But they, in themselves, do not constitute OD. Indeed, a defining characteristic of OD is that it is a form of planned change: a strategy in which goals have been identified and a design for achieving them has been laid out. The plan must be specific: identifying target populations, establishing a timetable, and committing resources necessary to its fulfillment. The plan also must be tailored specifically to the particular circumstances of the organization.

Emphasizing the importance of a plan for OD should not imply rigidity. Indeed, if the effort is initially successful, it is probable that the increasing involvement of participants will require modifying and shaping the plan over time. It is important to provide for this in the planning stages, lest the effort turn into just another in-service program. Conversely, however, haphazard introduction of bits and pieces of OD technology, without clear purposive planning and the commitment to carry it through, can do more harm than good.

It has been noted, for example, that the decision to undertake OD in an organization can, in itself, produce some organizational improvement: it is often a signal to members involved that the culture is changing and that new ideas and new ways of doing things are becoming more of a possibility and reality. Obviously, a badly mounted OD program or the sudden termination of one that has been started following the raising of hopes (because, perhaps, of the administrator's timidity or the lack of sufficient resources for the program) can result in an understandable backlash of feeling.

An OD program is a complex and sophisticated undertaking; it involves a wide range of possible interventions that deal with potentially sensitive matters. A highly qualified OD specialist often can facilitate the planning and carrying out of such a program by helping the administrator develop a practical OD design tailored to the specific realities of his or her organization. The designing of an OD project offers both the administrator and the behavioral scientist the rare opportunity to collaborate in a common cause.

9. Change agent.   OD is characterized by the participation of a change agent who has a vital and very specific role to play, at least in the initial stages of the change effort. Indeed, OD—in the various forms currently known to us—is impossible without a competent change agent. This person may have various official titles in different organizations; regardless, the term "consultant" is almost always used among OD practitioners to refer to the specialist who helps an organization design and carry out an OD program.

The consultant is so vital to the success or failure of OD that a substantial part of the literature is devoted to descriptions of his or her role, function, and specialized competencies, the nature of his or her relationships to client organizations, and so forth.

Finding an appropriate consultant and establishing an effective working relationship with him or her may well be the administrator's most crucial role in establishing OD in his or her school. Indeed, the need for consultant help has been the source of some of the thorniest problems in implementing OD. There can be much confusion, under the best of circumstances, about the consultant: what his or her role is, from whom he or she takes orders, what impact his or her presence has upon the usual relationships between administrators and teachers—these are some of the problem areas that commonly appear in OD work. They are the subject of considerable study and discussion among OD consultants themselves, as they attempt to shape their own roles in appropriate ways.

In general terms, consultants may be either from outside the organization (external consultants) or from within the organization (internal consultants). In its early history, OD efforts depended exclusively upon external consultants. Of course, the relationship of the external consultant to the organization is temporary and requires that extra money be found to cover the consulting fees. One reaction to this has been efforts to train individuals appropriately so that they may function as internal consultants;[37] typically, once such a position has been budgeted, it tends to become a long-term, institutionalized arrangement. It appears likely that the role of internal change agents, or consultants, will become increasingly visible and formalized in school districts in the years ahead. However, the need for external consultants to deal with particularly complex and difficult problems of change will probably not be completely eliminated.

Some limited progress has been made in developing procedures for carrying out certain crucial aspects of OD activities without the direct assistance of behavioral science consultants.[38] At this stage of the development of OD, however, the consultant is a key individual. Policy and administration problems in dealing with OD consultants are discussed later in this book.

10. Involvement of top-level administration. Inevitably, one must conclude from the social systems orientation of OD that one cannot change part of the system in constructive ways without affecting other parts of the system. For example, management cannot presume to change the organization without being part of the process. Organizational change is not a matter of "us" (the administration) changing "them" (the teachers and other subordinates) or even of changing "it" (the organization as some sort of entity detached from "us"). Administration must be an active partner involved in the development process to assure that all subsystems of the organizational system will stay appropriately linked together in the dynamic, interactive way. This is one of the identifying characteristics of the increasingly effective organization.

In operational terms, OD recognizes that organizations are hierarchical and will continue to be so. When subordinates see that the administration is doing something to organizations in the name of improving their effectiveness—something in which administrators are not involved except as observers—the subordinates are very likely to be wary and less than fully committed. On the other hand, if the administration is already interested in the undertaking, committed to it, and involved in visible ways, subordinates are much more inclined to view the effort as valid and will be more highly motivated to involve themselves. In any organization, subordinates tend to develop highly sensitive antennae that pick up reliable indications of what is really important at higher levels through all the static and noise that may surround the issuance of official statements.

This was illustrated in the case of a large suburban school district. Located in a highly industrialized community, the district was undergoing the stresses and strains related to the social and ethnic problems that have become so commonplace in recent years. The new superintendent—young, bright, articulate, energetic, and with an enviable record in other districts—moved early to bring the principals and other key administrators together and organize them as a team. With a new and greater opportunity to play a crucial role in establishing policy and dealing with districtwide problems, this group was soon involved in important, districtwide issues that had significant implications for each school. Unfortunately, the team quickly ran into difficulties: wrangling broke out, decisions arrived at in meetings were undercut by private deals made outside of the team (often involving school board members), and some members created an alliance to control voting on issues before the team on the basis of the self-interest of their departments or schools. A number of principals—who had enjoyed considerable autonomy under the previous superintendent to "wheel and deal" with school board members in behalf of their individual schools—felt that the whole team idea was simply a scheme to undermine them. The superintendent discussed these problems with the group and won easy agreement that a consultant should be brought in to help them find solutions.

During an exploratory meeting, the consultant was able to establish a basis for working with the group. In addition to agreeing upon some goals and some modes of operating, certain ground rules also were agreed upon. One, suggested by the consultant and quickly supported unanimously, was that all members of the group must attend each scheduled training session, if at all possible. This was a highly capable and sophisticated group, and, within a few meetings with the consultant, there was a general feeling that real progress was being made and that the training effort should be continued. At the session following that decision, the superintendent announced that—because of the eruption of an unforeseen crisis— he would have to rush off soon after the group convened.

At the next session, he strongly endorsed the training effort and expressed keen interest in it but had to hurry off to another emergency. At the subsequent session, three principals—after a decent interval—withdrew and hurried off to attend to "emergencies" at their schools. Needless to say, the superintendent's team members realized that, as soon as the original crisis had eased, the training program no longer was a high priority matter at the top, and they responded accordingly.

A sociotechnical view.   Those who are inexperienced in participative approaches to management often think of them as being "soft," "permissive," and incompatible with the structure, discipline, and power that characterize organizations. In fact, however, what is needed is a new, more effective, approach to management: an approach that stresses more functional administrative structures and seeks more effective organizational behavior. Although the new structures may well be more flexible and adaptable than those of the past, they will not be fuzzy or ill-defined; neither will the more effective work-related behaviors be lacking in clear, exact description and definition.

When the administrator confronts the need for more involvement of staff in decision making or seeks to move the organization in a more "organic" or self-renewing direction, does it mean that system, orderly procedures, and control must be abandoned? The answer is, of course, negative. In fact, quite the opposite is true: the need is to provide organizational structures that will enhance and facilitate the development of more adaptive decision-making styles to replace the rigid hierarchical structures characteristic of the mechanistic organization.

The shift in organizational system development, then, is not away from the clarity, order, and control associated with traditional views of organizational structure toward an ill-defined, disorderly, laissez-faire administration. What is sought, administratively, is a new and more functional basis for *task* analysis, *structural* arrangements, selection and use of *technology,* and selection and professional development of individual *people* and groups of people on the staff.

The rationality of this view—which is a sociotechnical orientation—becomes increasingly apparent when we acknowledge that technological change and innovation are likely to play an increasingly important role in organizational change in schools in the future. The function of the administrator, then, is to develop organizational structures that—while providing clearly for such imperatives as coordination of effort toward goal attainment—assure the development of more adaptive ways of integrating people, technology, task, and structure in a dynamic, problem-solving fashion.

Force-field analysis. How can one analyze an organizational situation so as to better understand how to deal with it? Force-field analysis has proven to be a useful analytic approach for both the researcher and the administrator.[39]

Basically, this approach sees a social or organizational *status quo* as a state of equilibrium resulting from the balance between two opposing sets of forces. There are forces for change, sometimes called *driving forces,* and these are opposed by forces for remaining unchanged, sometimes called *restraining forces.* When these force fields are in balance, as in Figure 8–2, we have equilibrium—no change. Obviously, when one or another of these forces is removed or weakened, the equilibrium is upset and change occurs, as shown in Figure 8–3. On a very simple level, such an imbalance can be brought about by the introduction of a new work technique or the acquisition of new skills by participants. But an organization is essentially a stable entity generally characterized by equilibrium; an imbalance of equilibrium will bring about readjustments that will again lead to a new organizational equilibrium. This simple concept can become very complex when applied to a large-scale organization. But it also can be a practical aid to the administrator who seeks to understand his or her organization better so as to facilitate either change or stability in the organization. The analytic process of identifying restraining forces and driving forces ranges from a very simple approach at the rudimentary level to rather sophisticated techniques.

Force-field analysis eventually led its creator, Kurt Lewin, to a fundamental three-step change strategy that has come into increasingly popular use. It is predicated on the notion that in order to effect organizational change, it is first necessary

FIGURE 8–2. Force field in equilibrium.

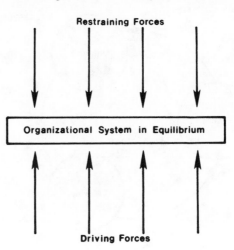

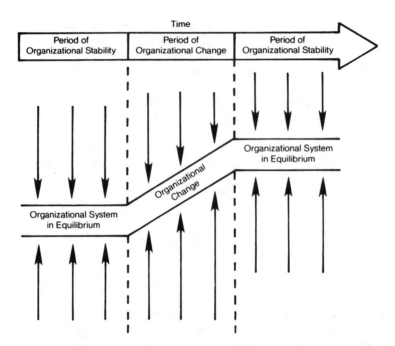

FIGURE 8–3.   Imbalance of force field causes organizational change until a new equilibrium is reached.

to break the equilibrium of the force field: that is, the organization must be *unfrozen*. Once that is done, it is possible to introduce *change*—to move the organization to a new level. But no one knows better than educational administrators how fragile change can be, and how easily the organization can slip back into its old ways. Therefore, the third step in the three-step change process is *refreezing*. This is an institutionalizing process that serves to protect and insure the long-range retention of the change. Of course, refreezing smacks of a new *status quo;* in Lewin's view, the desired amount of flexibility could be built in by establishing "an organizational set up which is equivalent to a stable circular causal process."[40] Unfreezing can be

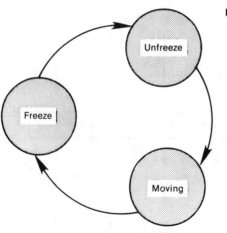

FIGURE 8–4.   A three-step change process as an ongoing life cycle of an organization.

a highly traumatic experience to a very rigid and resisting organization. But it can also be built in as a normal part of its life cycle, as suggested in Figure 8–4 in order to achieve greater organizational flexibility over time.

The value of a force-field analysis is diagnostic: it permits the preparation of plans for specific action designed to achieve the changes sought. The success of such a plan will depend in large measure upon the clarity with which the likely consequences of proposed action are perceived. Of the four major organizational subsystems—task, technological, structure, and human—only the human subsystem has the capacity to react differentially to differing conditions.

Great art and literature teem with depictions of heroic achievements of people moved by such feelings as love, faith, courage, and duty. Much of the literature on organizations is concerned with apathy, anger, frustration, and apprehensions of people and their great power to inhibit the organization's goal achievement. Although administrators must be deeply concerned with the work to be performed in the school, the structure of the organization, and the technology that is used, none of these has the capability of resisting plans for action. It is only the human subsystem that has that capability.

But it is not productive for the administrator to view opposition to change in any form—whether as outright resistance, apathy, skepticism, or whatever—as obdurate behavior.

If "increasing the driving forces" is interpreted by the administrator as meaning the stepped-up use of authority and power to get people behind the change effort, it is highly predictable that the result will be strong reactions against the change. Pressure generates counterpressure, and in the school setting, where the administrator's coercive power is sharply limited, it is not likely that the equilibrium of the force field can be broken by such an approach. At the very least, it is predictable that, as the pressure is relaxed—as it must be eventually—there will be a tendency for the organization to retreat to its old ways under the pressure of the restraining forces.

In school situations generally, it is likely to be more effective to help bring the restraining forces into the open as legitimate in the process of change. By creating a culture in which feelings can be expressed instead of secretly harbored, by opening communication and valuing the right to question and challenge, and by helping those who would oppose the forces of change to examine and deal with the concerns that cause their resistance, it is likely that (1) unforeseen probable consequences of proposed actions would be brought into the planning process and—perhaps more important—(2) the level of resistance will be diminished.

As the opposition contributes to shape and mold decisions, its views are also shaped, molded, and modified in the process. *To obtain this kind of participation requires the existence of a developmental, or growth-enhancing, organizational culture that characteristically*

a. is intellectually, politically, and aesthetically stimulating;

b. emphasizes individual and group achievement;

c. places high value on the personal dignity of individuals;

d. accepts divergent feelings and views in a nonjudgmental way;

e. is oriented to problem solving rather than to winning or losing in intraorganizational skirmishes.

The establishment of orderly problem-solving processes that provide maximum participation for those who will be affected by the change is necessary to develop the collaborative approach suggested here. Although the point of view is important, it must be accompanied by effective specific procedures for making it work, creating the climate needed and assuring that the way in which decisions are reached is understood and workable. Development of a new organizational culture and building the group skills for open, collaborative decision making require definite training and practice. These things are not achieved through cognitive understanding and determination alone: they require the development of new insights, new values and commitments, and new group process skills that are best taught and learned in problem-solving situations.

It must be remembered that the creation of a new organizational culture—a new environment for working and solving problems—requires participants to develop new and more effective responses to events, to act differently than they have done in the past. As every educator is keenly aware, such changes in human functioning do not often occur as a result of learning *about* the new, more effective ways of doing things. Opportunities must be provided wherein the new behaviors may be developed in practice: in short, *learning by doing* is required. The goal is to develop new and more productive norms of work-oriented behavior through reeducation.

Change is likely to be stabilized and maintained in the organization over time, when the new, more effective level of performance can be maintained without coercion and without continuous expenditures of administrative energy and vigilance to keep it going. Indeed, this is one practical criterion by which the administrator may judge whether or not change has been "accomplished."

An appropriate plan for organizational change must take cognizance of these realities. It must also recognize that the goal of changing an organization in significant ways presents a challenge in terms of difficulty and in terms of the time span required. There are no quick and easy solutions, though there will probably never be a shortage of those who claim to possess such solutions. Hersey's and Blanchard's admonition on this point is highly appropriate:

> Changes in knowledge are the easiest to make, followed by changes in attitudes. Attitude structures differ from knowledge structures in that they are emotionally charged in a positive or a negative way. Changes in behavior are significantly more difficult and time consuming than either of the two previous levels. But the implementation of group or organizational performance change is perhaps the most difficult and time consuming.[41]

RESEARCH ON THE EFFECTIVENESS OF OD

In reporting a major study of OD in schools, Fullan, Miles, and Taylor point out that a problem of assessing OD efforts to develop the self-renewal, problem-solving capacity of school systems and schools lies in the fact that many so-called OD projects are partial, incomplete, short-term activities lacking the planning, scope, and sustained effort required for success.[42] In many cases, for example, a few days of "human relations training" for teachers, or the use of an outside consultant for a few sessions, is incorrectly labeled an "OD project." Often the effort is limited to attempts to reduce conflict or otherwise to ameliorate unpleasant aspects of organizational culture, with little or no intention of significantly affecting organizational structure or processes of decision making. For reasons such as these, surveys of OD activities in education tend to show spotty success; yet, those school districts that are successful with OD generally tend to institutionalize it and maintain it over time. Not a few school districts now have OD school renewal projects that have been functioning for a period of years.

Philip Runkel and Richard Schmuck, at the Center for Educational Policy and Management (CEPM) at the University of Oregon, have conducted the most comprehensive research and development work in this field. They began their work in 1967, and in 1974 they published the findings of their studies up to that time. In assessing whether or not OD has been successful in a district or school, they caution against accepting superficial claims about *any* effort at change:

> Our experience in looking for outcomes has taught us that they are not simple....Editors of scientific journals and providers of funds should demand detailed documentation when a researcher claims that one or more schools have "installed" or "adopted" some particular new way of doing things. The depth and variety in the ways that a new structure such as team teaching can be installed or adopted in a school are stupefying, and so are the ways a principal can cover up with verbiage the fact that the innovation really has not taken hold in his school at all. Statements that go no farther than, "In a school that had adopted a team teaching the previous year,..." or "We shall install team teaching in X schools next year...," should never be accepted without skepticism.[43]

Their findings regarding OD in schools include these:

- Success is more likely when the school faculty senses a readiness to change and welcomes the OD project.
- Entering into OD may be the most critical phase of the project and requires a skilled and experienced OD consultant to avoid hidden pitfalls.
- Open, active support from administrators is critical to success.
- OD is more likely to be helpful in a school in which the staff is in substantial agreement on goals.
- An OD project can be thought of as consisting of four main phases: (1) entry, (2) diagnosis of organizational problems, (3) institutionalization, and (4) maintenance.

John Goodlad has been associated with studies of organizational change in public schools since the late 1940s. After witnessing the "continuing, frustrating failure of promising innovations to alter school practice in desired ways"[44] he undertook to lead a five-year research and development project addressing the problems of personal and institutional renewal in education. Goodlad started by pointing out that the conventional model for studying educational change is to manipulate certain instructional interventions (such as class size or teaching method) and to look for changes in pupil outcomes. As shown in Figure 8–5, such a research design treats pupil outcomes as the dependent variable and instruction (for example, methods and materials) as the independent variable. However, Goodlad's long-term observation of the difficulty of installing and sustaining instructional reforms led him to realize that "the explanatory thesis for this difficulty...is that the regularities of the school sustain certain practices, through expectations, approval, and reward. Teachers,

INDEPENDENT
VARIABLE

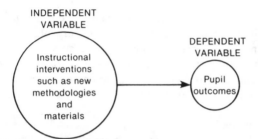

DEPENDENT
VARIABLE

FIGURE 8–5.   Conventional model for effecting and studying ends-means relationships when the focus is on instruction and pupil outcomes. From John I. Goodlad, *The Dynamics of Educational Change* (New York: McGraw-Hill Book Company, 1975), p. 113.

as individuals, usually are not able to run successfully against these regularities or to create the schoolwide structures and processes necessary to sustain new practices."[45] This suggested the need to focus on the entire culture of the school; and, further: "We see everything constituting the culture of the school—its operational curriculum, written and unwritten rules, verbal and non-verbal communication, physical properties, pedagogical regularities, principal's leadership behavior and so on...."[46] This led to research design in which the school's culture is the independent variable, and *both* (a) the behavior of the teacher and (b) pupil outcomes are seen as dependent upon that culture, while *at the same time* pupil outcomes are seen as dependent on teacher behavior (see Figure 8–6).

In practical terms, Goodlad judged that, although the relationships, as shown in Figure 8–7, probably correctly represent important elements of "reality" for schools, the design is much too complex for the practical study of schools in the "real world." He therefore settled on a study of the "causes" of the culture of the school, as shown in Figure 8–6.

The central proposition of Goodlad's research was "that entire schools can and should be regarded as malleable and capable of changing, and that, as schools change in their cultural characteristics, so do the people in them."[47] Further, a basic assumption was that, in order to succeed, a client school must exhibit an internal sense of need, a desire to change. The principal experimental intervention was to train faculty members of schools to engage in a four-step process called DDAE (dialogue, decision making, action, and evaluation), which is essentially an OD intervention aimed at developing self-renewal in the schools. A significant additional feature of Goodlad's work was to join the participating schools in this

FIGURE 8–6. A paradigm for studying ends-means-effects relationships and for improving schooling and learning. From John I. Goodlad, *The Dynamics of Educational Change* (New York: McGraw-Hill Book Company, 1975), p. 117.

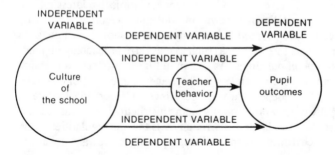

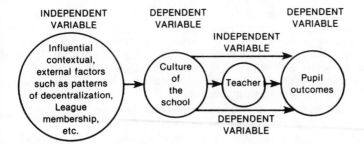

INDEPENDENT VARIABLE — DEPENDENT VARIABLE — DEPENDENT VARIABLE

INDEPENDENT VARIABLE

Influential contextual, external factors such as patterns of decentralization, League membership, etc.

Culture of the school → Teacher → Pupil outcomes

DEPENDENT VARIABLE

FIGURE 8-7. A paradigm for improving and studying educational practice with changes in the entire culture of a school the focus of attention. From John I. Goodlad, *The Dynamics of Educational Change* (New York: McGraw-Hill Book Company, 1975), p. 114.

five-year project into a "league" so that they could provide one another with a sense of mutual support and nurturance during the experimental period.

Goodlad reports that:

> In the high DDAE schools there were more cooperative teaching arrangements, more friendship networks among teachers, and more task-oriented communication among teachers. Teachers had more influence in decision-making, especially in areas affecting schools as total units. The quality of principal leadership was higher and principal influence depended more on competence. The principals in high DDAE schools were more apt to see teacher influence on schools as a desirable condition. These schools ranked higher on indices of school climate. By contrast, there were more self-contained classrooms in low DDAE schools. Teacher influence was more narrowly limited to areas affecting only a few people rather than the school as a whole and the principal was more apt to see teacher influence on schoolwide decisions as undesirable. The principal's influence was more likely to depend upon status and power to reward.[48]

The characteristics of high DDAE seemed to be associated in a school with significant potential for ongoing growth and self-renewal. But a visitor to such a school would have difficulty in isolating *an* innovation in that school because

> ...most of those being widely advocated were there: considerable use of audiovisual aids, especially by two or three children at a time and on their own; some of the new curricular materials, modified, flexible classroom space; multiage or non-graded groups and classes; use of parent volunteers in the instructional program; team planning, teaching, and evaluation.[49]

This kind of observation is characteristic of the self-renewing school: it is a growing and developing organization, not because of some agreement with an outside agency to employ a given innovation, but, rather, because it is continuously engaged in systematic problem solving and is able to select appropriate technology from all that is available.

SUMMARY

Although many ways of classifying strategies for planned, managed organizational change have been devised, this chapter used Robert Chin's three-part typology:

1. *Empirical-rational strategies* are based on the concept that change can be fostered by systematically inventing or discovering better ideas and making them readily available in useful form to schools. Adherents of this strategy are often confounded by the difficulties usually encountered in the processes of "installing" new practices in the "target" schools. Typical difficulties are (1) ignoring the new ideas, (2) resisting or rejecting the new ideas, or (3) modifying the idea or practice in such ways that, when put into practice, it has been significantly changed.

2. *Power-coercive strategies* are based on the use (or potential use) of sanctions to compel the organization to change. For example, a state education department might require each school district to draw up and implement a program of competency-based instruction in accordance with specific guidelines. This could be accompanied by specific required timetables, forms of reporting, and other techniques for monitoring compliance. Problems often encountered with this strategy include the problem that public school systems (and, certainly, what are sometimes called "state public school systems") are—at best—composed of relatively loosely coupled components, through which it is difficult to transmit precise orders and from which it is difficult to extract compliance. As I describe more fully in Chapter 10, *satisficing* is commonplace in organizational decision making: that is, adopting workable responses to demands (sufficient to avoid sanctions) but not seeking maximally effective responses when faced with an array of conflicting demands.

3. *Normative-reeducative strategies* are based on the notion of bringing about change in schools by improving their problem-solving capabilities as organizations. This requires shifting the normative values of the school's culture (interaction-influence system) from those usually associated with hierarchical (bureaucratic, mechanistic, classical) organization to more creative, problem-solving norms. This process is widely referred to as *organizational self-renewal*. Techniques and processes for bringing about organizational self-renewal focus on developing increased skills among the staff members of individual schools in studying and diagnosing their own organizational problems systematically and in working out solutions to them. The term *organization development* (OD) is widely applied to these techniques for increasing the self-renewal capacity of schools.

Research, largely carried out in the 1970s, appears to make it clear that these three strategic orientations to planned, managed change in education are complementary rather than competing. But the critical importance of helping schools to develop their own inner capacity for self-renewal was not widely understood (outside of the field of organizational behavior) until the failure of extensive applications of both empirical-rational and power-coercive strategies to achieve desired levels of success had produced widespread frustration and concern. By the decade of the 1980s, it was clear to thoughtful people concerned with education that the long-neglected area of developing self-renewal in schools would have to be addressed seriously if change in American schooling were to move forward. By thus improving the organizational health of schools, it appears possible to make schools more proactive than defensive and to reach out responsively to adopt new ideas and implement changing goals of society.

Though schools are organizations and, therefore, share much with other kinds of organizations, it must be remembered that we know relatively little about their specific organizational characteristics. Although research on the organizational characteristics of schools is increasing, until very recently our assumptions about them have been derived largely from studies in other kinds of organizations (for example, business firms, military organizations, government agencies). But schools do possess special properties (not all, necessarily, unique) that may well affect the ways in which they should deal with issues of stability and change. A common observation is, for example, that they are largely populated by a nonvoluntary clientele. Fullan, Miles, and Taylor point out six other special properties that undoubtedly must be considered in planning change.[50]

1. *Their goals are diffuse*, usually stated in general, even abstract terms with effectiveness measurement difficult and uncertain.

2. *Their technical capability* is low, with a weak specific scientific base underlying educational practice.

3. *They are loosely coupled systems*, which gives rise to coordination problems: activities are not always clearly connected to goals, and control (for example, accountability) is difficult to establish. (Recall the discussion in Chapter 1 that pointed out that this organizational feature of schools is not necessarily entirely negative: it also can be a source of flexibility and adaptability.)

4. *Boundary management is difficult* inasmuch as "the skin of the organization seems overly thin, over-permeable to dissatisfied stakeholders."[51]

5. Schools are *"domesticated"* organizations, noncompetitive, surviving in a relatively protected environment, and with little incentive for significant change.

6. Schools are part of a *constrained decentralized system:* sixteen thousand school districts in the United States with 89,000 buildings, each nominally autonomous, yet with many national constraints (for example, national textbook market, accreditation and certification requirements, statutes and case law).

SUGGESTED READING

GUEST, ROBERT H., PAUL HERSEY, AND KENNETH H. BLANCHARD, *Organizational Change through Effective Leadership*. Englewood Cliffs, NJ: Prentice-Hall, 1977.
This 174-page book presents a three-year longitudinal case study of change in a large manufacturing plant. The case itself originally was published fifteen years earlier, but in the publication suggested here, it has been extensively analyzed in terms of modern concepts of organizational behavior. Though not directly related to educative organizations, this small volume is very specific and helpful in showing how concepts of organization, motivation, leadership, climate, and change apply in dealing with "real-world" organizational problems. The views of such scientists as Lewin, Likert, Vroom, Hersey and Blanchard, Bales, and Herzberg—and many others that have been discussed in the present book—are well represented.

HERRIOTT, ROBERT E. AND NEAL GROSS, *The Dynamics of Planned Educational Change: Case Studies and Analyses*. Berkeley, CA.: McCutchan, 1979.
Based on the experience of five school districts that received substantial supplemental funding through the National Institute for Education to carry out comprehensive change efforts. Between 1972 and 1977 a social scientist (a sociologist or anthropologist) lived in each district recording the events that occurred during the planning and implementation of the change projects. The volume not only presents the five cases but offers five additional chapters of interpretations and recommendations by various specialists. Helpful in clarifying the difficulties encountered when a federal agency seeks to stimulate change at the local level.

MAEROFF, GENE I., *The Empowerment of Teachers: Overcoming the Crisis of Confidence*. New York: Teachers College Press, 1988.
Written by a professional writer who is a Senior Fellow at the Carnegie Foundation and was a consultant for the Rockefeller Foundation, and under a grant from the Rockefeller Foundation, this book strongly argues the case for teacher empowerment, which is an idea supported by both foundations. It includes an incisive analysis of the professional circumstances of public school teachers today and shows how, by restructuring schools to provide greater autonomy to teachers, they may be significantly changed. Maeroff believes, of course, that these changes will result in marked improvement in the performance of schools.

PINCUS, JOHN, "Incentive for Innovation in the Public Schools," *Review of Educational Research*, 44, no. 1 (1974), 113.

Noting that the record of American public schools in adopting innovation is uneven, with some innovations spreading rapidly, others slowly, and some hardly at all, the author concludes that the processes of innovation and adoption are complex; in this article he discusses these complexities. He uses a "marketplace" analogy, comparing public schools (bureaucratic, protected monopolies) with competitive private firms in terms of incentives for adopting and implementing innovation. This is, of course, the kind of thinking that underlies such ideas as magnet schools, youth endowment and voucher plans, and abolition of tenure. One conclusion: "...if externally encouraged innovative efforts are to avoid a great deal of waste motion, they must be based on a far more detailed appraisal of the reality of the schools as institutions than is now the case" (p. 135).

ROSOW, JEROME M. AND ROBERT ZAGER, WITH CASNER-LOTTO, JILL AND ASSOCIATES, *Allies in Educational Reform: How Teachers, Unions, and Administrators Can Join Forces for Better Schools*. San Francisco: Jossey-Bass Publishers, 1989.

Sponsored by the Work in America Institute, this edited book, written by various authors, draws upon case studies of reportedly successful alliances of teachers unions and school districts that have led to achieving what are described as lasting educational reform. Part Two of the volume, which reports "eleven models of excellence" from school districts, schools, and special programs is of special interest to those who want to discover "what's happening in educational reform at the school district level."

ROSSMAN, GRETCHEN B., H. DICKSON CORBETT, AND WILLIAM A. FIRESTONE, *Change and Effectiveness in Schools: A Cultural Perspective*. Albany: State University of New York Press, 1988.

By reporting and analyzing case studies of three high schools that were grappling with change, the authors provide the reader with a better understanding of the complex texture and meaning of educational reform. The lens through which they observe unfolding events in these schools brings the relationships between school culture and leadership into focus.

SCHMUCK, RICHARD A., PHILIP J. RUNKEL, JANE H. ARENDS, AND RICHARD I. ARENDS, *The Second Handbook of Organization Development in Schools*. Palo Alto, CA: Mayfield Publishing Company, 1977.

A classic, in its second edition, this is the bible for practitioners who want to know what organization development and organization self-renewal are all about. Filled with specific, practical, "how-to" help, aids, and advice for those who want to be involved in implementing the theory and concepts in a school or school system. Very strongly recommended.

WILLIAMS, RICHARD C., CHARLES C. WALL, W. MICHAEL MARTIN, AND ARTHUR BERCHIN, *Effecting Organizational Renewal in Schools: A Social Systems Perspective*. New York: McGraw-Hill Book Company, 1974.

This small volume describes and reports research conducted in eight elementary schools from the League of Cooperating Schools. Though all had been implementing the DDAE process, four of the eight had been adjudged low. The study is well based on the Getzels-Guba model of the school as a social system (recall the discussion in Chapter 3) and examines (1) leader behavior, (2) the "fit" between the personalities of teachers and their official role in school, and (3) the value orientations of school staffs compared with those of the immediate community (that is, parents of the children). This book does much to specify in practical terms some important differences between self-renewing schools and those that are not.

NOTES

[1]Seymour B. Sarason, *The Culture of the School and the Problem of Change* (Boston: Allyn & Bacon, Inc., 1971), p. 7.

[2]Matthew B. Miles, "Some Properties of Schools as Social Institutions," in *Change in School Systems*, ed. Goodwin Watson (Washington, D.C.: National Training Laboratories, NEA, 1967), p. 20.

[3]Paul R. Mort and Donald H. Ross, *Principles of School Administration* (New York: McGraw-Hill Book Company, 1957), p. 181.

[4]Paul R. Mort, "Educational Adaptability," in *Administration for Adaptability*, ed. Donald H. Ross (New York: Metropolitan School Study Council, 1958), pp. 32–33.

[5]"Kindergarten Education, 1967–68." *NEA Research Bulletin*, 47, no. 1 (March 1969), 10.

[6]Paul R. Mort and Francis G. Cornell, *American Schools in Transition* (New York: Teachers College, Columbia University, 1941).

[7]A. G. Grace and G. A. Moe, *State Aid and School Costs* (New York: McGraw-Hill Book Company, 1938), p. 324.

[8]Austin D. Swanson, "The Cost-Quality Relationship," in *The Challenge of Change in School Finance*, Proceedings of the Tenth Annual Conference on School Finance (Washington, DC: Committee on Educational Finance, National Education Association, 1967), pp. 151–65.

[9]Richard O. Carlson, *Adoption of Educational Innovations* (Eugene: Center for the Advanced Study of Educational Administration, University of Oregon, 1965).

[10]For a full description of PSSC, see Paul E. March, "The Physical Science Study Committee: A Case History of Nationwide Curriculum Development" (unpublished doctoral dissertation, Graduate School of Education, Harvard University, 1963).

[11]Two other taxonomies that are widely used are those developed by (a) Daniel Katz and Robert L. Kahn, and (b) Ronald G. Havelock. There is substantial agreement among the three taxonomies. For a discussion, see Robert G. Owens and Carl R. Steinhoff, *Administering Change in Schools* (Englewood Cliffs, NJ: Prentice-Hall, 1976), Chapter 4.

[12]David L. Clark and Egon G. Guba, "An Examination of Potential Change Roles in Education," in *Rational Planning in Curriculum and Instruction*, ed. Ole Sand (Washington, DC: National Education Association, 1967).

[13]Such as the Biological Sciences Curriculum (BSCS), the Physical Sciences Study Committee (PSSC), the Chemical Bond Approach Project (Chem Bond or CBA), and the School Mathematics Study Group (SMSG).

[14]Gerald Zaltman, David Florio, and Linda Sikorski, *Dynamic Educational Change: Models, Strategies, Tactics, and Management* (New York: The Free Press, 1977), p. 77.

[15]Robert Chin, "Basic Strategies and Procedures in Effecting Change," in *Educational Organization and Administration Concepts, Practice and Issues*, ed. Edgar L. Morphet and others (Englewood Cliffs, NJ: Prentice-Hall, 1967).

[16]Homer Garner Barnett, *Innovation: The Basis of Cultural Change* (New York: McGraw-Hill Book Company, 1953).

[17]Matthew B. Miles, *Innovation in Education* (New York: Columbia University Press, 1964), p. 14.

[18]Robert Chin and Kenneth D. Benne, "General Strategies for Effecting Changes in Human Systems," in *The Planning of Change*, 2nd. ed., ed. Warren G. Bennis, Kenneth D. Benne, and Robert Chin (New York: Holt, Rinehart & Winston, 1969).

[19]Group on School Capacity for Problem Solving, *Program Plan* (Washington, DC: National Institute of Education, June 1975), p. 1.

[20]Paul Berman and Milbrey Wallin McLaughlin, *Federal Programs Supporting Educational Change, Volume VIII: Implementing and Sustaining Innovations* (Santa Monica, CA: Rand Corporation, May 1978), p. iii.

[21]This study is fully reported in eight volumes under the general title, *Federal Programs Supporting Educational Change* (Santa Monica, CA: Rand Corporation).
Volume I: *A Model of Educational Change* by Paul Berman and Milbrey Wallin McLaughlin (1975).
Volume II: *Factors Affecting Change Agent Projects* by Paul Berman and Edward Pauley (1975).
Volume III: *The Process of Change* by Peter W. Greenwood, Dale Mann, and Milbrey Wallin McLaughlin (1975).
Volume IV: *The Findings in Review* by Paul Berman and Milbrey Wallin McLaughlin (1975).
Volume V: *Executive Summary* by Paul Berman, Peter W. Greenwood, Milbrey Wallin McLaughlin, and John Pincus (1975).
Volume VI: *Implementing and Sustaining Title VII Bilingual Projects* by Gerald Sumner and Gail Zellman (1977).
Volume VII: *Factors Affecting Implementation and Continuation* by Paul Berman and others (1977).
Volume VIII: *Implementing and Sustaining Innovations* by Paul Berman and Milbrey Wallin McLaughlin (1978).

[22]Group on School Capacity for Problem-Solving, p. 1.

[23]Ibid., p. 4.

[24]Ibid., p. 5.

[25]T. Barr Greenfield, "Organizations as Social Inventions: Rethinking Assumptions about Change," *Journal of Applied Behavioral Science*, 9, no. 5 (1973), 551–74.

[26]Chris Argyris, *Integrating the Individual and the Organization* (New York: John Wiley & Sons, Inc., 1964), p. 123.

[27]Matthew B. Miles, "Planned Change and Organizational Health: Figure and Ground," in Richard O. Carlson and others, *Change Processes in the Public Schools* (Eugene: Center for the Advanced Study of Educational Administration, University of Oregon, 1965), p. 17.

28Adapted from Miles, "Planned Change," pp. 18–21.

29Rensis Likert, *New Patterns of Management* (New York: McGraw-Hill Book Company, 1961).

30Gordon L. Lippitt, *Organizational Renewal: Achieving Viability in a Changing World* (New York: Appleton-Century-Crofts, 1969).

31Matthew B. Miles and Dale G. Lake, "Self-Renewal in School Systems: A Strategy for Planned Change," in *Concepts for Social Change,* ed. Goodwin Watson (Washington, DC: National Training Laboratories, NEA, 1967).

32Far West Laboratory, "A Statement of Organizational Qualification for Documentation and Analysis of Organizational Strategies for Sustained Improvement of Urban Schools" (paper submitted to Program on Local Problem-Solving, National Institute of Education, San Francisco, 1974).

33John I. Goodlad, *The Dynamics of Educational Change: Toward Responsive Schools* (New York: McGraw-Hill Book Company, 1975), p. 175.

34Gerald Zaltman, David H. Florio, and Linda A. Sikorski, *Dynamic Educational Change: Models, Strategies, Tactics, and Management* (New York: The Free Press, 1977), p. 89.

35Michael Fullan, Matthew B. Miles, and Gib Taylor, *OD in Schools: The State of the Art, Volume I: Introduction and Executive Summary.* Final report to the National Institute of Education, Contract nos. 400-77-0051-0052 (Toronto: Ontario Institute for Studies in Education, August 1978), p. 14.

36The following discussion of OD concepts and force-field analysis is from Robert G. Owens and Carl R. Steinhoff, *Administering Change in Schools* (Englewood Cliffs, NJ: Prentice-Hall, 1976), pp. 142–48.

37See, for example, Spencer Wyant, *Organizational Development from the Inside: A Progress Report on the First Cadre of Organizational Specialists* (Eugene: Center for the Advanced Study of Educational Administration, University of Oregon, 1972).

38Jack R. Gibb, "TORI Theory: Consultantless Team-building," *Journal of Contemporary Business,* 1 (Summer 1972), 33–34.

39The concepts of force-field analysis and the three-step cycle of organizational change are generally credited to Kurt Lewin, "Frontiers in Group Dynamics," *Human Relations,* 1 (1947), 5–41. The definitive work in this field by Lewin is *Field Theory in Social Science* (New York: Harper & Row, Publishers, Inc., 1951).

40Lewin, "Frontiers in Group Dynamics," p. 35.

41Paul Hersey and Kenneth H. Blanchard, *Management of Organizational Behavior: Utilizing Human Resources,* 3rd ed. (Englewood Cliffs, NJ: Prentice-Hall, 1977), p. 2.

42Michael Fullan, Matthew B. Miles, and Gib Taylor, *OD in Schools: The State of the Art* (Toronto, Ontario: Ontario Institute for Educational Studies, 1978), 4 volumes.

43Philip J. Runkel and Richard A. Schmuck, *Findings from the Research and Development Program on Strategies of Organizational Change at CEPM-CASEA* (Eugene: Center for the Advanced Study of Educational Administration, Center for Educational Policy and Management, University of Oregon, 1974), p. 34.

44John I. Goodlad, *The Dynamics of Educational Change: Toward Responsive Schools* (New York: McGraw-Hill Book Company, 1975), p. xi.

45Ibid., p. 113.

46Ibid.

47Ibid., p. 115.

48Ibid., p. 135.

49Ibid., pp. 139–40.

50Fullan, Miles, and Taylor, *OD in Schools,* p. 2.

51Ibid.

9

CONFLICT
IN ORGANIZATIONS

"The potential for conflict permeates the relations of humankind, and that potential is a force for health and growth as well as for destruction...No group can be wholly harmonious...for such a group would be empty of process and structure."

—James MacGregor Burns[1]

Thus far in this book I have emphasized the desirability of developing the organization as a system that enhances cooperative effort among people. But in the "real world" of educative organizations, a significant fact of life is the presence of conflict in many forms and at various levels of strength. It is clearly among the most "touchy" topics in the field of organizational behavior, undoubtedly because of the potential in every conflict situation for destructive outcomes. The central thesis of contemporary behavioral science applied to conflict is that—with diagnostic and management approaches now available—it is possible not only to minimize the destructiveness of conflict but also, in many cases, to deal with it productively.

Conflict is pervasive in all human experience. Indeed, it can occur even within a single individual (so-called intrapersonal conflict), typified by approach-avoidance conflict, the common situation in which the person feels torn between the desire to achieve two goals that are incompatible. This leads to feelings of stress and—not infrequently—behavior manifestations (for example, indecisiveness) and even physiological symptoms (for example, hypertension, ulcers). And, of course, conflict runs the gamut of social experience—between individuals, between groups, and between whole societies and cultures.

Conflict can occur *within* persons or social units; it is *intra*personal or *intra*group (or, of course, *intra*national). Conflict can also be experienced *between* two or more people or social units: so-called *inter*personal, *inter*group, or *inter*national conflict.

In this chapter, I am not attempting to deal with the broad, general phenomenon of conflict; I will confine the discussion to conflict in organizational life—*organizational conflict* (that is, *intra*organizational conflict). Most commonly, this involves interpersonal conflict and intergroup conflict.

THE NATURE OF CONFLICT IN ORGANIZATIONS

In classical management theory, the existence of conflict is viewed as evidence of breakdown in the organization: failure on the part of management to plan adequately and/or to exercise sufficient control. In human relations views, conflict is seen in an especially negative light and as evidence of failure to develop appropriate norms in the group.

Traditional administrative theory has, therefore, been strongly biased in favor of the ideal of a smooth-running organization, characterized by harmony, unity, coordination, efficiency, and order. Human relations adherents might seek to achieve this through happy, congenial work groups, while classical adherents would seek to achieve it through control and strong organizational structure. Both, however, would tend to agree that conflict is disruptive: something to be avoided.

One of the more dramatic developments in the literature on organizations has been a reexamination of these positions, resulting in some more useful views.

Definition of conflict. In the vast body of scientific literature, there is no consensus on a specific definition of "conflict."[2] There is general concurrence, however, that two things are essential to any conflict: (1) divergent (or apparently divergent) views and (2) incompatibility of those views.

Thus, Morton Deutsch tells us simply that "a conflict exists whenever incompatible activities occur."[3] But this incompatibility produces a dilemma: conflict becomes "the pursuit of incompatible, or at least seemingly incompatible, goals, such that gains to one side come out at the expense of the other."[4] We are confronted with the classic, zero-sum, win-lose situation that is potentially so dysfunctional to organizational life; everyone strives to avoid losing and losers seek to become winners. Though a conflict may originate as substantive (that is, "conflict rooted in the substance of the task"[5]), it readily can become affective (that is, "conflict deriving from the emotional, affective aspects of the...interpersonal relations").[6] To the Likerts, this affective involvement is a central characteristic of conflict in organizations, which they define as "the active striving for one's own preferred outcome which, if attained, precludes the attainment by others of their own preferred outcome, *thereby producing hostility*"[7] (emphasis added).

The focus of contemporary application of behavioral science to organizations is precisely this point: to manage conflict in the organization so that hostility can be either avoided or minimized. This is *not* the management of hostility; it is the management of conflict so as to reduce or eliminate hostility emanating from it.

Conflict different from attacks. There is a distinct difference between organizational conflict and its attendant hostility, on the one hand, and destructive attacks, on the other hand; to treat them alike can be a serious mistake. Kenneth Boulding suggests that we distinguish between malevolent hostility and non-malevolent hostility.[8] Malevolent hostility is aimed at hurting, or worsening the position of, another individual or group, with scant regard for anything else, including consequences for the attacker. Nonmalevolent hostility, on the other hand, may well worsen the position of others but is acted out for the purpose of improving the position of the attacker. Malevolent hostility is often characterized by the use of issues as the basis for attack, which are, in reality, not important to the attacker except as a vehicle for damaging the opposition.

Malevolent hostility can, in turn, give rise to what Richard Wynn has called "nefarious attacks."[9] These are characterized by (1) the focus on persons rather than on issues, (2) the use of hateful language, (3) dogmatic statements rather than questions, (4) the maintenance of fixed views regardless of new information or argument, and (5) the use of emotional terms.

The key difference between such attacks (whether "malevolent," "nefarious," or otherwise) and legitimate expressions of conflict lies in the motivation behind them, often not easily discernible. Although considerable (and often vigorous) conflict may erupt over such issues as improving school performance, ways of desegregating a school system, or how to group children for instruction, the parties to the conflict may well be motivated by essentially constructive goals. The key is whether or not the parties involved want to work with the system or are motivated by a wish to destroy it.

Warren Bennis has described, for example, how—in a period of student disruption at the State University of New York at Buffalo—he labored hard and long to deal with a student takeover of the campus, using his not inconsiderable skills as a third-party facilitator. But it was all to little avail. Looking back, Bennis came to realize that he really had not been in a two-party conflict-management situation at all.[10] The students—to the extent that they were organized—were committed to a set of political goals that had little to do with the educational goals that the university administrators embraced. In this case, the conflict was largely a device being used to achieve carefully masked goals. The student confrontations and rhetoric often were, in fact, malevolent with little intention of coming to agreement.

Any public education administrator needs to be sensitive to this problem and to be aware of the significant difference between attacks for the sake of destruction[11] and vigorous expression of essentially constructive—though sharply divergent and perhaps unwelcome—views.

Contemporary views of conflict. Conflict in organizations is now seen as inevitable, endemic, and often legitimate. This is because the individuals and groups within the human social system are interdependent and constantly engaged in the dynamic processes of defining and redefining the nature and extent of their interdependence. Important to the dynamics of this social process is the fact that the environment in which it occurs is, itself, constantly changing. Thus, as Chester Barnard pointed out, "inherent in the conception of free will in a changing environment"[12] are social patterns characterized by negotiating, stress, and conflict.

Effects of organizational conflict. Frequent and powerful conflict can have a devastating impact upon the behavior of people in organizations. Psychological withdrawal from the hostility often associated with conflict—such as alienation, apathy, and indifference—is a common symptom that keenly affects the functioning of the organization. Physical withdrawal—such as absence, tardiness, and turnover—is a widely occurring response to conflict in schools that is often written off as laziness on the part of teachers who have been spoiled by "soft" administrative practices. And outright hostile or aggressive behavior—including job actions, property damage, and minor theft of property—are far from unknown responses by teachers to conflict situations that appear to be "too hot to handle": totally frustrating.

Indeed, the behavioral consequences of conflict in educative organizations can be, to put it mildly, undesirable. Ineffective management of conflict (for example, a hard-nosed policy of punishment for "offenses," get-tough practices in the name of administering the negotiated contract, emphasizing the adversarial relationship between teachers and administration) can—and frequently does—create a climate that exacerbates the situation and is likely to develop a downward spiral of mounting frustration, deteriorating organizational climate, and increasing destructiveness, as shown in Figure 9–1. Obviously, the health of an organization caught in this syndrome tends to decline. Effective management of conflict, on the other hand (for example, treating it as a problem to be solved, emphasizing the collaborative essence of organizational life), can lead to outcomes that are productive and enhance the health of the organization over time, as shown in Figure 9–2.

The point to be emphasized is that conflict in itself is neither good nor bad; it is (in value terms) neutral. Its impact on the organization and the behavior of people is largely dependent upon the way in which it is treated.

The criterion: organizational performance. To speak of organizational conflict as good or bad, or as functional or dysfunctional, requires one to specify

FIGURE 9–1. An ineffective conflict-response-climate syndrome leads to a lower state of organizational health.

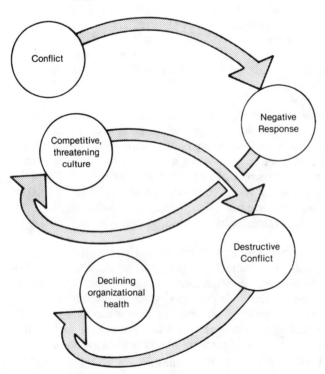

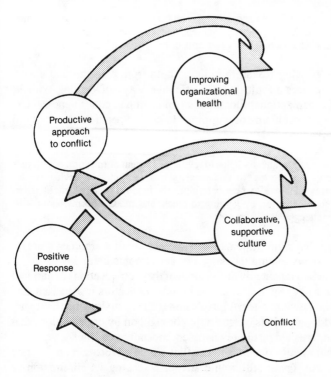

FIGURE 9–2. An effective conflict-response-climate syndrome leads to an improved state of organizational health.

the criteria used in judging. Some people—many with a "humanistic" bias—simply find conflict repugnant and seek to abolish it wherever it may be found. Others are concerned about the internal stress that conflict often imposes upon individuals. These, in themselves, are not of central concern in *organizational* terms. One would do well to keep in mind that—after all—there also are people who relish conflict, find it zestful, and seek it out. The issue, then, is the impact of conflict on the performance capability of the organization as a system.

Again, the problems of measuring the productivity of educational organizations and the discussion of the relevance of the school system's or school's internal conditions (that is, organizational culture, interaction-influence system) come to the fore. Thus, the functional or dysfunctional consequences of conflict on educative organizations are understood best in terms of organizational health, adaptability, and stability.

As has been seen, modern motivation theory makes clear that challenge, significance, and the need to solve problems are important attributes of work that people find interesting, enjoyable and—in a word—motivating. Also, as has been seen, concepts of participative leadership rest on the conviction that many people in the organization have good ideas and quality information to contribute to making better decisions in the organization. In this view, Kenneth Thomas observes:

> ...the confrontation of divergent views often produces ideas of superior quality. Divergent views are apt to be based upon different evidence, different considerations, different

insights, different frames of reference. Disagreements may thus confront an individual with factors which he had previously ignored, and help him to arrive at a more comprehensive view which synthesizes elements of his own and other's positions.[13]

Finally, there is growing reason to believe (both from research and expert opinion) that conflict causes people to seek effective ways of dealing with it, resulting in improved organizational functioning (for example, cohesiveness, clarified relationships, clearer problem-solving procedures).[14] Speaking of society in general, Deutsch observed:

> ...conflict within a group frequently helps to revitalize existent norms; or it contributes to the emergence of new norms. In this sense, social conflict is a mechanism for adjustment of norms adequate to new conditions. A flexible society benefits from conflict because such behavior, by helping to create and modify norms, assures its continuance under changed conditions.[15]

He went on to caution that rigid systems that suppress conflict smother a useful warning signal, thereby maximizing the danger of catastrophic breakdown.

We all have witnessed repeatedly the wisdom of these observations in national and international events of great and small magnitude. Educators in America also have seen it closer to home, where fearful explosions of pent-up hostility have, not infrequently, followed long periods of frustration brought on by organizations that thought they had either crushed or nimbly avoided impending conflict.

Although few who really understand conflict would advocate its deliberate use in organizational life, fewer still would advocate seeking its elimination or avoidance. Rather, by applying concepts of conflict management, the intent is to minimize the destructive potential, on the one hand, and make conflict as productive, creative, and useful as possible, on the other hand.

THE DYNAMICS OF ORGANIZATIONAL CONFLICT

Although numerous writers have compiled a long list of the causes of organizational conflict, Louis Pondy has classified most of them into three basic types of *latent* conflict:

1. When the organization's resources are insufficient to meet the requirements of the subunits to do their work, there is *competition for scarce resources* (for example, budget allocations, assigned teaching positions, space or facilities);
2. When one party seeks to control the activities "belonging" to another unit (and the second unit seeks to fend off such "interference"), the issue is *autonomy* (for example, protecting one's "turf");
3. When two parties in the organization must work together but cannot agree on how to do so, the source of conflict is *goal divergence* (for example, the school principal and the director of special education have differing views as to how mainstreaming issues are to be settled).[16]

A contingency view. These latent sources of conflict are unlikely to disappear from organizational life. It is, therefore, important to develop a culture that supports productive approaches to conflict management.[17] Because there are a number of causes of conflict—even when classified or grouped, as above—it is obvious that there is no one best way of managing conflict. As John Thomas and Warren Bennis put it:

> An effective paradigm incorporates what might be termed a "situational" or "contingency" framework, a point of view reflected in much of the current theoretical and empirical work in organizational theory. There is a primary emphasis upon diagnosis and the assumption that it is self-defeating to adopt a "universally" applicable set of principles and guidelines for effecting change or managing conflict.[18]

As a basis for the necessary organizational diagnosis, two concepts concerning conflict are often used: one seeks to understand the internal dynamics of the events that occur in the process of conflict; the other seeks to analyze the external influences that tend to structure the conflict.

A process view of conflict. Conflict between two parties appears to unfold in a relatively orderly sequence of events and—unless something intervenes—the sequence tends to be repeated in episodes. Each episode is highly dynamic, with each party's behavior serving as a stimulus to evoke a response from the other. Further, each new episode is shaped in part by previous episodes.

One model of such a process is suggested by Thomas (see Figure 9–3), in which an episode is triggered by the *frustration* of one party by the act of another (for example, denial of a request, diminishment of status, disagreement, or an insult). This causes the participants to *conceptualize* the nature of the conflict— often a highly subjective process that suggests ways of defining and dealing with perceived issues in the conflict. Indeed—as experimental research reported by Robert Blake, Herbert Shepard, and Jane Mouton makes clear—this step of

FIGURE 9–3. Process model of conflict episodes between two parties. Kenneth Thomas, "Conflict and Conflict Management," in *Handbook of Industrial and Organizational Psychology,* ed. Marvin D. Dunnette (Chicago: Rand McNally & Company, 1976), p. 895.

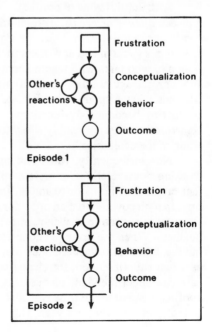

defining the issues and seeking alternative responses is frequently viewed by the parties to the conflict as a simple matter of victory or defeat. Alternatives other than winning or losing are easily overlooked.[19] This is followed by *behavior* intended to deal with the conflict. As Kenneth Thomas explains, understanding the bases for this behavior is a complex matter; but key elements surely include a mix of (1) a participant's desire to satisfy the other's concern (cooperative-uncooperative) and (2) the participant's desire to satisfy his or her own concern (assertive-unassertive).[20] *Interaction* of the parties follows, of course; this is a highly dynamic phase of the process. It can involve escalation or deescalation of the conflict, depending upon such factors as the trust level that is established, biases and self-fulfilling prophesies that get in the way, the level of competition between the participants, and the openness and sensitivity each has to the other. The *outcome* of all this—the last stage in an episode of conflict—is not merely some agreement on substantive issues but includes residual emotions (for example, frustration, hostility, trust—either increased or decreased). These outcomes have potentially long-term effects on the aftermath of a conflict episode, particularly as they set the stage for ensuing episodes.

In commenting on the aftermath as part of a sequence of episodes, Louis Pondy pointed out that:

> If the conflict is genuinely resolved to the satisfaction of all participants, the basis for a more cooperative relationship may be laid; or the participants, in their drive for a more ordered relationship may focus on latent conflicts not previously perceived and dealt with. On the other hand, if conflict is merely suppressed but not resolved, the latent conditions of conflict may be aggravated and explode in more serious form....This legacy of a conflict episode is...called "conflict aftermath."[21]

A structural view of conflict.   Although a process approach to conflict sees it as a *sequence of events,* a structural view tends to see conflict in terms of the *conditions that influence behavior.* For example, every organization has rules and procedures (written and unwritten, formal and informal) that regulate behavior (for example, who talks with whom about what). Rules and procedures often serve to avoid or manage conflict by clarifying such issues as how to proceed, when, and who has what responsibility. But, of course, they also can cause or exacerbate conflict by becoming dysfunctional, such as when they lead to rigid, repetitious behavior that does not readily allow for exceptions (the typical bureaucratic "hardening of the categories").

Not infrequently, rules and procedures so complicate the processes of working out a relatively simple conflict through direct negotiation that they in fact create conflict. For example, in one school district an elementary school principal discovered that an order for a certain kind of paper had been cut sharply by an administrative assistant in the office of the assistant superintendent for business. When the principal contacted the administrative assistant to straighten out the matter, she was reminded that her complaint should be routed through the assistant superintendent for elementary education who could take it up with the assistant superintendent of business, and so on. Needless to say, considerable conflict ensued, much time was lost, and the needed paper finally arrived at the school—in time for *next* year. The point is that some simple rearrangements in the way that even minor decisions are made and differences are negotiated can influence the course of conflict in organizations.

Another structural factor lies in the kinds of people found in the organization, with particular reference to their personality predispositions, for instance, their attitudes toward authority and the extent and flexibility of their responses to others. In selecting new personnel, for example, many school districts and schools are attracted to candidates who seem to "fit in," over candidates who might add diversity to the staff.

A further structural factor influencing the incidence and nature of conflict in an organization is the social norms of the organization: the social pressures, for example, to "stand up and fight" or "not to rock the boat." The creation of organizational cultures that smooth over friction and frown upon open challenge and questioning can make it very difficult to identify and confront conflict at all. Similarly, when secretiveness and restricted communication represent the organizational norm, it is difficult to know if a latent conflict exists, let alone to plan ways of dealing with it. Many administrators of educational organizations instinctively understand this and make it a rule to put as little communication in writing as possible, to assemble people for meetings as infrequently as possible, and—when meetings *must* be held—to be sure to control the proceedings tightly so as to minimize the "risk" of opening up issues that might "cause trouble."

Thus, the structural factors that shape conflict in organizations are strongly influenced by structural factors in the organization itself. In the words of the Likerts:

> The success of [an organization] is influenced greatly by its capacity to achieve cooperative coordination rather than hostile conflict among its functional departments and also to stimulate differences and then to capitalize on them by productive problem-solving leading to creative and acceptable solutions....Institutions based on traditional organizational theory...lack the capacity to deal successfully with the conflicts created by the new demands which recently legitimized values are placing on them..,.Repressive action brings costly backlash.[22]

They, of course, advocate developing a more responsive interaction-influence system through System 4 leadership, developing a supportive climate, de-emphasizing hierarchical status, and using consensus for productive (win-win) problem solving.

An open-systems view. Thus far I have been discussing organizational conflict entirely in terms of the internal functioning of educative organizations, and this will continue to be the focus of the chapter as a whole. It is, however, vital that one never loses the perspective that these organizations are open systems; they are interactive with their environments, and much that goes on within them reflects changes in the external environment.

In terms of conflict, a good case in point is P.L. 94-142, which was passed by Congress and signed into law on November 29, 1975. It is a classic example of power-coercive change strategy and probably set the stage for more widespread conflict in American public schooling—at all levels—than anything since the *Brown* school desegregation decision of some two decades earlier. At the highest levels it raised conflicting constitutional issues: the interpretation of the Tenth Amendment that education is a state responsibility and a matter of local control *versus* the view that P.L. 94-142 is an exercise of federal responsibility to assure full civil rights to equal opportunity for the unserved (and inadequately served) handicapped.

However, the law also raised conflicts all along the line, from Washington, DC, to the most remote school classroom in the land. For example, it sought to redefine the prerogatives of teachers to control instruction and related decision making, by mandating the inclusion of parents in a participatory role in planning individualized instruction and in a formalized appeal process. The parent—formerly an "outsider" confined to an advisory role—suddenly became one of the "insiders" with new authority in relationship to the teacher.

The ability of schools to deal productively with this conflict thrust upon them from the larger environment was unclear even as late as 1990 because external initiatives to mandate increasing control of the classroom decisions of teachers were still increasing in number and scope. It is, however, a clear and unambiguous illustration of how conflict—very much involving the internal functioning of schools and school systems—can be imposed upon them by rapid change in the external system.

Gerald Griffin and David Rostetter have speculated as to whether Randall Collins's five hypotheses on coercive efforts to deal with coercion and conflict might apply.[23] As they point out:

1. Coercion leads to strong efforts to avoid being coerced.

2. If resources for fighting back are available, the greater the coercion applied the more counter aggression is called forth.

3. If resources are not available but opportunities to escape are, the greater the tendency to leave the situation.

4. If resources for fighting back and opportunities to escape are not available, or if there are other strong incentives for staying in the situation (material rewards or potential power), the greater coercion that is applied the greater the tendency to comply with exactly those demands that are necessary to avoid being coerced.

5. If resources for fighting back and opportunities for escape are not available, the...tendency to dull compliance and passive resistance [is increased].[24]

In this view, coercion leads to a conflict-hostility-resistance syndrome *within* the organization, very unlike the synergistic, creative, problem-solving culture that characterizes effective organizations. Only time will tell what effect this federal initiative, based on traditional concepts of schools as organizations, will ultimately have.

APPROACHES TO ORGANIZATIONAL CONFLICT

When conflict arises, the almost instinctive response of the parties involved is to adopt a strategy—backed by determination—to *win*. To most people that means, *ipso facto*, that the other party will *lose*.

> Confrontation, non-negotiable demands, and ultimatums have become the order of the day as *the* way of dealing with deep-seated differences. One party marshals all its forces to compel the other party to do what the first has decided it wants. Confrontation is from

a fixed position and seeks to mobilize the power to win. Win-lose strategy is used in a variety of situations, such as struggles for civil rights; urban riots; student demonstrations and sit-ins; international conflicts; union-management disagreements; a hearing on next year's budget; a controversy between departments...or a controversy between professional staff and the lay board.[25]

The focal point of conflict management is the win-lose orientation and how to deal with it. It is important, *first,* to understand the dynamics and consequences of win-lose approaches to conflict and, *second,* to see what alternatives are available.

The win-lose orientation to conflict. The dynamics of win-lose conflict and their consequences for organizational behavior are well known. Group dynamicists in the 1950s and 1960s conducted extensive research on the phenomena of group conflict—including both experimental work and field observation studies (recall the discussion of group dynamics and human relations in Chapter 1).[26]

"A win-lose orientation to conflict is characterized by one basic element," Blake, Shepard, and Mouton observe. "The contesting parties see their interests to be mutually exclusive. No compromise is possible. One must fail at the price of the other's success...[and] hope is abandoned of being able to appeal to each other on the basis of reason."[27] The parties to the conflict come to believe that the issues can be settled in one of three ways: (1) a power struggle, (2) intervention by a third party who possesses some sort of power greater than either of them (and this can include public opinion or moral suasion), or (3) fate.

The consequences of this approach are twofold:

1. *Between the parties to the conflict.* Antagonisms deepen, hostility rises, hope of finding a mutually acceptable solution fades and—as it does—the search for such a solution ceases.

2. *Within the groups involved.* Spirits soar as members close ranks in preparation for battle. Differences of opinion, skepticism, and challenge of leadership or the "party line" are frowned upon: members are pressured to support the decisions taken, to conform, to "go along," to be loyal to the group or get out. Leadership gravitates rapidly to a very small number of people, who are usually forceful and aggressive. Thus diversity of opinion, the search for quality ideas, and the broad involvement of members in developing creative responses are snuffed out in the group. This not only hardens the group's position in the conflict itself but—more importantly—sets the stage for ineffective functioning of the group after the conflict eases.[28]

Experimental studies of conflict[29] make it clear that the perception of individuals and groups is very much involved in conflict—often becoming distorted as the episode unfolds. And, of course, "perception is the key to behavior. The way persons see things determines the way they will act. If their perceptions are distorted, the distortions are reflected in their behavior."[30] Thus, judgment is adversely affected by the conflict experience: one tends to become blindly loyal, to become hostile to members of the other group, and to denigrate not only their ideas but their worth as persons. Leaders of the opposition—formerly seen as mature, able people—are now seen as irresponsible and incapable. Indeed, even cognition is affected: in studying proposed solutions to the conflict, it becomes difficult or impossible to see merit in proposals put forth by "the other side," even though they may be in substantial agreement with one's own ideas. Thus, agreement becomes elusive. *Any* sign of questioning the position of one's group or any approval of proposals put forth from the other side is viewed by associates as "backing down." Winning becomes everything. The ability to "see" alternatives, to be objective, and to suspend judgment while seeking to understand—all are badly distorted as one increasingly shares the "gung-ho" drive of the group for "victory."

In terms of the process model of conflict (described earlier), win-lose is a way of conceptualizing the conflict and gives rise to predictable patterns of behavior in the interaction between parties to the conflict as the episode unfolds. But the consequences, it should be clear, are not limited to the shape and character of the conflict itself. Each of the groups involved in the conflict is powerfully affected in the aftermath. Usually, of course, hostility between the winning group and the losing group is intensified, and subsequent episodes may be expected.

Commonly, the losing group will reject its leaders; very likely it will, in time, begin reappraising what went wrong and start preparing to do better next time. Powerful emotional reactions (resentment—even hatred—and anxiety) are likely to continue to distort the group's functioning, reducing the likelihood that it will develop a climate supportive of self-renewal and creative problem solving. Thus, win-lose solutions to conflict tend to build long-term, dysfunctional behaviors resulting in a downward spiral of organizational climate, performance, and overall organizational health.

A central concern of conflict management, then, is to seek more effective ways of conceptualizing conflict as a basis for more effective behavior.

A contingency approach to conflict.   Contingency approaches to management are, of course, predicated upon the concept that diagnosis of the situation is necessary as a basis for action. In dealing with conflict, the contingency view is that there is not one best way of managing it under all conditions but that there are optimal ways of managing conflict under certain conditions. An important aspect of conflict management, then, is to consider (1) alternative ways of managing conflict and (2) the kinds of situations in which each of these various alternatives might be expected to be the most effective, not only in dealing with the critical issues but also in doing so in a way that strengthens the organization.

Diagnosing conflict.   In the first place, it is helpful to ascertain whether conflict *does* exist between the parties or whether a conflict only *appears* (to the parties) to exist. The criterion is whether or not the two parties seek goals that are actually incompatible.

Not infrequently, what appears to be a brewing conflict between two parties is, in fact, a misunderstanding. Recognizing the problems of distorted perception as discussed above, it is probable that a misunderstanding can be dealt with through explicit goal setting and improved communication. This often requires some training of individuals and groups in such skills as group goal setting and prioritizing, as well as in communication skills (for example, active listening, seeking feedback to check receiver's perceptions, using multiple channels).

If a conflict *does* exist, however (that is, the parties do have goals that are mutually incompatible), then it is necessary to select a method of dealing with it as productively as possible from among the many options available. *The general principle is that a win-lose approach tends to be the least productive, while a win-win approach—in which both parties win something (though not necessarily equally)—tends to be the most productive.*

Collaboration is a process in which the parties work together to define their problems and then engage in mutual problem solving. As a mode of dealing with conflict, this process requires, first, that the parties involved must want, actively, to try to use it (will give time and effort to participating). The process also requires that the people involved possess (1) the necessary skills for communicating and working in groups, effectively coupled with (2) attitudes that support a climate of openness, trust, and frankness in which to identify and work through problems.

In situations in which the *will* to do this exists in the groups but the skills are not well developed, a facilitator can be brought in to help the group to learn the necessary skills and engage in the collaborative processes (though the facilitator does not get involved in the substance of decisions, merely the processes for making them). This is the highest level of win-win conflict management because it leaves the groups with new skills and new understandings that they can use again and again in dealing with future problems. It is, of course, a form of organization development (organizational self-renewal). Not the least attribute of collaborative approaches to problem solving is the healthy sense of "ownership" or commitment to the solution arrived at that is unmatched by other approaches. In Likert's terms it is System 4 management; Blake and Mouton would call it 9, 9 style.

Bargaining, compromise, and other forms of splitting the difference have some elements in common with collaborative problem solving: (1) the parties must be willing to engage in the process (though sometimes they are legally required to do so); (2) there is some move toward collaboration (though usually this is restricted to the negotiators); and (3) the process is basically conciliatory and not in flagrant conflict with the organization's well-being. If the bargaining escalates to mediation and/or arbitration, the outside "third party" plays a role quite different from that of the group-process facilitator in a collaborative process: he or she *does* have the power to make judgments and impose decisions on the parties in conflict. Bargaining does seek to develop a long-term relationship between the parties and provides them with a mechanism for dealing with future problems. But bargaining is not a collaborative approach: it recognizes that the two parties are essentially adversaries and may use information as a form of power for strategic purposes.

Neither party wins in the typical bargaining/compromise situation, but, then, neither party is the loser. Although the term "bargaining" is readily associated with labor-management relations, negotiation processes are, in fact, widely employed within organizational settings to settle conflicts. For example, when two administrators confer to "work out" some problems between their divisions, it is not uncommon for them to use negotiating and compromise techniques systematically. And if the negotiations do bog down, they may take the problem to their immediate superordinate for mediation (a common feature of the so-called bureaucratic mode of conflict management).

Avoidance (withdrawal, peaceful coexistence, indifference) is often employed when dealing with conflict. Avoidance is useful (a) when it is not likely that the latent conflict really can be resolved ("live with it") or (b) when the issues are not so important to the parties as to require the time and resources to work them out. As Blake and his colleagues point out, avoidance can be in the form of a "cease-fire," wherein two groups engaged in a long-term struggle decide to keep in contact, still entrenched in their positions, but not to get locked into combat with each other.[31] An interesting outcome of various avoidance responses to latent conflict is that, although conflict is not inevitable, neither is agreement possible. Thus, though hostile aftermath is avoided, the underlying problems are not dealt with; the latent conflict—with all its hazardous potential—remains, ready to become manifest at any time.

Power struggle is, of course, the effort by each party to win, regardless of the consequences for the other party. Although conflict, in itself, may be seen as having some beneficial potential for organizations (or, at least, as being nondestructive), this mode of dealing with it is viewed almost universally as being destructive. It is the classic win-lose situation.

A CONTINGENCY APPROACH TO DIAGNOSIS OF CONFLICT

An important aspect of diagnosis for the conflict manager is to ascertain the way *each party* to the conflict has conceptualized the situation.

Kenneth Thomas contends that it is common, in a conflict situation, to emphasize the extent to which a party is willing to cooperate with another party but to overlook a second critical factor: the party's desire to satisfy his or her own concerns.[32] Thus, in his view, two critical behavioral dimensions shape the way one conceptualizes conflict:

1. *Cooperativeness*, which is the extent to which one wishes to satisfy the concerns of the other, and
2. *Assertiveness*, which is the extent to which one wishes to satisfy her or his own concerns.

These are seen as independent dimensions, as shown in Figure 9–4. Thus, in diagnosing conflict—*as conceptualized by the parties involved*—the issue becomes more than merely a matter of cooperating or "acting professionally": cooperation can be viewed as literally a sacrifice of one's own needs.

From this analysis, Thomas identifies five principal perspectives that may be used in conceptualizing conflict and behaviors commonly associated with those perspectives:

1. *Competitive* behavior is the search to satisfy one's own concerns at the expense of others if need be. As shown in Figure 9–5, it is a high competitive-high uncooperative orientation. The effect is domination of the situation (as, for example, in hard-nosed contract negotiations in which nothing is yielded and every advantage is exploited). It is the classic win-lose view of conflict.
2. *Avoidant* (unassertive-uncooperative) behavior is usually expressed by apathy, withdrawal, and indifference. This does *not* mean that there is an absence of conflict but that it has been conceptualized as something not to deal with. Hence, the latent conflict remains and may be viewed differently at another time.
3. *Accommodation* (high cooperativeness-low assertiveness) is typified by appeasement: one attends to the other's concerns while neglecting his or her own. This orientation

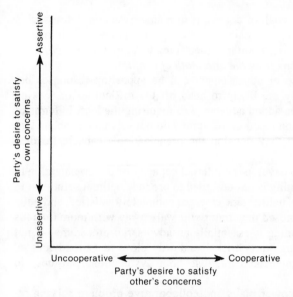

FIGURE 9–4. Assertiveness and cooperativeness are independent dimensions in conflict. Based on Kenneth Thomas, "Conflict and Conflict Management," in *Handbook of Industrial and Organizational Psychology,* ed. Marvin D. Dunnette (Chicago: Rand McNally & Company, 1976).

may be associated with a desire to maintain a working relationship even at some sacrifice of one's own interests.

4. *Sharing* orientation (moderate assertiveness-moderate cooperativeness) often leads to compromise (trade-offs, splitting the difference, horse-trading).

5. *Collaborative* orientation to conflict (high assertive-high cooperative) leads to efforts to satisfy fully the concerns of both parties through mutual problem solving. The solution to the conflict is a genuine integration of the desires of both sides. The concept is win-win.

This approach to the analysis of conflict helps to assess the kinds of strategies that might be most usefully employed in managing it (for example, bargaining,

FIGURE 9–5. Five orientations to conflict related to assertiveness and cooperativeness. From Kenneth Thomas, "Conflict and Conflict Management," in *Handbook of Industrial and Organizational Psychology,* ed. Marvin D. Dunnette (Chicago: Rand McNally & Company, 1976), p. 900.

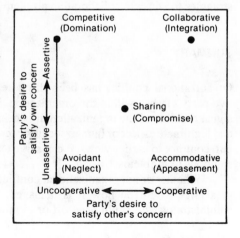

power, or collaboration). The goal, of course, is to manage the conflict in such a way that it will be as productive as possible for the organization while minimizing destructive consequences. It is important, therefore, to *consider the potential long-run consequences resulting from the aftermath of conflict.*

For example, avoidance or appeasement can be appealing responses because—in the short run—they are likely to head off the difficulties of seeking genuine solutions and have the added advantage of requiring the least in terms of organizational energy, time, and resources. But they do not solve the problem that triggered the conflict, nor do they develop the organization's capacity to deal productively with conflict.

Bargaining does help to develop the internal capacity of the organization to deal with conflict. But bargaining is not designed to produce optimal solutions: in the processes of horse-trading, neither side emerges completely satisfied, and quite likely the more skilled, hard-nosed negotiator will walk away with more than his or her opponent does. Bargaining is essentially an adversarial procedure—if not downright underhanded—using "dirty tricks" and wily ploys to gain advantage. These often engender resentment and mistrust, both dysfunctional attitudes in organizational life.

Competitive win-lose power plays and collaborative problem solving require the most energy, time, and resources. The essentially different consequences of each mode already have been described. Because the aftermath and long-term consequences of win-lose power struggles are well known to be dysfunctional and those of collaboration functional, few who are concerned about enhancing the organization's performance would fail to choose collaboration—whenever practicable—as the most desirable conceptualization of conflict, and competition as least desirable.

Because avoidance and appeasement are really *non*management of conflict, we are left with three basic general strategies for dealing with it: collaboration, bargaining, or power. Figure 9–6, which summarizes the essential characteristics of each of these strategies, also shows how bargaining incorporates certain features of *both* collaboration and power strategies. In this sense, bargaining serves as a bridge between power strategies and collaboration, making it *possible*—though far from inevitable—to move, over time, organizational processes from win-lose power struggles to win-win collaborative problem solving.

SUMMARY

Organizational conflict has been discussed in this chapter chiefly in terms of two-party clashes within the organization. Whereas conflict was once thought to signal a failure of the organization, it is being increasingly recognized as a normal and legitimate aspect of human social systems. Thus, conflict is not only inevitable but, contrary to earlier views, it can serve a useful function by stimulating creative solutions to problems.

Whether or not organizational conflict is destructive or constructive depends to a large extent on how it is managed. The day is over for the wily school administrator who could head off or terminate conflict with deft tricks or a swift

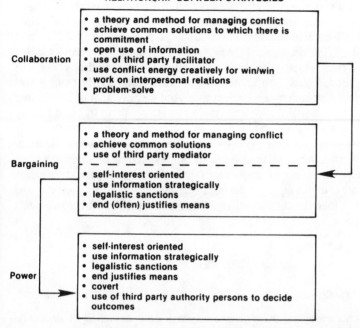

RELATIONSHIP BETWEEN STRATEGIES

Collaboration
- a theory and method for managing conflict
- achieve common solutions to which there is commitment
- open use of information
- use of third party facilitator
- use conflict energy creatively for win/win
- work on interpersonal relations
- problem-solve

Bargaining
- a theory and method for managing conflict
- achieve common solutions
- use of third party mediator
- — — — — — — — — — — — — — —
- self-interest oriented
- use information strategically
- legalistic sanctions
- end (often) justifies means

Power
- self-interest oriented
- use information strategically
- legalistic sanctions
- end justifies means
- covert
- use of third party authority persons to decide outcomes

FIGURE 9–6.   Relationship between conflict management strategies. From C. Brooklyn Derr, Managing Organizational Conflict: When to Use Collaboration, Bargaining and Power Approaches (Monterey, CA: Naval Postgraduate School, 1975), p. 12.

exercise of power. Healthy organizations—characterized by well-developed problem-solving mechanisms and a collaborative climate—are able to identify conflict and deal with it in a collaborative way that leaves the organization stronger and more well-developed rather than weakened and wracked with hostility.

Ways of handling conflict in school districts and schools have been heavily influenced by the people who have been consulted for advice or by third-party intervention. Especially with the spread of collective bargaining, school districts have turned increasingly for advice to people trained and conditioned to view conflict in adversarial, combative terms (lawyers and, not infrequently, professional negotiators and mediators), rather than to people trained and conditioned to view it as a phenomenon of organizational behavior (applied social scientists, organizational psychologists). Too often this has tended to produce essentially destructive, win-lose strategies and tactics. All too often it has been associated with the denigration of proposals to seek more productive approaches as being "unrealistic."

This chapter has proposed a way of diagnosing conflict in a given situation as a basis for choosing an appropriate management strategy. Clearly, there is no one best way of managing conflict in organizations. There are a number of ways, each suited to circumstances in a particular situation. The basic principle in choosing a way of managing conflict, however, is to use the approach most likely to minimize the destructive aspects (for example, hostility) and to maximize the opportunities for organizational growth and development (for example, to develop greater trust, to improve problem solving).

Finally, there is no more critical phase in conflict management than diagnosis of the situation. Not infrequently the processes of conceptualizing, or analyzing, conflict confuses effects with causes. For example, a superintendent of schools asked a consultant, "What are some of the ways that I càn deal with conflict in this school district?" When asked what kind of conflict he was talking about, the superintendent replied, "Well, you know, we had that teachers strike and it was pretty bad here. Now the teachers are back at work, but we have a lot of bad feeling everywhere. You know: hostility. We have to do something about it. What can we do?" While, as I have explained, hostility is an important aspect of conflict, it is important to bear in mind that hostility does not describe a conflict, itself. Hostility is an emotional reaction that is all too often part of the outcome or aftermath of an episode of conflict. But trying to ameliorate hostile feelings is, perhaps, dealing with a symptom rather than a cause. If we fail to diagnose the conflict correctly and deal with the causes, then the conflict will continue in latent form ready to manifest itself at a later time.

SUGGESTED READING

BECKHARD, RICHARD, "The Confrontation Meeting," *Harvard Business Review,* 45 (March–April 1967), 149–55.
    Description of "an activity that allows a total management group, drawn from all levels of the organization, to take a quick reading on its own health, and—*within a matter of hours*—to set action plans for improving it" (p. 149). Provides a specific design for a one-day meeting that can be used to deal with the stress of a crisis that helps the group (1) diagnose the situation, (2) set goals and priorities collaboratively, (3) develop a plan of action, and (4) implement the plan on both a short-range and a long-range basis.

BLAKE, ROBERT R., HERBERT A. SHEPARD, AND JANE S. MOUTON, *Managing Intergroup Conflict in Industry.* Houston, TX: Gulf Publishing Company, 1964.
    This small, readable book has become a classic in the literature of conflict. Explains many of the insights into organizational conflict that now are widely accepted. Draws upon experimental research as well as upon the authors' own practical experience. Includes a straightforward contingency analysis.

DERR, C. BROOKLYN, *Managing Organizational Conflict: When to Use Collaboration, Bargaining and Power Approaches.* Monterey, CA: Naval Postgraduate School, 1975.
    Proposes a contingency approach. Pointing out that collaboration, bargaining, and power approaches all are appropriate in the management of organizational conflict under certain conditions, the author explains how to diagnose the contingencies in different situations. Benefits and drawbacks for each strategy, under varying conditions, are discussed.

LIKERT, RENSIS, AND JANE GIBSON LIKERT, *New Ways of Managing Conflict.* New York: McGraw-Hill Book Company, 1976.
    After analyzing the causes of increasing organizational conflict, this book describes procedures for substituting System 4 ("win-win") problem-solving strategies for the "win-lose" approach that usually leaves one party to a conflict frustrated and embittered. A highly specific, practical, how-to book with some explicit applications to schools that should be helpful to practitioners.

WYNN, RICHARD, *Administrative Response to Conflict.* Pittsburgh: Tri-State Area School Study Council, School of Education, University of Pittsburgh, 1972.
    In this twenty-three-page monograph the author attempts to distill contemporary concepts of organizational conflict into practical advice for school superintendents, school board members, and other public school practitioners. Emphasizes that organizational climate appears to predispose an organization toward either productive conflict or destructive conflict and that the administrator influences this climate by his or her administrative style and values.

NOTES

[1]James MacGregor Burns, *Leadership* (New York: Harper & Row, Publishers, Inc., 1978), p. 37.

[2]Kenneth Thomas, "Conflict and Conflict Management," in *Handbook of Industrial and Organizational Psychology,* ed. Marvin D. Dunnette (Chicago: Rand McNally & Company, 1976), p. 890.

[3]Morton Deutsch, *The Resolution of Conflict: Constructive and Destructive Processes* (New Haven: Yale University Press, 1973), p. 10.

[4]Bernard Berelson and Gary A. Steiner, *Human Behavior: An Inventory of Scientific Findings* (New York: Harcourt Brace Jovanovich, Inc., 1964), p. 588.

[5]H. Guetzkow and J. Cyr, "An Analysis of Conflict in Decision-making Groups," *Human Relations,* 7 (1954), 369.

[6]Ibid.

[7]Rensis Likert and Jane Gibson Likert, *New Ways of Managing Conflict* (New York: McGraw-Hill Book Company, 1976), p. 7.

[8]Kenneth E. Boulding, *Conflict and Defense: A General Theory* (New York: Harper & Brothers, Publishers, Inc., 1962), pp. 152–53.

[9]Richard Wynn, *Administrative Response to Conflict* (Pittsburgh: Tri-State Area School Study Council, 1972), pp. 7–8.

[10]Warren G. Bennis, *The Leaning Ivory Tower* (San Francisco: Jossey-Bass, 1973).

[11]For advice on how to deal with "nefarious attacks," see Wynn, *Administrative Response to Conflict.*

[12]Chester I. Barnard, *The Functions of the Executive* (Cambridge, MA: Harvard University Press, 1938), p. 36.

[13]Thomas, "Conflict and Conflict Management," p. 891.

[14]The research (none of it in schools) has been summarized by Thomas, "Conflict and Conflict Management."

[15]Deutsch, *The Resolution of Conflict,* p. 9.

[16]Louis R. Pondy, "Organizational Conflict: Concepts and Models," *Administrative Science Quarterly,* 12 (September 1967), 296–320.

[17]Most writers in this field today use the term conflict *management,* connoting an ongoing organizational process that is heuristic and supportive of organization development over time. To many, the term conflict *resolution* carries the connotation of seeking final, conclusive solutions that will terminate even latent conflict—an unlikely event.

[18]John M. Thomas and Warren G. Bennis, *Management of Change and Conflict* (Baltimore: Penguin Books, 1972), p. 20.

[19]Robert R. Blake, Herbert A. Shepard, and Jane S. Mouton, *Managing Intergroup Conflict in Industry* (Houston, TX: Gulf Publishing Company, 1964).

[20]Thomas, "Conflict and Conflict Management," p. 900.

[21]Pondy, "Organizational Conflict."

[22]Likert and Likert, *New Ways of Managing Conflict,* p. 7.

[23]Randall Collins, *Conflict Sociology: Toward an Explanatory Science* (New York: Academic Press, Inc., 1975).

[24]Gerald Griffin and David Rostetter, "A Conflict Theory Perspective for Viewing Certain Problems Associated with Public Law 94-142" (paper presented at the American Educational Research Association, Atlanta, Ga., March 1978), p. 4.

[25]Likert and Likert, *New Ways of Managing Conflict,* p. 59.

[26]The research literature is rich and fascinating. See, for example, Muzafir Sherif and Carolyn W. Sherif, *Groups in Harmony and Tension* (New York: Harper & Brothers, Publishers, 1953); Muzafir Sherif and others, *Intergroup Conflict and Cooperation: The Robbers Cave Experiment* (Norman: Institute of Group Relations, University of Oklahoma Book Exchange, 1961); Morton Deutsch, "The Effects of Cooperation and Competition upon Group Process: An Experimental Study," *American Psychologist,* 4 (1949), 263–64; and—also by Deutsch—*The Resolution of Conflict.*

[27]Blake, Shepard, and Mouton, *Managing Intergroup Conflict,* p. 18.

[28]Likert and Likert, *New Ways of Managing Conflict,* p. 61.

[29]Such as the work of Deutsch, Blake, and Sherif mentioned above.

[30]Likert and Likert, *New Ways of Managing Conflict.*

[31]Blake, Shepard, and Mouton, *Managing Intergroup Conflict,* p. 63.

[32]Thomas, "Conflict and Conflict Management."

10

DECISION MAKING

"Decision-making processes represent the brain and nervous system of the organization."
—*Richard L. Daft*[1]

Since mid-century, decision making has been widely recognized as being at the heart of organization and administration. For example, in a landmark book published in 1950, Herbert Simon observed that "a general theory of administration must include principles of organization that will insure correct decision-making".[2] By 1959 Daniel E. Griffiths had proposed a theory that administration *was* decision making.[3] He maintained that first, the structure of an organization is determined by the nature of its decision-making processes; second, an individual's rank in an organization is directly related to the control exerted over the decision process; and third that the effectiveness of an administrator is inversely proportional to the number of decisions that he or she must personally make.

Griffiths' theory, which was highly influential in educational circles for many years, highlights two important concepts: (1) that the administrator's task is to see to it that an adequate decision-making process is in place in the organization, and (2) that, because such a process is in place, the effective administrator makes relatively few decisions personally, although those few may be particularly potent in their impact on the organization. In other words, the administrator's control rests not so much in personally making numerous decisions as it does in controlling the means by which decisions in the organization are made. In this view, the administrator's influence resides more firmly in creating and monitoring the processes through which decisions shall be made by the organization than in personally making large numbers of the many decisions that are required in any busy complex organization.

INDIVIDUAL VERSUS ORGANIZATIONAL DECISION MAKING

An important issue that enters many discussions of decision making is being raised here: the question of individual versus organizational decision making. On the one hand, there is the widely held expectation that persons in administrative positions will personally "be decisive." What that means is far from clear but is often taken to mean making decisions swiftly, without delay or temporizing, and clearly, with minimum ambiguity. It often also implies that the individual tends to make decisions that conform to certain accepted qualitative standards: that, for example, decisions are well-informed and ethically acceptable. Thus, discussions of administrative decision making often focus on the personal behaviors of individuals who are construed to be "decision makers."

On the other hand, since administration is defined as working with and through other people to achieve organizational goals, it is important to consider the mechanisms by which the organization (and not merely the individual) deals with decision making. In this perspective, the issue begins to turn on the ways in which the *organization* "acts" (or "behaves") in the process of making and implementing *organizational* decisions, rather than on the idiosyncratic behavior of the person in administrative office. For many of the clients of organizations (students and parents, for example) the individual roles of administrators in decision-making processes are obscure and perhaps irrelevant, whereas the "behavior" of the organization is highly proximate and relevant. In this view—while administrators may be seen as implicated—the vital decision-making functions are organizational.

This was illustrated by the situation in one university in which the heating system was constantly malfunctioning, classrooms were chronically unkempt, and student seating typically in disrepair. Students were astounded when, in the spring, an ambitious project was undertaken to beautify the campus by planting flowers and shrubs and setting sculptures among the trees. This, of course, prompted outcries from students, such as, "What is wrong with this university? It obviously doesn't care what happens in the classrooms. All that matters is what visitors see on the outside!" The implication was, of course, that—regardless of the persons who might be involved—somehow the decision-making processes of the university, as an organization, had gone awry.

The discussion of decision making in this chapter recognizes that the personal decision-making style of the administrator is important insofar as it gives rise to the ways in which the organization, as an entity, goes about the unending processes of identifying problems, conceptualizing them, and finding ways of dealing with them. The individual decision making of persons in administrative office takes on significance as organizational behavior chiefly because of its inevitable impact on the behavior of others as it affects the decision-making processes of the organization itself.

This emphasis on the responsibility of the administrator for the nature and quality of the decision-making processes used in an organization is compatible with the contemporary view that the administrator is a key actor in the development of the culture of the organization. That is, that decision-making practices are not so much the result of circumstances inherent in a given organization ("the kind of place a school is") as they are the choices of those in authority (namely administrators) as to how decisions *ought* to be made. These choices are closely tied to assumptions held by administrators on issues that are now familiar to the reader, such as:

- what motivates people at work;
- the relative values of collaboration vs. directiveness in the exercise of leadership in the workplace;
- the desirability of a full flo of information up, down, and across the organization;
- the best ways of maintaining organizational control and discipline;
- the value of involving people throughout all levels of the organization in decision making.

These views on decision making are also closely related to concepts of leadership which were discussed in Chapter 6. For example, Robert Tannenbaum and Warren Schmidt conceptualized leadership as being the ways in which the leader manages the decision-making process (see Figure 6–1). A number of others, notably Robert Blake and Jane Mouton (see Figure 6–5) and Victor Vroom and Philip Yetton (see Figure 6–9) have also explored the dense relationship between the behavior of leaders and the ways in which they manage the processes of making decisions in the organization.

RATIONALITY IN DECISION MAKING

Even an elementary understanding of contemporary approaches to decision making in organizations requires brief consideration of some of the ways in which we have learned to think about such things. We who live in the Western world tend to use and accept logic, rationality, and science when thinking about concepts such as decision making. This reflects generally held assumptions in our culture about the ways in which we "ought" to go about making decisions. These assumptions have formed the central core of our thinking about such matters.

During the three centuries since the Reformation, the history of Western thought and culture has been dominated by the rise of science, technology, and industry. Scientific thought, with its strong emphasis on logical rationality, has become virtually ingrained in the institutions of our culture. Thus, in seeking explanations of our experiences, we are accustomed to respect the rationality of logical positivism—in short, as I shall explain further in this chapter, we have strongly tended to see the solution to all sorts of problems as requiring the application of "engineering" approaches.

This was reflected in Max Weber's analysis of bureaucratic organization (see Chapter 1). It was epitomized by the work of Frederick Taylor (see Chapter 1) who, adapting the principles and methods of science to a form of "human engineering" in the workplace, sought to create a science of management which could be applied to everyday problems in the organization. Taylor called it Scientific Management and, as Donald Schön points out, "Taylor saw the...manager as a designer of work, a controller and monitor of performance...[seeking through these roles] to yield optimally efficient production."[4]

The concept of management as a science grew steadily during the first half of the century but World War II stimulated its development enormously. This was due to three factors associated with the war:

- The great emphasis on the roles of science and technology in winning the war.
- The development of operations research and systems theory (see Chapter 3). These involved the application of the rational logic of mathematics modeling to the solution of complex problems ranging from how to reduce the loss of shipping to submarine attack to how to increase the effectiveness of aerial bombing.
- The unprecedentedly vast scale of organizing that was required to manage the global dimensions of the conflict.

The post–World War II era was one of great optimism and energy as industry and business moved rapidly to exploit the ready markets that abounded as a result of the years of wartime shortages everywhere. Confidence in science and technology boomed and the rational, logical methods associated with science soared in acceptance and prestige. It was commonplace to refer to the wartime Manhattan Project as a model for conceptualizing and solving problems: "After all, if we could build an atomic bomb we ought to be able to solve this problem." Government expenditures for research surged to new heights on the "basis of the proposition that the production of new scientific knowledge could be used to create wealth, achieve national goals, improve human life, and solve social problems."[5]

As though to be sure that attention to the importance of the message did not lag, Russia launched Sputnik I in the fall of 1957. The United States reacted with another spasm of emphasis on the logic of applying mathematics and science to the solution of problems. Under the leadership of President Kennedy, a large-scale effort to develop new space technology was undertaken. Before long, the educational infrastructure of the nation found itself involved in meeting the demands of the space programs for scientists and mathematicians, as well as managers trained to apply the concepts of those disciplines to complex organizational challenges. The new rallying cry became, "If we can put a man on the moon, why can't we solve this problem?" The implication was, of course, that the National Space and Aeronautics Administration (NASA) had—since its inception under the presidency of Dwight Eisenhower—developed and demonstrated the effectiveness of a model for complex decision making that was applicable to all sorts of problems, social as well as technological.

During the post–World War II era another, similar, model—widely admired and emulated—was preferred by medicine. It emphasized clinical-experimental research as the basis of knowledge.

> The medical research center, with its medical school and its teaching hospital, became the institutional model to which other professions aspired. Here was a solid base of fundamental science, and a profession which had geared itself to implement the ever-changing products of research. Other professions, hoping to achieve some of medicine's effectiveness and prestige, sought to emulate its linkage of research and teaching institutions, its hierarchy of research and clinical roles, and its system for connecting basic and applied research to practice. The prestige and apparent success of the medical and engineering models exerted great attraction for the social sciences. In such fields as education...the very language...rich in references to measurement, controlled experiment, applied science, laboratories and clinics, was striking in its reverence for those models.[6]

Rational decision-making models. It is not surprising, therefore, that students of decision making tried to develop, and assist administrators to master, a *science* of making better-quality decisions through the analysis of decision-making processes. An early and very major contributor in this effort was Herbert Simon.

Simon's analysis was that there are three major phases in the process of making decisions. First, there is *intelligence activity.* Not surprisingly, in view of the influence of World War II on postwar thought, Simon used the term "intelligence" much as military people do: the search of the environment that reveals circumstances that call for a decision. The second phase is *design activity:* the processes by which alternative courses of action are envisioned, developed, and analyzed. The third phase in Simon's analysis is *choice activity:* that is, the process of actually selecting a course of action from among the options under consideration.[7]

Simon's great stature as a scholar and his popularity as a consultant to numerous prestigious corporations enhanced wide acceptance of his pioneering approach to decision making, which now stands as classic work. Many who were to follow would create a substantial literature devoted to efforts to improve upon his conceptualization, usually by elaborating the number of steps to be found in the process. Thus, one finds numerous models preferred in the extensive literature on decision making. Two basic assumptions, incorporated in virtually all of them, are based on Simon's work: the assumption that decision making is an orderly, rational process that possesses an inherent logic; and the assumption that the steps in the process follow one another in an orderly, logical, sequential flow (which some refer to as "linear logic"). Such models, and the assumptions upon which they are based, became important in the training of administrators and have been widely applied in planned, systematic ways to "real-world" organizations in the hope of improving their performance.

Peter F. Drucker, a leading organizational scholar whose thinking was very influential in corporate circles from the 1960s into the 1980s, listed the following steps in decision making:

1. Define the problem.
2. Analyze the problem.
3. Develop alternative solutions.
4. Decide on the best solution.
5. Convert decisions into effective actions.[8]

Such a formulation was seen as helping the administrator to organize decision making, make it more systematic, as an alternative to intuitive, perhaps haphazard, "knee-jerk responses" to the flow of events in the busy environment of organizational life. Drucker's model, much elaborated and detailed, was widely applied in American corporate and governmental organizations and was accepted by many as the essential logic of administrative thought.

Nevertheless, even as the number of models proliferated and efforts to install them in organizations intensified, a widespread disparity between the theoretic notions of the scholars and actual practices of administrators was also apparent. Therefore, further work to improve decision-making models went forward. It was noted, for example, that decision making usually does not terminate with either a decision or the action to implement a decision. In the "real world," decision making is usually an iterative, ongoing process whereby the results of one decision provide new information on which to base yet other decisions. Thus, "feedback loops" were added to some process models to ensure that the outcomes of decisions would be considered as future decisions were pondered.

Eventually recognition of this cyclic nature of decision-making processes caused some students of the subject to abandon conventional lists of steps and linear flow charts in favor of circular depictions. Both the feedback loop concept and the circular concept of decision-making processes illustrate two further assumptions commonly found in the literature on decision making: (1) that decision making is an iterative cyclical process that proceeds over time to provide successive approximations of optimal action, and (2) reaching optimal decisions is the central goal of decision making.

However, it has long been obvious that an organization tends not to search endlessly and relentlessly for the best way of achieving its goals. It will engage its decision-making procedures to seek alternative ways of doing things only when the organization's performance seems to be falling below some acceptable level. This "acceptable level" of performance is usually not the highest level of performance possible: rather, it is one that is good enough to fit the organization's perception of reality and values.[9] Moreover, once the organization senses the need to seek some alternative way of doing things, it tends to seek a course of action that is perceived as sufficient to alleviate the need for action. That is, it tends to make a decision that will relieve its proximate problem but is unlikely to seize the moment as occasion for moving to some optimal level of performance. This widespread tendency in organizations is called *satisficing*.

LIMITS ON RATIONALITY IN DECISION MAKING

As I have explained, much of the scholarly literature on decision making—both organizational and individual—represents the efforts of academicians to uncover and describe the logic assumed by them to be inherent in decision-making processes. And, based upon these efforts, a number of "models" of decision-making processes have been developed. These models, it has often been assumed, can be useful in facilitating the learning of this logic by administrators so that it may be applied in their work. Many people—including practicing educational administrators, legislators, and school board members trained at a time when these assumptions were essentially unchallenged—tend to persist in the belief that more rigorous application of these efforts to practice is essential to improving organizational performance.

However, ambiguity and uncertainty are dominant characteristics of the "real world" of the educational administrator. Organizations, their goals, their technologies, and their environments have become so complex that it is difficult to connect causes with effects, actions with outcomes. For example, the volatile nature of the economic, social, and political environments of the educational organization makes it difficult to predict the course of future events with any certitude. This condition is not limited to educational organizations by any means: it is of pressing importance in all forms of organizational life. This has caused researchers to reexamine organizational life more carefully in recent years and, in the process, to question old assumptions concerning the logic and rationality of decision making.

The gap between theory and practice.   Scholars commonly seek to improve the performance of administrators by instructing them in the application of rational, logical models of decision making to their work. One of the better examples, in the field of education, is found in a training manual called *Deciding How to Decide: Decision Making in Schools.*[10] Intended to be the basis for organizing and presenting an in-service workshop to teach administrators when and how to involve others in decision making, the manual is essentially an orderly presentation of the Vroom and Yetton model (described in Chapter 6), together with exercises to give those attending the workshop practice in using the model in lifelike situations. Because the models used as the basis attempt to establish new behavioral norms in the administrator's professional practice, they are often referred to as *normative models.*

However, research conducted in a variety of organizations makes it clear that practicing managers and administrators rarely actually use such models in their work. Henry Mintzberg, Duru Raisinghani, and Andre Theoret report that normative decision-making models have no influence on the behavior of middle- and upper-level corporate managers.[11] James G. March found that decision makers, in fact, tend to make sense of problems not by applying logical models to them but by assessing what kinds of options are actually available to be used in solving them.[12] Paul C. Nutt, after examining seventy-eight different organizations, concluded that

> Nothing remotely resembling the normative methods described in the literature was carried out. Not even hybrid variations were observed....The sequence of problem definition, alternative generation, refinement, and selection, called for by nearly every theorist seems rooted in rational arguments, not behavior. Executives do not use this process.[13]

The findings of a national survey of senior high school principals indicates a similar situation in that group of administrators.[14]

Thus we have an obvious gap between theory and practice. What does it mean? It could suggest that the administrators and managers whose behavior was studied by the researchers were ill-trained and therefore unable to use the decision-making models available to them. An equally plausible explanation is that the decision-making models espoused in the scholarly literature arise from assumptions about the nature of administrative work that do not reflect the conditions that the administrator on the job actually encounters. This leads us to consider research that describes the behavior of managers and administrators as it actually occurs on the job.

The nature of managerial and administrative work.   In 1973, Henry Mintzberg reported research that documented detailed descriptions of the activities of the chief executives of five organizations as they were observed in their daily work.[15] The executives whose behaviors were thus recorded were (1) the manager of a consulting firm, (2) the president of an industrial company, (3) the manager of a hospital, (4) a manager of a consumer goods concern, and (5) the superintendent of a suburban school district. This research strikingly reveals, first that the executive's work is very diverse and requires a broad range of skills; and, second, the pressure that appears to be inherent in the work. More specifically, Mintzberg developed five propositions from his observations:

1. Administrators and managers do a great deal of work, and do it at an unrelenting pace. Each day they attend a number of previously arranged meetings as well as a number of unplanned conferences and interactions, deal with a substantial volume of mail and paper work, handle numerous phone calls. There are seldom any real breaks in the work.
2. In doing their work, administrators characteristically devote a brief time to each of a large number of decisions and these tend to center around specific, well-defined issues and problems. Important and trivial activities arise in juxtaposition to one another in an unplanned, random way, requiring quick mental shifts from topic to topic. There are many brief contacts with people interspersed with planned meetings of prolonged duration and other activities (such as desk work, telephone calls, unscheduled meetings, and tours) worked into the daily schedule.
3. Administrators prefer to deal with active problems that are well-defined and non-routine. Routine information (such as recurring reports) is given low priority whereas "fresh" information (even if of uncertain quality) is given high priority.
4. Verbal communication is much preferred. (In Mintzberg's original study, it accounted for over three-fourths of the executives' time and two-thirds of their activities.)
5. Managers maintain working relationships with three principal groups: superiors, subordinates, and outsiders.[16]

This research suggests a great deal about the ways in which administrators go about making decisions, and particularly about why few seem to use formal decision-making models in their work. The rhythm of the administrator's workday comprises a driving force that evokes behavior in ways that are not likely to enter the mind of the contemplative scholar pondering the logic he or she seeks to find in the situation. As Mintzberg noted,

The work of managing an organization may be described as taxing. The quantity of work to be done, or that the manager chooses to do, during the day is substantial and the pace is unrelenting. After hours, the chief executive (and probably many other managers as well) appears to be able to escape neither from an environment that recognizes the power and status of his position nor from his own mind, which has been well trained to search continually for new information.[17]

Why do managers maintain such a pace and such a workload? Mintzberg thinks it is because the job is inherently open-ended and ambiguous:

The manager must always keep going, never sure when he has succeeded, never sure when his whole organization may come down around him because of some miscalculation. As a result, the manager is a person with perceptual preoccupation. He can never be free to forget his job, and he never has the pleasure of knowing, even temporarily, that there is nothing else he can do. No matter what kind of managerial job he has, he always carries the nagging suspicion that he might be able to contribute just a little bit more.[18]

In conducting his observations of the administrators he studied, Mintzberg developed a technique which required the frequent recording of code symbols that described behaviors being observed during numerous small time frames during the day. Eventually, these coded entries are reduced and arrayed statistically so as to produce a detailed quantified description of the observable behaviors that occurred over the total period of time during which observations were carried out.

A number of studies using the "Mintzberg technique" have examined the on-the-job behavior of such educational administrators as superintendents of schools and school principals.[19] These have substantially confirmed that Mintzberg's propositions apply to the work of school administrators. These administrators work long hours, at an unrelenting pace. Their work is characterized by many brief interactions, mostly verbal. Meetings, phone calls, and paper work account for almost every minute from the moment they enter the office in the morning until they leave in the afternoon or evening.

Mintzberg's use of the term "unrelenting pace" needs a little clarification here. One could conjure up the image of an assembly-line worker being driven at his task by the inexorable onrush of work coming down the line, never stopping, never varying. This is not what Mintzberg appeared to mean in describing the work of managers. In the manager's work situation, time becomes an important resource. Unlike the situation of the teacher, however, time for the administrator is a fluid resource rather than a constraining one.

For the teacher, critical time constraints (such as the school year, the school day, the bell schedule, and fixed constraints such as bus schedules and lunch schedules) sharply limit what he or she can or cannot do. Administrators, on the other hand, can—and often do—have considerable latitude to vary the pace of their work as seems appropriate to them. They can take extra time to carefully consider some even unimportant issues at length, if they wish, and seek to save time by making a series of rapid decisions on other matters. Or the administrator who wishes to do so can vary the use of time resources by stretching the workday into the evening, or the workweek into the weekend, and the workyear into the summer and holidays. This is, of course, what many educational administrators commonly do. Thus, the "unrelenting pace" is not at all necessarily an unvarying pace; it is one in which characteristically the work to be done is never completed, and there is always more to be done. One never knows when the task is finished.

These characteristics of administrative work combine with the ambiguity inherent in the educational system—and ambiguity arising from the unclear goals and priorities of schools and school systems, uncertain methods of evaluating administrative performance, and problematic preferences exercised by various constituency groups—to put considerable pressure on educational administrators. One result, and an additional source of pressure, is that they—like administrators in other fields—seldom stop thinking about their work.[20]

How administrators think.   Recent research suggests that a source of confusion in the minds of scholars who study organizations and the behavior of administrators in them may be the fact that academic people and administrators tend to think about administrative work in different ways. The models for decision making described in the beginning of this chapter are the products of persons conditioned in the belief that highly logical, linear thinking, sometimes called "scientific thinking," is the single most appropriate way of exploring problems and seeking alternatives in the decision-making process. Largely academics, such observers tend to expect to see administrators behave in much the same ways that they, themselves, do. They maintain, that is, "that thinking is visible in the form of long reflective episodes during which managers sit alone, away from the action, trying to make logical inferences from facts. Since observers do not see many episodes that look like this, they conclude that managers do not do much thinking."[21] Indeed, much of the in-service training for administrators that emphasizes the so-called models for decision making is little more than an effort to train administrators in formal methods of reflective thought. The assumption underlying such training is that one can improve the decision-making behavior of administrators by improving their skills in logical, reflective thought.

But why is it that researchers report so few occasions in which administrators are observed, as scientists frequently are, thinking reflectively—cogitating, mulling over a problem, considering alternatives in the dispassionate calm of a quiet retreat? Karl Weick proposes three possible explanations. First, they do think but not while they are on the job: "...they think at home, on airplanes, in the john, on weekends....Thus, the reason researchers do not see managers think is that managers do not think when the observers are around."[22] The second possibility is that, essentially, managers don't think because they have reduced uncertainty to such an extent and anticipate the future so very well that they are confronted by few situations in which they are perplexed or bewildered. The third possibility proposed by Weick (and the one he considers most likely) is that managers think all the time but researchers have missed that fact because, while the researcher looks for episodes evidencing reflective thinking, managers go at the thinking process quite differently. That is, thinking is inseparably woven into, and occurs simultaneously with, managerial and administrative action.

Thus, when administrators tour, read, talk, supervise, and meet with others, all of those actions contain thought and, indeed, they *are* the ways in which administrators do their thinking. "Connected ideas, which are the essence of thought," Weick explains, "can be formed and managed *outside* the mind, with relatively little assistance from the mind. This is how managers work, and this is why we are misled when we use reflection as an index of how much their work involves thinking."[23] Thus, most of the thinking that administrators do is woven into their actions when their actions are taken with attention, intention, and control; that is, they pay attention to what is happening, impose order on their actions, and correct their performance when it strays from accepted standards.[24]

In considering the ways in which administrators think about their work, it is important to bear in mind that the organizational environment in which the work is done is characterized by ambiguity, uncertainty, and disorder: it is, in a word, messy. Situations that require decisions are often fluid and, therefore, difficult to analyze even after the fact; they are subject to a number of interpretations, often conflicting; and (as will be explained more fully below) they are often not clearly bounded and labeled. In the daily flow of action, administrators typically engage in brief, spontaneous, face-to-face, verbal interaction with others. They are, in other words, constantly "fighting fires." But

> ...fighting fires, which managers do all the time, is not necessarily thick-headed or slowwitted. Firefighting has seemed like mindless activity because we have used

scientific activity as the ideal case for comparison, because we have thought of thinking as a separate activity that stops when people put out fires, because we have presumed that the only time people think is when they make distinct decisions or solve clearcut problems...and because we keep examining things as if they occurred in sequences rather than simultaneously.[25]

A crucial issue is implied in this view: whether administration is, or can be, a science in the traditional sense or whether it is, instead, an art or a craft. There are many who continue to pursue the notion of administration as the application of management science to organizational problems (much as engineering is the application of physics and mathematics to other sorts of real-world problems), as envisioned earlier in this century. Those holding this view tend, of course, to emphasize the development of technical rationality in organizational decision making. Others, however—cognizant of the great complexities of human organizations, and the uncertainty, instability, and uniqueness that are commonly found in them—recognize the importance of intuitive judgment and skill, the sense of proportion and appropriateness in the context of the traditions and values of the organization's culture. Schön, like Weick, finding the thinking of managers closely entwined with the action demanded in their work, observed:

> Managers do reflect in action. Sometimes, when reflection is triggered by uncertainty, the manager says, in effect, "This is puzzling; how can I understand it?" Sometimes, when a sense of opportunity provokes reflection, the manager asks, "What can I make of this?" And sometimes, when a manager is surprised by the success of his own intuitive knowing, he asks himself, "What have I really been doing?"[26]

Thus Schön makes clear that the term "art" has a twofold meaning in describing administration: intuitive approaches to understanding situations and also one's reflection, in a context of action, when one encounters events that are incongruent with his or her intuitive understandings.

The reader should note carefully that, in this discussion, we are talking about *trained* intuition.[27] The point is that we can learn—through both formal education and socialization into the organization's culture—to "see" a complex system as an organic whole as well as we can be trained (as we commonly are) to see individual parts of the whole. This crucial point is difficult for some observers to accept perhaps for two main reasons. One is that, in the strong tradition of technical rationality that has long been so emphasized in Western culture, the logic of breaking complex phenomena down into relatively simple, quantifiable parts has been thoroughly ingrained in many of us. It seems so sensible, so "right," that holistic approaches to complex problems are suspect. It is also probable that recent research on right- and left-hemisphere brain functioning is important to our understanding here. One mode of consciousness, associated with the left hemisphere, is generally described as analytic, rational, sequential, convergent, logical, objective, and linear. The other, associated with the right hemisphere, is characterized as intuitive, holistic, pattern-recognizing, artistic, subjective, and nonlogical. Unquestionably, emphasis has been placed on training left-brain functions in education that stresses logical-positivistic approaches to decision making. If we are to improve the way we apply right-hemisphere functioning to our decision making, it is likely that we will also have to improve our training strategies.[28]

Thus, it is argued that administrators are thinking all the time, that their thinking is closely intertwined with the actions (decisions) they take, and that everyday thinking almost never represents a sequence of steps. This suggests that formal models for decision making have little relevance to everyday administrative thinking and that to try to implement them would run counter to the "real world" as administrators experience it. In that world, problem situations are experienced holistically and the steps found in usual decision-making models are considered simultaneously rather than serially. This view suggests that emphasis on holistic thought—which seeks understanding of the complexities, interconnections, ambiguities and uncertainties of educational organizations—might be more fruitful in decision making than the linear-and-step models proffered in the past.

The influence of organizational culture on decision making. Earlier in this book, the concept of organizational culture was discussed as being at the core of understanding organizational behavior, such as decision making. Organizational culture involves the norms that develop in a work group, the dominant values advocated by the organization, the philosophy that guides the organizations's policies concerning employees and client groups, and the feeling that is evident in the ways in which people interact with one another. Thus, it clearly deals with basic assumptions and beliefs that are shared by those who are members of the organization. Taken together, these define the organization itself in crucial ways: why it exists, how it has survived, what it is about. In the process of developing and becoming part of the way of life in the organization, these values and basic beliefs tend to become solidly—almost unquestioningly—established as "the way we do things here." In this way, they shape the very view of the world that members bring to problems and decision making. We speak of "intuition" in the processes of thinking; organizational culture plays a large role in shaping that intuition in that the assumptions and beliefs that comprise the essence of organizational culture are largely taken for granted by participants. This is especially so in educational organizations inasmuch as those who work in them are generally highly socialized to the values and central beliefs of the organization through long years of commitment to them.

Consider the educational and work history of professionals in schools and institutions of higher education. Most of these people entered school at the age of five or (at the most) six years and have remained in educational organizations with only brief absences (such as for military service or child-rearing) virtually continuously throughout their formative years and the later years in which they established themselves as full adult members of society. As a result, they strongly tend to have "bought into" the values of education and educational organizations and, as professionals in these organizations, are highly committed to their core values, central beliefs, and goals. In the long process of being so thoroughly socialized into the organization—first as pupil, then as student and, ultimately, as professional—those who work in educational organizations tend strongly to accept the "rules of the game" for getting along and "the ropes" that must be learned in order to become accepted as a member.[29]

In other words, these individuals become members of a set of persons who have a long history of sharing common experiences. These shared experiences have, over time, led to the creation of a shared view of the world and their place in it.[30] This shared view enables people in the organization to make sense of commonplace as well as unusual events, ascribe meaning to symbols and rituals, and share in a common understanding of how to deal with unfolding action in appropriate ways. Such sense-making is described by Karl Weick as being central to understanding how people in organizations attribute credibility to interpretations that they have made of their experience.[31] Such a shared view is developed over a period of time during which the participants engage in a great deal of communicating, testing, and refinement of the shared view until it is eventually perceived to have been so effective for so long that it is rarely thought about or talked about any more: it is taken for granted.[32] This constitutes the development of an *organizational culture.* And it is culture that largely determines how one literally perceives and understands the world; it is the concept that captures the subtle, elusive, intangible, largely unconscious forces that shape thought in a workplace.[33]

Mintzberg's analysis, which is supported by a number of studies in educational organizations, makes clear that administrators spend little time in reflective thought: they are active, they spend much of their time communicating, interruptions are frequent, and they have little opportunity to be alone in peace and quiet. But, as Schön and Weick have pointed out, that does not necessarily mean that administrators do not think: it means that their thinking is closely intertwined with their action on the job.

But, is their thinking merely random, perhaps geared to the last person that they talked with or the latest crisis that has emerged? Probably not. Organizational culture is a powerful environment which reflects past experiences, summarizes them, and distills them into simplifications that help to explain the enormously complex world of the organization. In this sense, the organization—the school, the university—may be understood as a body of thought[34] that has evolved over time and that guides the administrator in understanding what is going on and how to deal with it. This body of thought embodies a highly complex array of subtleties, inconsistencies, and competing truths: it reflects the complexities and delicate balances of the administrator's world. Efforts to reduce this complexity through such simplification processes as imposing decision-making models on it are not likely to be very workable. In this view, therefore, the culture of the organization represents significant thinking prior to action and is implicit in the decision-making behavior of administrators.

The role and power of organizational culture to shape and mold the thinking and, therefore, the decision making of people in organizations is not a new concept by any means. However, as I described in Chapter 7, only in relatively recent years has it received widespread serious attention from organizational analysts and administrative practitioners alike as an approach to improving the decision making of organizations.

Closing the gap between theory and practice.   What guidance is there in the theoretic and research literature for practicing administrators attempting to implement these newer concepts in decision making? One answer is that in selecting an administrative style to use in practice, one needs to examine one's assumptions as to what is the most effective approach to administrative practice. Let us consider briefly how some of the important points of this book come together at this juncture to see where they lead us in administrative decision making.

Administration has been defined as *working with and through people to achieve organizational goals*. It has long been accepted (after Fayol) that the functions of administration are planning, organizing, leading, coordinating, and controlling. But the persistent puzzling issue throughout this century has been, what are the most effective ways of performing these functions? As I have described, there are conflicting ways to approach administrative practice: classical approaches and human resources approaches being the leading contenders among the currently competing systems of analysis through which administrative practice is interpreted. Except for those administrators who choose to pursue a mindless eclectic course in their professional work, the administrator must choose between these competing systems of analysis in deciding how to go about his or her professional work. The choice that the administrator chooses to embrace rests largely upon the assumptions about the nature of organizations and the people in them.

The assumptions that form the foundations of one's professional practice constitute, in the language of Chris Argyris and Donald Schön, a theory of practice. But we do not always practice what we preach: the actual theory of practice that one uses in deciding what to do is not always explicit, clear, and well-reasoned. Indeed, given human frailty, we often espouse one theory and actually act on the basis of another, perhaps conflicting, theory. And so we commonly witness administrators verbalizing their commitment to values that support improving the quality of work life in educational organizations while engaging in actions that are perceived by role referants to be antithetical to such improvement. Thus as individuals—often enlightened and well-intended—we act out the conflict between opposing ideas about organizations and people that has characterized organizational theory for decades.

There is a pattern in the history of the competition between the two major conflicting systems of analysis. Over the course of this century, the classical (or bureaucratic) approach has gradually lost credibility in the analysis of *educational* organizations, at least, as the organizational problems of schools and universities have deepened even as the application of bureaucratic attempts at solution grew and multiplied. Simultaneously, as more sophisticated research was pushed forward, the credibility and usefulness of human resources approaches grew steadily and that pattern seems likely to continue into the foreseeable future. This pattern is clearly evident in the body of research literature that has been discussed in this book.

In this book I have described modern human resources development (HRD) as being based upon the overlapping theories and concepts of such scholars as Douglas McGregor, Abraham Maslow, Frederick Herzberg, Chris Argyris, Rensis Likert, James March, Karl Weick, and William Ouchi.

McGregor described two sets of conflicting assumptions that administrators tend to hold about people and their attitudes toward work: Theory *X,* the belief that people are lazy and will avoid work if they can, and Theory *Y,* the belief that people seek responsibility and want to perform satisfying work. These concepts are now well understood by many administrators.

Maslow's concept of motivation is based on a hierarchy of prepotent needs in which satisfied needs are seen as not motivating people but in which yet unsatisfied needs can be motivators.

Herzberg's work identified "maintenance" factors, such as compensation and working conditions, as not being motivators but as being essential in order for such motivating factors as satisfaction arising from achievement in the work itself and a sense of autonomy on the job to be effective.

Likert conceptualized four management styles (System 1–System 4), each using different styles of leadership, motivation, and conflict management that have predictable outcomes in terms of organizational culture as well as end results in terms of organizational effectiveness. Further, and perhaps more important, Likert pointed out that it is the administrator—who has options from which to choose in deciding what the philosophy of management is to be, how communication is to be carried out, and how decisions shall be made in the organization—who bears major responsibility for the culture that develops in an organization.

Tannenbaum and Schmidt and Vroom and Yetton lent strong support to Likert's views by demonstrating that administrators are key actors in controlling decision making in the organization, and that this control is exercised by the decision-making style that administrators choose to use.

Argyris's work emphasized the need to develop greater harmony and consistency between the goals of organizations and the human needs of people who work in them, and that this requires replacing directive administrative styles with more participative styles.

James March pointed out that ambiguity and uncertainty characterize the natural state of affairs in organizations, rather than the patterns of predictability and order that administrators have traditionally sought to find in them. Thus, streams of problems, solutions, participants, and opportunities for making choices swirl around, occasionally resulting in decisions, though rarely arrived at in the orderly sequential fashion usually envisioned by formal rational decision-making models.

Karl Weick made clear that, instead of the close hierarchical cause and effect linkages that classical theory assumes to be present in organizations, the instructional activities of schools are characteristically loosely coupled. This loose coupling not only calls traditional assumptions about management methods into question, but opens new visions as to how schools can be managed so as to reduce the rigidity and ineffectiveness so frequently observed in them.

William Ouchi and others—including Terrence Deal, Rosabeth Moss Kanter, Edgar Schein, and Marshall W. Meyer—have explained that there are various ways of exercising administrative control in organizations. While traditional bureaucratic hierarchy is one way, and often thought to be the only way, in fact, the norms of the culture of an organization evolving through its history are an exceedingly powerful means through which administrators exercise influence over others. Further, they explain, the cultures of some organizations are more effective than others in implementing HRD concepts of motivation, leadership, conflict management, decision making, and change.

These HRD perspectives on organization provide a set of assumptions on which to base the practice of administration that are clear alternatives to classical perspectives. Whereas those who choose to use classical bureaucratic perspectives on organization continue to push hard for reducing ambiguity through increasing use of rules and close surveillance, striving for greater logic and predictability through more planning, increased specification of objectives, and tighter hierarchical control, contemporary best thinking in management emphasizes tapping the inner motivations and abilities of participants while recognizing that disorder and illogic are often ordinary characteristics of effective organizations. Taken together, the assumptions of HRD constitute a theory of decision making, the centerpiece of which is participative methods.

ISSUES IN PARTICIPATIVE DECISION MAKING

Much of decision making revolves around issues of participation in solving problems and making decisions. Participation is defined as the mental and emotional involvement of a person in a group situation that encourages the individual to contribute to group goals and to share responsibility for them.[35]

Notice that participation in this sense is "mental and emotional involvement"; this is the notion of "ownership" of (or "buying into") decisions. It is genuine ego involvement, not merely being present and "going through the motions." Such involvement is motivating to the participant, and thus it releases his or her own energy, creativity, and initiative. This is what distinguishes participation from *consent*, which is the major feature of voting on issues or approving proposals.[36] This ego involvement, this sense of "ownership," also encourages people to accept greater responsibility for the organizations's effectiveness. Having "bought into" the goals and the decisions of the group, the individual sees himself or herself as having a stake in seeing them work out well. This, in turn, stimulates the development of teamwork so characteristic of effective organizations.

The use of participative decision making has two major potential benefits: (1) arriving at better decisions and (2) enhancing the growth and development of the organization's participants (for example, greater sharing of goals, improved motivation, improved communication, better-developed group-process skills). As a practical guide for implementing participative processes in educative organizations, three factors in particular should be borne in mind: (1) the need for an explicit decision-making process, (2) the nature of the problem to be solved or the issue to be decided, and (3) criteria for including people in the process.

An explicit decision-making process. Participation can mean many things, as the work of Tannenbaum and Schmidt and Vroom and Yetton illustrate. All too often, the process, when not properly attended to, can be seen by participants as vague and ill-defined. Under such conditions people are not sure when to participate or what their proper role is in the process.

The most important decision that a group makes is to *decide how it will make decisions*. This is often one of the most inexplicit facts of organizational life: not uncommonly, people literally do not know who makes decisions or how they are made, let alone know how they individually may participate in the process. It is important, therefore, for the organization to develop an *explicit, publicly known* set of processes for making decisions that is *acceptable to its participants*.

The best time to grapple with this problem is before it is necessary to make a decision. One illustrative way of initiating this process is to convene a meeting of a school faculty (or other work group) for the purpose of reviewing the recent performance of the group. After selecting a few, *specific*, recent, decision-making episodes, the group can assess its experience by asking a few questions, such as these:

What were the processes by which this decision was reached? Do we all agree that we know how the decision was reached? How do we feel about that way of solving this problem? Should we use similar procedures next time, or should we make some changes? What suggestions are there for (1) identifying and defining problems, (2) deciding how to deal with them (and who should be involved), and (3) keeping everyone informed as to what is going on?

Simple steps such as these can begin to focus on the importance attached to the *way* that problems are defined and dealt with—a focus on group process. To be successful it must be accompanied by an emphasis on developing a climate in the group that supports open communication and stresses the skills required for revealing and working through differences among members of the group.

Readers who seek more specific suggestions and advice on developing explicit decision-making processes in the organization may find it useful to consult the following:

BRADFORD, LELAND P., *Making Meetings Work: A Guide for Leaders and Group Members*. La Jolla, CA.: University Associates, 1976.
  The old master shows—among other things—how to turn apathy and indifference into involvement and concern, how to use conflict constructively, and how to arrive at a decision.

DOYLE, MICHAEL, AND DAVID STRAUS, *How to Make Meetings Work*. Chicago: Playboy Press, 1976.
  Explicit "do-it-yourself" manual shows how to make meetings more productive by applying concepts of participative decision making. Excellent for staff development.

DUNSING, RICHARD J., *You and I Have Simply Got to Stop Meeting This Way*. New York: AMACOM, 1977.
  Emphasizes the need to tailor your approach to meetings, based on careful analysis of specific needs in your situation.

LIKERT, RENSIS, AND JANE GIBSON LIKERT, "Integrative Goals and Consensus in Problem Solving," in *New Ways of Managing Conflict*. New York: McGraw-Hill Book Company, 1976.
  Excellent short chapter clearly discusses the nature of consensus and its importance to group problem solving.

SCHINDLER-RAINMAN, EVA, AND RONALD LIPPITT, WITH JACK COLE, *Taking Your Meetings out of the Doldrums*. La Jolla, CA.: University Associates, 1975.
  A treasure-trove of detailed suggestings for making sure that meetings are productive and stimulating.

SCHMUCK, RICHARD A., "Developing Collaborative Decision-Making: The Importance of Trusting, Strong and Skillful Leaders," *Educational Technology*, 12, no. 10 (October 1972), 43–47.
  The entire issue of this journal is devoted to organization development in schools.

SCHMUCK, RICHARD A., PHILIP J. RUNKEL, JANET H. ARENDS, AND RICHARD I. ARENDS, *The Second Handbook of Organizational Development in Schools*. Palo Alto, CA.: Mayfield Publishing Company, 1977.
  (See annotation under Suggested Reading in Chapter 8).

SMITH, CAROL E., *Better Meetings: A Handbook for Trainers of Policy Councils and Other Decision-Making Groups*. Atlanta: Humanics Press, 1975.
  A "must" for those meetings that bring school staff members and community people together for joint decision making.

Emergent and discrete problems.   Participative decision making has salience primarily because it tends to produce decisions of better quality than those reached by even highly capable individuals. But some kinds of problems are best solved by expert individuals, whereas other kinds of problems are best solved by groups. To achieve the highest possible quality of decisions, therefore, it is necessary to analyze the situation. Indeed, one of the indicators of a highly skilled group is that its members are able to make such analyses, thereby knowing what problems the group should try to work through and what problems it should refer to appropriate experts.

Some problems have the following characteristics: (1) the elements of the problem are relatively unambiguous, clear-cut, and often quantifiable; (2) the elements of the problem are readily separable; (3) the solution to the problem requires a logical sequence of acts that may be readily performed by one person; and (4) the boundaries of the whole problem are relatively easy to discern. Problems of this kind may be called *discrete,* and they may well be solved best by an expert individual.

Some problems are quite different: (1) the elements of the problem are ambiguous, uncertain, and not readily quantifiable; (2) the elements of the problem are so dynamically intertwined that it is difficult to separate them on the basis of objective criteria (in fact, obtaining measurements may be difficult); (3) the solution to the problem requires the continued coordination and interaction of a number of people; and (4) the dimensions and nature of the problem cannot be fully known at the time of decision but will come into better view as iterative processes of dealing with the problem cause it to unfold over time. Such problems may be called *emergent.* The highest-quality solution to problems of this kind are likely to come from a group of people who (a) are in the best position to possess among them the knowledge necessary to solve the problem and (b) will be involved in implementing the decision after it is made.

A typical discrete problem in a school district is handling school supplies. The myriad problems involved in consolidated purchasing, warehousing, and distributing supplies to schools are relatively clear-cut and can be ordered into a logical sequence by an expert. Indeed, as compared with the skilled business manager— with his or her intimate knowledge of the budget, contract law, purchasing procedures, and the vagaries of the school supply market—a group of school district administrators trying to deal with the problem of getting the right supplies at the right price to the right places on time could well be a matter of the blind leading the blind. Similarly, laying out school bus routes for maximum economy and efficiency is normally a discrete problem. The use of mathematical models and computer simulations, now relatively common in larger districts, requires the use of experts who have the requisite technical skills and the techniques for grasping the full dimensions of the problem.

Policy issues in public education, on the other hand, are very often emergent problems. The matter of implementing competency-based education, for example, clearly meets the description of an emergent problem. Often the issue confronts school district administrators on the level of "How shall we implement the decision that has been handed down to us?" rather than in terms of "Should we do it?"

As every educator knows, concepts of competency-based education involve many facets of the school enterprise in dynamic interrelationship, and certainly the specialized knowledge of many individuals in the system must be brought to bear on the problem in highly coordinated fashion even to understand the problem. Therefore a decision to undertake such an endeavor will require commitment to the program by many people, continuous close collaboration and free flow of communication, and recognition that success depends upon an iterative process of decision making as the extent and implications of the problem become apparent.

Many of the problems encountered in the course of day-to-day administrative practice are, such as is this, emergent. Indeed, as education grows more complex there appears to be less and less certitude that many important issues can be resolved by experts who pass their solutions on to others to implement. Appropriate solutions require free and open communication among a number of individuals who pool and share information. Close collaboration is necessary to weigh and evaluate information in the process of developing an informed judgment as to which of several alternatives might be best. Commitment to the implementation of the solution is essential in order to maintain the collaboration that is the basis of the iterative processes of decision making.

Who should participate?   A commonly held erroneous assumption that is often made about participative decision making is that its intent is to involve everyone in every decision. Clearly, this is neither practical nor desirable. Edwin Bridges has suggested two rules of thumb for identifying decisions in which it is appropriate for teachers to participate:

1. *The test of relevance.* "[W]hen the teacher's personal stakes in the decision are high," Bridges states, "their interest in participation should also be high."[37] Problems that clearly meet this test concern teaching methods and materials, discipline, curriculum, and organizing for instruction.

2. *The test of expertise.* It is not enough for the teacher to have a stake in the decision; if his or her participation is to be significant, the teacher must be competent to contribute effectively. In dealing with the physical education department's program schedule, for example, English teachers may be fitted by training and experience to contribute little or nothing.

And, I add, there is a significant third test to use in deciding about which problems the teachers should be consulted:

3. *The test of jurisdiction.* Schools are organized on a hierarchical basis; the individual school and staff have jurisdiction only over those decision-making areas that are assigned to them, either by design or omission. Problems may be *relevant* to teachers, and the teachers may have the requisite *expertise,* but—right or wrong—they may not have *jurisdiction.* Participation in the making of decisions that the group cannot implement can lead to frustration at least as great as simple nonparticipation.

Desire of individuals to participate.   Another practical consideration is whether or not individuals themselves wish to be involved in the making of a decision. The demands of time and personal interest inevitably require each person in the organization to establish (albeit imprecisely, perhaps) some priorities for his or her own time and energies. Chester Barnard pointed out that there are some things in which some individuals simply are not interested: he spoke of such matters as falling within the individuals's *Zone of Indifference.*[38] To seek active involvement of teachers in matters to which they are essentially indifferent is, of course, to court resistance in various forms. It is common, for example, for school principals to seek involvement of teachers, either on a limited basis (for example, limiting participation to expressing views and opinions) or on low-level problems (reserving important decisions for themselves). There is little wonder that teachers are often indifferent to such participation.

There are areas of decision making in which teachers take great personal interest over a sustained period of time; in effect, this area may be described as a *Zone of Sensitivity*.[39] These matters represent "personal stakes," as it were, and could include such things as teaching assignments and evaluation of professional performance. When dealing with problems that fall within a staff's Zone of Sensitivity, a high degree of participation in a group-process mode of decision making would, of course, be indicated. The principal would enhance his or her authority with such involvement.

There is a third category of problems in which teachers have something at stake but not enough to make them especially concerned as individuals. These fall in the *Zone of Ambivalence*.[40] For example, it may be difficult for everyone on the staff to become concerned about preparing the agenda for a professional conference day or scheduling an assembly program. Thus, in order to avoid needless negative feelings from teachers who feel that they are already overburdened by the unnecessary bureaucratic demands of administrators, involvement of teachers with problems of this sort has to be selective. To be effective, such involvement should be restricted (for example, have a small representative group deal with the problem or simply be sure to keep everyone informed as the problem is processed to a decision).

Although there are undoubtedly clusters of issues to which teachers may be sensitive, ambivalent, or indifferent, it is not possible simply to assume these generalizations: some assessment should be part of the diagnosis in each situation. When the group is small it is possible to do this through discussion. In dealing with larger groups, it may be useful to employ a paper-and-pencil inventory as a diagnostic aid. One such technique used by Robert Owens and Edward Lewis in a large senior high school reveals that interest in participating in certain issues may be associated with certain characteristics of teachers. For example, experienced teachers and inexperienced teachers on the same school staff may have dissimilar views toward participation in dealing with specific issues.[41] Thus, Owens and Lewis reported that probationary teachers had much higher interest in learning about such things as the policies and rules of the school, the curriculum that they were to teach, and procedures for supervisory evaluation of their work. Older teachers were more concerned about maintaining traditions of the school and issues pertaining to their involvement in key decisions in the school.

TEAM ADMINISTRATION

Team administration emerged in the 1970s as a popular approach to administration in American school districts. A defining concept of team administration is participative decision making. Robert Duncan states it succinctly: "Team administration simply refers to genuine involvement—before the fact—of all levels of administration in goal-setting, decision-making, and problem-solving processes.[42] Similarly, a state association of school principals said:

> In place of the unilateral decisions which were made by the superintendent and passed down through the ranks to the level of final implementation, this new format would require a team approach to decision-making, providing an opportunity for all administrative and supervisory personnel to contribute...to the process....In return for this participation on the part of...principals, the superintendent must be willing to demonstrate his confidence in group processes; he must involve individuals so that they may feel a part of the decisions which are made...he must understand that this type of involvement is imperative if the principal is to consider himself a member of an administrative team.[43]

Harold McNally concluded: "The administrative team is a group formally constituted by the board of education and the superintendent, comprising both central office and middle echelon administrative-supervisory personnel, with expressly stated responsibility and authority for participation in school system decision making."[44]

Administrative teams vary considerably in the techniques used for participation in making decisions. Five techniques are commonly found. Ranging from the least participation to the maximum, they are:[45]

1. *Discussion.* Perhaps the simplest level of participation, the discussion of a problem is widely used to ascertain that team members are aware of the problem and that a decision about this problem must be made. When participation is limited to discussion, the administrator makes the decision, but he or she hopes that the others will accept the decision more readily than if he or she were to communicate the decision to them *before* discussion.

2. *Information seeking.* This technique of participation is more than mere discussion; it also involves the administrator's obtaining information so as to facilitate making a more rational, logical decision.

These types of participation are most useful for decisions that fall within the participants' zone of indifference; presumably, the decisions involved would not be of vital interest to them, and each actual decision would be made by the administrator. The essential purposes of involving others at these levels would be (1) to help the administrator make a better decision and (2) to enhance the likelihood that the decision will be accepted by the group when it is made. To decide matters outside the members' zone of indifference—and to allow them to participate actively—other forms of involvement will be used:

3. *Democratic-centralist.* Undoubtedly the most commonly used procedure, this method consists of the administrator's presenting the problem to the staff and asking for suggestions, reactions, and ideas. The administrator will make the decision, but he or she will try to reflect the staff's participation in the decision.

4. *Parliamentarian.* When the team members are actually to make a decision but it does not appear likely that unanimity or even consensus will prevail, the parliamentarian technique is often used. It offers the great advantage of specifically providing for minority opinions, conflict of ideas and values, and shifting positions in time as issues, facts, and values change. It has the distinct disadvantage of creating winners and losers.

5. *Participant-determining*. The essential characteristic of this procedure is that consensus is required of the group. It is one that would be used when (1) the issues are considered very important to the team members and (2) when it appears that consensus probably can be reached. Because consensus can be looked upon as pressure, the participant-determining method would probably not be used frequently. However, when it is used successfully, it is a powerful decision-making procedure.

A PARADIGM FOR DECISION MAKING

Confusion can be a very real hazard in organizational decision making. Unless participants know just what procedures the organization is using to arrive at decisions and what their own role and function will be in the procedures, the very advantages ascribed to "democratic" or participatory decision making may well be nullified. It would be difficult to find research support for the possible contention that ambiguity in the decision-making processes in a school is somehow a virtue. In addition to knowing *how* people are to participate in decision making, that is, what their role and functions will be, they must know *just when* they will participate.

It is also important that participants understand the orderly steps of the decision-making process as the organization moves toward a decision. These steps can be charted, and in so doing, some of the critical choices to be made can be seen more readily.

A skeleton of a proposed decision-making paradigm might resemble the one shown in Figure 10–1, which incorporates Bridges's suggestion that four steps typically are involved in reaching a decision: (1) defining the problem, (2) identifying possible alternatives, (3) predicting the consequences of each reasonable alternative, and (4) choosing the alternative to be followed.[46] In Figure 10–1 these four steps are identified by the numbers along the *time* dimension. In practice, individual administrators and their staffs might employ other series of steps, perhaps labeled differently; the suggested paradigm is readily adaptable to any sequence of decision-making behavior. Along the *behavior* dimension, a choice must be made as to who is going to perform each necessary decision-making function. Here, broken lines indicate choices of action that the administrator can elect to make: to involve the staff at any one step, at all of them—or, indeed, not to involve them at all.

In other words, when the administrator receives (or becomes aware of) information indicating the need for a decision, the choice is clear: the information either can be used or ignored. If the decision is to act on the information, one can logically proceed either (1) by defining the problem or (2) by giving the information to the staff and asking them to define the problem. From then on, the process of decision making can comprise any combination of participation that the decision makers desire. The administrator can handle every phase of the process alone or can utilize any combination of participation by the staff. But we must bear in mind that the administrator has no monopoly on the initiation of participation. The concept of participating decision making requires that all members have access to means of initiating decision-making processes.

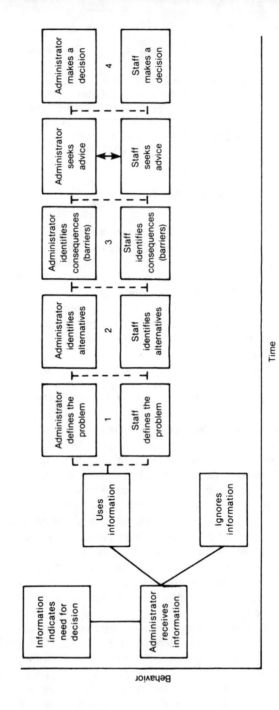

FIGURE 10–1. A paradigm for shared decision making in the school.

284

SUMMARY

The wish to simplify organizational decision making and render it more rational has spawned a large number of decision-making models, each of which seeks to reveal the order and logic of organizational life. A commonplace puzzle, however, is that administrators are infrequently observed—even after training—using such models in their work or spending prolonged periods of time in episodes of reflective thinking. Recent research is giving rise to the understanding that (1) educational organizations and administrative work are far more complex than had formerly been believed, and (2) administrators go about the thinking that precedes decision making in ways that differ significantly from that of scholars and researchers. Events in the organizational world rarely occur in neat sequence; more rarely still does one thing occur at a time. Rather, the administrator is typically confronted with ambiguous circumstances in which a number of events are unfolding simultaneously, various goals and values of the school may be in conflict, and truth may take several forms, yet the need for decisions presses inexorably on at a relentless pace.

Further, many organizational problems are ill-understood at the time that decisions must be made. They may be described as being emergent problems. That is they tend to be ambiguous, difficult to define, and the information needed to solve them is scattered among a number of people. Moreover, dealing with emergent problems leads to an iteration of diagnosis and solution by a process of successive approximation over time.

Under these conditions the theory of Human Resources Development (HRD)—derived from such concepts as loose coupling, organizational ambiguity, and organizational culture linked with HRD concepts of such things as motivation and leadership—supports the use of participative style in the management of decision making. Some suggestions for the management of participative decision making, drawn from the large and growing body of work in this field, have been discussed in this chapter.

SUGGESTED READING

BOLMAN, LEE G., AND TERRENCE E. DEAL, "Applying the Human Resource Approach," in *Modern Approaches to Understanding and Managing Organizations*. San Francisco: Jossey-Bass, 1984. Describes the basis for the HRM approach to decision making and practical considerations in applying it in practice. Includes discussions of participative methods, organizational democracy, and organization development.

CUNNINGHAM, WILLIAM G., "Decision Making," in *Systematic Planning for Educational Change*. Palo Alto, CA.: Mayfield Publishing Company, 1982. One of the better discussions of formal decision-making procedures based on conventional logical linear models. Features a description of decision tree analysis that can be very effective in dealing with discrete problems.

KANTER, ROSABETH MOSS, "Dilemmas of Participation," in *The Change Masters: Innovation and Entrepreneurship in the American Corporation*. New York: Simon & Schuster, Inc., 1983. As the title suggests, this chapter explores problems and apparent dilemmas confronting administrators seeking to implement participative decision-making methods and suggests ways of dealing with them.

WYNN, RICHARD, AND CHARLES W. GUDITUS, Team Management: Leadership by Consensus. Columbus, OH: Charles E. Merrill Publishing Company, 1984.

An excellent resource for readers who want a detailed, practical guide for implementing participative management in educational organizations.

NOTES

[1]Richard L. Daft, *Organization Theory and Design* (St. Paul: West Publishing Company, 1983), p. 344.

[2]Herbert A. Simon, *Administrative Behavior* (New York: Macmillan, Inc., 1950), p. 1.

[3]Daniel E. Griffiths, *Administrative Theory* (New York: Appleton-Century-Crofts, 1959), p. 89.

[4]Donald A. Schön, *The Reflective Practitioner: How Professionals Think in Action* (New York: Basic Books, Inc., Publishers,) p. 237.

[5]Ibid., p. 39.

[6]Ibid.

[7]Herbert A. Simon, *The New Science of Management Decision* (New York: Harper & Row, Publishers, Inc., 1960), p. 2.

[8]Peter F. Drucker, *Management: Tasks, Responsibilities, and Practices* (New York: Harper & Row, Publishers, Inc., 1974), pp. 19–20.

[9]James G. March and Herbert A. Simon, *Organizations* (New York: John Wiley & Sons, Inc., 1958).

[10]*Deciding How to Decide: Decision Making in Schools.* Project Leadership Presenter's Guide prepared by the Research-Based Training for School Administrators Project (Eugene: Center for Educational Policy and Management, College of Education, University of Oregon, 1983).

[11]Henry Mintzberg, Duru Raisinghani, and Andre Theoret, "The Structure of 'Unstructured' Decision Processes." *Administrative Science Quarterly,* 21 (June 1976), 246–75.

[12]James G. March, "Footnotes to Organizational Change," *Administrative Science Quarterly,* 26 (December 1981), 563–77.

[13]Paul C. Nutt, "Types of Organizational Decision Processes," *Administrative Science Quarterly,* 29 (September 1984), 446.

[14]National Association of Secondary School Principals, *The Senior High School Principalship* (Reston, VA: National Association of Secondary School Principals, 1978).

[15]Henry Mintzberg, *The Nature of Managerial Work* (New York: Harper & Row, Publishers, Inc., 1973).

[16]These five points are summarized from Mintzberg, *The Nature of Managerial Work,* pp. 28–48.

[17]Ibid., p. 30.

[18]Ibid.

[19]For examples see Van Cleve Morris, Robert L. Crowson, Emanuel Hurwitz, Jr., and Cynthia Porter-Gehrie, *The Urban Principal: Discretionary Decision-Making in a Large Educational Organization* (unpublished manuscript, University of Illinois at Chicago, 1981). This study was elaborated into a book by the same authors entitled *Principals in Action: The Reality of Managing Schools* (Columbus, OH: Charles E. Merrill Publishing Company, 1984). Also see Nancy J. Pitner, "Descriptive Study of the Everyday Activities of Suburban School Superintendents: The Management of Information" (unpublished doctoral dissertation, The Ohio State University, 1978).

[20]Mintzberg, *The Nature of Managerial Work;* Sune Carlson, *Executive Behavior: A Study of the Work Load and the Working Methods of Managing Directors* (Stockholm: Strombergs, 1951); Pitner, "Descriptive Study of the Everyday Activities of Suburban School Superintendents"; William H. Whyte, Jr., "How Hard Do Executives Work?" *Fortune* (January 1948), 108–11.

[21]Karl E. Weick, "Managerial Thought in the Context of Action," in *The Executive Mind,* ed. Suresh Srivastva (San Francisco: Jossey-Bass, 1983), p. 222.

[22]Ibid., pp. 222–23.

[23]Ibid., p. 222. Emphasis in the original.

[24]Ibid., pp. 226–27.

[25]Ibid., p. 236.

[26]Schön, *The Reflective Practitioner,* pp. 240–41.

[27]T. R. Blackburn, "Sensuous-Intellectual Complementarity in Science," *Science,* 172 (1971), 1003–1007.

[28]Louis R. Pondy, "Union of Rationality and Intuition in Management Action," in *The Executive Mind,* ed. Suresh Srivasta (San Francisco: Jossey-Bass, 1983).

[29]Edgar H. Schein, "Organizational Socialization and the Profession of Management," *Industrial Management Review,* 9 (1968), 115; John Van Manaan, "Breaking In: Socialization to Work," in *Handbook*

of Work, Organization and Society, ed. Robert Dubin (Chicago: Rand McNally & Company, 1976); R. R. Ritti and G. R. Funkhouser, *The Ropes to Skip and the Ropes to Know* (Columbus, OH: Grid, 1982).

[30]Edgar H. Schein, *Organizational Culture and Leadership* (San Francisco: Jossey-Bass, 1985), p. 6.

[31]Weick, "Managerial Thought."

[32]Schein, *Organizational Culture,* p. 7.

[33]Terrence E. Deal, "Cultural Change: Opportunity, Silent Killer or Metamorphosis?", in *Gaining Control of the Corporate Culture,* eds. Ralph H. Kilmann, Mary J. Saxton, Roy Serpa and Associates (San Francisco: Jossey-Bass, 1985).

[34]Karl E. Weick, "Cognitive Processes in Organizations," in *Research in Organizational Behavior,* Vol. 1, ed. Barry M. Staw (Greenwich, CT: JAI Press, 1979), pp. 41–74.

[35]Kenneth Davis, *Human Behavior at Work: Human Relations and Organizational Behavior,* 4th ed. (New York: McGraw-Hill Book Company, 1972), p. 136.

[36]Mary Parker Follett, "The Psychology of Consent and Participation," in *Dynamic Administration: The Collected Papers of Mary Parker Follett,* ed. Henry C. Metcalf and Lyndall Urwick (New York: Harper & Row, Publishers, Inc., 1941), pp. 210–12.

[37]Edwin M. Bridges, "A Model for Shared Decision Making in the School Principalship," *Educational Administration Quarterly,* 3, no. 1 (Winter 1967), 52.

[38]Chester I. Barnard, *The Functions of the Executive* (Cambridge, MA: Harvard University Press, 1938).

[39]Robert G. Owens and Edward Lewis, "Managing Participation in Organizational Decisions," *Group and Organization Studies,* 1 (1976), 56–66.

[40]Ibid.

[41]Ibid.

[42]Robert Duncan, "Public Law 217 and the Administrative Team," *Indiana School Boards Association Journal,* 20 (1974), 10.

[43]Ohio Department of Elementary School Principals, *The Administrative Team,* (1971), 2–3.

[44]Harold J. McNally, "A Matter of Trust," *National Elementary Principal,* 53 no. 1 (November-December 1973), 23.

[45]The five types of participation discussed here are from Edwin M. Bridges, "A Model for Shared Decision Making in the School Principalship," *Educational Administration Quarterly,* 3, no. 1 (Winter 1967), 52–59.

[46]Ibid., p. 53.

11

THE HOLOGRAPHIC
IMPERATIVE
AND QUALITATIVE
RESEARCH

"The formal disciplines create models and metaphors for the way things are.... Together these models and metaphors form a kind of atlas of mental maps of the actual world. They tell us what we know about the nature of things—what is real, what may be false, and what to pay attention to.... We are rarely conscious of them because they are usually implicit: paradigms tend to surface mainly when they are changing."
—*Peter Schwartz and James Ogilvy*[1]

There was a time when people believed that scientific thinking required us to extract phenomena from the real world, break them down into constituent parts and, after examining them closely, reassemble them, conceptually or actually, in order to understand how things happen. This is reductionist thinking and it derives from a rational model of thought: the belief that some rational order and system underlies the manifest confusion and ambiguities that are obvious in the world around us. Moreover, it has long been assumed that the most powerful scientific explanations would be those that could be proved by empirically testing theoretical propositions through mathematical algorithms.[2]

THE HOLOGRAPHIC IMPERATIVE

For a long time, students of organizational behavior believed the above statement. Indeed, much of the organizational theory that has been described in this book emerged from traditional rationalistic, reductionist thinking intended to produce mathematically demonstrable certitude. However, much of what has been described in this text came from a new and different kind of scientific thinking that is now emerging and that cuts across all of the scientific disciplines.

It has been called "the holographic imperative" because it emphasizes the need for holographic thinking, which entails "...viewing the problem in three dimensions, at many different levels of detail and from every angle...."[3] This new kind of thinking explains, in large part, the growing interest in organizational culture and organizational climate and how they help to explain the behavior of people at work. Through the examination of culture as an explanation of organizational behavior one views the organization in depth as a complex integrated whole for which there can be no single, simple explanation. Organizations and the behavior of people in them must be understood in different ways when viewed from different perspectives.

Importance of the new scientific thinking. The newer, holographic, kind of scientific thinking is essential and it is important. It is essential if we are to better understand the apparent disorder, ambiguities, and disjunctures in our organizational environments—both physical and social—that we have long ignored because they are difficult to study. James Gleick called this seeming inexplicable disorder that is so commonplace in human experience Chaos. In a remarkable 1987 best-selling book he described the new ways of thinking that scientists from all disciplines are using in the process of "making a new science." They are doing this, he explained, by trying to understand the complexities of the world we live in, rather than to concentrate on the neat bits of that world that can be easily separated from the whole for convenient study.[4]

It is holistic thinking, rather than the traditional reductionist thinking of science, and it represents a major shift in science. "We find strong evidence that a number of the underpinnings of our basic beliefs are under challenge," say James Ogilvy and Peter Schwartz. "That challenge is coming from a multifaceted revolution of the sort that we have experienced only a few times in the course of our civilization's history: the revolution that began more than a century ago and has gathered momentum ever since involves as great a change as the Copernican revolution or the emergence of the Enlightenment."[5]

We need not probe deeply into this new scientific revolution here. However, we must be aware that new ways of thinking about schools that reflect these major shifts in scientific thought are having great impact on the ways in which we study organizations and the behavior of people in them. In recent years, a new approach to organizational research that reflects the new way of thinking scientifically, called *naturalistic research*, has developed rapidly to challenge the traditional approaches to research that have been dominant in the study of educational organizations for generations.

In supplanting traditional rationalistic ways of thinking, naturalistic research methods have, in fact, made it possible for significant new knowledge of organizational behavior in education to develop. For example, the concepts of organizational culture have emerged as dominantly as they have in contemporary understanding of organizational behavior in schools precisely because reductionist views had become so unsatisfactory in explaining behavior in them that people sought more powerful holistic, holographic explanations.

While a shift in ways of thinking that is as fundamental as this is not simple and easy to understand, its importance requires that we become aware of the ways in which it differs essentially from the old ways of scientific thinking that are now being challenged. Studies of organizational culture exemplify the use of this kind of thinking as it is used in research on organizational behavior.

DESCRIBING AND ASSESSING ORGANIZATIONAL CULTURE IN SCHOOLS

The study of organizational culture presents nettlesome problems to the traditional researcher primarily because important elements of culture are subtle, unseen, and so familiar to persons inside the organization as to be considered self-evident and unworthy of discussion. Collecting, sorting, and summarizing data such as the significant historical events in the organization and their implications for present-day behavior, the impact of organizational heroes on contemporary thinking, and the influence of traditions and organizational myths is a task that does not lend itself to the tidiness of a printed questionnaire and statistical analysis of the responses to it. As the work of Ouchi, Peters and Waterman, Kanter, and Deal and Kennedy demonstrated, it is necessary to get inside the organization: to talk at length with people; to find out what they think is important to talk about; to hear the language they use; and to discover the symbols that reveal their assumptions, their beliefs, and the values to which they subscribe. For that reason, students of organizational culture tend to use field research methods rather than traditional questionnaire-type studies. This has raised vigorous debate in many schools of education as to the epistemological value of field research methods as contrasted with the more traditional statistical studies (of the experimental or quasi-experimental type) that have long been the stock-in-trade of educational researchers. In order to understand contemporary issues in organizational culture in education, it is essential to have some grasp of the research problems involved.[6]

As Egon Guba[7] has pointed out, there are several paradigms[8] for discovering "truth" or for "understanding." There is, for example, a judicial paradigm that has well-established rules of procedure, rules of evidence, and criteria for judging the adequacy of a given judicial proceeding. The judicial paradigm provides guidelines for behavior in courtrooms, hearings, and other judicial approaches to discovering "facts," "truth," and "understanding." Until recently the judicial paradigm has had little utility in educational inquiry but is now gaining popularity as an approach to educational evaluation.[9]

Another widely used paradigm for gaining understanding or discovering meaning is that of expert judgment. This is, of course, commonly used in the accreditation of educational institutions in which the site visiting team is expected to exercise expert judgment. Such an approach is commonplace in judging athletic performances and artistic efforts of many kinds.[10]

Two paradigms of systematic inquiry.   At the present time, two other—and distinctly different—paradigms vie for dominance in systematic inquiry in educational administration. These paradigms gained prominence in the 1950s with the so-called theory movement in educational administration. A major factor in the theory movement was the recognition that the social and behavioral sciences had much to contribute to the study of administration—not only theory, concepts, and knowledge drawn from these sciences, but also their research traditions. The history of the social and behavioral sciences, themselves, had been filled for over a century with epistemological issues related to the "two modes of thought,"[11] that is, deductive and inductive inquiry.

William James described the tender-minded and the tough-minded; others have spoken of the theoretical and the practical. "Hard vs. soft," "natural vs. social," "science vs. criticism," "quantifiers vs. describers," "rigor vs. intuition" are common clichés often used to describe the dichotomy between the "two modes of thought" in administrative and organizational research. Thus, in reducing the dialectic to simple and rigid polarities, and often coming close to moral judgments such as "good" or "bad," the complexities and nuances in these two approaches to "knowing," "understanding," and, not least important, thinking are obscured.

The issue of terminology. On the other hand, the lack of precision and clarity as to the essential characteristics of the two paradigms of administrative inquiry as well as their implications for methodology tends to obscure and confuse the criteria that are appropriate to use in judging methodological adequacy. How should these paradigms be described and what should they be called? This is not a simple issue. Indeed, it has generated increasing debate among inquirers and research methodologists in educational administration in recent years.[12]

In this discussion, the traditional, long-dominant paradigm is called *rationalistic* and is conceptualized as a paradigm that, while it embraces a number of research techniques, is essentially associated with deductive thinking and logical-positivist views of "knowing" and "understanding" social and organizational phenomena. The other major paradigm in administrative inquiry is labeled the *naturalistic* paradigm. It, too, includes a number of research techniques, but it is essentially based upon inductive thinking and is associated with phenomenological views of "knowing" and "understanding" social and organizational phenomena.

It is neither possible nor desirable to examine here all of the "shades of gray" that may or may not describe various methodological views that may or may not lie on a possible continuum between these two paradigms. Indeed, it is likely that emphasis on blurring the essential differences between the paradigms makes it more difficult to establish well-recognized criteria by which to assess the methodological adequacy of research. Therefore, in the following discussion, the rationalistic and the naturalistic paradigms are described as a relatively simple dichotomy—as prototypes, somewhat in the sense that Weber discussed the characteristics of ideal bureaucratic organizations in his classic work.

One recognizes, of course, that in the "real" world such prototypes are rarely encountered. Indeed, it can be reasonably argued that the traditional "rules" that govern rationalistic administrative inquiry are so rarely followed as to give rise to frequent expressions of concern about the quality of research in the field of educational administration. The central point to be made is that there are legitimate ways of conducting administrative inquiry other than the traditional (rationalistic) way, and that the use of other alternatives does not result in sloppy research.

It is recognized that both the naturalistic and the rationalistic paradigms represent legitimate modes of systematic inquiry. They are different paradigms arising from different perceptions of such things as the nature of social phenomena and ways of understanding them. Although the two paradigms often tend to compete for legitimacy and support, they are, in fact, complementary methods of investigation available for use in the knowledge-production process essential to informing educational administration.

The rationalistic paradigm. Of the two research paradigms, the rationalistic paradigm stands clearly as *the* dominant approach in educational administration. It is often called quantitative research though, as will be seen, this is a misnomer. It is commonly thought to be a methodology, which it really is not. However, this paradigm is more widely published, taught, accepted, and rewarded in educational research circles than any other approach,[13] and it has been well established as the dominant method of disciplined inquiry.

Clearly the epitome of the rationalistic paradigm is the controlled experiment, which Donald Campbell and Julian Stanley describe as

> ...the only means of settling disputes regarding educational practice, the only way of verifying educational improvements, and the only way of establishing a cumulative tradition in which improvements can be introduced without the danger of faddish discard of old wisdom in favor of inferior novelties.[14]

Little administrative research has used the controlled experimental research design, however.

In the rationalistic paradigm, nonexperimental research methods are considered inferior, but acceptable, methods if certain procedural safeguards to insure the basic integrity of the study are adequate. Essentially, the view is that what exists can be extrapolated from its environment and, because it exists, it exists in some measure and, thus, can be quantified. Some basic assumptions that underlie this set of notions about "procedural safeguards" and "integrity" are:

1. That certain parts of the real world, which are called "variables," may be singled out (literally or through statistical manipulation) from reality for study or treatment while other parts of the setting are controlled. Ideally, therefore, laboratory experimentation is the epitome of method because of the greater control it affords the inquirer.
2. That the inquirer and the subject under study are, and should remain, independent of one another. Typically this is facilitated by interposing "objective" data-gathering instruments between the inquirer and the subjects under study.
3. That context-free generalizations are not only possible but also the essential goal of inquiry.
4. That quantitative methods are inherently preferable to nonquantitative methods—thus leading to the common confusion between the concept of quantitative methods and the rationalistic paradigm itself.
5. That the use of a priori theory and hypothetico-deductive methods (typically hypothesis-testing) is important to the design of studies and to the cumulation of knowledge itself.
6. That a preordinate design should specify each step of the inquiry in advance, from data collection through its analysis.[15]

Operationally, research organized by the tenets of the rationalistic paradigm begins with an existing theory which is used to set up an articulated problem in advance of the inquiry. The next step is to convert the problem into dependent and independent variables. Having done this, the researcher proceeds to develop strategies and instruments attempting to control and uncover relationships between and among the naturally occurring variables through the design. Once the steps of the preordinate research design have been completed, the inquirer returns to the theory to interpret the results.[16]

Here, the term "rationalistic" will be used in referring to inquiries that (1) use formal instruments or other a priori techniques for categorizing as the primary basis for collecting data, (2) transform the data into quantitative expressions of one kind or another, and (3) attempt to generalize the findings in some formal way to some universe beyond that bounded by the inquiry. It is realized, of course, that this is not an exhaustive list of the characteristics of the "rationalistic" paradigm of inquiry, but they are viewed as the salient ones and, therefore, are regarded as modal characteristics.

The rationalistic paradigm is—by an awesome margin—the dominant, established tradition in systematic inquiry. Any competing paradigm must be compared and contrasted with this standard approach to inquiry in modern science.

The naturalistic paradigm.   The second of the two inquiry paradigms in science is the naturalistic paradigm. What is not always clear is that naturalistic inquiry is based on two sets of concepts which taken together provide a strong rationale for it as a research paradigm.[17] One set of concepts is the *naturalistic-ecological hypothesis,* which claims that human behavior is so significantly influenced by the context in which it occurs that regularities in those contexts are often more powerful in shaping behavior than differences among the individuals present. In this view, the behavior of people in schools is seen as powerfully influenced by the organizational context in which it occurs.[18] Thus, "if one wants to generalize research findings in schools, then the research is best conducted within school settings where all these forces are intact."[19]

The other set of concepts basic to naturalistic inquiry is the *qualitative-phenomenological hypothesis.* This essentially holds that one cannot understand human behavior without understanding the framework within which the individuals under study interpret their environment, and that this, in turn, can best be understood through understanding their thoughts, feelings, values, perceptions, and their actions.

The term "naturalistic" is appropriate as will be explained but, first, it should be made clear that the naturalistic paradigm is a different way of "knowing" than the rationalistic paradigm. It emanates from a basically different view of the six assumptions discussed earlier. The naturalistic inquirer posits that:

1. In the real world, events and phenomena cannot be teased out from the context in which they are inextricably embedded, and understanding involves the interrelationships among all of the many parts of the whole.

2. It is illusory to suppose that interaction between inquirer and subject might be eliminated. Indeed, this dynamic relationship can make it practicable for the inquirer, himself or herself, to become the data-gathering and processing "transducer."

3. Generalizations are suspect, at best, and knowledge inevitably relates to a particular context.

4. Qualitative methods—which emphasize both inner and outer knowledge of man in his world—are preferable. As William Filstead put it, "Qualitative methodology allows the researcher to get close to the data, thereby developing the analytical, conceptual, and categorical components of explanation from the data itself."[20]

5. Theory emerges from the data themselves in the sense that Glaser and Strauss describe "grounded theory."[21]

6. The naturalistic inquirer, believing in unfolding multiple realities (through interactions with respondents that will change both them and the inquirer over time) and in grounded theory, will insist on a design that unfolds over time and that is never complete until the inquiry is arbitrarily terminated as time, resources, and other logistical considerations may dictate.[22]

What does "naturalistic" mean?   It is important to start with some clear notion as to exactly what the term "naturalistic" means when it is applied to inquiry. Partly because the term has complex meanings, but mainly because it is at odds with awesomely well-entrenched traditional concepts regarding inquiry, it helps to try to define the term in two ways: (1) what it essentially means to inquirers and (2) how it differs from what may be called "rationalistic" inquiry.

The term "naturalistic" expresses one view as to the nature of reality. It is the view that the real world that we encounter "out there" is a dynamic system all of whose "parts" are so interrelated that one part inevitably influences the other parts. To understand the reality of that world requires acceptance of the notion that the parts cannot be separated, bit by bit, for careful examination without distorting the system that one seeks to understand. The parts must be examined as best as possible in the context of the whole. It is, essentially, a phenomenological view—as differentiated from a logical-positivistic view—of reality of the world.

On the one hand, the logical-positivist approach to understanding the complex world emphasizes singling out various "variables" for study while attempting to control other variables in the situation. The naturalist, on the other hand, views this as altering the situation, resulting in distortions of our understanding of reality. Thus, if one seeks to understand the realities of human organizations and the behavior of people in them, the naturalistic view would hold that those organizations must be examined in all the rich confusion of their daily existence. Human behavior must be studied *in situ* if it is to be understood.

The term "naturalistic" is used here in referring to inquiries that (1) primarily employ direct contact between investigators and actors in the situation as a means of collecting data, (2) use emergent strategies to design the study rather than a priori specification, (3) develop data categories from examination of the data themselves after collection, and (4) do not attempt to generalize the findings to a universe beyond that bounded by the study. Again, it is realized that many other characteristics may properly be associated with naturalistic inquiry, but to me these are the salient—and, therefore, modal—characteristics of naturalistic inquiry.

Are "naturalistic" and "qualitative" synonymous?   It is now possible to turn to the term "qualitative" in the context of the foregoing discussion. Although "naturalistic" alludes to *ways* in which one may seek to examine reality and these ways emphasize the wholeness and phenomenological interrelatedness of the real world, "qualitative" alludes to the *nature of the understanding* that is sought. Qualitative inquiry seeks to understand human behavior and human experience from the actor's own frame of reference, not the frame of reference of the investigator. Thus, naturalistic inquiry seeks to illuminate social realities, human perceptions, and organizational realities untainted by the intrusion of formal measurement procedures[23] or reordering the situation to fit the preconceived notions of the investigator. The qualitative nature of the resulting description enables the investigator to see the "real" world *as those under study see it.*

Thus, qualitative description is not necessarily the exclusive territory of the naturalistic inquirer. Positivists can, and do, use qualitative methods in their investigations. For example, data gathered through paper-and-pencil instruments can be (and often are) used as indicators of group norms or values or other social forces that influence behavior.[24] However, the *techniques* for uncovering and describing the qualities of these norms and values differ importantly between the two approaches. The naturalistic inquirer will in all likelihood regard gestures, language, and behavioral patterns of the subjects as significant descriptive data. The positivist, on the other hand, tends to search for understanding through data supplied by either the subjects or others using such standardized means as questionnaires and inventories or through analysis of demographic or other descriptive data. The *nature* of the quality of description yielded by these two approaches differs, however, in important ways: one yields lean, spare description stripped of the contextual references in which the data originated; the other yields what Clifford Geertz calls *thick description*.[25]

Thick description provides meaning of human behavior in the real world in such terms as cultural norms, deep-seated values and motives arising from cherished tradition, and community values. "Believing, with Max Weber, that man is an animal suspended in webs of significance he himself has spun," comments Geertz, "I take culture to be those webs, and the analysis of it to be therefore not an experimental science in search of law but an interpretive one in search of meaning."[26] Thus, thick description conveys very much the sense of the web of interrelated contextual factors that is associated with the situation under study. Thick description is more than mere information or descriptive data: it conveys literal description that figuratively transports the readers into the situation with a sense of insight, understanding, and illumination not only of the facts or the events in the case, but also of the texture, the quality, and the power of the context *as the participants in the situation experienced it.*

This qualitative characteristic of inquiry is well illustrated by Philip Cusick, who spent six months in a high school as a participant observer. He notes, for example, that teachers in the school routinely spent ten to fifteen minutes of the forty-minute class period checking excuses and passes and on other actions intended to control students.[27] Further, when teachers finally did attend to the lesson for that class period, inattentiveness on the part of some students and numerous interruptions from others greatly reduced the amount of time devoted to teaching and learning activities. Thus, he estimated that the average student spent less than one and a half hours a day mentally engaged in the processes of learning.[28] But Cusick's observations go beyond this sort of informing, which is relatively objective and quantified, to take on the richer meaning associated with thick description.

He discovered, for example, that teachers and administrators often ignored gambling and stealing among the students, and punished those who cut classes or violated school routine.[29] Students who did little work were reported to succeed academically as long as they paid strict attention to classroom routines and school rules.[30]

This sort of qualitative description of life in schools has been confirmed numerous times in a wide variety of sources such as those cited by Charles Silberman in "Education for Docility."[31] Such description "takes the reader there" and conveys a keen insight into the behavior of people in those schools. It is qualitatively "thick" in that much that is meaningful about the context-bound nature of the behavior under study is conveyed.

Judging the adequacy of a naturalistic study.   As the "domain assumptions"[32] that underlie rationalistic and naturalistic inquiry are basically different and essentially polar, so the criteria by which to judge the appropriateness of research design and methodological adequacy of studies representing the two domains are significantly different. The question arises as to which criteria are appropriate in judging the adequacy of a reported study.

In rationalistic inquiry, for example, the researcher seeks some slice of the "real" world[33] that is comprehensive enough to be generalizable. Therefore, in assessing the design of such a study one looks for representativeness of the sample, which is usually assured by either a random sample or a selected sample. And, if the response rate is adequate, it is possible to generalize the results to a large population which the sample represents. This is, of course, commonly referred to as external validity.

To minimize bias on the part of the investigator, the researcher seeks to eliminate subjectivity and maximize objectivity. At least a careful social distance is maintained between subject and investigator—often by interposing formal data-collecting instruments (such as paper-and-pencil questionnaires) between the two—in order to minimize affective bias (such as empathy) that arises from interactions. Normally the proximity of the investigator to the situation under study is minimized to assure maximum detachment from it.

In the rationalistic paradigm, the investigator seeks to control for the unknown and unknowable. For example, random procedures are normally used for selecting samples of subjects within the total population under study. Researchers may not even know what the differences are that they are seeking to cancel out: they need only to know that random distribution across groups should prevent any differences from making a difference.[34] If it is not feasible to select the sample of a population randomly, the investigator may seek to heighten control of unknown variables by matching population samples on the basis of "relevant variables." The remaining variables, having been declared irrelevant, are no longer considered to be intrusive in the realm under study.

One is concerned also in rationalistic inquiry with the need to be sure that the data-collection measures yield consistent results. If the tests are given again or if the interviews are replicated, will the same results be obtained or is there likely to be some drift leading to confounding interpretation?[35] Thus, researchers are concerned with the reliability of their data-gathering procedures such as instrument reliability, reliability between items, and reliability between and among raters and/or interviewers.

Certainly a preordinate research design is essential in rationalistic inquiry. It should specify in advance of initiating the study each step that will be taken to collect and analyze data in order to test the hypotheses or answer the research questions. Important in the design are the specified procedures by which the investigator will deal with issues of external validity, objectivity, internal validity, and reliability. When the preordinate design of research utilizing the rationalistic paradigm is evaluated, these are important criteria by which its adequacy is judged. In execution of the research and, finally, in examining the written research report, these are or ought to be important issues under consideration.

Because of the assumptions about the nature of reality and ways of understanding that reality in the naturalistic paradigm, the traditional concern for objectivity, validity, and reliability have little relevance for the design of naturalistic research. Michael Scriven's now-classic work on subjectivity and objectivity was a major contribution pointing out that what have traditionally been called "objective" and "subjective" have commonly been confused with the quantification of data, often masking the matter of subjective bias.[36] In short, Scriven made clear that quantification in research, usually accompanied by statistical manipulation of data, has come to be confused with objectivity, which is the *sine qua non* of rationalistic research.

In order to avoid unreliable, biased, or opinionated data, the naturalistic inquirer seeks not some "objectivity" brought about through methodology but, rather, strives for validity through personalized, intimate understandings of phenomena stressing "close in" observations to achieve factual, reliable, and confirmable data.[37] Whereas the rationalistic methodologist might pursue confirmation through the use of data from a number of subjects, the naturalistic methodologist often seeks to confirm through the intensive study of a small group or even a single individual.

The striving for generalizability has had powerful impact on the canons of the rationalistic paradigm of inquiry. However, Lee Cronbach has brilliantly argued that generalizations are not enduring: they do, in fact, break down over time in all fields of science, the physical and biological as well as the social sciences.[38] If the stars shift in their courses so as to render star maps obsolete and DDT fails to control mosquitoes as genetic transformations make them resistant to the compound, and as protons are apparently found to degenerate, it becomes clear that every generalization is less scientific truth than it is history. Further, it may reasonably be argued, of course, that the processes of developing generalizations in the "hard sciences" are appropriately different from the case in educational administration. Often in the physical and biological sciences, investigators seek generalizations based on a large number of like events, which must necessarily be observed indirectly. Thus, statistical methods facilitate the building of models that may be explanatory. In educational organizations, in contrast, there are relatively few events that may be described as "alike" and, what is more, these events often may be best observed directly.

But more germane to the present discussion is the inescapable conclusion that, far from achieving generalizations, rationalistic inquiry used in the study of social systems reveals "truth" very much embedded in the context in which it is discovered. This concept is crucial in administrative and organizational inquiry for, as Guba and Lincoln observe: "It is virtually impossible to imagine any human behavior that is not heavily mediated by the context in which it occurs."[39] Thus, the notion of discovering context-free generalizations in human social systems is seriously called into question by the naturalistic paradigm.

Characteristics of the naturalistic research plan. The inquirer in the rationalistic paradigm views research design as a sequence of discrete procedures bounded by a predetermined timeline. The naturalistic investigator views the design as providing an emergent plan for a highly interactive process of gathering data from which analysis will be developed. It is described here as an interactive process because data collection and analysis go on simultaneously, with the analysis giving direction to the data collection by suggesting what to check, when to seek confirmation, and how to extend the data collection itself. To be more specific, it is now in order to turn to a brief discussion of three elements that are ordinarily found in the plan of a naturalistic study—the research strategy, strategies for collecting data, and the audit trail. This is appropriate whether considering the proposal stage, the execution, or the reporting of naturalistic research.

The research strategy. Normally, the research strategy will provide for a rather broad-scale exploration at the outset that is simultaneously accompanied by checking for accuracy, seeking verification, testing, probing, and confirming as the data collection proceeds. Typically, the strategy will emphasize data gathering in the early phase of the project. Checking, verifying, testing, probing, and confirming activities will follow in a funnel like design resulting in less data gathering in later phases of the study along with a concurrent increase in analysis—checking, verifying, and confirming (see Figure 11–1).

In the early stage of such a study, perhaps 80 percent of the time and effort will be spent in gathering data while 20 percent will be devoted to analysis; in the latter stages of the study, this may be reversed with 80 percent devoted to analysis and 20 percent devoted to data collection (see Figure 11–2). An important element in the design of naturalistic research is starting with questions of broad scope and proceeding through a conceptual funnel—working with data all the while, ever trying to more fully understand what the data mean—making decisions as to how to check and how to verify as the investigation unfolds. It is important in the design of such a study that the investigator be fully prepared to look for unanticipated perceptions arising from the data as he or she gets closer and closer to the data over time.

FIGURE 11–1. General outline of the plan for a naturalistic study.

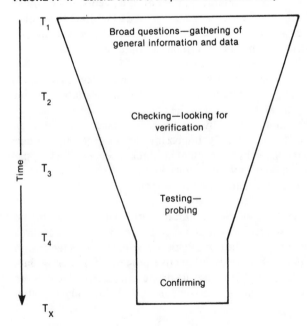

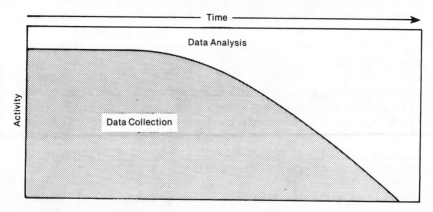

FIGURE 11–2. Typical pattern of data collection and data analysis in a naturalistic study.

The audit trail. Guba and Lincoln have proposed that an "audit trail" be carefully maintained throughout the course of a naturalistic study. This should consist of documentation of the nature of each decision in the research plan, the data upon which it was based, and the reasoning that entered into it.[40] The existence of a carefully documented audit trail makes it possible to do two important things: (1) to examine the procedures of the study, either while it is in progress or after the fact, in order to verify its consistency and credibility by independent external auditors, and (2) to make it possible to reproduce the study at another time.

An audit trail consists of deliberately leaving sufficient evidence so that someone external to the inquiry could review the processes and results of the inquiry and ascertain whether the processes were appropriate and the results were reasonable and credible. A basic component of the audit trail is the investigator's log. In this personal journal, the investigator meticulously records not only all contacts throughout the study from beginning to end, but also two other key kinds of information: (1) the reasoning and logic that entered into every decision as the investigation unfolded, and (2) the hunches, guesses, feelings, and perceptions of the investigator as they occurred during the course of the investigation.

But a log is not an audit trail; at best it is an annotated index to the audit trail. The trail itself will consist of numerous documents which carefully preserve the record of the investigation. Among them may be the following:

1. raw notes from interviews and observations;

2. edited summary notes of interviews and observations;

3. records of meetings about the research;

4. all documents used as data sources;

5. guidelines and "rules" used for content analysis of documents;

6. decision rules by which data were categorized;

7. interview guidelines;

8. completed documents that may have been commissioned as part of the study.

Guba has proposed that, particularly in the case of evaluation studies, an independent external auditor be employed to conduct an impartial audit and report on the reasonableness of the study's findings in light of the investigative procedures used.

Strategies for collecting data   It is important that the naturalistic research design (1) provide for multiple data sources and methods of collection, and (2) describe the techniques that were used to check and validate analyses as the research proceeded. The procedures used to implement these strategies are important in determining the credibility of any naturalistic study. Six procedures relevant to data gathering in naturalistic inquiry are described in the next section.

Procedures to enhance credibility.   When confronted with the bewildering, dynamic patterns of interrelated people, events, and contexts in organizations, investigators are necessarily called upon to "make sense" of the confusion. At the same time, they are called upon to demonstrate that the steps they have taken in this sense-making process yield credible explanations. How, for example, does the researcher using the naturalistic approach sort out the complex patterns of behavior in an organization so as to discern what is "really" happening? And, having done so, how do researchers assure themselves and others that they understood what was "really" happening and were not misled by the intrusion of bias and various sources of error? How can the findings of such inquiry be accepted as credible interpretations of reality? Answers to questions such as these must be provided by the naturalistic inquirer, and these answers must be in harmony with the basic assumptions of the naturalistic paradigm—the holistic perspective on reality, the multiple factors of causation, the likelihood that truth may not be singular and that there may be many "truths" in a situation, and the certainty that the truths are all context-bound. Such a study, then, will utilize a number of techniques intended to enhance its credibility. Six of these techniques considered essential to the design of naturalistic inquiry will be briefly discussed.

Prolonged data gathering on site.   Time—an extended period of time—spent immersed in the situation is important. It provides for entry into the situation, "learning the language," and becoming accepted, trusted, and ultimately relatively unnoticed. Time permits the researcher to see the atypical in the situation against a backdrop of broad trends so that he or she can sort the significant from the passing event. Time also permits the researcher to check his or her deepening perceptions of what is happening and to examine his or her own biases and attitudes in terms of the situation under study. In short, time is essential to permit the researcher to shift from predispositions, through early impressions, to a deeper level of understanding. Throughout the period of prolonged data gathering, the inquirer's log should record a chronicle of the struggle to understand—the thickening of description and the deepening of insight into the situation under study.

Triangulation.   The investigator uses a number of sources of information and data, not necessarily about different things but also perhaps about the same things. For example, as themes begin to arise from interviews or documents or observation, they are cross-checked with other sources so as to verify them, to check the accuracy of information, and to test different actors' perceptions of given events. Whenever possible, the researcher should use multiple data-gathering techniques including interviews, document analysis, self-reports, questionnaires, observation, and other approaches. This ensures the potential for cross-checking and verifying data.

Member checks. The investigator continuously corroborates data, information, and perceptions with relevant others in the organization being studied. Quite literally he or she may go to an actor in the situation and say, "Some people say that [such and such] is typical of the way things get done here. What do you think?" The process of member checks is perhaps the single most important means available to the naturalistic inquirer for establishing the credibility of an inquiry. Again, the researcher's log and the audit trail should include careful documentation of member checks and how the feedback from them was used in the inquiry.

Referential adequacy materials. Wherever possible the investigator should create and maintain a file of materials from the site that relate to findings and interpretations. This can include all sorts of relevant documents (for example, handbooks, copies of memos, and other ephemeral materials). It might well also include video tapes, audio tapes, photographs, and films. These materials can help preserve over time some sense of the context in which observations were made and thus aid in recall of events. The investigator must make careful judgments, however, in balancing, on the one hand, the wish to have a complete video tape record of the study with, on the other hand, the need not to intrude excessively into the setting under study, thereby changing the context.

Thick description. In the course of prolonged observation, the investigator will be carefully triangulating, conducting member checks, corroborating information, and collecting referential adequacy materials *all for the purpose of developing thick description.* This calls for synthesizing, integrating, and relating observations in such a way as to "take the reader there." This is not an easy task and it will be treated further, below.

Peer consultation. It is desirable, particularly in the case of lengthy observational studies, to be able to disengage from the setting and discuss the progress of the work and the nature of the experience with qualified peers who are interested.[41] For the graduate student investigator this might be a meeting with the thesis director or other members of the thesis committee who are skilled in naturalistic methods. Peer consultation provides opportunities while the inquiry is still in progress to check one's thinking, to raise questions and concerns, and to talk through problems of which the investigator may or may not be aware. Again, the investigator's log should record peer consultation, note the nature of the feedback received, and reveal how the study has been redirected as a result.

Characteristics of the naturalistic research report. In reporting rationalistic research, language becomes important and words significant. For example, persons under study are routinely referred to as *subjects,* a term etymologically derived from the Latin word *subjectus,* meaning literally to place one under, put one under, another's authority.[42] Form also becomes important and is highly standardized. Speaking to this point, Eisner observed,

> ...the standardization of style is considered a virtue. One is supposed to identify the problem, review the literature, describe the instruments and population, report the treatment, present and discuss the results and, finally, project possible implications. If, in this format, any sense of the personality of the investigator shines through, it is to be neutralized. This is accomplished by requiring that writers use the third person singular or the first person plural instead of using the I form. The people studied are referred to as "subjects" or "S's" and whatever uniqueness particular individuals might have are [sic] to be disregarded.[43]

A distinctive characteristic of the naturalistic research report is that it is usually written in ordinary language. In contrast with research reports in the rationalistic paradigm, naturalistic inquirers rarely refer to "subjects" let alone "S's." More commonly they speak of *respondents*—from the Latin word *respondens*, meaning responding, answering.[44] The difference between this term and the rationalistic paradigm's use of *subject* is not inconsequential; the latter clearly reveals the intent of the rationalistic inquirer to control the subjects (or, at least, control what happens to them) as opposed to the naturalistic inquirer's intent to *understand* what the respondent experiences, knows, believes, feels, and values.

A second characteristic of the naturalistic research report is that it is trustworthy. It must be based on trustworthy data collection and analysis procedures, a few of which have been discussed. But the report itself must be plausible, carefully documented, and provide corroboration from multiple sources. In short, it is valid, meaning not only that it is accurate or based upon well-corroborated evidence, but also that it provides rich, thick description. Judgments and conclusions in the report should be demonstrably reasonable, meaning that they are well connected to the evidence and supportable by a carefully maintained audit trail.

Third, as should all research reports, it should be well organized. Its parts should be well interconnected and follow a clear plan of exposition. The report should be as free of jargon as possible, but it should be lively and rich in thick description that "takes the reader there."

And, fourth, the report should be fair and ethical. The evidence in it should not have been obtained under false pretenses and the report should scrupulously observe agreements as to confidentiality, either explicit or implied, that were entered into during the study. Certainly it is as important to safeguard the rights of respondents as it is to safeguard the rights of subjects in rationalistically designed research. The problem of defining and specifying ethical behavior, as all researchers know, grows more complex with time.

Among naturalistic inquirers there is some debate as to how much the investigator should interpret his or her observations for the reader. Some, such as Roger Barker[45] contend that events and conditions should be described, leaving the reader to interpret the meaning; others, such as Louis Smith and W. Geoffrey,[46] attempt to provide thick description supplemented by interpretation. However, a basic purpose of the naturalistic research report is to "take the reader there"—to provide a report that yields a rich sense of understanding events and of having insight as to their meaning or, more likely, meanings. Therefore, an important factor in judging the adequacy of a naturalistic research report is the clarity with which the texture and quality of the findings are transmitted to the reader.

There are numerous classic examples in this regard that are instructive. One thinks, for example, of William Whyte's description of the bowling matches between the Norton Street gang and another young men's group.[47] In reading it, one comes to understand the social relationships that were played out between the groups and the individuals in them. By describing the bowling match in careful detail, Whyte enables the reader to "see" how this one incident portrayed behavior that he had seen many times before in the neighborhood in other contexts.

As an illustration, the following quotation from a section of a study of the schooling of hearing-impaired children is apropos. It is an example of thick description, portrayed in ordinary language in a lively manner—all important criteria in judging the adequacy of a naturalistic research report.

"SOUNDS IN A SILENT WORLD"

The silent world of the deaf can only be inferred by the hearing observer; he cannot fully know it. It is a world apart from the experience of that observer. It has a different language, different customs, and different values. Its inhabitants rely upon different senses in interpreting their experiences. The citizens of the silent world think differently, linking concepts which have arisen from experience, rather than creating syntactical arrangements of language which describe experience. They seek associations among those who are like themselves and derive enjoyment from their companionship. They find it difficult to cope with the citizens of the hearing world, who speak a language foreign to them, who have values different from their own, who make demands upon them which are often incomprehensible, and who, in turn, often fail to understand them when they strive to make themselves understood.

They and their hearing associates live in two distinctly different cultures. They have agreed upon names for these cultures. One is called the deaf world. The other is called the hearing world. The symbolism of these conventional terms is not accidental.

Sometimes the relatives and the educators of the citizens of the silent world desperately desire for them to move into their world. Seldom is that their desire, and seldom is it possible. They are content, rather, to remain in the company of their deaf friends and to seek fulfillment in the world of silence.

The hearing individual who wishes to enter the silent world may get his passport in order and move among the natives. He may even go so far as to learn the language. It is a strange and foreign one. It also requires the use of a totally different communication system. No longer can he rely on speaking or writing but must learn a new alphabet and new concept-symbols which are expressed in an entirely different medium, manual signs. He may even develop considerable dexterity in the use of this strange language and "speech," but at best it will remain a second language. It is not his native tongue. He must be prepared to remain forever alien. He is not equipped to experience the reality of the deaf person's world. He can only infer that reality, handicapped as he is by his own cultural differences. To step into that world is a cultural shock.

Surprisingly, the silent world is a noisy place. Contrary to one's expectations, upon entering that world he is immediately struck by the volume of sound. But the sounds are not those normally encountered. The citizens of this world have been taught to accompany their use of the native sign language with the use of oral speech, even though they, themselves, cannot hear that speech. The result is striking. It is a speech the visitor is unprepared for.[48]

SUMMARY

Scientific thinking has, for a long time, been dominated by rationalistic, positivistic, reductionist ideas. The traditional concept of scientific research, methodologically celebrated in the controlled laboratory experiment as the epitome of scientific method, has therefore long been established in the study of organizational behavior as the standard of scientific rigor.

Within the last century, however, a new approach to scientific thinking has been developing in all of the sciences, not merely in the social and behavioral sciences. The new scientific thinking emphasizes the need to take a *holographic* view of the phenomena that we wish to study, a view that is holistic, a view that examines the context as well as the parts. This has, of course, required the development of rigorous research methods that are compatible with the new view. Among these are qualitative, naturalistic methods of field research.

Qualitative, naturalistic research methods—such as ethnography—offer a way to study the behavior of people in educational organizations that use the newer, holographic, holistic approach to scientific understanding. Since about 1980 there has been an upsurge in the use of these methods in the study of organizational behavior in educational organizations.

Qualitative, naturalistic research methods have been described and discussed as a legitimate method of choice in the study, for example, of organizational culture. Qualitative, naturalistic research is viewed as a way of seeking "truth" or understanding in organizations that is different from "truth" or understanding as traditional scientists have conceptualized it. It is an alternative research method, well suited to certain kinds of research questions but not necessarily superior to or inferior to other research methods.

The essential theory of qualitative research has been described and the research procedures used to implement the theory have been discussed. Further, these have been compared and contrasted with traditional quasi-experimental research so as to differentiate clearly between the assumptions and the procedures properly used by the two approaches.

SUGGESTED READING

BOGDAN, ROBERT C., AND SARI KNOPP BICKLEN, *Qualitative Research for Education: An Introduction to Theory and Methods.* Boston: Allyn & Bacon, Inc., 1982.
This is an excellent introduction to qualitative research theory and methods. In 252 easy-to-read pages, Bogdan and Bicklen provide an authoritative, yet highly lucid, overview that conveys with considerable clarity what qualitative research is and why. A very useful book for those who want to get a clearer grasp of what qualitative research is and for those who want to plan and carry out a study.

FETTERMAN, DAVID M., *Ethnography Step by Step.* Newbury Park, CA: Sage Publications, Inc., 1989.
This small book does just what its title promises. As is true of most how-to-do-it volumes, it shows only one way to do ethnography, which is the qualitative study of culture. It is a reliable guide to the basics of a standard approach to qualitative research. Its 7-page bibliography is superb.

MARSHALL, CATHERINE, AND GRETCHEN B. ROSSMAN, *Designing Qualitative Research.* Newbury Park, CA: Sage Publications, Inc., 1989.
As the title suggests, this book concentrates on the issues and procedures for designing the qualitative study. In addition to providing an excellent orientation to the research process, it is a

mine of practical advice and suggestions. The 10-page bibliography overlooks some standard references; nevertheless, it is a good one. A fine book for anyone considering launching a qualitative study.

NOTES

[1]Peter Schwartz and James Ogilvy, *The Emergent Paradigm: Changing Patterns of Thought and Belief.* Menlo Park, CA: SRI International, 1979, p. 4.

[2]See, for example, the classic work of Daniel E. Griffiths, *Administrative Theory* (New York: Appleton-Century-Crofts, 1959).

[3]Richard F. Tucker, " 'Holographic' Science to Meet Energy Needs." *Scientific American* (March 1990), p. 128.

[4]James Gleick, *Chaos: Making a New Science* (New York: The Viking Press, 1987).

[5]Schwartz and Ogilvy, *The Emergent Paradigm,* p. 1.

[6]The following section is adapted from Robert G. Owens, "Methodological Rigor in Naturalistic Inquiry: Some Issues and Answers," *Educational Administration Quarterly,* 18, no. 2 (Spring 1982), 1–21.

[7]Egon G. Guba, "ERIC/ECTJ Annual Review Paper: Criteria for Assessing the Trustworthiness of Naturalistic Inquiries," *Educational Communication and Technology Journal,* 29 (Summer 1981), 75–91.

[8]Thomas S. Kuhn, *The Structure of Scientific Revolutions,* vol. 2, no. 2, *International Encyclopedia of Unified Science,* 2nd ed. (Chicago: University of Chicago Press, 1970).

[9]Robert L. Wolf, "The Use of Judicial Methods in the Formulation of Educational Policy," *Educational Evaluation and Policy Analysis,* 1 (January–February 1979), 19–28.

[10]Elliot W. Eisner, "On the Differences between Scientific and Artistic Approaches to Qualitative Research," *Educational Researcher,* 10 (April 1981), 5–9.

[11]James B. Conant, *Two Modes of Thought: My Encounters with Science and Education* (New York: Trident, 1964).

[12]See, for example, R. Lindgren and R. Kottkamp, "The Nature of Research: A Conference Report," *UCEA Review,* 22 (Winter 1981), 2–4; and A. L. Jefferson, "Qualitative Research: Implications for Educational Administration, a Conference Report," *UCEA Review,* 22 (Winter 1981), 5–6.

[13]Ray C. Rist, "On the Relations among Educational Research Paradigms: From Disdain to Detente," *Anthropology and Education,* 8, no. 2 (May 1977), 42–48.

[14]Donald T. Campbell and Julian C. Stanley, *Experimental and Quasi-Experimental Designs for Research* (Chicago: Rand McNally & Company, 1963), p. 2.

[15]Robert E. Stake, *Evaluating the Arts in Education* (Columbus, OH: Charles E. Merrill Publishing Company, 1975).

[16]Francis A. J. Ianni, "Field Research and Educational Administration," *UCEA Review,* 17 (February 1976).

[17]Stephen Wilson, "The Use of Ethnographic Techniques in Educational Research," *Review of Educational Research,* 47, no. 1 (Winter 1977), 245–65.

[18]For examples, see Roger G. Barker, *Ecological Psychology* (Stanford: California University Press, 1968): Dan C. Lortie, "Observations on Teaching as Work," in *Second Handbook on Research on Teaching,* R. M. Travers, ed. (Chicago: Rand McNally & Company, 1973); James G. March, "American Public School Administration: A Short Analysis," *School Review,* 86, no. 2 (February 1978), 217–49; and Seymour Sarason, *The Problem of Change and the Culture of the School* (Boston: Allyn & Bacon Inc., 1971).

[19]Wilson, "The Use of Ethnographic Techniques," p. 248.

[20]William J. Filstead, *Qualitative Methodology* (Chicago: Markham, 1970), p. 6.

[21]Barney G. Glaser and A. L. Strauss, *The Discovery of Grounded Theory* (Chicago: Aldine Publishing Co., 1967).

[22]Guba, "ERIC/ECTJ Annual Review Paper," p. 8.

[23]Robert L. Wolf and Barbara Tymitz, "Ethnography and Reading: Matching Inquiry Mode to Process," *Reading Research Quarterly,* 12 (1976–1977), 5–11.

[24]Jack D. Douglas, ed., *Understanding Everyday Life: Toward Reconstruction of Sociological Knowledge* (Chicago: Aldine Publishing Co., 1970).

[25]Clifford Geertz, "On the Nature of Anthropological Understanding," *American Scientist,* 63 (January–February 1975), 47–53.

[26]Clifford Geertz, *The Interpretation of Cultures* (New York: Basic Books, Inc., Publishers, 1973), p. 5.

[27]Philip Cusick, *Inside High School* (New York: Holt, Rinehart & Winston, 1973), p. 29.

[28]Ibid., pp. 42–68.

[29]Ibid., p. 160.

[30]Ibid., p. 61.

[31]Charles E. Silberman, *Crisis in the Classroom* (New York: Random House, Inc. 1970).

[32]Alvin W. Gouldner, *The Coming Crisis in Western Sociology* (New York: Basic Books, Inc., Publishers, 1970).

[33]Kenneth Carlson, "Ways in Which Research Methodology Distorts Policy Issues," *Urban Review*, 11 (Spring 1979), 3–14.

[34]Ibid., p. 5.

[35]Michael Q. Patton, *Alternative Evaluation Research Paradigm* (Grand Forks: University of North Dakota Press, 1975).

[36]Michael Scriven, "Objectivity and Subjectivity in Educational Research," Chapter V, in *Philosophical Redirection of Educational Research*, 71st Yearbook, Part 1, National Society for the Study of Education, L. G. Thomas, ed. (Chicago: University of Chicago Press, 1972).

[37]Rist, "On the Relations," p. 46.

[38]Lee J. Cronback, "Beyond the Two Disciplines of Scientific Psychology," *American Psychologist*, 30 (February 1975), 116–27.

[39]Egon G. Guba and Yvonna S. Lincoln, *Effective Evaluation* (San Francisco: Jossey-Bass, 1981), p. 62.

[40]Ibid., p. 122.

[41]Jack T. Murphy, *Getting the Facts* (Santa Monica, CA: Goodyear Publishing Co. Inc., 1980), pp. 71–72.

[42]Robert L. Wolf, "An Overview of Conceptual and Methodological Issues in Naturalistic Evaluation," (paper presented at the annual meeting of the American Educational Research Association, Boston, April 1980), p. 4.

[43]Eisner, "On the Differences," p. 7.

[44]Wolf, "An Overview of Conceptual and Methodological Issues," p. 3.

[45]Barker, *Ecological Psychology*.

[46]Louis M. Smith and W. Geoffrey, *The Complexities of an Urban Classroom* (New York: Holt, Rinehart, & Winston, 1968).

[47]William F. Whyte, *Street Corner Society*, 2nd ed. (Chicago: University of Chicago Press, 1955).

[48]James R. Upchurch, "A Description of a School Culture by Teachers of Hearing Impaired Children" (unpublished doctoral dissertation, Indiana University, 1980), pp. 69–74.

AUTHOR INDEX

A

Abbott, Max G., 39
Adler, Mortimer Jerome, 54
Adorno, Theodore W., 87
Allen, Vernon L., 87
Anderson, Carolyn S., 207
Anderson, James G., 86
Arends, Jane H., 278
Arends, Richard I., 278
Argyris, Chris, 15, 49, 50, 55, 128, 163, 164, 241, 275, 276
Aronson, Elliot, 87
Atkinson, John W., 120, 130
Ayer, Fred, 7

B

Baird, Leonard L, 179, 208
Baldridge, J. Victor, 207
Bales, Robert F., 11, 12, 39, 239
Barker, Robert G., 179, 204, 208, 302, 305, 306
Barnard, Chester I., 14, 43, 54, 72, 87, 167, 207, 245, 261, 280, 287

Barnett, Homer Garner, 217, 241
Barth, Roland S., 40
Bass, Bernard M., 15, 133, 164
Beck, E.T., 99
Beckhard, Richard, 260
Beckman, J., 100
Bell, Cecil H., Jr., 87
Bell, Colleen, 96, 97, 100, 101
Benne, Kenneth D., 66, 67, 87, 218, 241
Bennis, Warren G., 43, 54, 65, 66, 67, 87, 133, 134, 163,164, 241, 245, 249, 261
Berchin, Arthur, 240
Berelson, Bernard, 129, 261
Berman, Paul, 53, 55, 86, 241
Bernard, J., 99
Berrien, F. Kenneth, 56, 86
Bertalanffy, Ludwig von, 56, 57, 86
Bicklen, Sari Knopp, 304
Bidwell, Charles E., 25, 40, 54, 86
Bishop, Lloyd, 208
Blackburn, T.R., 286
Blake, Robert R., 52, 55, 139, 140, 141, 150, 151, 153, 164, 249, 250, 255, 260, 261, 264
Blanchard, Kenneth H., 130, 155, 156, 157, 158, 165, 194, 204, 239, 242

Blau, Peter M., 15
Bogdan, Robert C., 304
Boguslaw, Robert, 87
Bolman, Lee G., 38, 285
Bonney, Merl E., 70, 87
Boulding, Kenneth E., 244, 261
Bowers, David G., 15, 200, 206, 209
Boyan, Norman J., 100, 101
Boyer, Ernest L, 54, 160, 165, 182, 208
Bradford, Leland P., 278
Bridges, Edwin M., 280, 283, 287
Brookover, Wilbur, 160, 165, 183, 208
Burns, James MacGregor, 135, 162, 163,
    164, 165, 243, 261

C

Callahan, Raymond E., 7, 39
Campbell, Donald T., 292, 305
Carlson, Kenneth, 306
Carlson, Richard O., 126, 130, 212, 213,
    241
Carlson, Sune, 286
Carroll, J.B., 86
Cartwright, Dorwin, 39, 136, 164
Carver, Fred D., 130
Chapple, Eliot Dismore, 15
Charters, W.W., Jr., 99
Chase, Richard B., 130
Chase, Susan, 96, 97, 100, 101
Chemers, Martin M., 164
Chin, Robert, 213, 216, 218, 221, 237, 241
Clark, Bernard, 167, 207
Clark, David L., 214, 241
Cohen, Allan R., 205, 207
Cohen, Michael, D., 23, 24, 40
Cole, Jack, 278
Coleman, James S., 183, 184, 208
Collins, Randall, 252, 261
Conant, James B., 305
Conway, James A., 40
Coons, Alvin E., 39, 92
Cornell, Francis G., 212, 240

Corwin, Ronald G., 86
Croft, Don B., 60, 86, 92, 93, 165, 167, 175,
    186, 187, 188, 207, 208
Cronbach, Lee J., 297, 306
Crow, Mary Lynn, 70, 87
Crowson, Robert L., 40, 286
Cubberly, Elwood P., 7, 39
Cullers, Benjamin, 209
Cummings, Robert, 39
Cunningham, Luvern L., 39, 55, 165
Cunningham, William G., 285
Cusick, Philip, 295, 306
Cyr, J., 261

D

Daft, Richard L., 262, 286
Davis, Kenneth, 287
Deal, Terrence E., 28, 38, 40, 161, 165, 170,
    171, 181, 204, 205, 206, 207, 276,
    285, 287, 290
Derr, C. Brooklyn, 259, 260
Deutsch, Morton, 244, 248, 261
Diamond, Stanley, 163
Dickson, William J., 14, 39
Douglas, Jack D., 305
Dowling, William, 129
Doyle, Denis P., 47, 55
Doyle, Michael, 278
Drucker, Peter F., 150, 165, 166, 206, 266, 286
Dubin, Robert, 287
Duncan, Robert, 281, 287
Dunnette, Marvin D., 86, 208, 257, 261
Dunsing, Richard, 278

E

Ebel, R.L., 40
Edson, Sakre Kennington, 88, 95, 99, 100
Eisner, Elliot W., 302, 305, 306
Elshof, A.T., 100
Enns, Frederick, 164

Epstein, Joyce L., 160, 165, 185, 208
Etzioni, Amitai, 15, 39

F

Fayol, Henri, 4, 5, 6, 7, 8, 39
Fetterman, David M., 304
Fiedler, Fred E., 92–93, 143–50, 164
Filstead, William, 293, 305
Firestone, William A., 40, 54
Fishel, A., 101
Fleischman, Edwin A., 164
Florio, David H., 241, 242
Follett, Mary Parker, 9, 287
Forehand, Garlie A., 178, 208
Frasher, James M., 101
Frasher, R.S., 101
Frederiksen, Norman, 101
French, Wendell L., 87
Frenkel-Brunswik, Else, 87
Fullan, Michael, 223, 234, 239, 242
Funkhouser, G.R., 287

G

Gadon, Herman, 205
Garland, Parnell, 149, 164
Gates, Philip E., 165
Gauthier, William Joseph, Jr., 209
Gearing, Fred O., 163
Geertz, Clifford, 295, 305
Geoffrey, W., 302, 306
Gephart, William J., 165
Getzels, Jacob W., 68–71, 73, 87, 92, 100, 162, 165
Gibb, Jack R., 242
Gilbreth, Frank B., 4
Gilmer, B. Von Haller, 178, 208
Gittel, Marilyn, 15
Glaser, Barney G., 293, 305
Glatthorn, A.G., 40
Gleick, James, 289, 305
Goffman, Erving, 62, 63, 86
Goodlad, John I., 45, 54, 80, 85, 87, 160, 165, 182, 204, 208, 235, 236, 237, 242

Gouldner, Alvin W., 13, 15, 122, 123, 126, 130, 306
Grace, A.G., 241
Greenfield, T. Barr, 20, 40, 241
Greenwood, Peter, W., 241
Griffin, Gerald, 252, 261
Griffiths, Daniel E., 18, 40, 60, 61, 62, 94, 100, 101, 262, 286, 305
Gross, Neal, 18, 40, 86, 239
Guba, Egon G., 68, 87, 92, 214, 241, 290, 297, 299, 300, 305, 306
Guditus, Charles W., 285
Guest, Robert H., 239
Guetzkow, H., 261
Gulick, Luther, 8, 39
Gump, Paul V., 179, 208

H

Hack, Walter G., 39
Haire, A. Paul, 207, 208
Hall, Richard H., 39
Halpin, Andrew W., 39, 60, 70, 71, 86, 87, 92, 93, 138, 160, 164, 165, 167, 175, 186, 187, 188, 207, 208
Hanson, Marjorie, 100
Harris, Edwin F., 164
Hartle, Terry W., 47, 55
Hartley, Eugene L., 39
Havelock, Ronald G., 241
Heller, Robert W., 40
Helriegel, Donald, 85, 87, 127, 130, 131
Hemphill, John K., 39, 92, 101, 134, 164
Henry, Nelson B., 73
Henry, William E., 130
Herriott, Robert E., 86, 239
Hersey, Paul, 130, 155–58, 165, 194, 204, 239, 242
Herzberg, Frederick, 102, 106, 114–19, 128–30, 204, 239, 275, 276
Hoffman, Nancy, 100
Homans, George, 13, 129, 207
Hoslett, Schuyler Dean, 129
Hoy, Wayne, 20, 40
Hughes, Clarence, 209
Hurwitz, Emanuel, Jr., 40, 286

I

Iannaccone, Laurence, 206
Ianni, Francis A.J., 305

J

Jacobson, S.L., 40
James, William, 80, 290
Jefferson, A.L., 305
Jencks, Christopher, 183, 184, 208
Jennings, Helen H., 12, 39, 93
Johnston, Gladys, 95, 100
Jones, E., 100

K

Kahn, Robert L., 65, 87, 241
Kanter, Rosabeth Moss, 29, 40, 96, 97, 101, 175, 176, 181, 205, 207, 276, 285, 290
Kast, Fremont E., 87
Katz, Daniel, 136, 164, 241
Kennedy, Alan A., 40, 161, 165, 170, 181, 205, 207, 290
Kerlinger, Fred W., 86
Kilmann, Robert H., 207, 287
Koch, James L., 87
Kottkamp, Robert, 305
Kuh, George, 100
Kuhn, David G., 130
Kuhn, Thomas S., 130, 305

L

Lake, Dale G., 222, 242
Lakomski, Gabrielle, 100
Lawler, Edward E., III, 120, 121, 130, 204
Lawrence, Paul R., 81, 87
Leavitt, Harold J., 76, 86, 87
Levine, Sarah L., 205
Levinson, Daniel J., 87
Lewin, Kurt, 12, 39, 208, 225, 231, 232, 239, 242

Lewis, Edward, 281, 287
Lieberman, Ann, 206
Lightfoot, Sara Lawrence, 160, 165, 204
Likert, Jane Gibson, 197, 198, 209, 249, 260, 261, 278
Likert, Rensis, 15, 51, 52, 55, 136, 141, 158, 164, 182, 193, 194, 196–204, 209, 221, 222, 239, 242, 249, 255, 260, 261, 275, 276, 278
Lincoln, Yvonna S., 297, 299, 306
Lindgren, R., 305
Lindzey, Gardner, 87
Lippitt, Gordon L., 53, 55, 222, 242
Lippitt, Ronald, 278
Litwin, George H., 207
Lonsdale, Richard C., 62
Lorsch, Jay W., 81, 87
Lortie, Dan C., 86, 129, 305
Luthans, Fred, 126, 130, 152–54, 165
Lutz, Frank R., 206
Lwoff, Andre, 86
Lyman, K.D., 100

M

Maccoby, N., 164
Maeroff, Gene I., 239
Mann, Dale, 241
Mann, Richard D., 133, 164
March, James G., 23–25, 40, 54, 76, 86, 87, 207, 268, 275, 276, 287, 305
March, Paul E., 241
Marrow, Alfred J., 15, 206
Marshall, Catherine, 304
Martin, W. Michael, 240
Maslow, Abraham H., 92, 93, 106–10, 112, 114, 118, 130, 204, 275, 276
Maughan, Barbara, 207
Mayer, J.P., 39
Mayo, Elton, 10, 159
McCarthy, Martha, 100
McClelland, David C., 129, 155
McGreal, Thomas, 209
McGregor, Douglas M., 1, 15, 37, 38, 48, 52, 55, 79, 102, 106, 109, 141, 170, 275

McLaughlin, Milbrey Wallin, 53, 55, 86, 241
McNally, Harold J., 282, 287
McNamara, Vincent, 149, 164
McReynolds, Charles, 163
Metcalf, Henry C., 287
Meyer, John W., 26, 27, 40, 54, 204, 206
Meyer, Marshall W., 38, 54, 167, 207, 276
Miles, Matthew B., 60, 211, 222, 223, 234, 239–42
Miller, Jill Y., 100
Miller, Van, 16, 39
Mintzberg, Henry, 38, 268–70, 274, 286
Miskel, Cecil, 20, 40, 207
Mitchell, Douglas E., 129
Mitchell, Tedi K., 129
Mitchell, Terence R., 164
Moberg, Dennis, 87
Moe, G. A., 241
Montenegro, X., 100
Moore, S.E., 100
Moos, Rudolf, 185, 208
Moreno, Jacob L., 11, 39
Morphet, Edgar L., 241
Morris, Van Cleve, 40, 286
Morse, Nancy C., 164
Mort, Paul R., 42, 54, 211–13, 240
Mortimore, Peter, 207
Mouton, Jane Srygley, 53, 55, 139–41, 150, 151, 153, 164, 249, 250, 255, 260, 261, 264
Murphy, Jack T., 306
Murray, Henry A., 189, 208
Myers, M. Scott, 127

N

Naisbett, John, 161, 165
Nanus, Bert, 133, 134, 163, 164
Newberg, N.A., 40
Newcombe, Theodore M., 39
Nowell, Irene, 92, 100
Nutt, Paul C., 268, 286
Nystrand, Raphael O., 39

O

Ogawa, Rodney, 207
Ogilvy, James, 288, 289, 305
Oller, Sakre, 100
Olsen, Johan P., 23, 24, 40
O'Reilly, Robert, 149, 164
Ortiz, Flora Ida, 95, 100, 129
Ott, J. Steven, 206
Ouchi, William, 168, 170, 181, 207, 275, 276, 290
Ousten, Jane, 207
Owens, Robert G., 78, 87, 169, 192, 208, 241, 242, 281, 287, 305

P

Panttaja, Leon A., 40
Parsons, Talcott, 39, 87
Pasmore, William A., 86
Patterson, Kerry J., 207
Patton, Michael Q., 306
Pauley, Edward, 241
Perrow, Charles B., 15, 56, 86
Peters, Thomas J., 28, 38, 40, 161, 165, 170, 171, 181, 205, 207, 290
Pfiffner, John M., 74, 87
Pincus, John, 241
Pitner, Nancy J., 286
Pondy, Louis R., 248, 250, 261, 286
Porter, Lyman W., 110, 111, 118–21, 130, 204
Porter-Gehrie, Cynthia, 40, 286
Pottker, J., 101
Presthus, Robert V., 15, 124, 125, 130
Purkey, Stewart, 31, 32, 40, 41

Q

Quinn, Robert R., 87

R

Raisinghani, Duru, 268, 286
Redl, Fritz, 13

Reddin, William J., 151, 153–55, 165, 204
Reif, William E., 126, 130
Richman, Joel, 189, 190
Rist, Ray E., 305
Ritti, R.R., 287
Robbins, Stephen P., 87, 118, 130
Roethlisberger, Fritz J., 13, 14, 39
Rokeach, Milton, 87
Rosenzweig, James E., 87
Ross, Donald H., 42, 54, 240
Rossman, Gretchen B., 304
Rostetter, David, 252, 261
Rowan, Brian, 26, 27, 40, 54, 204
Runkel, Philip J., 235, 242, 278
Rutter, Michael, 167, 207, 208

S

Sanford, R.N., 87
Sarason, Seymour B., 165, 179, 180, 204,
    206, 208, 211, 240, 305
Sarbin, Theodore, R., 87
Savage, Ralph M., 117, 130
Saxton, Mary J., 207, 287
Sayles, Leonard R., 15
Schaef, Anne Wilson, 98, 101
Schein, Edgar H., 29, 40, 99, 163, 170, 171,
    207, 276, 286, 287
Schindler-Rainman, Eva, 278
Schmidt, Gene L., 117, 130
Schmidt, Warren H., 137, 204, 264, 276, 277
Schmuck, Patricia, 91, 97, 99, 100
Schmuck, Richard A., 235, 242, 278
Schön, Donald A., 19, 20, 39, 264, 272,
    274, 275, 286
Schwartz, Peter, 288, 289, 305
Scott, W. Richard, 15, 86, 206
Scriven, Michael, 297, 306
Seashore, Stanley E., 15, 206
Seemen, Melvin, 126, 130
Selznick, Philip, 13, 167, 207
Sergiovanni, Thomas J., 50, 51, 55, 112,
    113, 117, 118, 130, 132, 159, 163,
    165
Serpa, Roy, 207, 287
Shakeshaft, Charol, 92, 93, 98, 99, 100, 101

Sheats, Paul, 66, 67, 87
Shepard, Herbert A., 249, 250, 260, 261
Sherif, Carolyn W., 261
Sherif, Muzafir, 13, 15, 39, 261
Sherman, J.A., 99
Sherwood, Frank P., 74, 86, 87
Sherwood, John J., 88
Shils, Edward A., 39
Siepert, Albert F., 55, 164, 199, 201
Sikorski, Linda A., 241, 242
Silberman, Charles E., 295, 306
Silver, Paula, 94
Simon, Herbert A., 14, 208, 262, 266, 286
Sizer, Theodore, 160, 165, 182, 204, 208
Slocum, John W., Jr., 85, 87, 127, 130, 131
Smith, Alan, 207
Smith, Carol E., 278
Smith, Dorothy E., 100
Smith, Louis M., 302, 306
Smith, Marshall S., 31, 32, 40, 41
Snöek, J. Diedrick, 87
Speizer, J.J., 100
Sproull, Lee, 38
Srivastva, Suresh, 286
Stake, Robert E., 305
Stanley, Julian C., 292, 305
Starratt, Robert J., 135, 164
Staw, Barry M., 287
Steiner, Gary A., 129, 261
Steinhoff, Carl R., 78, 87, 189, 192, 208,
    241, 242
Stent, A., 100
Stern, George G., 160, 165, 188, 189, 193,
    208, 221
Stinchcombe, Jean, 206
Stockard, J., 100
Stogdill, Ralph M., 133, 164
Straus, David, 278
Strauss, A.L., 293, 305
Sumner, Gerald, 241
Swanson, Austin D., 241

T

Tack, M.W., 100
Taguiri, Renato, 167, 168, 207, 208

Tannenbaum, Robert, 137, 204, 264, 276, 277
Taylor, Frederick W., 4–8, 10, 39, 47, 71,
  87, 264
Taylor, Gib, 223, 234, 239, 242
Thelen, Herbert A., 73
Theoret, Andre, 268, 286
Thomas, John M., 261
Thomas, Kenneth, 247, 249, 250, 256, 257,
  261
Thomas, L.G., 306
Thompson, James D., 22, 40
Thompson, Victor A., 15, 126, 130
Tomlinson, E., 100
Townsend, Robert, 43, 54
Travers, R.M., 305
Tucker, Richard F., 305
Tyack, David B., 39
Tymitz, Barbara, 305

U

Upchurch, James R., 306
Urwick, Lyndall, 8, 39

V

Vidich, Arthur J., 163
Villadsen, A.W., 100
Vroom, Victor H., 106, 120, 130, 149, 150,
  152, 164, 165, 194, 204, 239, 264,
  268, 276, 277

W

Wall, Charles C., 240
Walton, Richard, 131
Warren, Carol A.B., 100

Waterman, Robert H., Jr., 28, 38, 40, 161,
  165, 170, 171, 181, 205, 207, 290
Watson, Goodwin, 240, 242
Wax, Murray L., 163
Weber, Max, 5–7, 264, 295
Weick, Karl E., 25, 40, 54, 204, 271, 272,
  274–76, 286, 287
Weiner, Stephen, 38
Whyte, William Foote, 13, 15, 303, 306
Whyte, William H., Jr., 286
Wickstrom, Rodney A., 117, 130
Wilkins, Alan L., 207
Williams, Richard C., 240
Wilson, Bruce L., 40
Wilson, Stephen, 305
Wilson, Woodrow, 3, 7, 14, 36, 38
Winer, B.J., 40
Wolcott, Harry F., 15
Wolf, David, 38
Wolf, Robert L., 305, 306
Wolfe, Donald M., 87
Wolman, Benjamin, 12, 39
Wyant, Spencer, 242
Wynn, Richard, 245, 260, 261, 285

Y

Yeakey, C.C., 100
Yetton, Philip W., 149, 150, 152, 165, 264,
  268, 276, 277
Yukl, Gary A., 163

Z

Zacharias, J.R., 213
Zaltman, Gerald, 241, 242
Zander, Alvin, 136, 164
Zellman, Gail, 241

SUBJECT INDEX

A

Accountability, and motivation, 103
Activities Index (AI), 189 (*see also*
  Climate, organizational)
Administration:
  ancient systems, 2
  as academic discipline, 2–3
  bureaucratic assumptions, 44–47
  civil services, 2–3
  and concept of social systems, 16–17
  defined, 18, 274–75
  Fayol's principles of, 5
  Follet's principles of, 9–10
  functions of, 5
  historical development, 2–38
    human dimensions of organization,
      37–38
    human relations movement, 10–13
    human resources development, 23–32
    impact of industrial revolution, 3–10
    organizational behavior movement,
      13–16
    rise of classical theory, 7–10
    human resources assumptions, 35–36,
      275–77

Taylor's principles of scientific
  management, 9–10
Administration, educational:
  and concept of social systems, 16–18
  early theory and research, 16–17
  and social sciences, 16–18
Administrative (*see also* Administration,
  historical development):
  thinking, impact of industrial revolution
    on, 3–10, 270–73
  work, 268–70
Agricultural model of change, 216
Alexander the Great, 2
Ambiguity in educational organizations, 18
American Association of School
  Administrators, 13
American Telephone and Telegraph
  Company, 127
Anarchies, organized, 23–24
Androcentrism, 89–90
Assertiveness, in conflict, 256–58
Association for Supervision and
  Curriculum Development, 13
Assumptions (*see also* Culture,
  organizational):
  Classical (bureaucratic) theory, 44–47

Assumptions (*see also* Culture, organizational) (*cont.*)
human resources development theory, 28, 47–53
Attacks, *see* Conflict
Authoritarian leadership, *see* Theory, leadership
Authoritarian personality, 70
Avis Rent-a-Car, 43

B

Behavior, organizational:
defined, 68–70
Behavior Patterns A and B, 49–51
Board of Regents, *see* New York State
Bureaucracy, *see* Theory, organization, bureaucratic
Business-Higher Education Forum, 54

C

Caesar, 2
California, 46, 200
California Business Roundtable, 46
Canada, 117
Career-bound and place-bound, 126
Career ladders, 45
Catholic Church, 2
Change, organizational (*see also* Theory, change):
change agent, 228–29
empirical-rational, 214–18
life cycle, (*figure*, 232)
normative-reeducative, 219–30
power-coercive, 218
Chicago, 10, 103
Civil services, 2–3
Classical organization theory, 7–10 (*see also* Theory, organization)
Climate, organizational (*see also* Theory, culture):
affective aspects, 167–68, 176
defined and described, 60, 167–68, (*figure*, 169)

feminocentric critique of research on, 92–93
perception, 175
satisfaction, 175
Closed system, *see* Theory, social system
College Characteristics Index (CCI), 189
(*see also* Climate, organizational)
College Entrance Examination Board, 55
Colorado, 46
Columbia University, 211
Conflict defined, 244–61 (*see also* Theory, conflict)
Consideration, defined, 138–41 (*see also* Theory, leadership)
Contingency theory, 29–30 (*see also* Theory, contingency)
Control Press, 189–93 (*see also* Climate, organizational)
Cooperativeness in conflict, 256–58 (*see also* Theory, conflict)
Corning Glass Works, 127
Cosmopolitans and locals, 122–24
Coupling (*see also* Theory, organization):
loose coupling, 25–26
Thompson's concepts, 22–23
Culture, organizational:
affective aspects, 175–76
as bearer of authority, 28–29
as control mechanism, 28–29
defined and described, 28–29, 167–68, (*figure*, 169), 171–74, 268–69, 273–74
growth-enhancing, 234
and leadership, 159–61
and multiple cultures, 146–48, 176–77
organizational effectiveness, 181–86
research on, 168–71
school size, 179–80
socialization, 173–74
symbolism, 174
in systems theory, 58

D

Decision making (*see also* Theory, decision):

defined and described, 262–63
emergent and discrete problems,
    278–80
garbage can model, 24–25
participative decision making issues,
    277–81
rational-logical, 20–21
Democratic supervision, 11
Development press, 189–93 (*see also*
    Climate, organizational)
Donnelly Mirrors, 127

E

Educational administration (*see also*
    Administration, educational):
and concept of social systems, 17
defined, 18
early theory and research, 17–18
and social sciences, 17–19
Education Commission of the States, 45
Effective schools research, 30–33
Elementary and Secondary Education Act
    (ESEA), 213
Empirical-rational strategy of change,
    214–18 (*see also* Theory, change)
Ethnography, *see* Research, naturalistic,
    and Qualitative research
Europe, 37
Exception Principle, 8
Expectancy theory of motivation, 119–22
    (*see also* Theory, motivation)

F

Feedback, 43
Feminocentrism, 90–94
Florida, 46
Followership related to leadership,
    161–62
Force-field analysis, 231–34
Foreign Service of U.S. State Department, 3
Formal organization, 17
Fortune (magazine), 127
Frito-Lay, 170

G

Gaines Pet Food Manufacturing
    Corporation, 127
Garbage can model of organizational
    choice, 24–25
General Motors Corporation, 2
General systems theory, *see* Theory, general
    systems
Georgia, 117
Great Britain, civil services, 2–3
Grid leadership concepts, 138–42 (*see also*
    Theory, leadership)
Group, defined, 134–35
Group dynamics, defined, 11
Group norms defined and described, 66–68,
    177–78

H

Hawthorne effect, 39, 103–6
Hawthorne plant (Western Electric), 10, 14
Health, organizational, *see* Organizational
    health
Hierarchy in organizational structure, 8–9
    (*see also* Theory, organization).
Hierarchy of needs theory, 107–14 (*see also*
    Theory, motivation)
Human relations (*see also* Western Electric
    Company research):
concepts of, 10–13
defined, 15–16
Hawthorne effect, 103–6
impact on school administration, 13
Western Electric Company research, 103–6
Human resources development (HRD),
    35–37, 166–67, 275–77 (*see also*
    Theory, human resources
    development)

I

Idiographic-nomothetic, 68–75
Illinois, 103

Imperial Chemical Industries, 127
Indifferents, 124–25, (*figure*, 125)
Industrial revolution, impact on
    organizational thought, 3–7
Informal organization, 14
Initiating structure, *see* Theory, leadership
Innovation, defined, 217
Interaction-influence system, 194–96,
    (*figure* 195–96) (*see also* Culture,
    organizational and Climate,
    organizational)
Interdependence and organizational
    coupling, 22–23
International Business Machines
    Corporation, 127

J

Job enrichment defined and described,
    126–28
Johnson & Johnson Products, Inc., 170

K

Kindergarten as example of educational
    innovation, 212
Knowledge production and utilization
    (KPU), 214–18

L

Laboratory method of personal growth
    training, 13
Leadership, 132–63 (*see also*, Theory,
    leadership)
Least Preferred Co-Worker Scale (LPC),
    144–48, (*figure*, 145)
Linking pin concept, 202–4
Loose coupling, 25, 53 (*see also* Coupling
    and Organizational coupling)
Loosely coupled systems, 47–48 (*see also*
    Organizational coupling and
    coupling)

M

Managerial Grid, 139–40, (*figure*, 140)
Massachusetts Institute of Technology, 213
Milwaukee, 32
Minneapolis, 32
Motivation (*see also* Theory, motivation):
    accountability, 103
    defined, 102
    expectancy theory, 119–22
    extrinsic-intrinsic factors, 114–18
    Herzberg's theory, 114–18
    Maslow's theory, 107–14
        feminocentric critique of, 92–93, 109
    Porter's theory, 110–12

N

National Aeronautics and Space
    Administration (NASA), 265
National Commission on Excellence in
    Education, 44
National Defense Education Act (NDEA),
    213
National Institute of Education (NIE), 216,
    219
National Research Council, 10
National Science Board Commission on
    Precollege Education in
    Mathematics, Science, and
    Technology, 55
Neoclassical administrative concepts, 10, 23
New Jersey Bell Telephone Company, 14, 43
New York, 32, 113
New York State Board of Regents, 46
Nomothetic, 68–75
Normative-reeducative strategy of change,
    219–30
North Carolina, 46
North Dakota, 46

O

Open system, *see* Theory, social system

Organization (*see also* Theory, organization):
control in, 27–30
defined, 20, 57, 75–76
formal and informal, 14
Organization development, 223–30
Organizational behavior, defined, 15–16
Organizational behavior movement, 13–15
Organizational change, *see* Theory, change
Organizational climate, *see* Climate, organizational
Organizational Climate Descriptive Questionnaire (OCDQ), 186–88
Organizational Climate Index (OCI), 188–93
Organizational conflict, *see* conflict
Organizational coupling (*see also* Loose coupling):
loosely coupled systems, 47–48
schools as dual systems, 26
tight coupling in schools, 27–28
Organizational culture, 167–75 (*see also* Culture, organizational)
Organizational health, defined and described, 221–22
Organizational self-renewal, *see* Organization development
Organizational theory (*see also* Theory, organization):
bureaucratic, 5–6, 44–47
classical, 7–10, 44–47
contingency, 29–30
defined, 43
holographic, 288–89
human resources, 35–36, 275–77
informed by experience and research, 43
middle-range, 22–23
sources of, 43
uses of, 42
Organized anarchies, 23–24

P

Participative decision making, *see* Theory, decision
Pennsylvania, 212

Person-environment interaction, 68–69, 177–78
Personnel relations, 13
Physical Science Study Committee (PSSC), 213
Planning, rational models, 79–81
Planning-Programming-Budgeting Systems (PPBS), 32, 79
Power-coercive strategy of change, 218 (*see also* Theory, change)
Power, and leadership, 135–36, 161–63
Profile of a School (POS), 193–204
Program Evaluation Review Technique (PERT), 79
Pyramids, administration required to build, 2

Q

Qualitative research methods, 21 (*see also* Research, qualitative/naturalistic, and Research, rationalistic)

R

Rand Corporation, 219
Reform, educational, 33–35
Regents, New York State Board of , 46
Research, development, and diffusion (RDD) strategy of change, 214–17 (*see also* Theory, change)
Research:
on effectiveness of organization development, 233–37
feminocentric critique of administrative research, 92–94, 97–99
informs organization theory, 43
methods used in studying effective schools, 30
naturalistic methods, 96, 289–303
qualitative/naturalistic defined and described, 198, 289–303
rationalistic compared to naturalistic, 289–303

Research: (*cont.*)
  rise of qualitative methods, 21
  Western Electric studies, 10–12
Right to Read program, 219
Role, *see* Theory, role
Russia, 265

S

St. Louis, 32, 212
San Diego, 32
Saskatchewan, 117
Scalar principle in bureaucratic theory, 8
School reform movement, 33–35
Schooling as a process, *see* Theory,
  organization, and Theory, social
  system
Schools:
  and ambiguity, 19, 88
  bureaucratic characteristics, 42
  as dual organizations, 26–28, 53–54
  organizational characteristics of effective
    schools, 32–33
Scientific management, 4, 7–8, 264–65
Secretariat of the United Nations, 3
Self renewal, organization, *see*
  Organization development
Sensitivity training, 13
Social conformity, 96
Social systems (*see also* Theory, systems,
  and Theory, social systems)
Socialization, 48, 166, 273–74
Sociogram, (*figure*, 12)
Sociotechnical system theory, *see* Theory,
  sociotechnical, and Theory,
  organization
South Africa, 37
Southern Regional Education Board, 55
Span of control in bureaucratic theory, 9
Sputnik I, 265
State University of New York at Buffalo,
  43, 245
Structure, organizational, 54 (*see also*
  Theory, organization)
Symbolic leadership, 162 (*see also* Theory,
  leadership)

Symbolism, 174–75
Syracuse, N.Y., 189
System, basic concepts of, 57–58 (*see also*
  Theory, system)
System theory, *see* Theory, organization,
  and Theory, social system

T

Task Force on Education for Economic
  Growth, 55
Team administration, 281–83
Tennessee, 46
Texas Instruments, 127
T-Group training, 13
Theory:
  defined and described, 43
  emerging scientific concepts of, 288–89
  change:
    agricultural model, 216
    cost-quality relationships, 212
    empirical-rational, 214–18, (*figure*,
      215)
    life cycle (*figure*, 232)
    normative-reeducative, 219–30
    power-coercive, 218
    RDDA model (*figure*, 211)
    strategies, 213–14
    systems, 224–25
  classical, 7–10, 44–47
  conflict:
    assertiveness-cooperativeness,
      256–58, (*figure*, 257)
    classical views, 243–44
    conflict defined, 244
    contingency theory, 254–59, 259–62
    effects of conflict, 246–47
    management strategies (*figure*, 259)
    open systems theory, 251–52
    process theory, 249–50, (*figure*, 249)
    structural theory, 250–51
  contingency in conflict, 254–59
  culture, *see* Culture, organizational
  decision:
    limits on rationality, 267–75
    organizational culture, 273–74

Theory: (*cont.*)
   participative, 277–78
   rational models, 265–67
   theory-practice gap, 274–77
   thinking and, 270–73
general systems, defined and described, 57
human relations, 10–16
human resources development (HRD),
   47–48
   central to understanding organization,
      37–38
   defined, 35–36, 275–77
   goal of, 166
   organizational concepts, 35–36
   schools as dual systems, 35–36
leadership:
   behavioral, 162
   classical, 161
   consideration, defined, 138–41
   contingency, 142–58
   cultural, 159–60
   defined, 126, 132, 158–61
   Fiedler, 143–149
      feminocentric critique of, 92–93
   grid concepts, 138–142
   Hersey and Blanchard, 155–58
   human relations, 161–62
   initiating structure, defined, 138,
      (*figures*, 138–39)
   new perspectives, 158–61
   organizational culture, 159–63
   power, 127–28, 134–35
   Reddin, 151–55, (*figures*, 154)
   successful and effective, 155–56
   symbolic, 159–60
   trait theory, 133–34
   two-dimensional, 136–42
   Vroom-Yetton, 149–51, (*figure*,
      152)
motivation (*see also,* Motivation):
   defined, 102
   expectancy theory, 119–22
   Herzberg's theory, 114–18
      feminocentric critique of, 92–93
   Maslow's theory, 107–14
      feminocentric critique of, 92–93
   Porter's theory, 110–12

Theory X-Theory Y, 45
organization:
   bureaucratic, 5, 7–9, 44–47, 48–53
   characteristics of schools, 239
   classical, 44–47, 161–62
   culture, 166–68, (*figures*, 169, 173),
      172–74
   decision making, 273–74
   human relations, 10–13, 243
   human resources, 35–38, 166–67,
      275–77
   linking pin, 202–4, (*figures*, 202, 203)
   middle-range theories, 22
   organic system defined, 80–81
   organizational health, 221–22
   organization development, 223–30
   role, 60–75
   schools as dual systems, 27–28,
      53–54
   self-renewal, 223–30
   social systems, 58–62
   sociotechnical systems, 75–79, (*figure*,
      78), 230–31
   system 1-system 4, 194–96, (*figure*,
      195–96)
   Theory X-Theory Y, 48–53, 136,
      168–70
   Theory Z, 168–70
organizational climate (*see also* Climate,
   organization):
   closed climate, 188
   defined and described, 60, 167–72,
      (*figure,* 169)
   Organizational Climate Description
      Questionnaire (OCDQ),
      298–301
   Organizational Climate Index (OCI),
      301–6
   open climate, 188
   Profile of a School (POS), 193–204
organizational culture, 28–29, 167–68,
   (*figure,* 169), 171–74, 268–69,
   273–74 (*see also,* Culture,
   organization)
organization development, 223–30
   defined, 223
   role defined and described, 61–68

Theory: (*cont.*)
  social system:
    defined and described, 57–59
    Getzels-Guba model, 68–75, (*figure*, 73)
    feminocentric critique of, 92–93
    input-output concept, 58–59, (*figure*, 59)
    open-closed system, 59–60
    related to contingency theory, 81–84
    related to role, 68
    subsystem-suprasystem, 60–61
  sociotechnical system, 75–79, (*figure*, 78)
Theory X-Theory Y, 48–53 (*see also* Theory, organization)
Theory Z, *see* Theory, organization
Thick description, 295, 301
3M, 170
Tradition, in organizational culture, 172–74
Traveler's Insurance Company, 127
Twentieth Century Fund, 55

U

Uncertainty characteristic of organizational life, *see* Ambiguity
United Airlines, 127
United States Congress, Senate Committee on Labor and Welfare, 129
United States Department of Education, 212
Unity of command in bureaucratic theory, 8
Upward mobiles and indifferents, 124–26

V

Vocational Education Act, 219

W

Weldon Manufacturing Company, 167
Western Electric Company research, 10, 14, 37, 103–6